Gregg Typing, Series Six

Typing 2

Advanced Course

Alan C. Lloyd, Ph.D.
Director, Typing Instructional Services
Gregg Division
McGraw-Hill Book Company

Fred E. Winger, Ed.D.
Former Professor
Office Administration and Business Education
Oregon State University

John L. Rowe, Ed.D.
Late Chairman
Business and Vocational Education
University of North Dakota

Jack E. Johnson, Ph.D.
Assistant Professor
Office Administration and Business Education
University of Wisconsin, Eau Claire

Gregg Division | **McGraw-Hill Book Company**

New York   St. Louis   Dallas   San Francisco   Auckland   Bogotá
Düsseldorf   Johannesburg   London   Madrid   Mexico   Montreal   New Delhi
Panama   Paris   São Paulo   Singapore   Sydney   Tokyo   Toronto

contributors

The following typewriting instructors assisted the authors in developing the manuscripts for the **Typing 2** program. Both the authors and the publishers gratefully acknowledge their invaluable contributions.

Robert Gryder, Ed.D.
Arizona State University
Tempe, Arizona

Rebecca A. Hall
Centerville Public Schools
Centerville, Ohio

Robert N. Hanson, Ed.D.
Northern Michigan University
Marquette, Michigan

B. Scot Ober, Ph.D.
Gregg Division
McGraw-Hill Book Company

Robert P. Poland, Ph.D.
Michigan State University
East Lansing, Michigan

Albert D. Rossetti, Ed.D.
Montclair State College
Upper Montclair, New Jersey

Patsy C. Smith, Ed.D.
Georgia State University
Atlanta, Georgia

COVER DESIGNER
Graphic Concern, Inc.

TEXT DESIGNER
Betty Binns

EDITING MANAGER
Elizabeth Huffman

EDITING SUPERVISOR
Evelyn Belov

BOOK EDITOR
Trent Duffy

ART DIRECTOR
Frank Medina

DESIGN SUPERVISOR
Edwin Fisher

PRODUCTION SUPERVISOR
Laurence Charnow

Library of Congress Cataloging in Publication Data

Main entry under title:

Typing 2.

    Fifth ed. published in 1973 as v. 2 of Typing 300, by
J. L. Rowe, A. C. Lloyd, and F. E. Winger.
    Includes index.
    1. Typewriting. I. Lloyd, Alan C. II. Rowe,
John L., date. Typing 300. v. 2.
Z49.T956   652.3'024   77-5423
ISBN 0-07-038244-1

Typing 2 is a cornerstone of a comprehensive instructional system: Gregg Typing, Series Six. It includes the best features of the five prior editions.

At the same time, it introduces many exciting new features, some of which will prove to be landmark innovations for the future as well as for the present.

the "series six" program

Gregg Typing, Series Six, is a two-year program of typing instruction that includes:

Textbooks. *Typing 1, General Course,* is the text for the first year; *Typing 2, Advanced Course,* is the text for the second year.

Workbooks. Each half of each textbook is accompanied by a correlated workbook entitled *Learning Guides and Working Papers.* All four workbooks provide a variety of reinforcement and enrichment exercises in addition to stationery.

Instructional Recordings. The *Keyboard Presentation Tapes for Typing 1* (cassettes) offer training correlated with the textbook keyboard lessons.

Transparencies. The three volumes of transparencies include one on the alphabet keys, one on the number and symbol keys, and one on production work.

Manual and Key. The *Teacher's Manual and Key* includes discussions of teaching methods, keys, tests, and other instructional aids.

the best of the past

Typing 2 retains many features created for prior books by the same authors and now well tested by millions of learners. For example:

Performance Goals. Specific goals are cited for all skill-building and production exercises.

Controlled Copy. All skill-building and production material is controlled in length, difficulty, and vocabulary to ensure the learner's achievement of the performance goals.

Work Experience. Production work is done in simulated offices (twice as many as previously) with office layouts, narrative directions, etc., to invest every task with real work experience.

Double-Blocked Copy. Most timed-writing selections double-block to expedite proofreading.

Drills for Electrics. Many skill drives include special drills for electric machines.

We-23 Drills. Pair pattern and other number drills appear throughout the program.

Sentence Warmups. Every lesson's warmup covers speed, accuracy, numbers, and editing.

Visual Guides. Each workbook includes visual placement guides for letters and manuscripts.

Learning Guides. Each workbook contains "programmed" learning guides on technicalities.

the exciting new features

In addition to retaining and enhancing the best features of its predecessors, *Typing 2* provides many significant new features, including these:

Dual Lesson Structure. Each lesson is structured for presentation and completion either as a single unit or as two mini-units. Thus the program is functionally designed for courses organized on either a class-period or a modular basis.

National Geography. To make the names, places, and products of this country more familiar, each state is the subject of one or more timed writings and the locale of a production project.

Job Simplification. To increase output power, *Typing 2* gives more assignments on fewer ways to arrange production. It also standardizes placement in letters, reports, and tables.

Remedial Clinics. *Typing 2* provides 18 period-length "skill clinics" for optional practice.

End-of-Part Reviews. The Review at the end of each Part includes exercises that summarize the coverage of the preceding 12 lessons.

Instant-Scoring Aids. The 12-second sprint scales, 30-second speed-check counts, and sustained-writing speed markers (see page 2) save time and ensure accuracy in computing scores.

Homework Sheets. Each workbook has six advanced Skill Gainers—games, drills, timings, and other challenges—for typing at home.

Work Simulations. For experience in composing at the machine and cooperating in an office atmosphere, *Typing 2* has 11 two-person *interaction* simulations—9 in the text (one period each) and 2 in the workbooks (four periods each).

Tests. A full program of tests that may be reproduced for classroom use is provided in the *Teacher's Manual and Key.*

our thanks

We wish to express our appreciation to the many classroom teachers, graduate students, and students who assisted us in planning and developing this publication. We particularly wish to thank the scores of graduate students and hundreds of classroom teachers who shared with us the data on which the goals and standards of this publication are based. ***The Authors***

contents

PART

v

†"L" is line for line; "U" is for unarranged (listen for the bell).

d Timing is doubled for 5′ writing.

* Arranged in equal 1′ paragraphs for piecemeal practice.

JOB 144-1: TRANSMITTAL LETTER

Workbook 331 □ Body 142 + subject □ SI 1.31FE □ Edit to supply missing elements □ ■ 15'/0e

This letter is to mr earl k strong, at 18 mountain pass road, palm springs california 92262. It needs a centered, underscored subject line, subject: bill of sale

mr randolph has asked me to acknowledge receipt of your certified check for $3,500 for the antique sofa that you have purchased from him. mr randolph has also asked me to tell you two more things:

1 he has executed a bill of sale [cap *bill* and *sale*] for the sofa. it is enclosed with this letter.

2 the sofa has been picked up and crated by a fine trucking firm long haul, inc. the company will have a truck leaving for the west coast [cap *w* and *c*] near the end of this week, which means that the sofa ought to be delivered to you by the first of the month. the insurance receipt for it is also enclosed.

it has been a pleasure to handle this matter for you and mr randolph. if ever you get to charleston, it would be a pleasure for me to meet you. yours very truly steven w kelso and list the two enclosures: bill of sale and insurance receipt

JOB 144-2: BILL OF SALE

Workbook 332 or use legal-ruled paper and type the document completely □ ■ 25'/0e

BILL OF SALE

Know all Men by these Presents,

That I, Foster G. Randolph, 1213 Peach Lane, Charleston, South Carolina, party — of the first part, for and in consideration of the sum of three thousand five hundred dollars ($3,500) — lawful money of the United States, to me — — — in hand paid, at or before the ensealing and delivery of these presents by Earl K. Strong, 18 Mountain Pass Road, Palm Springs, California, party — of the second part, the receipt whereof is hereby acknowledged, have bargained and sold, and by these presents do — — — grant and convey unto the said party — — — of the second part, his — — executors, administrators and assigns one antebellum antique sheraton sofa, described in the attached schedule. —

To have and to hold the same unto the said party — — of the second part, his — — executors, administrators and assigns forever. And do — — for my — — — — — — heirs, executors and administrators, covenant and agree, to and with the said party — — — of the second part, to warrant and defend the sale of the aforesaid sofa — — — — — — — — — — — — — — — hereby sold unto the said part of the second part, his — — executors, administrators and assigns, against all and every person and persons whomsoever.

In Witness Whereof, I — — have hereunto set my — hand — and seal — the twentieth — — — — — day of May — — — — in the year one thousand nine hundred and (this year)

Sealed and Delivered in the presence of

_____   _____ [L.S.]
Robert N. Snyder   Foster G. Randolph

SCHEDULE OF THE FOREGOING BILL OF SALE:

One (1) antique sheraton sofa, upholstered in original 1845 silk cloth with gold and blue stripes, as illustrated and defined on page 9 of the Hawley Brothers catalog of antique antebellum furniture!

PART 1

WELCOME TO WORK-EXPERIENCE TYPEWRITING!

This advanced course in typing will qualify you for employment as a professional typist. At the end of this course you will be able to type at least 50 words a minute (almost without error) for as long as it takes you to type a page of work. You will be able to produce just about anything that can be done on a typewriter. You will receive directions, office style, and fulfill them as a professional typist does.

The course begins with an intensive review. Part 1 will help you regain your basic skill to at least the 40-words-a-minute level. It will also help you recall how letters are placed on a letterhead, how tables are typed in open and ruled arrangements, how business reports are prepared, and how everyday forms are filled in.

Ready? Then start with Lesson 1 below.

goal A

■ To review course procedures: machine settings, practice routines, other essentials.

WHAT THE DIRECTIONS MEAN

□ *"Spacing—1" means "set the machine for single spacing."*
□ *"Line—60" means "set margin stops for a 60-space line" (20–85).*
□ *"Tabs—5 and center" means "set a tab stop 5 spaces in and at the center."*
□ *"Drills—3" means "type each line of drill three times."*

Directions: *Spacing—1. Line—60. Tabs—5 and center. Drills—3.*

GETTING READY

1. Confirm paper guide:
a. Set the carriage or carrier so that the print-point indicator is at 50.
b. Crease the paper at top center.
c. Insert the paper; slide it right or left until the crease is at the print point.
d. Slide the guide to the edge of the paper.
e. Note the setting so you can check it at a glance hereafter.

2. Make the machine adjustments given in the Directions. If you use 50 as the center and add 5 spaces for the warning bell, your margin settings will be:

Line—50: 25 and 80.
Line—60: 20 and 85.
Line—70: 15 and 90.

WARMUP REVIEW

Edit line 2.

1 I am to go to work for the audit firm by the eighth of May. 12

2 we saw john drew and bob crane with anne carr and sue hale. 12

3 Jacqueline was vexed by the folks who got the money prizes. 12

4 She moved out of Rooms 10, 28, and 39 into Rooms 47 and 56. 12

|1 |2 |3 |4 |5 |6 |7 |8 |9 |10 |11 |12

1   1   1

goal

■ To demonstrate how well you can arrange data as an open leadered table and a ruled table.

JOB 143-1: OPEN LEADERED TABLE

Workbook 330 □ Spacing 2 □ Line 50 □ Styled like a financial statement □ ■ 20'/0e

Center the adjacent table on workbook page 330 or on a full-size plain sheet. Spread the table to fill a 50-space line, and use leaders to tie the two columns together. Confirm (correct if necessary) that the items are in alphabetic sequence.

JOB 143-2: RULED TABLE

Workbook 331 □ Spacing 2 □ Line as necessary □ Ruled style □ ■ 20'/0e

Retype the adjacent table, centering it on workbook page 331 in ruled arrangement. Position the two columns only 6 spaces apart (the Pittsburgh item takes two lines, divided any way you prefer). Arrange the items from highest amount due (Rutherford) to lowest (Western).

Foster and Foster, Inc.
ACCOUNTS RECEIVABLE
As of April 30, 19—

Customer	Amount Due
Alexander's Hardware	$ 450.75
Burton, Rita N.	63.25
Denton and Denton Sons	1,200.00
Jordan, Robert and Susan	975.50
Fredericks, Richard T.	265.00
Rutherford Pharmacy	1,976.45
Leslie, Alice Anne	14.60
Louis, T. K.	39.40
Norton Tailoring, Inc.	437.15
Pittsburgh Duplicating and Printing Company	865.25
Southside Pharmacy	491.80
Truman, Stanford E.	80.80
Western Household Supply, Inc.	4.50
TOTAL OUTSTANDING ACCOUNTS	$6,864.45

 goal

■ To demonstrate how well you can type a standard business letter and produce a standard legal document.

Take a 3-minute writing to set the base for your improvement practice. Your goal is to type at least three copies of this paragraph in the 3 minutes.

5	To build expert typing skill, you must quickly observe	12
6	that it is very important to get off to a good start in any	24
7	work that you do. If you do not learn this, you just might	36
8	become a lazy typist.	40

|1 |2 |3 |4 |5 |6 |7 |8 |9 |10 |11 |12   SI 1.27FE

12-SECOND SPRINTS

Take four 12-second timings on each of these sentences. Your goal on each is to type at least 40 wam (words a minute) without error.

The scale indicates speed in words a minute.

9	A skill sprint is a short dash to type fast with no errors.	12
10	A girl and a small dog ran down the long lane to the shore.	12
11	If that guy is to get in the act, he must get here in time.	12

12" SPEED: 25 30 35 40 45 50 55 60

SPEED CHECK

Take three 30-second timings. Your goal on each is to type at least 40 wam without error. Your speed is the number under which you stop—or the even number between.

12	01 03 05 07 09 11 13 15 17 19 21 23 It is not the size, but just the quickness, of your fingers	12
13	25 27 29 31 33 35 37 39 41 43 45 47 that builds every extra word per minute in a timed writing.	24

POSTTEST

Repeat the Pretest above. Score your work and note your improvement.

goal B

■ **To type 40 or more wam within 3 minutes and 2 errors.**

PRETEST

Speed scores are for 3' TW. Circled numbers are 1' goals.

Directions *(reconfirm):* Spacing—1. Line—60. Tab—5.

Take a 3-minute writing to measure your skill on copy of normal difficulty. Your speed is the last tiny number (above the line) that you pass.

14	1 2 3 4 One outstanding thrill of a lifetime is to visit a big	12
15	5 6 7 8 sailing ship. As you stand on the wood deck and raise your	24
16	9 10 11 12 eyes to the towering masts and their jigsaw puzzle of ropes	36
17	13 ① 14 15 16 and sails above you, it is inevitable that your breath will	48
18	17 18 19 20 quicken and visions of pirate ships, hull down on a horizon	60
19	21 22 23 24 of flame, will stir your imagination. One seems hopelessly	72
20	25 26 ② 27 28 dull if he or she feels no excitement when visiting a ship,	84
21	29 30 31 32 or doesn't wish to hear the thunder of the roaring cannons.	96
22	33 34 35 36 If ever there's an opportunity for you to visit such a ship	108
23	37 38 39 40③ of olden days, move heaven and earth to see that you do so.	120

|1 |2 |3 |4 |5 |6 |7 |8 |9 |10 |11 |12   SI 1.38N

goal

■ To demonstrate how well you can type on printed forms and produce a report with an approval line.

Directions: *Spacing—1. Line—85.*
Warmup—page 270; then begin Job 142-1.

JOB 142-1: BUSINESS FORMS

Workbook 327 □ ■ **Three forms 20′/0e**

1. Invoice 8314 to mr fred i beauchamp at 727 grafton street in manchester new hampshire 03104 for merchandise shipped to his home [the same address]. The sale is to be credited to our salesman, rex turner. Items are:

3 cases paint brushes (D11) @ 30.00 90.00
3 cases paint brushes (P16) @ 40.00 120.00
2 cases paint brushes (J23) @ 50.00 100.00

Merchandise was rushed by prepaid air express, for which there are delivery charges of 13.50. (Be sure to check every detail, including the total line and the amount-due line.)

2. Receipt dated today for $50.00 payment on credit account by todd eggleston.

3. Another receipt, also dated today, for $123.47 paid by mrs ruth day morgan in full settlement of credit account.

JOB 142-2: BUSINESS REPORT

Workbook 328 □ **SI 1.60H** □ ■ **20′/0e**

KICKING THE FOOTNOTE   14
Training Department Bulletin 121   37
Prepared by Vanessa Vickle   54
[*Today's date*]   64

THE PROBLEM   68

Few things are quite as annoying to a   78
typist (even to a veteran!) as a footnote for 87
which insufficient space has been left at   95

the bottom of the page. The page has to be   105
retyped.   106

Your training department has two sugges-   116
tions to offer.   119

SUGGESTION 1   123

Continue with superior figures in the text   134
of the report in the traditional manner, but 143
put all the footnotes in a special "back-   151
notes" section at the end of the report.   159
Phrase them in the usual way, with the   167
usual abbreviations.   171

Entitle the page NOTES on line 13. Start-   182
ing three lines below, type each backnote   190
as a numbered, single-spaced paragraph. In- 198
dent the start of the paragraph five spaces. 208
Follow the number of the note by a period   216
and two spaces. (See Sabin, The Gregg   228
Reference Manual, pp. 278–279.)   241

SUGGESTION 2   244

It may not be necessary to provide so   254
many details in our footnotes as we have   262
traditionally done, particularly so when the 271
report will have a bibliography that gives   280
the publisher, the city, the date of publica- 289
tion, and so on.   292

It might then be practical to include a   302
condensed version of the footnote details   310
in parentheses right in the text, like the   319
Sabin reference above. How much is essen-   327
tial? You need just enough for the reader   336
to find the reference. A second reference to 345
Sabin could be even briefer (Sabin, 285).   354

Authorized and Approved [*signature line*]   360
Stewart Mann, Training Dept.   373

Type each line twice, plus once more if you typed either of the key letters incorrectly in the Pretest.

24 A art amp act aide amen asked B bad bat bit brag brim brand 12
25 C cat car cap crop crow check D dad dye due drag down drums 12
26 E elm eve ear etch east erase F fir fan few fame from flown 12
27 G gap gag gal game glow glory H hat has hop have hold helps 12

28 I its imp ill into ibex ideal J jar jot joy jump join juice 12
29 K key kit kid kiln kill kings L lob lie lag late lake laugh 12
30 M mat mad may more mist music N nor not nag norm noon nasty 12
31 O oak odd old over oath olive P pat pay pad pour past proud 12
32 Q aqa aqa que quip quid quick R row rip rid reap rake right 12

33 S sit sky sip sing stay sting T top tip try tame task throw 12
34 U urn ups use upon used unite V vet vex vat vote vase vague 12
35 W was wow wag when what white X sxs sxs six oxen axis exact 12
36 Y you yet yap yard year young Z zap zig zoo zeal zest zooms 12

POSTTEST

Repeat the Pretest at the bottom of page 2. Score your work and note your improvement.

goal A

■ To review horizontal spacing and centering.

LESSON 2

Directions: *Spacing—1. Line—60. Tab—5.*
Drills—3. WB—5–6.

WARMUP REVIEW

Edit line 2.

1 It would be nice if I did not start work until late in May. 12
2 we asked bill to point out tim clark and hugh green for us. 12
3 Jeff quietly moved his dozen boxes by using my power truck. 12
4 Bob lost checks Nos. 10, 28, and 39; I lost Nos. 47 and 56. 12
   |1 |2 |3 |4 |5 |6 |7 |8 |9 |10 |11 |12

HORIZONTALS

Spacing—2.
Tab—center.

Pica or Elite. To determine whether your machine has pica or elite spacing, type 10 periods and compare your typed line with the adjacent lines.

Centering. Center the carriage or carrier; then backspace once for every two strokes the line will occupy.

   Practice: Center the adjacent three lines. The letter T should align.

```
PICA SPACING          . . . . . . . . . .
(10 to inch)
ELITE SPACING         . . . . . . . . . . . .
(12 to inch)

          How to Achieve

        Horizontal Centering

          With Typewriters
```

(Continued on next page)

1   1   2

3

goal

■ To demonstrate how well you can type on ordinary paragraph copy.

Directions: *Spacing—1. Line—85. Warmup—page 270; then adjust machine for timed writings.*

JOB 141-1: TIMED WRITING

Workbook 325–326 □ Spacing 2 □ Line 70 [lines end even] or 60 [lines do not end even], as your teacher directs □ Tab 5 □ ■ 50 wam/5′/2e or 50 wam/10′/5e

Take either (a) two 5-minute writings, one on each column and average the scores or (b) one 10-minute writing on the entire selection, as your teacher directs.

	1			2	1+2

Survey after survey tells us that making a good correction is an annoyance or problem that bothers nine typists out of ten. It would, of course, be great if our fingers could gain so much skill that they never made an error. But the cold truth is that our minds wander and are easily distracted; and when attention slips, the fingers do also. One cannot rationalize that making errors is excusable or is natural, but one must admit that it is just as human to err on a typewriter as on anything else. Making corrections is a technique in which typists have to become expert if they hope to stay in the business of typing.

9 / 17 / 25 / 33 / 42 / 51 / 59 / 66 / 75 / 83 / 92 / 99 / 107 / 115 / 123 / 126

The starting point in expertness in making corrections is tools. There is no doubt about it, you have to have a kit of tools the right shape and size and quality for the work to be done. For example, you need not one but two erasers—a soft pencil eraser for use on carbons and an ink eraser for use on the original—and you do not make a good correction without using both. Yet, a high proportion of typists try to make both categories of corrections with just one eraser (and then they wonder why their erasures are poor). A sloppy erasure is a sure sign of a lazy typist who doesn't get and use both erasers.

135 / 144 / 152 / 160 / 168 / 176 / 184 / 193 / 201 / 210 / 218 / 226 / 234 / 243 / 250

However, there are ways to make corrections quite independent of erasers, thanks to new things that have come on the market that allow the typist to cover up or lift off any error. The trouble with these helps is that you can't use them on the carbon, only on an original. Still, with copying machines being used instead of carbon paper, much typing consists only of originals; so the new aids really are useful.

9 259 / 17 267 / 25 275 / 34 284 / 43 293 / 51 301 / 60 310 / 68 318 / 76 326 / 84 334

There are at least three ways to cover errors. The cleanest one is a white liquid that comes in a bottle like nail polish; you simply paint over an error. Another way that is just as good is using slips of paper coated with chalk; you position the paper over the error and type the error again, exactly over itself—the error seems to vanish. If you have half a line to change, you could use correction tape, the third way to cover errors; it has an adhesive side and comes in rolls from which you tear off whatever you need to hide an error.

93 343 / 102 352 / 111 361 / 119 369 / 128 378 / 136 386 / 144 394 / 152 402 / 161 411 / 169 419 / 177 427 / 185 435 / 193 443 / 194 444

The prize method, of course, is to lift the error off the page—all you need is one of the new "correcting" typewriters that has twin ribbons: a black one that prints carbon on the paper and a white one that, being sticky, picks the carbon right off the paper, like magic.

203 453 / 212 462 / 220 470 / 229 479 / 237 487 / 245 495 / 250 500

|1 |2 |3 |4 |5 |6 |7 |8   SI 1.42N |1 |2 |3 |4 |5 |6 |7 |8   SI 1.42N

HORIZONTALS
(Continued)

Spread Centering. From the center, backspace once for *each* stroke (except the last) the line *would occupy if it were not spread.* When you type it, space once between characters and three times between words.
Practice: Spread-center the three adjacent lines.

```
  S P R E A D I N G   N A M E S
F O R   S P E C I A L   D I S P L A Y
     M a r c h   1 ,   1 9 - -
```

Block Centering. Using the longest line of the group, backspace from the midpoint to center it; then begin all the lines there. (Set margin stop.)
Practice: Block-center the three adjacent lines.

```
A Block-Centering Technique

Aligns Everything

At the Left
```

Pivoting. From one space beyond the desired ending point, backspace once for each space the displayed line will occupy.
Practice: Arrange the adjacent three lines to end at 80.

```
Backspace Pivoting Technique

 Justifies Typewritten Words

                At the Right
```

goal B

▪ **To type 30 wam on number-filled copy within 2′/2e.**

Directions: *Spacing—1. Line—60. Drills—2.*

PRETEST

Take two 2-minute timings, then average your speed scores and error scores.

Speed markers are for 2′ TW.

```
5  The Class of 1977 will hold its annual reunion on August 16    12
6  with a dinner at the Hotel McAdams, 3344 West 55 Street, in    24
7  Woodlawn.  Tickets will be ten dollars.  Make your reserva-    36
8  tion with Janet Carr, 2288 East 199 Street, Woodlawn 64116.    48
9  Be sure to write Janet before 7/25 or phone her before 8/8.    60
   |1   |2   |3   |4   |5   |6   |7   |8   |9   |10   |11   |12   SI 1.36N
```

PRACTICE

Type each line twice—or more if you wish.

```
10  112 121 113 131 114 141 115 151 116 161 117 171 118 181 119
11  223 232 224 242 225 252 226 262 227 272 228 282 229 292 220
12  334 343 335 353 336 363 337 373 338 383 339 393 330 303 331
13  445 454 446 464 447 474 448 484 449 494 440 404 441 414 442

14  556 565 557 575 558 585 559 595 550 505 551 515 552 525 553
15  667 676 668 686 669 696 660 606 661 616 662 626 663 636 664
16  778 787 779 797 770 707 771 717 772 727 773 737 774 747 775
17  889 898 880 808 881 818 882 828 883 838 884 848 885 858 886

18  990 909 991 919 992 929 993 939 994 949 995 959 996 969 997
19  001 010 002 020 003 030 004 040 005 050 006 060 007 070 008
20  ;½; ;½; ½p½ p½p p½p ½p½ ½pop½ ½pop½ ½p½ p½p p½p ;p; ;½; ;½;
21  ;½; ;¼; ¼;¼ p½p p¼p ¼p¼ ¼pop¼ ¼pop¼ ¼p¼ p¼p ;¼; ;¼; ¼;¼ ¼;¼
```

POSTTEST

Repeat the Pretest above. Score your work and note your improvement.

1 **2**

JOB 140-1: CIVIL SERVICE TABULATION TEST

Plain paper □ ■ 20'/0e

Center on a full page, in any attractive arrangement you prefer, the handwritten table at the foot of page 276. The illustration here is one option.

Civil Service Scoring. From a possible score of 40%, deduct:
5% for uneven top/bottom margins.
5% for uneven left/right margins.
5% for uneven between-column areas.
2% for each error of any kind.

JOB 140-2: CIVIL SERVICE 7-MINUTE TIMED WRITING TESTS

Plain paper □ **Spacing 2** □ **Line 70** □ **Tab 5** □ ■ **20'/0e**

Copy *line for line* the material below; the lines will not end even. Type for 7 minutes. Repeat the effort and turn in whichever paper gives you the higher score.

Civil Service Scoring. Your speed score is the number at the end of the last line you copy completely. Your accuracy score is 30% minus 3% for each error. Total the speed and accuracy scores.

Total Test Score. Combine the table-test score and the timed-writing test score.

JOB 140-3: COMPLETION CARDS

5″ x 3″ cards or slips □ ■ **5'/0e**

7-Minute Speed Score

Line—70.
Spacing—2.
Tab—5.
SI 1.51FH

I wish to call attention to the fact that the summary of the permanent appropriations found in the committee report indicates that there is an increase of more than five million dollars in this item over the appropriations for the similar item last year. In these permanent appropriations that we can do nothing about, there is this constant increase by which the hands of the Congress itself are tied, and tied firmly.	1% 3% 5% 7% 9% 11%

We must meet the obligations of interest on the public debt. We must also meet the payments under the various trust funds that have been established. Cutting down on these items means that we must default or repeal the laws under which those trust funds have been accumulated; to do either of these things is unthinkable to someone of conscience.

13% 15% 16% 17% 18%

But, glance at the balance of the appropriation bill; it amounts to more than one billion dollars for the regular activities of these two departments. You will find item after item where the Appropriations Committee's hands are completely tied so far as reducing the major items of this bill is concerned. Under the circumstances, we cannot change the appropriation to pay the salaries that the Congress has imposed.

19% 20% 21% 22% 23% 24%

Typing the whole selection in 7' equals 45 wam.

The only thing this subcommittee could do in the direction of reducing expenditures might be to challenge the necessity as to the number of personnel who are needed in the department to perform certain tasks or functions. When this committee attempts to do that, it seems to me, we are attempting to place ourselves in the position of the executives who have been appointed to conduct the work of the postal department.

25% 26% 27% 28% 29% 30%

---

⑫ **140**

goal A

■ To review vertical spacing and centering.

Directions: *Spacing—1. Line—60. Tab—center. Drills—3. WB—7–8.*

VERTICAL SPACING

1	1½	2	2½	3
1				
1	1½	2		
1	1½		2½	3
1		2		
1	1½		2½	
1	1½	2		3

WARMUP REVIEW

Edit line 2.

1   I may be able to work for that firm on the last day of May.   12
2   we hired ann bray and ray mahr but not tom day or liz ford.   12
3   Would Elizabeth request that Jack pay for fixing my silver?   12
4   Pages 10, 28, and 39 need to be returned; 47 and 56 do not.   12

|1 |2 |3 |4 |5 |6 |7 |8 |9 |10 |11 |12

BLANK LINES

To leave blank space, advance the paper 1 line more than the number of lines to be left blank. For 6 blank lines in the top margin, begin on line 7. To leave 2 blank lines below a page number, space down 3 lines. In this book, arrow signals tell how many lines to drop down.

Practice 1:   Type the tinted area of the adjacent illustration of the start of a report page. Leave a 1-inch (6 lines) top margin.

Practice 2:   Type the tinted area of the adjacent illustration of a letter closing. Leave 3 blank lines for the signature.

```
                              1
                              2
                              3
                              4
                              5
                              6
              Page 4  ↓3      7
                              8
                              9
ke to purchase.  By and large, 10
```

```
I'm looking forward to seeing you at    1
e in Houston.                           2
                                        3
                                        4
  Sincerely yours,  ↓4                  5
                                        6
                                        7
                                        8
Ronald S. Cains                         9
District Sales Manager
```

SPACE WITH RULED LINES

Lines made of underscores are usually preceded by and followed by 1 blank line. To get this space, *single-space before typing the line and double-space after it.*

Practice: Type the tinted area of the adjacent table.

```
NAL SALES  REPRESENTATIVES  ↓1    1
_____     2
                                  3
           Salespersons           4
                                  5
_____     6
                                  7
           17                     8
            8
```

VERTICAL CENTERING

Lines to page:
Full size—66.
Half size—33.

Full metric—70.
Half metric—35.

For vertical centering, (a) count the lines, including blank ones, that the material will occupy when typed; (b) subtract the line count from the number of lines available on your paper; (c) divide the difference by 2, counting any fraction as a whole line, to find the number of the line on which to start typing.

Practice 4:   Center the adjacent display, single-spaced, on a half sheet.

Practice 5:   Center the same display in double spacing on a full sheet.

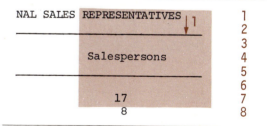

```
    A Paper Submitted to

Dr. Margaret C. Johnston

   In Partial Fulfillment

Of Readings in Education

    January 15, 19--
```

1   3

5

10. it was commodore perry who yelled dont give up the ship

11. get a reporter he said for i have a statement to make

PART 2. SPELLING

Some of the words shown in *italics* are misspelled. Type all 13 italic words, spelling all of them correctly. Use double spacing and a 70-space line, but type only the italic words. Do not type the numbers. Start 1 inch below the end of Part 1.

A common carrier is a carrier of chattels and [12] *passingers.* Some of the [13] *familair* common carriers are railroads, [14] *buses,* streetcars, and [15] *airplains.* When hauling goods, a common carrier [16] *furnishes* each shipper with a [17] *bill of loading,* which is an acknowledgment of the [18] *reciept* of goods plus an agreement to [19] *delliver* them to the [20] *consignee,* whose name is [21] *speciafied,* in exchange for proper [22] *renumeration.*

PART 3. OFFICE TERMINOLOGY

Type each of these sentences, inserting the word or words required to make each statement correct and complete. Use the back of the same paper on which you typed Parts 1 and 2.

Begin an inch from the top. Use double spacing and a 70-space line. In this part type the sentence numbers, following each by a period and two spaces.

23. A ream of paper usually contains about ____ sheets of paper.

24. The two common sizes of typewriter type are ____ and ____.

25. A form for requesting desk supplies is a stock ____.

26. A check that contains an explanation of what it is for is a ____ check.

27. A pencil-like tool used in drawing on stencils is a ____.

28. Index cards that overlap in trays are ____ ____ [*two words*] cards.

29. The place where visitors are received is called the "____ center."

30. The card on which is stamped the time of arrival and departure is a ____ card.

31. The IBM typewriter with a correction key is the ____ ____ [*two words*].

32. The original copy used in hektographic [*chemical*] duplicating is the ____.

33. Inverting parts of a name for filing is ____ the name.

JOB 140-1

See directions on page 277.

THE PUBLIC DEBT OF THE UNITED STATES
(Figures in Millions)

Year	Amount of Debt	Change From Previous Decade
1870	$ 2,436	$ 1,220 +
1880	2,090	346 −
1890	1,132	958 −
1900	1,263	131 +
1910	1,146	117 −
1920	24,299	23,153 +
1930	16,185	8,114 −
1940	42,967	26,782 +
1950	257,357	214,390 +
1960	286,330	28,970 +
1970	370,918	84,588 +

- To type 30 wam on symbol-filled copy for 3' within 2 errors.

IF YOU'RE USING A TYPE-ELEMENT MACHINE

Your printing element may have some special characters. For example, the figure 1 on the top row may be 1/! or 1/± or [/]. The ½/¼ may be !/°. Explore all the characters on your element.

Directions: *Spacing—1. Line—60. Drills—2+.*

PRETEST

Take two 3-minute timings and average your speed scores and error scores.

```
      1                    2                    3                    4
5  Dear Sir:  I am writing to ask you to check on an order for       12
             5                    6          7                   8
6  $4,000 worth of 5% bonds that I placed with West & Co. some       24
         9              10①          11                 12
7  time ago.  As of this date (9/26), I have heard nothing; it       36
        13               14                15               16
8  seems to me that I should have had a request for the money.       48
                                                                     49
             17            18            19              20②
9  Dear Sir:  About ten days ago I placed an order for $1,000+       61
           21            22          23                24
10 worth of items for my variety store.  The acknowledgment of       73
          25              26               27              28
11 the order is on your form #7799.  The items sell at a price       85
        29              30③                31              32      33
12 of 19¢ to 39¢ (the majority @ 29¢).  I need them right now!       99
   |1   |2   |3   |4   |5   |6   |7   |8   |9   |10  |11  |12
                                                             SI 1.36N
```

Speed markers are for 3' TW. Circled numbers are goals.

Note: Underscored words are counted three times.

SYMBOL PRACTICE

Type each line twice, plus once more if you typed the symbol incorrectly in the Pretest.

```
13  1!1 !1! !1! a!a !a! !2! !3! !4! !5! !6! !7! !8! !9! !0! !1!
14  2@2 @2@ @2@ s@s @s@ @3@ @4@ @5@ @6@ @7@ @8@ @9@ @0@ @1@ @2@
15  3#3 #3# #3# d#d #d# #4# #5# #6# #7# #8# #9# #0# #1# #2# #3#
16  4$4 $4$ $4$ f$f $f$ $5$ $6$ $7$ $8$ $9$ $0$ $1$ $2$ $3$ $4$

17  5%5 %5% %5% f%f %f% %6% %7% %8% %9% %0% %1% %2% %3% %4% %5%
18  6¢6 ¢6¢ ¢6¢ j¢j ¢j¢ ¢7¢ ¢8¢ ¢9¢ ¢0¢ ¢1¢ ¢2¢ ¢3¢ ¢4¢ ¢5¢ ¢6¢
19  7&7 &7& &7& j&j &j& &8& &9& &0& &1& &2& &3& &4& &5& &6& &7&
20  8*8 *8* *8* k*k *k* *9* *0* *1* *2* *3* *4* *5* *6* *7* *8*

21  9(9 9(9 0)0 0)0 (1) (2) (3) (4) (5) (6) (7) (8) (9) (0) (9)
22  0-0 0-0 0-0 -;- -2- -3- -4- -5- -6- -7- -8- -9- -0- -0- -0-
23  0_0 0_0 0_0 _1_ _2_ _3_ _4_ _5_ _6_ _7_ _8_ _9_ _0_ _0_ _0_
24  ;=; ;=; ;=; =;= =;= =;= ;+; ;+; +;+ +:+ 1+0 2+8 3+9 4+7 5+6
```

Only rarely can a learner type whole lines without looking up. Can you?

POSTTEST

Repeat the Pretest above. Score your work and note your improvement.

1   3   6

JOB 138-2: LETTER OF RECOMMENDATION

Workbook 323 □ Body 122 + subject □ SI 1.41N □ ■ 15'/0e

Type the following letter in any style you prefer; the illustration is just one acceptable option. Supply all missing parts and punctuation.

This letter has a subject line, "Inquiry about Doris Yengel." The letter is to Mr. L. G. Fordyce, Personnel Bureau of Casler & Son, Inc., at 1400 West Hill Street in Richland Center, Wisconsin, ZIP 53581.

I was glad to receive your letter about Miss Doris Yengel and to learn that she is being considered for a promotion to a top post with your firm. Paragraph. Miss Yengel was my secretary for three years right after she graduated from high school. She enrolled in night school classes at a local college and in a short time matured into an efficient and effective worker. She left my staff when my own firm promoted her to a fine job in another department. Paragraph. I am pleased to commend Miss Yengel to you. She is pleasant to work with and pleasant to work for. She will do well whatever duties are involved in the new assignment and I congratulate both you and her.

Yours very truly Stephen Canaris

[In case you and your teacher feel that you should try the letter a second time, another letterhead is on the back of the first one.]

JOB 138-3: COMPLETION CARDS

5″ x 3″ cards or slips □ ■ 5'/0e

LESSONS 39/40

Directions: Spacing—1. Line—85. Warmup—page 270; then begin the preliminary qualifying test below.

goals

■ To pass a preliminary general knowledge test. ■ To pass a Civil-Service style performance test: timing, draft.

JOB 139-1: QUALIFYING GENERAL TEST

Plain paper □ Line 70 □ Start line 7 □ ■ 20' or less

This test consists of typing correctly 33 sentences containing problems. Possible score is 100%, from which 3% is deducted for each sentence containing a technical or typographic error.

PART 1. CAPITALS AND PUNCTUATION

Type the following sentences correctly in double spacing on plain white paper. Do not type the sentence numbers. Do not erase.

1. the official postal abbreviation for south carolina is sc
2. when can i see you al about your mark in the english test
3. mr bowling has been department head since october 15 1975
4. the letters were smeared wrinkled and creased incorrectly
5. this is what mary ordered new shoes a suit and three blouses
6. they moved their offices from 2d avenue to 119th street
7. mr a d main and his wife mrs ann main live next door
8. he begged cried and pleaded both judges were unimpressed
9. did you read john wests famous article downwind destiny

WORD-DIVISION CAUTIONS

Don't divide words if you can avoid it.

Always know how many spaces you can type after hearing the margin bell.

Don't use word divisions you see in newspapers or books as a guide; use only those you find in a dictionary.

LESSON 4

Directions: *Spacing—1. Line—60. Drills—2. WB—9–10.*

WARMUP REVIEW

Edit line 2.

```
1  I came to work for that firm and have been here since then.   12
2  call tim gray and may barr and ask them to see jan and wes.   12
3  Did Jack pay for fixing my silver when Elizabeth requested?   12
4  Please clean rooms 10, 28, and 39, but not rooms 47 and 56.   12
   |1   |2   |3   |4   |5   |6   |7   |8   |9   |10  |11  |12
```

WORD-DIVISION RULES

Absolute Rules. Any word division that agrees with these three rules is acceptable.

1. Never divide abbreviations, contractions, or words pronounced as one syllable.

2. Divide only between whole syllables.

3. Divide only if you can leave on the upper line a syllable of two or more letters (such as *un- done*) and can carry to the next line a syllable of at least three letters (such as *un- did*) or two letters and a punctuation mark (such as *un- do!*).

Practice 1: If these words can be divided, hyphenate them correctly. (Key: see left margin.)

```
a. ARAMCO        e. thoughtful
b. better        f. party
c. strained      g. teacher?
d. couldn't      h. aground
```

Preference Guides. When space permits you to choose alternative places at which to divide a word, so that lines end within 3 spaces (plus or minus) of the desired margin, be guided by these:

4. Try to divide compound words between the elements of the compound. Do not add a hyphen to an already hyphenated word. *Brother- in-law* is preferred to *broth- er-in-law*. Divide solid compounds between the elements of the word. Thus *under- state* is better than *un- derstate*.

5. Try to divide between, not after, two accented vowels that occur together. *Recre- ation* is better than *recrea- tion*.

6. Try to divide after, not before, a one-letter syllable in the middle of a word. *Ana- lyst* is better than *an- alyst*.

Practice 2: Type these words, showing by a hyphen and a space the preferred division.

```
          i. inven- tion
i. in ven tion     m. sis ter-in-law
j. dy na mite      n. de lin e ate
k. pos i tive      o. up per hand
l. de vi a tion    p. de vi ous
```

7. Try to divide after, not within, a compound (double) prefix. For example, *intro- duction* is better than *in- troduction*.

8. Try to divide before, not within, a compound (double) suffix. *Mobili- zation* is better than *mobiliza- tion*.

9. Try to avoid separating elements that are read together, like page and number, month and day, title and last name.

10. Try to avoid dividing the last word of the first line of a paragraph or a page. Try not to divide the last word of more than two consecutive lines.

Practice 3: Type these words, showing the best division by a hyphen and a space.

```
q. lik a ble      u. e lec tric
r. prob a bly     v. mar a thon
s. ar thri tis    w. pho to graph ic
t. suit a ble     x. per il ous
```

a. ARAMCO
b. bet- ter
c. strained
d. couldn't
e. thought- ful
f. party
g. teach- er?
h. aground

i. inven- tion
j. dyna- mite
k. posi- tive
l. devi- ation
m. sister- in-law
n. deline- ate
o. upper- hand
p. devi- ous

q. lik- able
r. prob- ably
s. arthri- tis
t. suit- able
u. elec- tric
v. mara- thon
w. photo- graphic
x. peril- ous

JOB 137-1: TIMED WRITING PREVIEW

Plain paper □ **Spacing 2** □ **Line 70** □ **Tab 5**

Read the entire selection. Practice any words that you recall having had trouble with previously. Then, to regain the feeling of listening for the margin bell, type the first paragraph without looking up. Finally, prepare for the 10-minute writing: insert clean paper on which, at the right margin 1½″ from the bottom, you have marked a bottom-margin reminder line.

JOB 137-2: TWO 10-MINUTE TIMED WRITINGS

Plain paper □ **Spacing 2** □ **Line 70** □ **Tab 5**

Type the following material for 10 minutes, striving to maintain a 50-wam pace within 5 errors. Score by the Net method (deduct 1 wam for each error). Circled numbers are 1-minute goals at 50 words a minute.

EMPLOYMENT REFERENCES

Before a company will add someone to   8
the payroll, the employer has to know a lot   17
of things about the newcomer. Workers are   26
too expensive for the company to take a   34
chance on; so therefore you are asked to fill   43
in a job application form and come in for   51
an interview. Experience has shown that the   60
bright surface that anybody can put on dur-   69
ing the interview may be only skin deep, so   78
the applicant for a job that is a real prize is   87
likely to be asked for a reference list.   96

The employer will not phone or write the   105
reference persons unless you almost have   113
the job. The final step in hiring you is the   122
check on the references, for the person who   131
interviews you wants to confirm the deci-   139
sion. If your references come through for   148
you, you have the job.   153

Whom should you use as your references?   162
Of course the names must be ones that the   170
employer will respect. No one would be in-   179
fluenced by the words of your relatives, for   188
example, or of a friend your own age, or of   197
someone whose own work is inconsequen-   204
tial. The use of any such names would hurt   213
your chances. A list of names is expected   221
to include the name and address of a per-   229
son such as a school official, who would   238

|₁ |₂ |₃ |₄ |₅ |₆ |₇ |₈

confirm your skills and training; of someone   247
else who knows you as an employee, and   254
will confirm your work attitude and drive;   263
and of someone of a religious affiliation   271
who can testify to your character.   279

But note that you can never use the name   288
of anyone as a reference without permis-   296
sion. Acting as a reference is a nuisance   304
from which most people flinch, and anyone   313
who is used as a reference without an okay   321
is not likely to support you when the chips   330
are down. The normal procedure is to speak   339
to the person, like "Miss Green, may I use   347
your name as an employment reference?"   355
If you do not see her, then you should   363
write a letter to ask permission, "Dear Miss   372
Green: On the strength of working for you   381
last summer, may I use your name as an   389
employment reference? I would be very,   397
very grateful for your permission."   404

Your request must be accompanied by an   413
addressed card or a stamped and addressed   421
envelope, to expedite your getting approval   430
quickly. If you don't receive an answer, you   439
don't ask again; you realize that the answer   448
is no, and you turn to someone else with   456
your inquiry.   459

If you have not yet arranged for persons   469
to serve as references, now is the time to   477
do so. When you apply for a job, you will   486
need references; if you are wise, you will   494
get your reference list ready.   500

|₁ |₂ |₃ |₄ |₅ |₆ |₇ |₈   SI 1.41N

(Before repeating the 10-minute writing, type three times each (a) any line in your work that contains an error and (b) one additional line of the material.)

JOB 138-1: JOB APPLICATION FORM

Workbook 321 □ ■ **25′/0e**

Fill in the workbook form to apply for the highest office job for which you are qualified. Be sure to do both sides of the application form.

■ To review and practice the service keys of the typewriter.

PRETEST

Speed markers are for 3′ TW.

Caution: Only a very determined person can type this page without looking up. Can you?

Directions: *Spacing—2 for TW, 1 for drills. Line—60. Drills—follow directions. Tab—5.*

Take a 3-minute timing on lines 5–10. To force the use of the margin-release key at the end of each line, set margins exactly at 20 and 80 (indicated by Ⓜ).

```
     Ⓜ              1                2                3            4 Ⓜ
 5      We are fortunate today that Bill Jason, the famous inventor    13
           5            6            7            8            9
 6  of our SLEEP-EZ tablets, is with us today; we welcome Dr. Jason.   27
                    10                       12                13
 7      We all hope Dr. Jason will tell us how he created SLEEP-EZ.    41
       14            15            16            17        18     19
 8      This product has assisted millions, I really mean millions,   57
               20            21            22            23
 9  to get a good night's rest.  We think SLEEP-EZ is international.   71
           24            25            26            27        28
10      Ladies and Gentlemen, Dr. William Jason, SLEEP-EZ inventor!   85
     |1   |2   |3   |4   |5   |6   |7   |8   |9   |10  |11  |12  |13
```

PRACTICE

Do each drill twice, plus once more if you handled the Pretest inefficiently.
Spacing—1. In lines 11–12, return the carriage or carrier after each word.

Return.
M = manuals.
E = electrics.

11M aide burn cold dice edge fast gift quit when rate then vase   12
12M why elm rap the and sap den red for got cat van bat sad was   24

11E open part hard jade keep lame near made yelp head pear next   12
12E hat yet use job not mad kit lot ode pan her jet yes pat not   24

Shift Key.

13 A An Ann B Bo Bob C Ca Cal D Da Dan E Ev Eve F Fa Fay G Gus   12
14 H Ha Hal I Id Ida J Ji Jim K Ka Kay L Li Liz M Ma Mat N Ned   24
15 O Ol Oli P Pa Pat R Ra Rae S Sa Sam T Te Ted V Va Val W Wes   36
16 A Ad Ada B Be Ben C Ca Cam D De Dee E El Eli J Ja Jan S Sal   48

Shift Lock and Release.

17 The SHIFT LOCK makes Miami appear as MIAMI, Tulsa as TULSA.   12
18 BEN-GURION was once a PRIME MINISTER, not DIRECTOR-GENERAL.   24
19 Do NOT type a CAPITAL in lower case; always use UPPER case.   36
20 MS. ANN VINCENT-DALE, 21 FEAR STREET, EAU CLAIRE, WI 54701.   48
                                                    Reset: Ⓜ

Margin Release.
Copy line for line.

21   I hope to get on my bus by two or three. If I miss my   12
22 ride, I must take the next bus. It may not be here by four   24
23 and that means that I will have to take my car for the day.   36
24 Do you think we shall find a place to leave my car in town?   48
                                                    Reset: Ⓜ

Space Bar.

25 q z p r a ' w x o . s l e c i , d k r v u m f j t b y n g h   12
26 Write again . . . and again . . . and again . . . and stop.   24
27 He types 1 or 2 or 3 or 4 or 5 or 6 or 7 or 8 words faster.   36
28 art tan nod day yes sit tar ran not tab bat tea air rat tag   48
    |1 |2 |3 |4 |5 |6 |7 |8 |9 |10 |11 |12

(Continued on next page)

① 4

JOB 136-1: FINANCIAL STATEMENT

Plain paper ☐ **Spacing 2** ☐ **Line 60** ☐ ■ **20'/0e**

Center a copy of the financial statement on page 272 on a full sheet in the style indicated.

JOB 136-2: 5-MINUTE TIMED WRITING

Plain paper ☐ **Spacing 2** ☐ **Line 70** ☐ **Tab 5**

Take a 5-minute writing on the following selection, responding carefully to the bell (lines do not end even). Score by the Net method (deduct 2 wam for each error). Circled numbers are 1-minute goals at 50 wam.

JOB INTERVIEW

If you are asked by an employer to come 9
for a personal interview or a test of your 17
skills, there is an interest in you as a 26
prospective employee. Now you must get 34
yourself prepared for a good impression. 42

First, make a list of the things you 51
should take with you on the chance they 58
might be useful. You will want to take port- 67
folios of your best typewriting, for example. 78
You will want to bring pencils, paper, an 86
eraser, correction fluid, pocket-size diction- 94
ary, and a small note pad on which to jot 103
notes. If you have had correspondence 111
about this interview, bring along copies so 120
you will recall what you said and also the 128

|₁ |₂ |₃ |₄ |₅ |₆ |₇ |₈

names of all the people involved. Bring 136
along your social security card, your letters 145
of recommendation, all the names and 152
addresses and other things you need for 160
filling in an application form, and so on. 169

Second, plan in equal detail exactly what 178
you must do to prepare yourself: what you 187
will wear that will be neat and business- 196
like, what extra pains you must take with 204
regard to your grooming, and the like. To 213
put your best forward is quite important: 221
knowing you appear fairly decent gives you 229
confidence; and the interviewer gets a good 239
picture of how you will fit into the pattern 248
of the other employees. 252

Third, because the interviewer is sure to 261
talk about his firm, do some research on it. 271
Find out what its principal products are, 279
what services it performs, where its main 287
branches are located, and the work done 296
where you are interviewed. 300

|₁ |₂ |₃ |₄ |₅ |₆ |₇ |₈   SI 1.42N

(If you repeat the timed writing, before doing so, type three times (a) each line on your paper that contains a typing error and (b) the line after the last line you finished in the 5 minutes.)

JOB 136-3: COMPLETION CARDS

5" x 3" cards or slips ☐ ■ **5'/0e**

UNIT 35

LESSONS 37/13 8/13

Directions: *Spacing—1. Line—85. Warmup—page 270; then turn to page 274 and begin Job 137-1.*

Set a tab every tenth space; then type lines 29–31, tabbing and backspacing to use the tabulator as shown here and to make each column of words even on the right.

Tab and Backspacer.

Ⓜ	Ⓣ	Ⓣ	Ⓣ	Ⓣ	Ⓣ
29	bet	bets	better	per	pert	perch
30	tea	tease	teacher	leg	legal	legend
31	the	then	these	sea	seal	seam

POSTTEST

Repeat the Pretest on page 8. Score your work and note how much you have improved.

ACTIVITIES	20 MIN.	40 MIN.
Warmup alone	3'	—
Warmup, Plus	—	8'
Pretest once	3'	—
Pretest twice (averaged)	—	6'
Practice drills	11'	20'
Posttest once	3'	—
Posttest twice (averaged)	—	6'

CLINIC **1**

Directions: *Spacing—1. Line—60. Warmup drills—2; others, as directed.*

goal

■ **To use intensive drill to improve basic skill.**

WARMUP, PLUS

For the "Warmup," type lines 1–4 three times. For the "Plus," type four 12-second sprints on lines 1 and 2 for speed gain or on lines 3 and 4 for accuracy gain.

1	It is nice to know that he may have the job if he wants it.	12
Edit line 2.	2 we drove through idaho, nevada, utah, colorado, and kansas.	12
	3 Max and Kay reviewed the subject before giving Paul a quiz.	12
	4 Read Chapters 10, 28, and 39; summarize Chapters 47 and 56.	12

12" SPEED: |25 30 35 40 45 50 55 60|

PRETEST

Take two 1-minute timings on lines 5M–7M if your machine is manual or on lines 5E–7E if it is electric. Proofread both timings; then average the scores.

Manuals only.

5M	The editor failed to qualify for a gift of rayon stockings.	12
6M	The two tailors usually wait to clip the yellow waist line.	24
7M	He zoomed by the raised balloon and ran for a railway line.	36

|1 |2 |3 |4 |5 |6 |7 |8 |9 |10 |11 |12|

Electrics only.

5E	Eleven redwood trees were free from excess grass and weeds.	12
6E	A tax is assessed on gas we use but not on the beef we eat.	24
7E	Bees made wax in the vase, and deer made beds in the grass.	36

PRACTICE

Type many copies of each drill: lines 8M–11M for manuals, 8E–11E for electrics.

Manuals only:
Up reaches without left-hand runs.

8M	qualify tailors valued zoomed waist raise bail clip sky sly	12
9M	railway dailies yellow gained pairs mails mail harm jar ill	24
10M	usually kingdom lacked oblige quail taken wait walk way ran	36
11M	balloon calling sailed editor fails rayon deny gift yes par	48

Electrics only:
Left-hand runs without inward motions.

8E	assessed erasers desert verbs sewer dress vase deer wax bed	12
9E	decrease dressed drawer weeds grass based bass beef sew eve	24
10E	reserved reverse exceed trees fever deeds bees grew gas raw	36
11E	asserted deserve excess taxes erase brass tree free bee red	48

POSTTEST

Repeat the Pretest. Score your work and note your improvement.

April 30 (4/30):

Transportation to airport	7 50
Flight from Cincinnati to Pittsburgh ...	33 00
Car rental first day	25 00
Hotel William Penn	28 00
Meals	4 75
Tips, tolls, parking meters, miscellaneous	5 00

May 1 (5/1)

Car rental second day	12 50
Flight from Pittsburgh to Cincinnati ...	33 00
Transportation from airport	7 50
Total .... ■ 156 25	

2. Prepare a voucher check for "Payment in full for the expenses incurred on your trip from Cincinnati to Pittsburgh and return, April 30 and May 1, 19--." It is Check 4271.

(Duplicate forms are provided on workbook page 316 for your use if you and your teacher think you should try this employment test a second time.)

JOB 134-3: COMPLETION CARDS

5" x 3" cards or slips □ ■ 5'/0e

Directions: Spacing—1. Line—85. Warmup—page 270.

goals

■ To fill in a job application. ■ To pass an accounting-clerk typing test: financial summary and TW.

JOB 135-1: JOB APPLICATION FORM

Workbook 317 □ ■ 30'/0e

Fill in the workbook form to apply for the highest office job you are capable of handling.

JOB 135-2: FINANCIAL STATEMENT PREVIEW

Plain paper □ Review page 134 □ Spacing 2 □ Line 60 □ ■ 10'/0e

Rehearse the arranging and typing of the financial summary shown below. Use ruled-table form.

CONNER AND TRUMP, INC.
Summary of Financial Results
For the Quarter Ended March 31, 19 --

Summary Items	This Year	Last Year
Operating revenue	$172,508	$166,073
Income before taxes on income and minority interests	78,228	59,849
Provision for taxes on income	32,215	30,975
Minority interest in earnings of subsidiaries	2,758	2,659
Net income	$43,255	$26,215
Average number of common shares	31,665	28,077
Earnings per common share	$ 1.37	$ 0.94

goals A

■ To review the standard business letter. ■ To produce a letter within 10'/3e.

Directions: *Spacing—1. Line—60. Drills—2.*

1	It is but a short time for us to wait for our ride to town.	12
2	we drove through iowa, illinois, and indiana--but not ohio.	12
3	Jack would pay for fixing my vanity if Elizabeth requested.	12
4	Mark the chalkboards at 10, 28, 39, 47, and 56 centimeters.	12

|1 |2 |3 |4 |5 |6 |7 |8 |9 |10 |11 |12

JOB 5-1: LETTER

Workbook 13 □ Body 133
□ SI 1.31FE □ ■ 10'/3e

"Welcome to Ace Forms!" says Lincoln G. Clark, purchasing agent. You meet his staff, Ms. Foster and Ms. Ely. "I have some letters for

you to type when you're set," he continues.

In the files you find the carbon of a letter that shows Mr. Clark's preferences: date on line 15, address beginning 5 lines below it, date and closing lines starting at the center, standard punctuation after the salutation and closing, and so on. You study it carefully.

"I thought this was ready to sign," says Mr. Clark, showing you the letter on page 11, "then I saw it was addressed to the wrong person. Please do it over, addressing it to Mr. T. L. Drake, Postal Press Co., Bankers Trust Building, 406 Sixth Avenue, Des Moines, IA 50307. Be sure to correct the salutation and the reference in the body too."

goals B

■ To produce a letter within 10'/3e
■ To review envelope typing.

JOB 5-2: LETTER

Workbook 15 □ Body 115
□ SI 1.31FE □ ■ 10'/3e

"Now I want to let a printer know that I will be in his town," says Mr. Clark. He dictates:

Mr. T. G. Skaff, Jr. / Skaff Forms Printing Co. / 373 West Lawn Street / North Platte, NE 69101 / Dear Mr. Skaff: /   16   24   30

On November 14 and 15 I will be in North Platte to attend a meeting of the   37   48

Central Association of Purchasing Agents.   54

Would it be possible for me to visit your plant the next day, the 16th? If it is, I would be pleased to stay over an extra day to make the visit.   63   71   80   85

Our company, as you may know, is now looking for one or two new printers and new presses to help us take care of our growing business. The result of my visit could be our placing large orders in your hands.   94   102   109   117   126   127

Although the date is some weeks off, I would appreciate an early reply so that I might make arrangements. / Sincerely yours, / Lincoln G. Clark / Purchasing Agent / URS / cc Fred Cox   136   145   155   169   171

goals

■ To fill in a job application. ■ To pass a clerk-typist employment test: timed writing and two forms.

Directions: Spacing—1. Line—85. Warmup—page 270.

Note: Lines will not end even in the TW.

JOB 133-1: JOB APPLICATION FORM

Workbook 313 □ ■ 30'/0e

Assuming that you can market the skills you now have and that you will graduate at the end of this term, make an application [fill in the form] for the highest job you are capable of handling.

JOB 133-2: TIMED WRITING PREVIEW

Plain paper □ Spacing 2 □ Line 70 □ Tab 5

Type the timed-writing selection below, going as rapidly or as slowly as you wish, to determine the line endings (they do not end even; bring each line as close to 70 as you can) and words to practice. Then practice difficult words.

JOB 134-1: 5-MINUTE TIMED WRITING

Plain paper □ Spacing 2 □ Line 70 □ Tab 5

Take a 5-minute writing; score by the Net method (deduct 2 wam for each error). Circled numbers are 1-minute goals at 50 wam.

JOB HUNTING

When you have completed your training 9
and are ready to hunt for a job, how do 16
you go about it? Of many possible methods, 25
here are five excellent ones that thousands 34
before you have used successfully. 41 ①

First, get in touch with everyone you 50
know who might learn about vacancies in 58
your line of work. Tell all of them that 67
you're looking. Such people not only know 75
what openings will occur but also how 83
much they pay, what kind of applicant is 91 ②
wanted, and everything else. Try relatives, 100
friends, acquaintances from church, alumni, 109
and so on. 111

|1 |2 |3 |4 |5 |6 |7 |8

Second, talk with people at school whose 120
duties involve helping trainees find posi- 129
tions. Let them know you are ready and 136
what you can do best so that they will 144 ③
remember you when an inquiry comes from 152
some employer. Do not badger them, how- 160
ever; sometimes they are overwhelmed by 168
the avalanche of students who want job 175
interviews at the same time. 182

Third, think of putting in your request 191
with an employment agency, both the free 200 ④
public ones run by the government and the 207
private ones that charge fees. It is especially 217
good to do this if you have some unusual 225
skill, like the fluent command of a foreign 235
language. 237

Fourth, look at the want ads in the news- 246
papers. Even if you find nothing you want 254 ⑤
to seize upon, at least you can ascertain the 269
current salary scale for beginners in the 276
kind of employment you seek. 278

Fifth, if there is some firm in your com- 288
munity for whom you would especially like 295
to work, tell the company. Firms have 303 ⑥
much interest in persons who live close, 311
who have relatives already working for 319
them, or who want to work there. [*Start over.*] 325

|1 |2 |3 |4 |5 |6 |7 |8   SI 1.42N

JOB 134-2: EXPENSE VOUCHER, VOUCHER CHECK

Workbook 315 □ ■ Both within 15'/0e

1. Prepare an expense voucher for John Vance, 7020 Pickway Drive, Cincinnati, Ohio 45238, for the following expenses:

Purchasing (816) 555-3200

Ace **BUSINESS FORMS COMPANY**

920 Main Street / Kansas City, MO 64105

JOB 5-1

See page 10.

① September 12, 19--

4

8

② Mr. Ferdinand Santiago
Program Chairman
CAPA Convention
Interstate Stationery Company
2424 Dodge Street
Omaha, NE 68131

13
16
19
25
29
32
33

Dear Mr. Santiago:

37
38

③ Thank you for the invitation to speak at the CAPA
Convention, Monday, November 14. This meeting will
give me a chance to express some views I have on
devising better means of controlling stock items.

48
58
68
78
79

I have always been extremely interested in meetings
of CAPA and have gone to some of the past sessions.
Many of my colleagues have told me how very much
they are looking forward to the North Platte meeting; I think it will be a good one, Mr. Santiago.

90
100
110
120
130
131

I would surely like to hear a good talk on the topic
of forms design. Have you asked anyone to speak on
this subject? This is an area in which a good deal
of change is taking place; I think you could draw a
good crowd at such a session.

142
152
163
173
179
180

④ Sincerely yours,

185

188

⑤ Lincoln G. Clark
Purchasing Agent

192
196
197

⑥ URS
cc George Deeg

198
201

Remember. In a standard business letter: ① The date starts at the center of line 15.
② The inside address begins 5 lines below the date. ③ Line length is 5″ (pica 50, elite 60)
unless the letter is very short (under 75 words, use 4″ line—40 pica or 50 elite spaces) or
very long (over 225 words, use 6″ line—60 pica or 70 elite spaces). ④ Closing lines start
at center. ⑤ Signer's name is always typed. ⑥ Reference initials are yours, the typist's.

IN PART TWELVE . . .

1. The objective is to give you several experiences in taking employment tests so that you will coolly breeze through both the final examination of this course and your real employment tests.

2. At the same time, you are to boost your skill by 1 more word a minute, to 50 words a minute within 1 error on 3-minute writings, 2 errors on 5-minute writings, and 5 errors on 10-minute writings.

3. The schedule is therefore organized in this manner:

Unit 34: Sample Tests

Lessons 133–134:
    Clerical job applica-
    tion and test:
    TW, forms

Lessons 135–136:
    Accounting Clerk
    application and test:
    TW and financial
    statement

Unit 35: Sample Tests

Lessons 137–138:
    Secretarial job
    application and test:
    TW, letter

Lessons 139–140:
    Civil Service typing
    test: general
    information, TW,
    rough draft

Unit 36: Examination

Lesson 141: TW,
    objective information
    test

Lesson 142: Letter,
    financial statement

Lesson 143: Report,
    table

Lesson 144: Forms,
    organization chart

4. At the start of each practice period, turn to this page and type at least one set of sprints (four 12-second writings) on one sentence from each of the three groups below. Spacing 1, line 85.

SPEED RECALL

1   The chairman of the wood firm
2   paid the man and the boy for the ancient map they had.   17
3   got the new auditor to fix the mistake in panel eight.   17
4   had a neighbor who got bit by a lamb when she held it.   17

12" WAM: 45   50   55   60   65   70   75   80   85

ALPHABET RECALL

5   Max is quite lazy, but I know
6   he would love to get involved with my project in golf.   17
7   he would have no trouble adjusting to a piano factory.   17
8   he would enjoy having a chance to jump from a balloon.   17

12" WAM: 45   50   55   60   65   70   75   80   85

NUMBER RECALL

9   When asked to type numbers, he
10   did so by threes: 3 and 6 and 9 and 12 and 15 and 18.   17
11   included dollars: $10 and $28 and $39 and $47 or $56.   17
12   did some we—23 drills: we 23 or 94 it 85 up 70 to 59.   17

12" WAM: 45   50   55   60   65   70   75   80   85

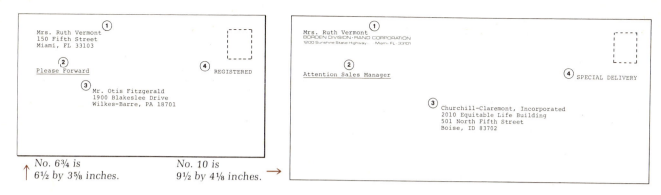

Do You Remember? ① Type the writer's name above printed return address or as first line of a typed return address (start 5 spaces in on line 3). ② Insert on-arrival directions, if any, below return address on line 9, underscored. ③ Begin address on line 12, 2 inches from edge (small envelope) or on line 14, 4 inches in (large envelope). ④ Special mail service, if any, goes in all caps on line 9 or 10, ending 5 spaces from right edge. **Practice typing addresses from Lesson 6 on Workbook 17–18.**

---

goal A

■ **To produce two letters (Jobs 6-1 and 6-2), each within 10'/3e.**

LESSON 6

Directions: *Spacing—1. Line—60. Warmup—repeat lines 1–4, page 10.*

JOB 6-1: LETTER

Workbook 19 □ Body and postscript 133 + 20 for attention line □ SI 1.33FE □ ■ 10'/3e

"I'll need a room reservation in North Platte," says Mr. Clark as he begins to dictate the following letter to you.

Holiday Inn, Inc. / Jct. US 83 and I-80 / North Platte, NE 69101 / ATTENTION INN-KEEPER *Type that in all caps at the left margin.* / Ladies and Gentlemen: /   16 20 21 26

Please reserve a double room for me for November 12 through November 15. I would like to have a room in the price range of $20 to $25.   34 42 50 54

Since I will be arriving by rail on the 12th, I will need to have a courtesy car pick me up at the train station and take me to the Inn. I will also need a car to commute to and from North Platte College,   64 71 80 88 97

where I will be going to a few meetings.   105

It is urgent that this room be held for me, even if there should be some delay in my train arrival time of 6 p.m. Therefore, Ace Forms will guarantee payment of this reservation.   114 122 131 139 142

Yours truly, / Lincoln G. Clark / Purchasing Agent / URS / *Oh, I want to add a postscript. (Start it a double space below your initials. Introduce it with "PS.")*   154 160

PS: If a deposit is required to hold this reservation for late arrival, please let me know.   169 177 179

JOB 6-2: LETTER

Workbook 21 □ Body 97 □ SI 1.35N □ ■ 10'/3e

"Send this letter to Mr. Sitz, telling him the title of my talk," says Mr. Clark. He dictates:

goal

■ To type at least 49 wam for 5'/2e.

Special Note: *Review 11 here consists only of the indicated timed writings because Part 11 itself was a production review in depth preparatory to the employment tests in Part 12.*

Directions: Spacing—1. Line—85.
Warmup—page 259.
TWs: Spacing—2. Line—70. Tab—5.

TWO 5-MINUTE TIMED WRITINGS

Type the TW in each column; then average the scores.

When the test is done, someone may take your papers for scoring, but the odds are that you will be asked to proofread it yourself. If the company is a small one, the person giving you the test might feel that you can mark it better than others anyhow; if the company is one of the large ones that has a personnel department, you'll be asked to mark your paper as one more demonstration: you're not guaranteed the job if you find all the errors, but you sure won't get the job if you don't find all the errors! So the proofreading is an important part.

Now, one thing to remember as you check your work: no one tells you to hurry it up. In classroom typing tests, you always are racing the clock; nine times out of ten you do not have enough time to check your work carefully, so you get a habit of skimming the work. Not so in the employment test. Oh, you can't sit there doodling, but no one will put pressure on you so long as you are obviously going over your work. So take time to do it right. There are no acceptable excuses.

You place your papers down on the table top with the test itself on the left side of your paper. You read half a line of the test and hold the place with a finger; then you read those words on your paper and hold the place with a finger. Half a line by half a line, you go over your test word for word.

SI 1.35N

CHECKING YOUR SPEED SCORE

If you are told to figure out your speed score, you must inquire about the system you are to use. In one system, called Net, you must deduct ten words for each error; this means cutting your speed by one word a minute on a 10-minute writing or cutting it two words a minute on a 5-minute writing. In the other system, called Gross, you do not penalize the speed score for any errors; you just divide the words by the minutes, and there's your speed. Accurate typists and most firms prefer the Net system, since typists with many errors are weeded out.

The system makes a difference; so when you write down your speed score, identify what it is, as "55 gross" or "55 net" words a minute.

OTHER REMINDERS

When you take a job test, you are almost always watched, because the way you behave under the pressure of a test is a good clue to how you will act under the pressure of a job. If you keep your cool when keys jam, ribbon breaks, or other disaster strikes, knowing that your poise withstood the disaster might be more important than the scores. If you are taking the test with others, watch how you act toward them before and after the test; the level of harmony or disharmony greatly interests the employer, who then may or may not consider this matter.

SI 1.36N

Mr. Hugh T. Sitz / CAPA Program Editor /   15
1303 Locust Street / Des Moines, IA 50309 /   23
Dear Mr. Sitz: /   28

This year it is my good fortune to be the   38
guest speaker at CAPA's annual luncheon   46
meeting in North Platte.   51

Mr. Drake asked me to brief you on my   61
talk and its contents. The title of my talk   70
is "Computer Control of Stock." In part,   78

it will relate to the following items: 86
Indent these items five spaces; allow two   ..
spaces after the number and period.   ..

    1. A computer approach to stock control.   97
    2. Equipment required for the new system.   107
    3. MIS and its effect on purchase base.   116

I look forward to seeing you at the meet-   126
ing. / Sincerely yours, / Lincoln G. Clark /   152
Purchasing Agent / URS   159

goal B

■ To type 40 wam for
   3'/2e.

Directions: *Spacing—1. Line—60. Tab—5.*
Drills—4.

12-SECOND SPRINTS

Each line four times.

1 Vince found their power lines were fewer than Bob had said.   12
2 When Ann said that they were out of the red, they were not.   12
3 Their man and one or two of ours had to beg to get a reply.   12

12" SPEED: 25 30 35 40 45 50 55 60

POWER DRILL

Up reaches without jump combinations.

4 weather voltage slides sticks waits views send rule jar mat   12
5 elastic ashamed anchor cleans badly argue kits host use see   12
6 medical enlarge plight highly fruit color jets life hop few   12
7 workers budgets woolen throat sides deals rise owed who ray   12

|1 |2 |3 |4 |5 |6 |7 |8 |9 |10 |11 |12

SKILL BLITZ

Summary:
3' TW.
Remedials.
3' TW.

A "blitz" is an intensive effort to boost speed without increasing errors. The effort concentrates on immediate and sustained repetition, as shown below.

1. Take a 3-minute writing, repeating lines as shown. Omit all blank lines. The circled numbers show where you should be at the end of each minute if you type 40 words a minute.

2. Type, half a dozen times, each word on which you made an error, hesitated, jammed keys, or stopped.

3. Repeat the 3-minute writing and try to surpass your goal.

8   Why must the blank between columns be six spaces? One   12
9   Why must the blank between columns be six spaces? One   24
10 Why must the blank between columns be six spaces? One   36

11 good reason: specialists say eyes cannot jump horizontally   48
12 good reason: specialists say eyes cannot jump horizontally   60
13 good reason: specialists say eyes cannot jump horizontally   72

14 over three quarters of an inch, and the six spaces is quite   84
15 over three quarters of an inch, and the six spaces is quite   96
16 over three quarters of an inch, and the six spaces is quite   108

Circled numbers are 1' goals.

17 within that width.   112
18 within that width.   116
19 within that width.   120

|1 |2 |3 |4 |5 |6 |7 |8 |9 |10 |11 |12   SI 1.42N

■ 3'/2e

1   6   13

Type lines 13–15 three times each as a Preview. Type them quick, quicker, very quick!

Spacing—1.
Line—60.

13 anticipation signature requisite resource compiled know how   12
14 painstaking exercises carefully therefore despite will need   12
15 corrections collections executive reference pursues compose   12

Take a 5-minute TW as a Pretest. Type each line of your typing that has an error three times as Practice; then repeat the Preview. Repeat the 5-minute TW as a Posttest.

Spacing—2.
Line—50.
Tab—5.

Circled numbers are 1′ goals.

16 Despite the painstaking care that the typist exercises on each   14 | 136
17 letter, with concern for how it is placed on the page, how much   26 | 148
18 space is left for the signature, how carefully the corrections have   40 | 162
19 been made, and so on, all of us know that what is requisite is a   53 | 175
20 good message. Letters must speak.   60 | 183
21 Any office worker who pursues a career as an aide to an execu-   73 | 196
22 tive will often need to compose a letter. A wise trainee will   86 | 209
23 therefore seize each chance to collect good letters for reference   99 | 222
24 use. The letters in this collection have been compiled in antici-   112 | 235
25 pation of the day when they will prove a resource.   122 | 245

■ 5′/2e

|1 |2 |3 |4 |5 |6 |7 |8 |9 |10 |11 |12 |13 |14   SI 1.41N

goal

■ To prepare a portfolio of typed forms or of samples of letters.

LETTER OF ACKNOWLEDGMENT	LETTER OF CONGRATULATIONS	LETTER OF REGRET
Acknowledging receipt of letter	Congratulating a person on the occasion of his retirement	Writer regrets that he cannot accept invitation to speak

LESSON **132**

Directions: Spacing—1. Line—85.
Warmup—page 259; then start project.

COLLECTION If you have a workbook, prepare a portfolio on forms typing. If you do not have a workbook, assemble a compilation of model letters for various messages.

Forms Portfolio. Workbook pages 301–311 provide forms on which you can quickly retype the following representative samples:

☐ Fill-in postal card: page 37, Job 16-3 (1)
☐ Data card, 5″ x 3″: page 39, Job 17-1 (1)
☐ Visible index card: page 40, Job 17-3 (1)
☐ Invoice: page 177, Job 79-1 (1)
☐ Monthly statement: page 177, Job 79-1 (3)
☐ Voucher check: page 178, Job 80-1 (No. 2-63)
☐ Expense voucher: page 178, Job 80-2 (1)
☐ Personnel roster: page 157, Job 71-1
☐ Interoffice memo: page 158, Job 72-1
☐ Stock requisition: page 46, Job 21-1 (1)
☐ Purchase requisition: page 46, Job 21-2 (1)
☐ Request for quotation: page 47, Job 21-3 (1)
☐ Purchase order: page 47, Job 22-1 (No. 9449)

Letters Collection. Collect and identify in the top right corner [on a file folder label or 2″ x 2″ block of colored paper, mounted on the paper] samples of different kinds of letters. You may have saved letters you can use or you may wish to retype on plain paper some given on the pages below.

☐ Acknowledgment, 43, 164, 192, 217, 247
☐ Appreciation, 86, 216, 217
☐ Answer to inquiry, 199, 200
☐ Confirmation, 165, 247
☐ Congratulations, anniversary, 241; retirement, 242, victory, 191
☐ Get well, 216, 242, 243
☐ Information, 75, 165, 187, 193
☐ Inquiry, 11, 50, 230–232
☐ Insurance, re claims, 199, 200
☐ Invitation, 11, 252
☐ Notification, 223
☐ Regrets, 247
☐ Reservations, 12, 94, 206, 207, 257
☐ Transmittal, 129, 144, 211, 238, 257

goal A

■ To type 40 wam for 5'/3e on copy of normal difficulty.

Directions: *Spacing—1. Line—60. Tab—5.*
Drills—3.

WARMUP REVIEW

Edit line 2.

1 Hey, note how well my fingers are flying on the keys today! 12
2 the skiffs were named doria, nancy lou, jojo, and susan ii. 12
3 Howe typed a dozen requisitions for jet black moving boxes. 12
4 A man put markers at 10 km, 28 km, 39 km, 47 km, and 56 km. 12

|1 |2 |3 |4 |5 |6 |7 |8 |9 |10 |11 |12

PRETEST

5-minute TW.

5   In the past this company has established no set policy 12
6 for the typing of tables. A typist has prepared tables for 24
7 reports in a form that has been the quickest and easiest to 36
8 use. As a result the number of table styles that have been 48
9 used has nearly equaled the number of tables that have been 60
10 typed! To minimize this problem for typists, the following 72
11 guidelines have been prepared for the typing of all tables. 84
12   All tables must be typed in one of two styles--open or 96
13 ruled. To use as little space on the page as necessary and 108
14 yet prepare copy that is easy to read, just six spaces will 120
15 be used between all columnar data. Unless the table has an 132
16 excess of horizontal lines, the data will be double-spaced. 144
17   Words in the first column must be aligned at the left. 156
18 Dollar signs should be aligned at the top and bottom of the 168
19 column. The first item and last item (if it is part of the 180
20 total line) should be preceded by the dollar sign. Numbers 192
21 should always be aligned at the right. 200

Tiny figures are speed counters for 5' writings.

■ 5'/3e

|1 |2 |3 |4 |5 |6 |7 |8 |9 |10 |11 |12   SI 1.38N

PRACTICE

TW vocabulary.

Type each drill three times; then repeat lines 22–24 for accuracy gain or lines 25–27 for speed gain.

22 established necessary quickest problems equaled column open 12
23 styles--open prepared typists, minimize aligned policy page 12
24 horizontal guidelines preceded columnar easiest excess item 12

|1 |2 |3 |4 |5 |6 |7 |8 |9 |10 |11 |12

25 table style typed space lines data, words first signs right 12
26 past form that have been used this open page easy just read 12
27 has set for the had use all one two yet six and no in as if 12

POSTTEST

Repeat the Pretest. Score your work and note your improvement.

goal

■ To compile and annotate a collection of legal papers or financial statements.

PERSONAL WILL	BUILDING PERMIT	BALANCE SHEET
With legal rules With signature lines With witness signature lines With all caps With 10-space indentions	Fill-in form Identifications on signature lines Bottom half not for typist	Double-spaced With leaders With all-cap heading lines With last two columns only 2 spaces apart With single and double rules

Directions: Spacing—1. Line—85.
Warmup—page 259.

COLLECTION Collect and annotate a group of legal documents or financial statements—whichever you prefer or whichever you have more examples of to build on.

1. What Pages? Use any you have typed and saved in this course. You may retype any you wish. You may compose and type new papers to involve more examples.

2. How to Annotate. Use file folder labels or a sheet of colored paper on which you rule off 2″ x 2″ boxes. Fill in one for each page of work; tell what the page illustrates and call attention to its salient features: spacing, rulings, alignments, and so on. Your score on the project is the number of items on the checklist that you are able to illustrate. Note pages to refer to.

LEGAL CHECKLIST

Bid specifications, 210, 235: ruled □ unruled □
Building permit, 210–213: ruled □ unruled □

Contracts: employment, 258, ruled □ unruled □; painting, 234, ruled □ unruled □ other □
Minutes of meeting, 122: single-spaced □ double-spaced □
Proxy, 119: single-spaced □ double-spaced □
Stockholders: notice, 224 □ report, 116, 133 □
Sublease agreement, 245, 246 □
Will, 250, 251: ruled □ unruled □

FINANCIAL STATEMENT CHECKLIST

Accounts receivable, 180: single-spaced □ double-spaced □
Balance sheet, 182: single-spaced □ double-spaced □
Financial summary: in report, 111–112 □
Income: statement of, 108, 126, 181, 188 □
Operations: consolidated statement, 77, 118, 134 □ summary in letter, 110, 228 □
Tax itemizations: expenses, 125 □ depreciation, 126 □

---

goal A

■ To type 49 wam/3′/1e.

goal B

■ To type 49 wam/5′/2e.

3-MINUTE TW SKILL DRIVE

Spacing—2.
Line—50.
Tab—5.

Speed markers are for 3′ TW. Circled figures are 1′ goals.

■ 3′/1e

TO BE EFFICIENT

□ *Adjust the machine first.*
□ *Insert the paper next.*
□ *Read the material.*
□ *Then remind yourself of your goals for today.*

Directions: Spacing—1. Line—85.
Warmup—page 259.

1. How many different forms are there? Experts judge that there | 13
2. are about fifteen thousand, when you include not only tax forms | 26
3. but also insurance forms, legal forms, billing forms, payroll | 39
4. checks and forms, and lots of others you can name. | 49
5. Since no typist could practice all the forms there are, how | 13 | 62
6. many should the typist experience? Well, it's not the quantity | 26 | 75
7. so much as the varied typing problems: typing on lines, between | 39 | 88
8. lines, between words, between rules, beside guides. | 49 | 98
9. The forms in this collection illustrate most of the demands | 13 | 111
10. made on the typist. The forms are of many kinds and sizes, but | 26 | 124
11. the important aspect of them all is the variety of manipulations | 39 | 137
12. which they require of the typist who will use them. | 49 | 147

SI 1.44N

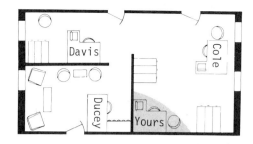

goals B

■ To review arrangement and production of business tables.
■ To produce one table (Job 7-1) within 15'/3e.

Directions: *Spacing—1. Line—clear. Tab—clear.*
WB—23–24.

JOB 7-1: TABLE

Plain paper □ **Full sheet** □ ■ **15'/3e**

"I hope you like to type tables!" exclaims Dick Cole, head of the Training Department, after introducing you to his staff, Paul Davis and Carol Ducey.

"You see," says Mr. Cole, "our training department has three duties. One is conducting orientation courses for new employees. A second duty is conducting courses to help employees who want to qualify for promotions and salary increases. It's the third duty, building staff efficiency, that your work today will involve."

"We want all our typists to use open or ruled style for tables,

so we are preparing a handbook about tables. We are at the point of developing the model tables we will use in the handbook." He gives you the clipping shown below. "Please type an exact copy of this table," Mr. Cole says.

Do You Remember? Before you insert paper for a table, you take four steps: (1) clear the margin and tab stops, (2) figure the top margin, (3) backspace-center to establish the left margin, and (4) space over to set the tab stops for the additional columns. Read the notes below, but do not type any of them.

Display column headings by underscoring and centering them over the columns.

Arrange the items in a definite pattern. Items here are from highest to lowest percentage.

Align words at the left.

An asterisk follows an item referred to in a footnote; in a footnote, the asterisk precedes the information.

Separate a footnote from the table itself by a 1-inch line. Center or block a 1-line footnote.

Table 1

AUTO PARTS RETAIL PRICE INCREASES

Fordette Accessories Division

Name of Part	1975	Current	Increase
Cruise Control	$ 99	$134	35.4%
Tinted Glass	24	31	29.2%
Power Seats	116	138	19.0%
Power Steering	124	142	14.5%
AM/FM/Tape	337	372	10.4%
Power Windows*	129	140	8.5%
Vinyl Roof	114	123	7.9%
Power Brakes	56	61	7.0%

————————

*4-door models

Open style table.

Put 6 spaces between columns unless there is some special reason for more or fewer.

Repeat the % sign after each number if the column heading does not clearly indicate that the figures under it are percentages.

Align numbers at the right. Align decimals.

Align the $ sign at the left of the longest amount entry in the column. Count a $ sign in the width of the column, but count it only if that helps when centering the heading and the column.

TO INCREASE ACCURACY

□ *Focus on typing smoothly.*
□ *Keep cool.*
□ *Type with fingers only.*
□ *Keep wrists still.*

Directions: Spacing—1. Line—85.
Warmup—page 259.

goal A

■ To type 49
wam/3'/1e.

goal B

■ To type 49
wam/5'/2e.

**3-MINUTE TW
SKILL DRIVE**

Spacing—2.
Line—50.
Tab—5.

Take a 3-minute TW as a Pretest. Take up to ten 1-minute TWs as Practice; trying to type each paragraph within 1'/0e. Repeat the 3-minute TW as a Posttest and note improvement.

1   Some say that legal papers are hard to type, and they are the   13
2   first time you do them; but then they seem to become easy. After   27
3   all, those legal lines that mark the margins are the only built-in   40
4   visual guides you will find in all you type.   49

5   A legal document is no more than a carefully worded agree-   12   61
6   ment between two parties; to give the paper an extra touch or   25   74
7   two, it is traditional to embellish it with all caps, lines of under- 38   87
8   scores, fancy language, and deep paragraph indention.   49   98

9   The only thing simpler to type than a wholly typed legal paper   14 112
10 is a legal form on which dates, amounts, and words or parts of 26 124
11 words are typed in gaps left in the printing. It is hard to realize 40 138
12 how any mystique about legal work came about.   49 147

|1 |2 |3 |4 |5 |6 |7 |8 |9 |10 |11 |12 |13 |14   SI 1.38N

**Speed markers
are for 3' TW.
Circled numbers
are 1' goals.**

■ 3'/1e

**5-MINUTE TW
SKILL DRIVE**

Spacing—1.
Line—60.

Type lines 13–15 three times each as a Preview.

13 arrangement placement financial ultimate complex demands on   12
14 concentrate production demands numerals editions expense of   12
15 statements operations analysis exercise caution; setting by   12

Take a 5-minute TW as a Pretest. Type each line of your typing that contains an error three times as Practice and repeat the Preview. Repeat the 5-minute TW as a Posttest.

Spacing—2.
Line—50.

Circled numbers
are 1' goals.

16 One kind of production work that demands the ultimate of any   13 135
17 typist is the typing of financial statements. The arrangement of 26 148
18 the work isn't so complex; it's the typing and lining up of so   39 161
19 many numerals that put the typist down to second gear.   50 173

20 It should slow you down a little, but not so much. True, the   63 186
21 first time you do a statement of operations or expense analysis, 76 199
22 you will exercise caution; but once you have worked out a place- 89 212
23 ment setting, the next dozen editions of the statement are quite 102 225
24 a snap: you copy the setup of one from the file, freeing your   115 238

■ two copies 5'/2e   25 mind to concentrate on all the numbers.   122 245

|1 |2 |3 |4 |5 |6 |7 |8 |9 |10 |11 |12 |13 |14   SI 1.43N

goals A

■ To produce one table (Job 8-1) within 15'/3e. ■ To review the typing of ruled tables.

JOB 8-1: TABLE
Plain paper ☐ Open style ☐ ■ 15'/3e

Directions: Spacing—1. Line—clear. Tab—clear. Warmup—page 14 (repeat).

"Great!" says Mr. Cole when Table 1 is done. "I will need another table in that same open style, so I wrote one out."

Handing you the table below, Mr. Cole says, "I need some blank space after every three typed lines. I made a mistake: I arranged the data by percents instead of prices. Please arrange the data by prices—highest first."

"That would make 'LeGrand S9' first," you note.
Mr. Cole nods his approval.

You study the job closely. You note (1) the title line, <u>Annual Price List Report</u>, should be in all caps; (2) the column headings need underscoring; and (3) no percent signs appear in Column 2 because "percent" is in the heading.

Table 2
ANNUAL PRICE LIST REPORT
Markwards Auto Company

Model	Percent of Increase	Markup	Price
Le Grand S8	13.5	$ 102	$5,822
Valdair	13.2	98	3,690
Parland	10.5	75	6,692
Fordette GT	9.2	67	5,139
Lindholm	8.5	53	5,660
Fordette	7.1	50	4,606
Le Grand GT	7.0	46	6,514
Volmair GT	6.0	45	4,850
Camarae GT	5.8	42	4,657
Camarae	4.9	39	3,737
Le Grand S9	4.1	37	6,902
Volmair	3.4	27	3,588

4
20
36
46
66
79
86
93
102
109
116
125
132
139
147
154
160

Type lines 13–16 three times each as a Preview. Type them slow, fast, very fast.

```
13  horizontally solutions problems display shorter quite right    12
14  exasperated line--that slightly somehow depress above other    12
15  half-space ordinarily carriage, spacing holding every space    12
16  like to have to when it this is that is move it this was an     12
```

Take a 5-minute TW as a Pretest. Type each line of your typing that contains an error three times as Practice; then repeat the Preview above. Repeat 5-minute TW as a Posttest.

Spacing—2.
Line—50.
Tab—5.

Circled numbers are 1' goals.

SALE
PRICE

■ 5'/2e

```
17   Typists who really like to solve problems in display become    13  135
18  exasperated if they have to center two lines horizontally, one  26  148
19  above the other, when one is just one stroke longer. In this case, 39  161
20  the two lines are ordinarily begun at the same point; but somehow  52  174
21  the result does not look quite right.                           60  183
22   The solution, of course, is half-spacing the shorter line—that 74  197
23  is, move it in by typing every letter a half space past its usual 87  210
24  place. You do this by using the half-space key if you have one,  100 223
25  or holding the space bar down as you depress each key, or press- 113 236
26  ing slightly on the left knob of the carriage.                  122 245
```

|1 |2 |3 |4 |5 |6 |7 |8 |9 |10 |11 |12 |13 |14   SI 1.40N

goal

■ To compile and annotate examples of display typing.

```
ORGANIZATION CHART      REVISED ITINERARY     NOTICE FOR
Underscore used to      New draft tele-       BULLETIN BOARD
  make boxes              scopes old one      Artistic lettering
Spread-centered         Vertical centering   Lines justified
  title                 Regular centering    Pivoting used to
Colons used to            of title             align bottom
  serve as lines                             Centered horizon-
Inserting typing                               tally
  in boxes
```

LESSON 128

Directions: *Spacing—1. Line—85.*
Warmup—page 259; then start the project.

DISPLAY PROJECT Collect and annotate a group of display pages that illustrate as many of the items on the adjacent checklist as possible.

1. What Displays? Use any you have typed and saved in this course. You may retype any you wish. You may compose and type new ones to involve more features.

2. How to Annotate. Mount a colored file label in the top right corner of the paper or rule in colored ink a 2″ x 2″ box in that corner. In this corner identify what the display is and list the items from the checklist that are illustrated. Do not type the same item more than once. Your score on this project is the number of checklist items you can illustrate (plus any other items you include that are not on the list).

3. High Quality. Since you may someday show your project to a possible employer, include in it only error-free work of which you can be proud.

DISPLAY CHECKLIST

Alignment of two adjacent pages: horizontal sequence ☐ vertical sequence ☐
Artistic borders: example 1 ☐ example 2 ☐
Artistic lettering: example 1 ☐ example 2 ☐
Centering, horizontal: regular ☐ spread ☐ block ☐
Centering, vertical: full page ☐ half page ☐
Colons: aligned to serve as vertical line ☐
Justifying lines: lines only ☐ with display lettering too ☐
Pivoting: signature to ad ☐ other ☐
Scope: organization chart with boxes ☐ organization chart without boxes ☐ bulletin board notice ☐ advertisement ☐ two-page table ☐ certificate 1 ☐ certificate 2 ☐ typing data in preprinted boxes ☐ creative revision to make work smaller ☐

■ To produce two tables (Jobs 8-2 and 8-3), each within 10'/2e.

JOB 8-2: TABLE

Plain paper ☐ **Ruled style** ☐ ■ **10'/3e**

Giving you the clipping below, Mr. Cole says, "Please make a copy of this table—the first of two ruled tables I need for the booklet."

"Will it still be 'Table 3' in your report?" you ask.

"Yes, let's use the same number," he says.

JOB 8-3: TABLE

Plain paper ☐ **Ruled style** ☐ ■ **10'/2e**

"For the final table," says Mr. Cole, "please type another copy of the table on page 16—but this time it is to be different in four ways:

"1. Type it, of course, in ruled style.

"2. Renumber it. Make it 'Table 4.'

"3. Arrange the items alphabetically—the 'Camarae' model will be the first one.

"4. Group items by fours, not by threes."

Do You Remember? When typing a ruled table: (1) Six spaces are always left between columns. (2) One blank line is always left above and below a ruled line. (3) All the ruled lines must be the same length. Study the margin notes in the table below for a further review.

Arrange the items in a definite pattern. This one is alphabetic.

Display the column heads by centering each above its column. Align all headings at bottom.

Place an asterisk (it does not count in column width) after an item referring to a footnote. Precede the footnote by an asterisk.

Block any summary word like "Totals" or "Averages."

Table 3

FORDETTE TEST SITE RESULTS

Markwards Auto Company

Test Site	Miles Driven	Percent Of Total
Brandenberg	117	15.6
Crescent	72	9.6
Donley	20*	2.7
Merced	293	39.0
Odello	34	4.5
St. Croix	59	7.8
Saratoga	108	14.4
Van Ness	48	6.4
TOTALS	751	100.0

*Automobile experienced mechanical problems at 20.1 miles (see report).

Ruled style table.

Tables in a series are numbered and displayed as shown here.

To get 1 blank line above and below a ruled line, single-space before typing the line and double-space after typing it.

Do not repeat the % sign after each number if the column heading clearly indicates that the figures under it are percentages.

Arrange as shown here any footnote with more than one line.

goal

■ To compile and annotate a collection of reports.

REPORT: AGENDA	OPERATIONS REPORT	COMMITTEE REPORT
Single-spaced Enumerated paragraphs Title without a subtitle Runover lines in 4 spaces One-page Job	Title and subtitle Body includes financial report Includes footnote First page of two	Double-spaced All-cap sideheads Group "signature" at bottom Includes a list

LESSON 126

Directions: Spacing—1. Line—85. Warmup—page 259; then start the project.

REPORTS PROJECT Collect and annotate a group of reports, and typed pages like reports, that illustrate as many of the checklist items as possible.

1. What Reports? Use any you have typed and saved in this course. You may retype any you wish. You may compose and type new ones to involve the checklist.

2. How to Annotate. Mount a colored file label in the top right corner of the paper or rule in colored ink a 2″ x 2″ box in the corner. In the area identify which items in the adjacent checklist are shown in the page. Do not type the same checklist item more than once. Your score on this project is the number of checklist items (plus any other characteristics that might not be included in the checklist) you can illustrate. All the pages included in the collection should be error-free—work of which you can be proud.

REPORTS CHECKLIST

Length: one page ☐ second page ☐ other page ☐
Margins: 6″ centered ☐ 6″ + wide left margin ☐
Spacing: single ☐ double ☐
Paper: plain ☐ plain, to be headed memo-style ☐ printed form with sideheads preprinted ☐
Body includes: financial data ☐ table other than financial data ☐ enumerated paragraphs ☐ set-in display paragraph ☐ list ☐ other ☐
Headings: centered title ☐ subtitle line(s) ☐ by-line ☐ subheads *at* left margin ☐ subheads *in* left margin ☐ run-in paragraph headings ☐
Scope: stockholders' notice ☐ operations report ☐ trip report ☐ committee report ☐ agenda ☐ minutes ☐ newsletter ☐ itinerary ☐ speech ☐
Paragraph indentions: none ☐ 5 spaces ☐ 10 spaces ☐

goal A

goal B

■ To type 49 wam/5′/2e.

3-MINUTE TW SKILL DRIVE

Spacing—2.
Line—50.
Tab—5.

Speed markers are for 3′ TW. Circled figures are 1′ goals.

■ 3′/1e

LESSON 127

Directions: Spacing—1. Line—85. Warmup—page 259.

Take a 3-minute TW as a Pretest. Take up to ten 1-minute TWs as Practice, trying to type each paragraph within 1′/0e. Repeat the 3-minute TW as a Posttest.

1	The papers in this collection are ones which I prepared in	13
2	my typing course. They show how to solve some of the	24
3	unique problems that the typist who wants to be ranked as a	36
4	"pro" finds exciting, or at least a challenge, to solve expertly. ①	49
5	Some of the problems have to do with placing typed copy	12 · 61
6	inside of a box. Some involve placing a box around typed	24 · 73
7	copy, centering one line above or below some other, lining up	36 · 85
8	typing on adjacent pages, and using ruled lines as decorations. ②	49 · 98
9	What these papers have in common is the fact that they are	13 · 111
10	not typed according to principle or to match a copy in the	25 · 123
11	file cabinet. Each is the creative solution to an original prob-	37 · 135
12	lem that had to be analyzed and executed with no guidance. ③	49 · 147

SI 1.44N

goals

■ To find which of two motions is harder, then to practice them proportionately.
■ To improve speed with no loss of accuracy.

ACTIVITIES	20 Min.	40 Min.
Warmup	3'	—
Warmup, Plus	—	8'
Pretest once	3'	—
Pretest twice*	—	6'
Practice drills	11'	20'
Posttest once	3'	—
Posttest twice*	—	6'
*Average the scores.		

Directions: Spacing—1. Line—60. Drills—3.

WARMUP, PLUS

The "Warmup" is lines 1–4, to be typed three times. The "Plus" is four 12-second sprints, to be typed on lines 1 and 2 to boost speed or on lines 3 and 4 to improve accuracy.

Edit line 2.

1 Show her what a nice day it is so that she may take a walk. 12
2 He crossed the forest, missouri, pembina, and snake rivers. 12
3 The many jovial men expressed a quick welcome to big Fritz. 12
4 Those five passengers are 10, 28, 39, 47, and 56 years old. 12

12" SPEED: 25 30 35 40 45 50 55 60

PRETEST

Take a 1-minute writing on each group to find which is harder for you.

Adjacent-key motions.

5 Werner built three new walks between the newer dress shops. 12
6 Asa has offered to trim several cherry trees within a week. 24
7 Eloise hopes to return and has offered to assist her class. 36
8 Louise saw the port as she was walking over the sandy soil. 48
9 Cher reserved a viewing spot near that new shopping center. 60

|1 |2 |3 |4 |5 |6 |7 |8 |9 |10 |11 |12

Proximate motions.

10 Willis loves to look for a place to swim, hike, and wander. 12
11 Kim hopes to travel in every kind of vehicle before spring. 24
12 Nina likes to walk on the river bank while the water rises. 36
13 Georgean goes to every traveling circus within this region. 48
14 Edwin believes he will be selected to build those exhibits. 60

PRACTICE

20-Minute Routine. Type the drills for the harder motion three times, for the easier motion twice.

40-Minute Routine. Type the drills for the harder motion six times, for the easier motion four times.

Drills on adjacent-key motions.

15 er newer flower serious spotter reserves samplers reserving 12
16 ui build quilts builder require building quilting buildings 24
17 as basis assure glasses eastern casualty roasters canvasses 36
18 we fewer viewer weavers welcome weakness welcomes westerner 48
19 oi point choice boilers spoiler appoints adjoined appointed 60

|1 |2 |3 |4 |5 |6 |7 |8 |9 |10 |11 |12

(Continued on next page)

1 2

goal A

■ To type 49 wam/3'/1e.

goal B

■ To type 49 wam/5'/2e.

TO INCREASE SPEED

☐ Move only fingers.
☐ Sit still; don't squirm.
☐ Squirt short words.
☐ Type very smoothly.

Directions: Spacing—1. Line—85.
Warmup—page 259.

3-MINUTE TW SKILL DRIVE

Spacing—2.
Line—50.
Tab—5.

Speed markers are for 3' TW. Circled numbers are 1' goals.

■ 3'/1e

Take a 3-minute TW as a Pretest. Take up to ten 1-minute TWs as Practice, trying to type each paragraph within 1'/0e. Repeat the 3-minute TW as a Posttest.

1   The reports and similar displays in this set of examples are   13
2 ones that I prepared in my typing class and that illustrate what   26
3 can be done in the standard format of a six-inch line with title   39
4 and subtitle and some subheads to guide a reader.①   49
5   Some of the papers are spaced double, mostly the ones that fit   14   63
6 on one sheet with that spacing; but the majority are spaced single   27   76
7 to save paper, filing space, time for duplicating and collating,   40   89
8 postage, and all the other costs of handling.②   49   98
9   One mark of business reports is subheadings. Typed at the left   14   112
10 margin or centered, they reveal at one quick glance the organiza-   26   124
11 tion and contents of the report. They are therefore important aids   40   138
12 in getting the recipient to read the report. ③   49   147

|1 |2 |3 |4 |5 |6 |7 |8 |9 |10 |11 |12 |13 |14   SI 1.44N

5-MINUTE TW SKILL DRIVE

Spacing—1.
Line—60.

Type lines 13–15 three times each—faster and faster and faster—as a Preview.

13 communications expression meeting minutes papers typed like   12
14 subsequently newsletters editions include beyond files fact   12
15 sideheadings "business" organized notices typist likes plan   12

Take a 5-minute TW as a Pretest. Type each line of your typing containing an error three times as Practice; then repeat the Preview above. Repeat the 5-minute TW as a Posttest.

Spacing—2.
Line—50.
Tab—5.

Circled numbers are 1' goals.

■ 5'/2e

16   The expression "business reports" includes a great many papers   14   136
17 that are not reports but should be typed like them. These③include   27   149
18 the agenda for meetings, the minutes that you type subsequently,   40   162
19 notices of many kinds, newsletters, and the①like.   50   173
20   What all these papers have in common, beyond the fact that   63   186
21 they are part of the communications plan that fits④the way busi-   75   198
22 ness is organized, are sideheadings and files. The sideheadings   88   211
23 tell us what the paper is all about; the copy in②the file shows the   102   225
24 typist how the boss likes to have these things set up. There are   115   238
25 no new papers, only new editions.⑤   122   245

|1 |2 |3 |4 |5 |6 |7 |8 |9 |10 |11 |12 |13 |14   SI 1.43N

20	se	loses	senses	secrets	serving	exercise	expenses	sensitive	12
21	in	lines	lining	finding	fringes	printing	mailings	buildings	24
22	ex	exits	expert	exports	complex	exhibits	flexible	expensive	36
23	li	lines	filing	linking	linings	climbing	limiting	millinery	48
24	be	begin	before	believe	liberty	believes	beginner	beginning	60

|1 |2 |3 |4 |5 |6 |7 |8 |9 |10 |11 |12

POSTTEST

Repeat the Pretest on page 18. Score your work and note your improvement.

goals A

■ **To review arrangement and production of business reports.**
■ **To produce a one-page report within 20'/5e.**

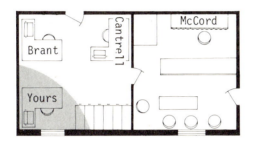

UNIT 3

LESSON **9**

Directions: *Spacing—1. Line—60. Drills—3. WB—25—26.*

WARMUP REVIEW

Edit line 2.

1 What would it be like to fly on and on and on to the stars?   12
2 bob and jack made the first team; tom and bill, the second.   12
3 Bud Fritz got a quick, jovial welcome from many expressmen.   12
4 Bob was No. 10; Jack, 28; Tom, 39; Bill, 47; and Fritz, 56.   12

|1 |2 |3 |4 |5 |6 |7 |8 |9 |10 |11 |12

JOB 9-1: REPORT

Plain paper □ **SI 1.40N** □ ■ **20'/5e**

Maurice McCord, product manager (radios and clock radios) at Eastinghouse Electric, welcomes you and introduces you to staff members Mrs. Barbara Brant and Mr. Paul Cantrell.

"I have two reports to be retyped," says Mr. McCord, "because they are addressed to my boss . . . er, I mean, my superior . . . with her old title, marketing director. But now she is our vice president for marketing, and I would not want the reports to use her old title—especially since we are so proud of her!"

He gives you the one-page report on page 20 and says, "This is the first one. Type it as it is arranged here—but address it to 'Ms. Tina Parker/Vice President, Marketing.'"

You study the page.

"Single-spaced?" you ask thoughtfully. You expected to see double spacing.

"Why double-space?" asks Mrs. Brant. "It takes twice as much paper, collating time, and file space when you double-space. You will find that business offices rarely use double spacing!"

1 ▶ **2** **9**

19

As a Preview, type lines 13–15 three times each, speeding up each repetition.

13 infrequently courses execute correct column tables data set

14 duplicates machines persons similar month's office desk you

15 organize business aligning however, numbers length copy top

Take a 5-minute TW as a Pretest. Type each line of your typing that contains an error three times as Practice; then repeat Preview above. Repeat the 5-minute TW as a Posttest.

Spacing—2.
Line—50.
Tab—5.

Circled numbers
are 1′ goals.

16 One of the things that most persons learn in typing courses is ③ | 14 | 136

17 how to organize and execute the tables that list business data. At | 27 | 149

18 a real office desk, however, a typist infrequently does so. In the ① | 41 | 163

19 office files are duplicates of similar tables from last week's or | 54 | 176

20 month's data. You copy them. | 60 | 183

21 You insert the table from the file into your machine and square ④ | 74 | 197

22 it at the aligning scale, just as though you were going to correct | 87 | 210

23 it. Then you set stops to serve the columns before you. Last, ② | 100 | 223

24 when you back out the file copy, count the number of blank lines | 113 | 236

■ 5′/2e

25 in its top margin so you can match that, also. ⑤ | 122 | 245

|1 |2 |3 |4 |5 |6 |7 |8 |9 |10 |11 |12 |13 |14

goal

■ To compile and
annotate a group
of tables.

BUSINESS TABLE	BUSINESS TABLE	BUSINESS TABLE
Open style	Open style	Ruled style
One-line title	Two-line subtitle	Two-line title
Column headings	Two-line column	Column headings
underscored	heading	not underscored
Totals percent	Totals dollars	Three horizontal
Three columns	Footnote centered	rules
	Two columns	Four columns

LESSON 124

Directions: *Spacing—1. Line—85.*
Warmup—page 259; then start the project.

TABLE PROJECT Collect and annotate a group of tables that illustrate as many of the items in the adjacent checklist as possible.

1. What Tables? Use any you have typed and saved in this course. You may retype any you wish. You may compose and type new ones to involve the features.

2. How to Annotate. Mount a colored file label in the top right corner of the paper or rule in colored ink a 2″ x 2″ box in the corner. In the area identify which features in the adjacent checklist are shown in the table. Do not type the same checklist item more than once. Your score on this project is the number of checklist items you can illustrate (plus any other items you include that may not be in the checklist).

TABULATION CHECKLIST

Styles: open ☐ ruled ☐ boxed ☐ with leaders ☐
Titles: in one line ☐ in two lines ☐
Subtitles: one line ☐ two lines ☐ with date ☐
Column heads: underscored ☐ not underscored ☐ two
  lines ☐ three lines ☐ triple meaning ☐
Columns, number: three ☐ four ☐ five ☐ more ☐
Columns, spacing: single ☐ double ☐ grouped ☐
Rules, horizontal: two ☐ three ☐ four ☐
Rules, vertical: three ☐ four ☐ more ☐
Totals: figures ☐ dollars ☐ percents ☐
Footnote: centered ☐ left margin ☐ two-line ☐
Contents: table in letter ☐ in a report ☐
Sequence: alphabetic ☐ high-to-low ☐ other ☐

① SPECIAL REPORT ON CLOCK RADIOS

Submitted to Ms. Tina Parker
Marketing Director
②

By Maurice McCord
Product Manager

GOOD SALES   2
                                                                    3
Until about a month ago, most retail outlets felt that clock   15
radios were very slow items, but there has been a sharp rever-   27
③ sal because demand for them has become high in the past four   40
weeks. This new demand applies to the whole wide range of   51
digital clock radios.   56
                                                                    57
As a result of the high demand, August sales have been quite   69
good. Most of our best retailers have built up inventory so   81
that they will have about a dozen or so models from which the   94
buyer may pick. Sales have been sufficiently high to restore   106
much of our confidence in our long-range sales design.   117
                                                                   118
④ NEXT YEAR   120
                                                                   121
We do not plan to add any other models next year. We shall   133
try to promote our current line and make changes and/or ad-   144
ditions wherever possible. Some of the reasons we have put   156
little emphasis on new product development have been rising   168
costs, tight money, and parts shortages. The average price   180
of a clock radio is expected to rise next year; this increase   193
in price should not hurt our sales.   200
                                                                   201
SALES PROBLEMS   204
                                                                   205
These radios have done a lot for us in our sales, but they   217
have also caused us a few problems   For instance, we have had   229
to lower the prices on some of the older models so our sales   241
would improve to some extent. Further, we have had to expend   254
more advertising money for this product because of the severe   266
competition in clock radios.   272

⑤

NOTE: To save space,
office workers fre-
quently type business
reports with 1 blank
line (rather than the
customary 2) above a
side heading.

Do You Remember? In a business report typed on plain paper. ① Title is all caps, centered, on line 13. ② Receivers and senders are separate single-spaced groups of lines, centered. ③ Body takes 2 blank lines above, single spacing, a 6-inch line (centered if report is not to be bound), blocked paragraphs. ④ Side headings are blocked left, all caps, with 2 blank lines above and 1 below. ⑤ Bottom margin is at least 1 inch.

BUSINESS LETTER	BUSINESS LETTER	PERSONAL LETTER
Average length	Baronial short	Very short length
Date at center	Date at right	Address typed under body
Salutation known addressee	Salutation for firm	Personalized complimentary close
Enclosure	Listed enclosures	List in the body
	PS with "PS"	

Directions: *Spacing—1. Line—85. Warmup—page 259; then start project.*

LETTER PROJECT Collect and annotate a group of letters that illustrate as many of the items on the adjacent checklist as possible.

1. What Letters? Use any you have typed and saved in this course. You may retype any you wish. You may compose and type new ones to involve the features.

2. How to Annotate. Use file-folder labels or sheet of colored paper on which you rule off 2″ x 2″ boxes. Fill one in for each letter—identify which features in the adjacent checklist are shown in the letter—and then mount the label or square (staple, tape, or glue) in the top right corner of the letter. Do not type the same checklist item more than once. Your score on this project is the number of items on the checklist you are able to include, plus the number of other items not included on the checklist.

LETTER CHECKLIST

Body length: average □ very short □ baronial short □ very long □ second page □

Date: at center □ at right □ at left □

Salutation: known person □ unknown person □ business firm, unknown people □

Attention line: at left □ centered □

Subject line: at left □ centered □ "Re" □

Paragraphs: blocked □ indented □ set in □ enumerated □ with list □ with table □

Company name: all caps □ under writer's name □

Writer's name: normal □ reference position □

Copies: cc notation □ bcc notation □

Enclosures: listed □ not listed □

Postscripts: with "PS" □ without "PS" □

Bottom: approval line □ coupon □

goal A

- To type 49 wam/3′/1e.

goal B

- To type 49 wam/5′/2e.

LESSON 123

Directions: *Spacing—1. Line—85. Warmup—page 259.*

3-MINUTE TW SKILL DRIVE

Spacing—2.
Line—50.
Tab—5.

Speed markers are for 3′ TW. Circled figures are 1′ goals.

■ 3′/1e

Take a 3-minute TW as a Pretest. Take up to ten 1-minute TWs as Practice, trying to type each paragraph within 1′/0e. Repeat the 3-minute TW as a Posttest.

```
 1    The tables in this collection are ones which I have produced in      14
 2  my typing class and which show the normal problems in typing         26
 3  up tables: titles, subtitles, column heads, plus two or more         38
 4  columns with six spaces left blank between columns.①                 49
 5    The space between the columns can be more or less, but six    13   62
 6  spaces seem just right: they place the columns close enough for  26  75
 7  easy reading yet far enough apart for clarity. Besides, six spaces is 40  89
 8  a good number when one sets up the machine!②                    49   98
 9    The tables in this portfolio cover all three main styles: the  14   112
10  open, the ruled, and the boxed. Ruled lines are frequently used  26  124
11  to organize parts of a table so they will be clearer. Some typists 40  138
12  think rules also make tables more attractive.③                 49   147
```

SI 1.39N

goal B

■ To produce the first page of a two-page report (Job 9-2) within 20'/5e.

JOB 9-2: REPORT, PAGE 1

Workbook 27 □ SI 1.36N □ ■ 20'/5e

"Here's another style we use (next column) for our reports," says Mr. McCord as you both examine the style manual. He points out these features:

① **Heading.** Data completing guide words are filled in; title becomes subject line.

② **Receivers and Senders.** Identified in heading.

③ **Body.** Two blank lines above, single-spaced, 6-inch line (¼ inch to the right if report is to be bound), blocked paragraphs.

④ **Side Headings.** Blocked left, all caps, 2 blank lines above and 1 blank line below (only 1 blank line above shown here to save space).

⑤ **Bottom Margin.** At least 1 inch.

"Now please type the second report (below)," says Mr. McCord. (If you don't have the workbook form, arrange the work like Job 9-1.)

To: Ms. Tina Parker   3
       Vice President, Marketing   7

From: Maurice McCord   11
          Product Manager   16

Floor or   Floor and Ext.
   Branch: 29   or Branch: 16 X2182   20

Subject: Sales Trainees' Briefing   26

Date: October 12, 19--   30

The first part of the week, you said to me   41
that you will soon need some data that you   49
could use in a talk you will give to our   57
sales trainees about radios. What I have   66
written below might provide our new peo-   74
ple with a pretty good idea as to what they 82
should talk about when selling radios.   91

The topics that I thought you might want   100
to suggest to the group are: 106
       Versatility   111
       Ease of Hearing   117
       Ease of Tuning   123

The following details should give the   132
trainees a good grasp of some of the items 141
to present in radio talks (from the cus-   149
tomer's viewpoint):   153

VERSATILITY   157

There are three questions that should be an- 166
swered on this topic: 171
   1. How versatile is the speaker?   181
   2. How many stations can this radio   189
        pick up?   193
   3. From what distance can a station be 202
        picked up?   207

If you purchased a radio that did not cost   216
you very much, you might not be able to   224
pick up more than just a few AM stations, 233
those nearest you.   237

There is something you can do to im-   245
prove FM reception, though. Most FM   252
radios have an antenna that can be adjusted 261
so that you receive a better signal. A better 270
FM signal may also be picked up if you   278
move the set to some other part of the   286
room.   287

goal A

■ To type 49 wam/3'/1e.

goal B

■ To type 49 wam/5'/2e.

TO INCREASE ACCURACY

☐ *Keep wrists still.*
☐ *Type with fingers only.*
☐ *Spell long words.*
☐ *Avoid speed pushes.*

Directions: *Spacing—1. Line—85.*
Warmup—page 259.

3-MINUTE TW SKILL DRIVE

Spacing—2.
Line—50.
Tab—5.

Speed markers are for 3' TW. Circled figures are 1' goals.

Take a 3-minute TW as a Pretest. Take up to ten 1-minute TWs, trying to type each paragraph within 1'/0e as Practice. Repeat the 3-minute TW as a Posttest.

1   The letters in this portfolio are ones which I have produced   13

2 in my typewriting class and which show the normal arrange-   25

3 ment of a business letter: the date and closing lines starting at   38

4 the center and all other lines beginning at the margin.   49

5   Some employers like their letters to be more unique and ask   13 | 62

6 for adjustments, such as indenting the paragraphs or shifting   25 | 74

7 the date to either the right or left margin. A number of com-   38 | 87

8 mon changes like these are included among these letters.   49 | 98

9   To maximize the efficient use of the machine in letter typ-   13 | 111

10 ing, it is the modern trend to apply the same line length for   25 | 123

11 most letters, margins to be altered only for the very long and   38 | 136

■ 3'/1e

12 very short. Samples of all three are in this collection.   49 | 147

|1 |2 |3 |4 |5 |6 |7 |8 |9 |10 |11 |12 |13 |14   SI 1.44N

5-MINUTE TW SKILL DRIVE

Spacing—1.
Line—60.

Type lines 13–16 three times each as a Preview.

13 "Ladies and Gentlemen" or "Dear Madam or Sir" "yours" rule: 12

14 complimentary important person, writer either under name is   24

15 accordingly signature business greeted assume below used in   36

16 salutation reference addressee closing reader woman must be   48

Take a 5-minute TW as a Pretest. Type each line in which you have made an error three times as Practice; then repeat the Preview. Repeat the 5-minute TW as a Posttest.

Spacing—2.
Line—50.
Tab—5.

17   Here are four points that are important when you type a   12 | 134

18 business letter. The first: that the name of the writer may be   25 | 147

19 placed either below the signature or in the reference line.   37 | 160

20 Another one: "yours" usually should be part of a complimen-   49 | 172

21 tary closing. A third: When the addressee is a known person,   62 | 185

22 the name is to be used in the salutation.   70 | 193

Circled figures are 1' goals.

23   Now, the fourth: When addressing a firm, or a person whose   83 | 206

24 name and sex you do not know, your salutation must reflect   95 | 218

25 that the reader is either a man or woman and must be   105 | 228

26 phrased accordingly as "Ladies and Gentlemen" or "Dear   116 | 239

■ 5'/2e.

27 Madam or Sir," as appropriate.   122 | 245

|1 |2 |3 |4 |5 |6 |7 |8 |9 |10 |11 |12 |13 |14   SI 1.44N

goal A

■ To produce the second page of a two-page report (Job 10-1) within 10'/2e.

JOB 10-1: REPORT, PAGE 2

Plain paper ☐ SI 1.22E ☐ ■ 10'/2e

Directions: *Spacing—1. Line—60. Drills—3.*

WARMUP REVIEW

Edit line 2.

1 He said he might go back to his job by the end of the week. 12
2 bob is robert, jack is john, sue is susan, peg is margaret. 12
3 Max placed work before joy and had a zest for quiet living. 12
4 Place 10 in group 28, 39 in group 47, but do not assign 56. 12

|1 |2 |3 |4 |5 |6 |7 |8 |9 |10 |11 |12

5-MINUTE WRITING

Using Spacing 1 and Line 50, take a 5-minute writing on the report on page 20, beginning with "Good Sales." Your goal: 40 wam/5'/3e or better.

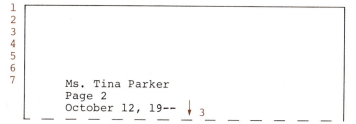

Ms. Tina Parker
Page 2
October 12, 19-- ↓ 3

Page 2 headings: Letters and reports on forms start on line 7; block the name of the addressee, the page number, and the date.

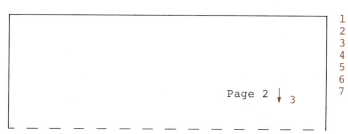

Page 2 ↓ 3

Reports on plain paper have the page number on line 7, ending at the right margin.

EASE OF HEARING 291

Most of what you want to say on this 300
topic was researched a couple of weeks ago 308
for the paper we prepared for our meeting 317
with the York office. Here is an outline 325
of what was included in that report: 333
Page 2 heading (*style shown above at left*)

1. How large should the speakers be? 343
2. Should a headset be used for smaller 354
    units? 358
3. How should a speaker be tested? 369

EASE OF TUNING 373

Check to see how easy the set is to 381
tune. You should hear just one station at 389
a time. If you hear more than one signal, 398
you can be certain that either you are too 407
far away from the station or the quality 415
of the tuner is poor. 419

These are some of the common items 427
with which our sales trainees are going to 436
have to acquaint themselves. I will have the 445
rest of the report on your desk by the early 454
part of next week. If you have any ques- 462
tions or would like to talk to me about any 471
of these topics, please feel free to call me. 481

Maurice McCord / URS *Note: Start* 488
writer's name at or near the center.

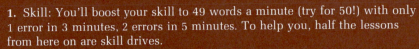

IN PART ELEVEN . . .

1. Skill: You'll boost your skill to 49 words a minute (try for 50!) with only 1 error in 3 minutes, 2 errors in 5 minutes. To help you, half the lessons from here on are skill drives.

2. Production: You will do no new production. Instead, you will build six compilations ("Portfolios" they are called) of work you have done or will do to illustrate what you can type well.

3. The schedule of skill and production lessons for Part Eleven:

Lessons in Unit 31	Lessons in Unit 32	Lessons in Unit 33
121 Skill	125 Skill	129 Skill
122 Letters	126 Reports	130 Documents
123 Skill	127 Skill	131 Skill
124 Tables	128 Display	132 Messages

4. The experiences and practice in Part Eleven will enable you to answer two questions that any employment interviewer would ask you: "How well can you type?" and "What can you type well?"

5. At the start of each practice period, turn to this page and type at least one set of sprints (four 12-second writings) on one sentence from each of the three groups below. Spacing 1, line 85.

SPEED RECALL

1 The two new men and the boy
2   got paid for the work they did for the girl at the lake.   17
3   lent the chairman of the auditors a map for their panel.   17
4   got both of us to lend them a hand with the visual aids.   17

12" WAM: 45 50 55 60 65 70 75 80 85

ALPHABET RECALL

5 Jack requested Elizabeth to
6   help with retraining my brown foxes to jump over fences.   17
7   give many extra prizes for the crossword puzzle contest.   17
8   help us pay for having the new locket fixed for Marjory.   17

12" WAM: 45 50 55 60 65 70 75 80 85

NUMBER RECALL

9 We had to measure exactly how
10   long sticks of 10 cm, 28 cm, 39 cm, 47 cm, or 56 cm are.   17
11   many liters we used to drive 10, 28, 39, 47, and 156 km.   17
12   far it is between 1028 39th Street and 3948 56th Street.   17

12" WAM: 45 50 55 60 65 70 75 80 85

Directions: *Spacing—1. Line—60. Tab—5.*
Drills—4.

1 Mary can type very fast on copy that has short, easy words.   12
2 Kay says that she can fix the vase that fell from the desk.   12
3 The four of them had to get to the bus by the time it left.   12

12" SPEED: 25   30   35   40   45   50   55   60

4E authors perform oblige prefer types speed wise task bed old   12
5E covered speaker soiled wished walks rider tied send raw ran   12
6E implies resumed upland talent fault defer kits love saw hot   12
7E highway noticed liquid follow cries baked deep bulb dry hit   12

|1 |2 |3 |4 |5 |6 |7 |8 |9 |10 |11 |12

4M cabinet scholar embark vacant scale cabin rave tank act cat   12
5M package tactful warmly places racks think face gave van tax   12
6M machine knowing mainly intact haven caves palm camp wax bat   12
7M factory examine facial Dacron abide badly baby able cap tab   12

8   Just why do expert typists use single spacing for most   12
9   Just why do expert typists use single spacing for most   24
10   Just why do expert typists use single spacing for most   36
11 of their reports? ① A dozen answers can be given, but one is   48
12 of their reports? A dozen answers can be given, but one is   60
13 of their reports? A dozen answers can be given, but one is   72

14 that single spacing is quick. It can ②conserve money, time,   84
15 that single spacing is quick. It can conserve money, time,   96
16 that single spacing is quick. It can conserve money, time,   108

17 space, and effort.   112
18 space, and effort.   116
19 space, and effort.③   120

|1 |2 |3 |4 |5 |6 |7 |8 |9 |10 |11 |12   SI 1.40N

CHECK YOUR POSTURE

☐ *Feet firmly on the floor.*
☐ *Back erect, leaning forward slightly.*
☐ *Hands low, fingers curled, wrists close.*
☐ *Head turned to face the copy.*

LESSON 11

Directions: *Spacing—1. Line—60 Tab—5.*
Drills—3.

1 The home row keys are easy to find as you type, type, type.   12
2 new york, los angeles, chicago, and philadelphia are large.   12
3 Joan saw six azure kites drift quickly by very huge maples.   12
4 The party governed during 1910, 1928, 1939, 1947, and 1956.   12

|1 |2 |3 |4 |5 |6 |7 |8 |9 |10 |11 |12

REVIEW JOB 2: CONTRACT

Legal-ruled paper □ Top margin 2″
□ Spacing 1 □ Tabs 10 and center
□ ■ 15′/0e

[*Title*] EMPLOYMENT CONTRACT   24

THIS CONTRACT, made and concluded   34
this [*Substitute today's date.*] seventeenth   38
day of March, 19--, by and between the   45
Cooperative of Vista Apartments, of 902   54
Valley Drive, Charleston, West Virginia,   62
Party of the First Part, and Ballard W.   69
Jones, of 906 Valley Drive, Charleston, West   78
Virginia, Party of the Second Part.   86

ARTICLE 1. The said Party of the Second   96
Part covenants and agrees to and with the   104
Party of the First Part to furnish his ser-   114
vices to the said Party of the First Part for   122
management of the apartment complex for   130
a period of one (1) year, to begin June 1,   139
19--, and end May 30, 19--; and the said   147
Party of the Second Part covenants and   154
agrees to perform faithfully all duties as   162
stated in the previously written job descrip-   173
tion for the said position.   178

ARTICLE 2. And the said Party of the   188
First Part covenants and agrees to pay the   195
said Party of the Second Part for the same,   205
the sum of twelve thousand dollars   211
($12,000) in twelve (12) equal monthly   218
installments of one thousand dollars   227
($1,000) to be paid on the last working day   235
of each month during the stated period of   245
employment. ↓₃   247

IN WITNESS WHEREOF, the parties to   257
this contract have set their hands and seals,   265
the day and year aforesaid.   272

[*Arrange signature lines in left half.*]   ..
Party of the First Part: / Crit M. Johnson,   294
President / Witness to Signature   308

[*Arrange signature lines in right half.*]   ..
Party of the Second Part: / Ballard W. Jones   329
/ Witness to Signature   341

REVIEW JOB 3: TABLE

Plain paper □ Arrange the data
below in any good way you prefer;
illustration here is just one
option □ Center horizontally and
vertically □ Arrange items highest
to lowest by sale price □ ■ 15′/0e

Description	Regular Prices	Sale Prices	
BARGAINS FOR THE WEEK OF MARCH 23-29		24	
		35	
		53	
"BIG LEAGUE" OFFICIAL BASKETBALL: tough composition cover with deep pebble finish and molded seams	$13.00	$ 8.95	125
"BIG LEAGUE" WOOD TENNIS RACKET: laminated wood construction with perforated grip, nylon stringing	12.00	7.95	175
"BIG LEAGUE" STEEL TENNIS RACKET: stainless steel frame, braided nylon stringing, leather grip	14.50	8.55	150
"BIG LEAGUE" CROQUET SET: carrying rack with 6 mallets, 6 balls, 9 arches, and 2 stakes	35.00	25.95	176
"BIG LEAGUE" FIELDER'S GLOVE: cowhide leather, fleeced wrist strap, right-hander model only	14.50	9.95	200

Take a 5-minute writing to serve as a basis for improvement and practice goals.

5   When typewriters first came on the market, most of the | 12
6   parts were made by hand. One part that was quite difficult | 24
7   to make was the gear for advancing paper around the platen. | 36
8   Because of the small size of the cylinder that was used, it | 48
9   was not possible to make a gear with enough cogs around the | 60
10 edge to allow less than what appeared to be double spacing. | 72
11   So, the first letters typed in any office were double- | 84
12 spaced. The internal parts of the typewriter did not allow | 96
13 typists to single-space. When a more usable gear was made, | 108
14 many people started to single-space the letters they typed. | 120
15 It was not long before single spacing became popular in the | 132
16 office and was employed often in the typing of other tasks. | 144
17   Today, double spacing is seldom used for text material | 156
18 in reports. The trend is to single-space this work so that | 168
19 less paper will be used. The completion of a job in single | 180
20 spacing will also result in better use of time by those who | 192
21 are involved with typewriting production. | 200

■ 5'/3e

Speed markers are for 5' TW.

|1 |2 |3 |4 |5 |6 |7 |8 |9 |10 |11 |12   SI 1.40N

Type, three times each, the drill lines indicated in this guide table.

Pretest errors	0–2	3–5	6–+
Type lines	22–28	23–29	24–30

22 first parts small used, typed space often other trend paper | 12
23 text this work that less will also time thus when more made | 24
24 the one use for did not and was job who are may by of to it | 36

|1 |2 |3 |4 |5 |6 |7 |8 |9 |10 |11 |12

25 weather voltage slides sticks waits views send rule jar mat | 12
26 elastic ashamed anchor cleans badly argue kits host use see | 24
27 medical enlarge plight highly fruit color jets life hop few | 36

|1 |2 |3 |4 |5 |6 |7 |8 |9 |10 |11 |12

28 typewriters difficult platen. cylinder usable seldom hand. | 12
29 production completion appeared internal became better allow | 24
30 typewriting advancing employed material single result tasks | 36

Repeat the Pretest. Score your work and note your improvement.

goals

- To type 48 or more wam 5'/2e
- To produce two short letters, an employment contract, and a table—each Job within 15'/0e.

Directions: Spacing—1. Line—60. Tab—5.
Warmup—page 240.

5-MINUTE TW

Spacing—2.
Line—60.
Tab—5.

Speed markers are for 5' TW.

1 Dear Madam or Sir: I thank you for your recent letter in reply 14
2 to my request for reservations at the Yellowknife. 24
3 I can understand how the golf tournament has put rooms at a 37
4 premium, and I am pleased to accept the facilities you have 49
5 offered me. I enclose a deposit of a hundred dollars. 60
6 Mrs. Young and I will arrive late on Thursday evening, May 12; 74
7 we're delighted to know we have the accommodations. 84
8 Dear Madam or Sir: Thank you for writing me about the need 97
9 for a deposit on the rental auto you will hold for me. 108
10 I do realize how the big golf tournament has put autos at a 121
11 premium, and I am delighted to have the auto which you are 133
12 saving. I am enclosing a deposit of a hundred dollars. 144
13 I will need to pick up the car on Friday morning about seven 157
14 o'clock and to return it on Sunday about six o'clock. 168
15 Dear Mr. LaTerre: I am writing to confirm the date of my visit 182
16 to your plant, something I am really anticipating. 192
17 I will get to Yellowknife by train, arriving very late in the 205
18 evening of Thursday, May 12. I will stay at the Inn on Ellis 218
19 Street. I shall be enjoying the Midnight Sun Golf Tournament on 231
20 Friday, as you know, and will look for you at the golf club. I 244
21 have left the entire day open on Saturday and can therefore fit 256
22 any schedule you may wish to suggest. 264
23 I cannot tell you how much I am looking forward to the visit 277
24 to your community and to the pleasure of meeting you. We have 290
25 done business for so long that we simply must meet! 300

|1 |2 |3 |4 |5 |6 |7 |8 |9 |10 |11 |12 |13 |14   SI 1.40N

REVIEW JOB 1: TWO SHORT LETTERS

Workbook 297 or baronial half sheets □ **Bodies 70 and 78**
□ **SI 1.55FH and 1.46FH** □ ■ **15'/0e**

Type the first two letters above for the signature of Roger D. Young, Sales Manager. Address them as follows:

1. Reservations Clerk, Yellowknife Inn, 1600 Ellis Street, Yellowknife, NWT ["NWT" *is the abbreviation for "Northwest Territories."*] X1A 1Z4.

2. Rental Manager, Host Rent-a-Car, 1800 West Ninth Street, Yellowknife, NWT X1A 2Y5.

On the envelopes, type the code below CANADA as the bottom line, or following CANADA on the same line.

goals B

■ To review arrangement of postal cards. ■ To produce four postal cards (Job 11-1) within 20'/4e.

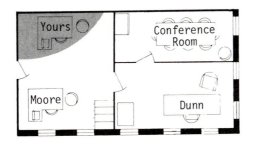

Directions: *Adjust your typewriter for Job 11-1.*

JOB 11-1: FILL-IN POSTAL CARD

Workbook 29–30 or 5½" x 3¼" slips of paper □ ■ 20'/4e

You work for Mrs. Moore, secretary to John Dunn. You have been hired to help with a rush project.

"We have to fill in some postal cards for acknowledging recent orders," says Mrs. Moore. "Use a salutation on the message side." She gives you the model card (below) to follow.

September 28, 19--

Dear Mr. Reeves:

Thank you for your order of September 25, 19--.

Your order will be shipped on September 29, and you should receive it shortly.

If your order does not arrive within 10 days, please write or call me at your convenience.

Susan Moore, Secretary

URS

Postal Card 1: Mr. Frank Reeves, 210 Duke Dr., Colorado Springs, CO 80918. Order placed Sept. 25; shipped, Sept. 29.

Postal Card 2: Mr. Joe Day, 611 Lee St., Denver, CO 80215. Order placed Sept. 26; shipped, Sept. 30.

Postal Card 3: Mrs. Amy Green, 3444 Spruce St., Pueblo, CO 81004. Order placed Sept. 24; shipped, Sept. 28.

Postal Card 4: Mr. Terry Malone, 690 Cook St., Denver, CO 80206. Order placed Sept. 25; shipped, Sept. 29.

① Susan Moore

signal RADIO COMPANY
Colorado Building
4232 Carson Street
Denver, Colorado 80239

② Mrs. Carolyn Ramsey
246 Clark Circle
Colorado Springs, CO 80915

③ August 13, 19--

④ Dear Mrs. Ramsey:

Thank you for your order of August 10, 19--.

⑤ Your order will be shipped on August 15, and you should receive it shortly.

If your order does not arrive within 10 days, please write or call me at your convenience.

⑥ Susan Moore, Secretary

⑦ URS

⑧

Do You Remember? On the address side of the postal card: ① Return address (if typed) begins on line 3, ½" from the edge, or, if it is printed, then the writer's name is typed above it. ② Mailing address begins on line 12, 2"-from left edge. On the message side: ③ Date begins on line 3, at center. ④ Salutation begins on line 5; body starts on line 7. ⑤ Half-inch side margins are used. ⑥ Sender's name begins at center. ⑦ Reference initials are used. ⑧ Insert dates.

goals A

■ To review the arrangement of invoices. ■ To produce three invoices (Job 12-1) within 15'/3e.

LESSON **12**

Directions: *Spacing—1. Line—60. Drills—2. Warmup—page 23.*

goal A

■ To produce a two-page memo within 20'/0e.

goal B

■ To produce a one-page itinerary within 15'/0e.

Directions: *Spacing—1. Line—60. Warmup—page 240; then begin Job 120-1.*

JOB 120-1: TWO-PAGE MEMORANDUM

Plain paper □ **Spacing 2** □ **Line 7″** □ **Tabs 13 and center** □ **Top 1″** □ **Needs 11 commas** □ ■ **20'/0e**

"Next," says Miss Lido, "is the following interoffice memo. Please note that Mr. Young likes the 'wide open' style—double-spaced, headings displayed in the side margin in all caps, and so on. Let me dictate from the notes he gave me."

[*Title*] Interoffice Memorandum 15

[*Heading: align at margin and tab 13*] To All Department Heads / From Roger D. Young / Date today / Subject Absence During My Trip to Canada, and Other Topics 19 27 37 44 45

[*Sidehead*] Absence / from my / office 58

As you may have heard by now Mrs. Young and I will leave for a two-week trip to Canada during May. We will be touring part of the time as well as attending the wedding of our grandson and taking care of a little bit of business. Miss Lido will have a copy of my itinerary and schedule. 66 75 84 94 104 114 121

[*Sidehead*] Who's in / charge? 130

While I am away Keith Alden my assistant sales manager will be acting sales manager. See him for all matters that you would normally take up with me. 141 148 157 164

[*Sidehead*] Meetings / schedule 174

Because many of you have said that having a sales meeting every Wednesday morning is more often than we need or more frequent than you can afford the time for I think we will change the meetings to the first and third Wednesday of each month. I would like to have your reaction to this suggestion. Unless there is some serious objection we will start this new 182 191 198 208 217 227 235 245 254

schedule on Wednesday May 2. 260

[*Sidehead*] Christmas / advertising / campaign The president has indicated that he would like us to begin planning at once for the Christmas campaign. So that you can all get a head start I have asked Alice Strang and Earl Forsythe to come up with some suggestions for our new store and counter displays. [*Page 2 heading, when needed:* All Department Heads / Page 2 / Today's date ↓₃] 273 282 293 302 311 320 330 332 352 354

[*Sidehead*] New fur / suppliers 362

Although my forthcoming trip to Canada will be the first real vacation that Mrs. Young and I have taken in more than five years I do plan to spend some time in Whitehorse in an effort to find some new supplier or suppliers for our fur shop. If you have any leads or if you would like to define exactly what we should hope to buy please let me hear from you. 373 382 391 399 408 418 428 437 443

[*At center*] Roger D. Young / urs 449

JOB 120-2: ITINERARY

Plain paper □ **Use any clear arrangement (the one shown is optional)** □ ■ **15'/0e**

"Oh!" Miss Lido exclaims. "Mr. Young wants the itinerary retyped —all on one page. Try to figure out how to do it!"

JOB 120-3: COMPLETION CARDS

5″ x 3″ cards or slips □ ■ **5'/0e**

Do You Remember? When typing an invoice: ① The left margin is set 2 spaces from the guides. ② First line of the body begins on line 2 below the ruled line. ③ Numbers align at right; words align at left. ④ Total line begins under the letter "D" in the word "Description." ⑤ If the shipping address and the billing address are the same, type "Same" after "Ship To." ⑥ Ship To and Date start at the tab setting.

JOB 12-1: INVOICES

Workbook 31 or plain paper

☐ ■ 20′/4e

"Now, let's catch up a little by completing these three invoices," says Mrs. Moore.

"How shall we ship the orders?" you ask.

"By United Parcel Service," says Mrs. Moore.

Invoice 81293: Billed and shipped to Mr. Stephen Lusk, 26027 Amie Ave., Torrance, CA 90503. 2 receivers (Set 58) @ $48, for $96. 1 headset (Set 16) @ $27. 3 transmitters (Set 5) @ $8, for $24. Total order is $147.00.

Invoice 81294: Billed and shipped to Hi-Phonic Sales, 175 Clover Dr., Cory, CO 81414.

NO.	SET	DESCRIPTION	UNIT PRICE	AMOUNT
1	17	Radio Transmitter	48.50	48.50
3	8	Receiver	58.00	174.00
2	35	Speaker	38.00	76.00
		TOTAL		298.50

12 relay switches (Set 32) @ $.15, for $1.80. 4 receivers (Set 58) @ $48, for $192. 1 headset (Set 16) @ $27. Total order is $220.80.

Invoice 81295: Billed to Purchasing Department, Benson Hardware, 12548 Marion St., Denver, CO 80241. Shipped to Mr. John Ames, same address. 6 receivers (Set 60) @ $52, for $312. 5 transmitters (Set 3A) @ $7, for $35. 2 mini-headsets (Set 11) @ $14 for $28. Total order is $375.00.

JOB 12-2: TWO MEMOS

Workbook 32 or 5½″ x 8½″ slips of paper ☐ Use current date ☐ ■ 20′/4e

"Mr. Young, president of the company, has approved extended leaves for Mrs. Karla Berg and Mr. Daniel Smith," Mrs. Moore says. "We have to send memos to each of them."

"Oh!" you exclaim, "then we can use the same message for both—just change names and dates."

"Right," says Mrs. Moore. She dictates:

Memo 1: *To* Mrs. Karla Berg / Marketing Department / *From* Della Banks / Personnel Department / *Subject* Approval of Leave (dates of leave—October 1 through October 15).

Memo 2: *To* Mr. Daniel Smith / R&D Office / *From and Subject* same as above (dates of leave—October 7 through October 28).

Memo Message: Your request for a leave has been approved by this office. The leave will start at 4:30 p.m. on (fill in appropriate date) and will end at 8:30 a.m. on (fill in appropriate date).

Please complete your leave-of-absence form and return it to me this week. / DB / URS

Do You Remember? When typing an interoffice memo: ① Left margin is set 2 spaces from guides. ② Two lines may be used for long name and title. ③ Body starts 3 lines below "Subject." ④ Sender's initials begin at center, 2 lines below body. ⑤ Reference initials are used.

"I think I have worked out the details of his itinerary," says Miss Lido. "If you can figure out my writing, please type this for him. Don't go to a lot of

trouble. If I know him, he will change his plans."

"No arrival and departure hours?" you ask.

"No, that information will be on his tickets," Miss Lido replies. "Do it quickly—say, in 20 minutes—and don't crowd things. If you use two pages, okay."

ITINERARY FOR MR. AND MRS. ROGER D. YOUNG

May 9-23, 19--

May 9-11

Carrier   Pacific Western Airlines 101, Seattle to Vancouver
               Pacific Western Airlines 303, Vancouver to Edmonton

Destination   Home of Roger D. Young, Jr.
               562 103d Street, Edmonton, Alberta

Highlights   Attend wedding of grandson
               Visit Alberta Game Farm
               Visit family
               Visit Queen Elizabeth Planetarium

May 12-14

Carrier   Northern Alberta Railway 561, from Edmonton to Yellowknife

Destination   Yellowknife Inn, Ellis Street
               Yellowknife, Northwest Territories

Highlights   Participate in Midnight Sun Golf Tournament (May 13)
Highlights   Tour the Consolidated Mining and Smelting Company (May 14)

May 15

Carrier   Host Rent-a-Car

Destination   Indian Village Campground No. 3
               Hay River, Northwest Territories

Highlights   Sightseeing, fishing, camping

May 16-18

Carrier   Transair Limited 701, from Yellowknife to Whitehorse, Yukon Terr.

Destination   Holiday House, Highway 5, Whitehorse, Yukon Territories

Highlights   Three-hour cruise up the Yukon River (May 17)
               Hike up Mt. Kennedy (May 18)
               Meeting with Miles Canyon Trading Co. officials to discuss purchase of fur apparel

May 19-20

Carrier   British Columbia Railways 72B, Whitehorse to Vancouver, British Columbia

Highlights   "Midnight Sun" overnight trip; Pullman bedroom reserved

May 21

Carrier   Pacific Western Airlines 100, from Vancouver, British Columbia, to Seattle

Destination   Home

May 23

Highlights   Return to office in time for 10 o'clock departmental-reports meeting

goals

- To type 40 or more wam for 5'/3e.
- To correctly produce a report, a letter, a table, and a printed form.

Directions: Spacing—1. Line—50.
Warmup—page 19.

5-MINUTE TW

Spacing—2.
Line—50. Tab—5.
Omit lines 4, 11,
and 19.

Speed markers are
for 5' TW.

■ 5'/3e

1 This suggestion is the result of the request you made in the   12
2 last issue of our paper for ideas we all could use to cut down on   26
3 routine expenses.   30

4   **USE SINGLE SPACING**

5 I have seen that a great many of the reports turned in routine-   43
6 ly, month after month or quarter after quarter, are typed in double   57
7 spacing. This practice is tempting because it makes all reports   70
8 seem to be thicker and more imposing, but the use of single spac-   84
9 ing could save us lots of paper and time and money, and I urge   95
10 that we give it a try.   100

11   **WHERE THE ECONOMY COMES**

12 If single spacing is used instead of double, the typing would   113
13 need about one-third less paper. The paper savings would be siz-   126
14 able, but the giant savings, in my judgment, would come from   138
15 handling less paper. We would save a third of the room in our   151
16 files or notebooks. We would save a third of the time in making   163
17 copies, in collating the pages of each report, and in postage on   177
18 copies we mail.   180

19   **HOW TO EFFECT THE CHANGE**

20 To effect all these savings, we need only an executive memo to   194
21 use single spacing for reports. The matter should not be made op-   207
22 tional, since the majority of our typists would double-space sim-   219
23 ply to embellish the reports their superiors produce.   230
24 I know that this suggestion concerns a small matter, but it   243
25 could save many, many big dollars.   250

|1 |2 |3 |4 |5 |6 |7 |8 |9 |10 |11 |12

SI 1.40

1

1

27

**5-MINUTE
PIECEMEAL
PRACTICE**

Spacing 1 for 1' TWs;
spacing 2 for 5' TW.

Take up to ten 1-minute writings until you are able to type each paragraph within
1'/0e; then take a 5-minute writing to achieve your goal of 48 wam/5'/2e.

Speed markers are
for 5' TW.
Circled numbers
are 1' goals.

1   There are many cities in Canada that offer great shows and   13
2   luxury restaurants and fine stores. There are vacation spots of   26
3   every kind you can think of, from beaches or lakes for swimming   39
4   to mountains for skiing and woods for camping.   48
5   But what Canada has that no one else has are the bleak parts of   62
6   the Northwest Territories, which comprise almost a third of the   75
7   nation. So few people live in some parts that it is easy to find   88
8   places where no human has ever set foot.   96
9   People like to go up to the Yukon, where pure gold was first   109
10 discovered in Canada. Although the early miners made the trip by 122
11 walking or piloting very small rafts, today you and the other   135
12 tourists can arrive by plane, train, or ship.   144
13 Just as life in Canadian cities is fine, so is hunting and fishing 158
14 and life in the wilds. Every year thousands of backpackers find   171
15 that one place they can get a little peace and quiet is along the 185
16 camping trails of a Canadian forest.   192
17 One of the unique things about Canada is the fact that it has   205
18 two official languages, English and French. Both of them are used 219
19 on stamps and coins, road signs and maps, and official announce-   231
20 ments. Nearly ten percent can speak both.   240

|1 |2 |3 |4 |5 |6 |7 |8 |9 |10 |11 |12 |13 |14   SI 1.38N

goal B

■ To produce an
itinerary within
20'/0e.

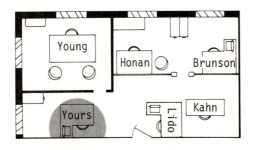

Directions: *Adjust machine for Job 119-1,*
on page 255.

Roger D. Young is sales manager of Northern Service and
Supplies of Seattle. His support team is Bob Honan, Wes
Brunson, Cher Kahn, Tina Lido, and you. Miss Lido is
coordinating the efforts to get things ready for a business-
personal trip by him and Mrs. Young to western Canada.

REVIEW JOB 1: REPORT

Plain paper □   Review page 20 □   SI 1.42N □   ■ 15'/5e

Type the report on page 27 in the style of the one on page 20, preceded by, "This report, "Economy Suggestions," is submitted to Dr. Weldon Jules, Vice President, Budgets and Personnel, by Ben Johnson, Assistant to Ms. Parker."

REVIEW JOB 2: MEMO

Workbook 35 □   Review page 26
□   SI 1.43N □   ■ 10'/3e

Type the following memo, using today's date.

To: Ms. Tina Parker / Vice President, Marketing / *From:* Weldon J. Jules / Vice President, Budgets and Personnel / *Subject:* Ben Johnson's Economy Suggestion / 13 20 28 34

I read Ben Johnson's suggestion with interest and checked it with a number of our typists. I found that all of them think his suggestion is a fine one, one that they would welcome. 43 51 60 69 72

So, I think we should take action on it. If we prepare a memo from the two of us to Mr. Young, I think he would be quite willing to issue an executive memo that would put the idea to the test. / WJJ / urs 81 89 98 106 119

REVIEW JOB 3: LETTER

Workbook 35–36 □   Review page 11
□   SI 1.36N □   ■ 10'/3e

Type the following letter on Workbook 36 and address the envelope on Workbook 35. Use standard form, as illustrated on page 11.

Today's date / Mr. Lincoln G. Clark / Purchasing Agent / Ace Business Forms Company / 920 Main Street / Kansas City, MO 64105 / 13 20 27 28

Dear Mr. Clark: I wish to acknowledge your recent letter in which you gave me the title of the talk you will give at the fall 39 47 56

meeting of the Central Association of Purchasing Agents. I appreciate also the brief outline of the comments you will make. 64 73 81

I am enclosing a form that lists projectors, tape and cassette players, and other kinds of presentation aids that will be available for the use of all speakers who wish to have them. 89 99 108 115 119

Please check the items on the list that you wish to have at hand when you speak, return the list to me, and rest assured that whatever you want will be at the right place at the right time. 129 137 144 154 159

Cordially yours, / Hugh T. Sitz / CAPA Program Editor / URS / Enclosure 173 179

REVIEW JOB 4: OPEN TABLE

Plain paper □   Review page 15
□   ■ 15'/3e

Type the following table in open style. Double-space the body of the table.

PROGRAM PARTICIPANTS			6
Fall Meeting of the CAPA			13
Name	*Day*	*Program*	27
Allen	Monday	Panel	32
Clark	Wednesday	Address	39
Fedderhand	Monday	Panel	45
Gagner	Tuesday	Address	51
Innizzi	Tuesday	Address	58
Johnson	Monday	Panel	64
Lemoyne	Wednesday	Panel	70
Norton, A.	Tuesday	Address	77
Norton, R.	Monday	Address	84
Perlman	Wednesday	Panel	90
Stevenson	Wednesday	Panel	97
Succretti	Tuesday	Panel	103
Tompkins	Tuesday	Panel	110
Vionoffski	Wednesday	Address	117
Walker	Tuesday	Address	123

goal A

■ To produce an
oversize table
within 15′/0e.

JOB 118-1: RULED TABLE

Plain paper, turned sideways
☐ ■ 15′/0e

Referring to the schedule on page 252, Ms. McKechnie says,
"I need three copies of this information. Can you arrange it as
a table?"

You can—if you turn the paper sideways.

JOB 118-2: COMPLETION CARDS

5″ x 3″ cards or slips ☐ ■ 5′/0e

*Directions: Spacing—1. Line—60.
Warmup—page 240.*

JOB 117-2: FORM LETTER
1. Typed by George Jenkins
2. Proofread with Jeanne McBride
3. No problems in preparing this job.

goal B

■ To type 48 wam
for 5′/2e.

**5-MINUTE TW
SKILL DRIVE**

Speed markers are
for 5′ TW.
Circled figures
are 1′ goals.

Directions: Spacing—2. Line—60. Tab—5.

Take a 5-minute writing as a Pretest. For your Practice, type three times any line in
which you made an error or with which you had difficulty. As a Posttest, repeat
the 5-minute timing.

1 Canadians are quite proud of their large and beautiful country. 14
2 The nation covers most of the upper half of North America and 26
3 has a land mass that is larger than that of the United States. In 40
4 fact, Canada is the second largest country in the world; Russia is 54
5 the only nation with more land. Although Canada is a bigger area 67
6 than the United States, it has only a tenth as many people. Most 80
7 of these live in the southern third of the nation since a great deal 94
8 of northern Canada is made up of woods and tundra and frozen 106
9 wasteland. 108
10 For people who don't care to hunt for big game or fish for 121
11 salmon or even whales to the north, there are the large cities. 133
12 Montreal is the largest city in the country and is the second 146
13 largest French-speaking city in the whole world. The soaring new 159
14 buildings in Montreal contrast sharply with those in the capital 174
15 city of Ottawa, which is known for the Gothic style of stately old 187
16 government and other buildings. 192
17 Canada is an exciting place, rich in scenic beauty and natural 206
18 resources. The citizens of this nation, who are as friendly as you 219
19 could wish, have successfully harnessed the resources to make 232
20 Canada one of the richest of all nations. 240

|1 |2 |3 |4 |5 |6 |7 |8 |9 |10 |11 |12 |13 |14

SI 1.45N

■ 5′/2e

goal

□ *Team up with someone who types about as well as you do. One of you will be Typist A; the other, Typist B.*

□ *Read the appropriate column below; do what it says. Use professional standards throughout.*

□ *Give your teacher a copy of each memo and the final table.*

CREATIVE CO-OP 1: DEVELOPING ORIGINAL TABLES

TYPIST A

Your assignment is to prepare (without asking *any* questions) a table, "Our Favorite Cars." Do this assignment in the following steps:

1. START A DRAFT

With the left margin at 20 and tab at 45, double-space a list of the names of 10 persons you know (family, friends, anyone) and the cars they drive. If you do not have enough names, ask your classmates the kinds of cars they would prefer driving.

2. WRITE A MEMO

Draft and type a memo to Typist B, your survey consultant. Tell B you are enclosing a list of persons and their cars. Ask B to add 5 or 10 more names and cars to your list and then to return it to you.

(You will be asked to serve as consultant to Student B. As soon as you receive B's request, stop everything and take care of it!)

3. FINISH THE TABLE

When you get your list back, count the times each car is mentioned. Type your final table (with carbon) and arrange the cars according to popularity. Name the cars in column 1; give the number of times each is listed in column 2. Show in two subtitle lines who prepared the list and who was the survey consultant.

TYPIST B

Your assignment is to prepare (without asking *any* questions) a table, "Best Music Groups." Do the assignment in three steps:

1. LIST YOUR FAVORITES

With the left margin at 30, double-space a list of as many musical groups as you can—classical, country, rock, soul, and so on. You should have at least 10 groups in the list.

(Student A will be asking you to serve as a consultant. When Student A asks you to help, drop everything and help him or her at once.)

2. WRITE YOUR CONSULTANT

Compose and type a memo to Student A, who is your consultant. Ask student A to add any groups he or she might wish to and to rank the groups from "1" (best) to whatever is the total number of groups, like "10" or "12" (lowest), and to then return the list to you.

3. FINISH THE TABLE

When your list is returned, type it in final copy (with carbon) as a two-column, double-spaced table. List the musical groups alphabetically in column 1 and their rank in column 2. Indicate in two subtitle lines who prepared the list and who was the survey consultant in preparing the list.

SESSION	TOPIC—SUBJECT	SUGGESTED SPEAKER	SUGGESTED CHAIRPERSON
8:30–10:00	Fund Raising	Paul Schaefer, Director Financial Services Institute 131 11th Avenue Calgary, Alberta T2G 0X5	Dr. Russell Brennan Carroll Brooks, Ltd. 200 Eaton Avenue Selkirk, Manitoba R1A 0W6
10:30–12:00	Consumer Affairs	Andre Glover, Vice President Retail Merchants Association 400 Laurier Avenue West Ottawa, Ontario K1A 0H4	Hellena Friedman Director of Research Goodman & Boyce 1019 Wharf Street Victoria, BC V8W 2Y9
2:00–3:30	Volunteer Activities	Lydia Greer, President Urban Aid Society Seventh Floor SPC Building Regina, Saskatchewan S4P 2Y9	Alvin Randall 491 Portage Avenue Winnipeg, Manitoba R3B 2E7

JOBS 117-1, -2, -3: FORM LETTERS

Workbook 291–294 or baronial (5½" x 8½")
plain paper □ **Body 97** □ **SI 1.57H** □
Needs 7 additional commas □ ■ **3 letters**
within 20'/0e

"Please send the following letter to each of the three persons we want as a speaker," says Ms. McKechnie. "Insert the correct names and addresses, and be sure to get the right subject and time in the second paragraph."

Dear --: It is my privilege to extend to you   40
for the Directors of the Association an   48
invitation to speak at our convention, to be   57
held in Montreal the week of August 13-17.   66

We know that you have long been in-   74
volved in [*Insert correct topic.*] so we   80
should like you to speak on that subject at   89
the [*Insert correct time.*] session on August   95
14.   96

If I may have your acceptance as soon as   105
possible I will see that you receive all the   114
details about the meeting room the audience   123
size and so on as rapidly as the full pro-   133

gramme is confirmed. / Cordially yours, /   142
Eleanor McKechnie / Managing Director /   154
urs   155

JOBS 117-4, -5, -6: FORM LETTERS

Workbook 293–296 or baronial plain paper
□ **Body 97** □ **SI 1.53FH** □ ■ **3 letters within**
20'/0e

"Now, modify that letter so we can send it to each of the persons we want to serve as a chairperson," says Ms. McKechnie. "We can use the letter almost as it is if we're sure we send each copy to the right person."

In the first paragraph, change "to speak at our convention, to be held in Montreal the week of" to "to chair a meeting at our Montreal convention the week of . . . ."

In the second paragraph, change "to speak on that subject" to "to chair the meeting on that subject . . . ."

The third paragraph and the closing of the letter will be the same as those in the first letter.

The six projects of
Part 2 use the
following states as
their locale:

Unit 4: Alabama,
Mississippi

Unit 5: New Mexico,
Arizona

Unit 6: Alaska,
Hawaii

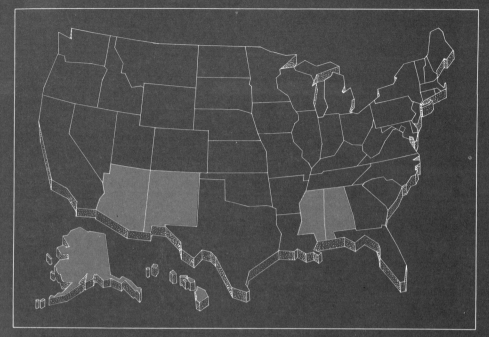

In Part 2 you begin the pattern that will be used in the rest of this book:

1. In each unit you have two work-experience projects of about an hour's business typing. You also have two skill drives in the middle of the unit and a clinic at the end of it:

3. Unless your teacher specifies otherwise, you will now begin to correct all your errors in production assignments. Use whatever means you and your teacher wish—eraser, correction paper,

Project 1	Project 1		Skill Drive 2	Project 2 2	
Project 1	Skill Drive 1		Project 2	Project 2 2	Clinic

2. Each project takes place in a business office in a different state, so by the time you complete *Typing 2*, you will have become familiar with the kinds of products and the names of places in all 50 states of the United States. Some Canadian provinces and Caribbean islands are treated similarly. The timed writings tell more about all these places.

correction fluid, or for certain machines, you can use the lift-off correction tape designed for them.

4. At the beginning of typing practice each day, warm up from the material on the introductory page, like that below. Throughout Part 2, you will turn to the drills here. From each of the four sets of sentences, type one sentence four or more times.

SPEED RECALL	1A The six girls held a social to pay for a visit to the lake.	12
	1B The man got a snap of an authentic whale by the big island.	24
ALPHABET REVIEW	2A Holly acquired a prize for jumping backwards over six feet.	12
	2B Paul reviewed the subject before giving Max and Kay a quiz.	24
NUMBER REVIEW	3A The runners were numbered "10," "28," "39," "47," and "56."	12
	3B I typed receipts for $10, $28, $39, $47, and $56 yesterday.	24
THINKING WHILE TYPING Edit these lines.	4A Please me call when come you into town; we to want see you.	12
	4B We shall give better you service; that a is sincere pledge.	24

|1 |2 |3 |4 |5 |6 |7 |8 |9 |10 |11 |12

by my executrix hereinafter named.

SECOND: I hereby give, devise, and bequeath all my estate and property, real and personal, of whatsoever nature and wheresoever situated, to my beloved wife, Anna Frances Easton.

THIRD: I hereby appoint my wife, Anna Frances Easton, as the sole executrix of my estate; and I direct that no bond be required of her in the performance of her duties. ↓₃

IN WITNESS WHEREOF, I have hereunto set my hand and my seal on this [*Spell out today's date.*] of [*Spell out the month.*] in the year one thousand nine hundred and [*Spell out the year.*] ↓₄ [*Start signature line at the center.*] _____ (LS) [*"LS," or locus sigilli, means "place of the seal" and is like the 10-space paragraph indentions, the use of all caps, and the use of ruled lines typical of legal writing. The following witness block is called the "Acknowledgment."*] ↓₃

THE ABOVE INSTRUMENT, consisting of this page only, was subscribed by the said Noel G. Easton in our presence and acknowledged by him to each of us; and he at the same time declared the above to be his Last Will and Testament; and we, at his request, in his presence and in the presence

of each other, have signed our names as witnesses hereto on the date last above written. ↓₃

_____ Residing at _____ ↓₂

_____ Residing at _____ ↓₂

_____ Residing at _____

JOB 116-2: WILL

Legal-ruled paper □ ■ 15′/0e

"Next," says Mr. Easton, "please type the same will, but substitute my wife's name for mine, and make the appropriate changes for 'his' and 'him,' 'her' and 'hers.' Name me executor. In other regards, the two wills are to be exactly alike."

JOB 116-3: COMPLETION CARDS

5″ x 3″ cards or slips □ ■ 5′/0e

Directions: *Spacing—1. Line—60. Warmup—page 163. Drills—repeat Clinic 14 on page 179.*

CLINIC 20

---

goal A
■ To produce three short letters.

goal B
■ To produce three short letters.

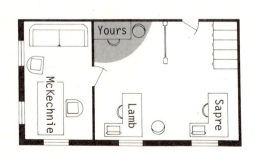

You work for Ms. Eleanor McKechnie, managing director of a business service club, Service Wheels, Ltd., in Scarborough, Canada.

"Service Wheels will hold its annual convention in Montreal in August," Ms. McKechnie says, "and right now I have to line up the speakers and chairpersons for the various meetings."

She gives you the schedule on page 252. "These are the people we want and the assignments we'd like them to accept, so let's write them and ask."

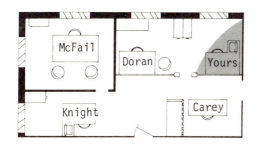

Directions: *Use the Warmup on page 30; then do Job 13-1.*

JOB 13-1: MAILING LIST

Workbook 37 or plain paper □ ■ 20′/0e

You have been hired by Forest Products, Demopolis, Alabama, and you work for Thomas McFail, General Manager. Kay Doran, a staff member, introduces you to Lisa Knight and Don Carey, also on the staff.

Mr. McFail calls you to his office.

"We're pleased to have you with us," he says. He continues, "I have received a number of requests for our regional dealers' list. It's changed substantially since the last time it was sent out, and we need to update it."

Mr. McFail gives you the revised list (page 32) and says, "Please retype this, ready for duplicating. Abbreviate everywhere possible. Omit all punctuation marks. Arrange the list alphabetically by city. Single-space the list, but double-space after each alphabetic group of cities."

If you do not have Workbook 37, arrange the list as a four-column table on a full sheet of plain paper.

goal B

■ To prepare two sets of labels, each set within 10′/0e.

JOB 13-2: ENVELOPE LABELS

Workbook 38 □ Spacing 1
□ ■ 10′/0e

"Now I'd like you to prepare envelope labels we can use when we mail the list to all our dealers," says Mr. McFail.

Use Workbook 38. If you do not have it, convert a plain paper to a sheet of labels: type a line of periods across the paper every sixth line, then turn the paper sideways and type a line of periods on lines 17 and 34.

JOB 13-3: PACKAGE LABELS

Workbook 39 □ Spacing 1
□ ■ 10′/0e

When you have finished the envelope labels, Mr. McFail says, "Now, please prepare package labels we can use to ship packets of brochures to each dealer whose ZIP Code number begins with '35.'"

If you do not have Workbook 39, divide a sheet of paper into ten labels that you type like this:

FOREST PRODUCTS INCORPORATED
255 Main - Demopolis, Alabama - 36732

Eagle Designers
722 Lantana Way NW
Huntsville, AL 35811

FOREST PRODUCTS INCORPORATED

JOB 115-1: ORIGINAL TABLE

Plain paper ☐ Use any arrangement you prefer, not necessarily the one shown ☐ ■ 10'/0e

"First I'd like to dictate a list of Mrs. Easton's properties," says Mr. Easton, "so you can type the data in a table. Ready?"

Title: Properties of Anna Frances Easton | 22
Column headings: Number, Description, and | 36
Location. There are six items: | 43

5 cottages with two bedrooms each, in | 49
Maya Cove, Tortila / British Virgin Islands | 63

8 beach houses with two bedrooms each, | 69
in West End, Tortila / British Virgin Islands | 84

1 12-acre farm, in Virgin Gorda / British | 97
Virgin Islands | 100

1 tourist hotel, "Easton House," in [*note* | 106
spelling] Treasurisle / British Virgin Islands | 118

2 condominiums, at 212 Palm Drive / | 127
Miami Beach, Florida | 133

1 six-room single-family dwelling, at | 139
4568 Tamarack Hills / Springboro, Ohio | 152

JOB 115-2: ORIGINAL TABLE

Plain paper ☐ Use any arrangement that will enable you to complete the table in 10 minutes ☐ ■ 10'/0e

"Now please tabulate a list of my properties," says Mr. Easton.
He dictates:

Title: Properties of Noel G. Easton | 19
Column headings: Number, Description, and | 30
Location. There are five items: | 38

1 103-acre farm with buildings, 1 mile | 49
north of Springboro, Ohio, on State Route | 61
741 | 62

1 150-acre farm with buildings, 3 miles | 74
east of Wilmington, Ohio, on Stone Road | 85

1 350-acre farm with buildings, 4 miles | 96
west of Salina, Kansas | 102

1 5-acre shopping center with 12 busi- | 114
nesses, intersection of State Routes 741 and | 126
73, in Springboro, Ohio | 130

1 tourist hotel, "Easton Inn," in Apple | 140
Bay, Tortila / British Virgin Islands | 149

---

goal A
■ To produce a short will within 20'/0e.

goal B
■ To produce a short will within 15'/0e.

JOB 116-1: WILL

Legal paper ☐ Start line 9
☐ Tabs 10 and center ☐ ■ 20'/0e

"Now," says Mr. Easton, "before leaving on this trip, I'd like to dictate my will. Type it on legal-ruled paper, please."

Title, centered between the ruled lines: | ··
Last Will and Testament of Noel G. Easton | 27
I, Noel G. Easton, of the City of Spring- | 37
boro, County of Warren, State of Ohio, be- | 46
ing of sound and disposing mind and | 53

LESSON 116

Directions: *Spacing—1. Line—60.*
Warmup—page 240. Editing—note capitalization.

memory, do hereby make, publish, and | 61
declare this to be my Last Will and Testa- | 69
ment, hereby revoking and canceling all | 77
former Wills and Codicils by me at any | 85
time made. ↓₃ | 87

FIRST: I hereby direct that all my just | 98
debts and funeral expenses be paid and dis- | 106
charged as soon as possible out of my estate | 116

FOREST PRODUCTS DEALER LIST FOR Alabama

City	Dealer	Street Address	ZIP
Andalusia	Creative Woodcraft ~	369 Main St	36420
Anniston	James Woodworks Incorp.	72 Walnut Dr	36201
Athens	Stlen Woodcraft	554 1st St	35611
~~Atmore~~	~~Absey Construction~~	~~801 Circle Dr~~	~~36502~~
~~Bessemer~~	LaCoure and Associates	206 7th Ave ~~184th Ave~~	35501 ~~36020~~
Birmingham	Pilot Wood ~~Co~~ Inc	3542 Belmont Rd	35210
Brewton	Midtown Supplies	1088 Arbor Blvd	36426
Decatur	Home of Economy	44 N 5th St	35601
Demopolis	Key Lumber Co	110 Newport Ave	36732
Dothan	Carhart Lumber Company ~	83 Clairemont Ave	36301
Enterprise	Powell's Home Building	362 Bruce St	36330
Florence	Drake Woodworks Inc	180 Grave Ave	35630
Hartselle	Roberts on Lumber Co	55 Forest Park Dr ~	35640
Huntsville	Eagle Designers	772 Lantana Way NW ~	35811
Jasper			
Mobile	Interstate Wood Co ~	168 Seale St	36617
Montgomery	Hoffmann Products	901 Orlando Dr	36110
Ozark	Ozark Lumber Products	22 W Dale St	36360
~~Phenix City~~	~~R&M Home Supplies Inc~~	~~661 Hatley Ave~~	~~36867~~
Prichard	Astor Display Company ~	382 N Fairmont Dr	36610
Prattville	Woodline Co Inc	23 W Main St	36067
Selma	Selma Lumber Co	750 Acker Blvd	36701
Sylacauga	Ted Brown and Son Inc	563 Ellis Drive ~	35150
Talladega	Berkshire Woods	710 Benchley St	35160
Tuscaloosa	Dissler Brothers Inc ~	430 King St	35401
Tuskegee	Raymond Brothers Inc	1112 Crescent St	36083

LESSON 14

Directions: *Warmup—page 30. Then begin Job 14-1, page 33.*

goal A

- To type 48 wam for 5'/2e.

CHECK THAT YOUR

☐ Feet are firmly on the floor.
☐ Back is erect, leaning forward.
☐ Hands are motionless.
☐ Fingers do all the reaching.

Directions: Spacing—1. Line—60. Warmup—page 240.

5-MINUTE PIECEMEAL PRACTICE

Spacing 1 for 1' TWs; spacing 2 for 5' TWs.

Take up to ten 1-minute TWs, trying to type each paragraph within 1 minute without errors; then take an overall 5-minute TW to achieve 48 wam/5'/2e.

```
 1      Close your eyes and fly away on an imaginary trip to a        12
 2  land where beauty and time are unlimited, where white sands       24
 3  stretch for miles, where the sun dazzles your eyes and tans       36
 4  your skin, where the sea is turquoise--visit the Caribbean!       48
 5      Begin with island hopping over to Jamaica, where sandy     12 | 60
 6  beaches make white fringe around the base of each mountain.    24 | 72
 7  Dance all night to the music of the steel drums in Kingston    36 | 84
 8  Bay; then doze and sail all day beneath the glittering sun.    48 | 96
 9      Next, make a quick stop in Haiti and meander up a path     12 | 108
10  through the rain forests to a mountain peak from which vast    24 | 120
11  plantations of sugarcane and some new industrial plants are    36 | 132
12  seen.  Walk over the border to the Dominican Republic also.    48 | 144
13      Now sail over to the Leeward Islands:  Aruba, Bonaire,     12 | 156
14  and Curacao.  The last is the biggest jewel, but the others    24 | 168
15  also glitter:  Aruba with its gorgeous beaches, and Bonaire    36 | 180
16  with waters so clear they were meant only for scuba divers.    48 | 192
17      For your finale, visit the Windward Islands.  You will     12 | 204
18  love the trees and flowers of Martinique, the looming peaks    24 | 216
19  and palms of Saint Lucia, the pulsing music of Grenada, and    36 | 228
20  on all of them the sun and sand and sea and tropical green.    48 | 240
    |1   |2   |3   |4   |5   |6   |7   |8   |9   |10  |11  |12        SI 1.40N
```

Speed markers are for 5' TW. Circled figures are 1' goals.

- 5'/2e

goal B

- To produce two tables from unarranged data, each within 10'/0e.

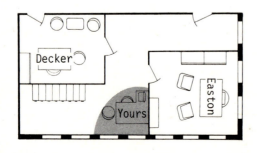

Directions: Adjust machine for Job 115-1.

You work for a lawyer, Noel G. Easton, who is about to leave with his wife for Miami and the British Virgin Islands to inspect their properties. Before starting on the trip, Mr. Easton would like you to make tables listing their real estate holdings.

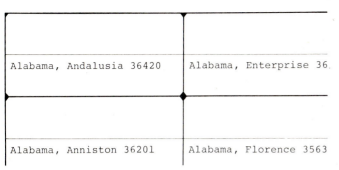

Alabama, Andalusia 36420	Alabama, Enterprise 36.
Alabama, Anniston 36201	Alabama, Florence 3563

File folder labels: Type the entry under which the folder will be filed, one line below the light line in the middle of the label.

JOB 14-1:   FILE FOLDER LABELS

1.   Prepared by Janice Holter

2.   Proofread with Ellen O'Rigby

3.   No problems in preparing this job.

Completion card: Attach one to each job, listing who typed it, who helped proofread it, and any problems encountered.

JOB 14-1: FILE FOLDER LABELS

Workbook 40 □ ■ 10'/0e

"Finally," says Mr. McFail, "please prepare a set of file labels —one for each dealer in the state—so we can get our files cleaned up." You type one-line entries like this, indented 3 spaces and typed just under the dividing line:

    Alabama, Andalusia 36420

JOB 14-2: COMPLETION CARDS

Four 5" x 3" cards or slips of paper □ ■ 10'/0e

At the end of this project, and after all other projects, give your work to your teacher. Attach a card to each job listing who typed it (you, of course), who helped you proofread it, and what problems—if any—you encountered.

goal B

■ **To type 41 wam for 3'/2e.**

Directions: *Spacing—1. Line—60. Tab—5.*

12-SECOND SPRINTS

Directions on page 2.

1 Helen typed three fewer lines than David thought she would.   12
2 The desk was moved over to the left and was not moved back.   12
3 For the rest of the day we will go to the fair in the city.   12

12" SPEED: 25 30 35 40 45 50 55 60

SKILL BLITZ

Directions on page 13:
1. 3' timing.
2. Corrective practice.
3. 3' timing.

Circled numbers are 1' goals.

4   Alabama lies as cozy as can be in the cotton belt. It   12
5   Alabama lies as cozy as can be in the cotton belt. It   24
6   Alabama lies as cozy as can be in the cotton belt. It   36
7 is just as rich in wood pulp, coal from the mines, and iron   48
8 is just as rich in wood pulp, coal from the mines, and iron   60
9 is just as rich in wood pulp, coal from the mines, and iron   72
10 and steel. Bauxite mines in the state have grown at a very   84
11 and steel. Bauxite mines in the state have grown at a very   96
12 and steel. Bauxite mines in the state have grown at a very   108

■ **3'/2e**

13 quick pace in recent years.   113
14 quick pace in recent years.   118
15 quick pace in recent years.   123

|1 |2 |3 |4 |5 |6 |7 |8 |9 |10 |11 |12   SI 1.19E

3-MINUTE TW

With a goal of 41 wam for 3 minutes within 2 errors, take one or more 3-minute timings at the top of page 34.

2   14   33

goal A

■ To produce a ruled table from unorganized data.

JOB 114-1: RULED TABLE

Plain paper □ ■ 15'/0e

"Bad luck!" exclaims Señor Fernandez. "The computer is not functioning. It has lost our reservations count for all seven S/S/S Motels for the week of June 12!"

He continues, "I called our six other motels and got their information, and I have ours. So, please take and type the following table":

Title: Reservations Inventory   15

Subtitle: For Week of June 12, 19--   33

Subtitle: Condensed Summary As of [to-day's date]   57

Column heads: Location, Rooms, Reserved   76
S-W, and Reserved T-S   81

Arecibo, 322, 116, 182			103
Humacao, 110, 76, 89			111
Isabela, 124, 24, 92			120
Luquillo, 220, 121, 187			129
Mayaguez, 180, 73, 114			137
Ponce, 214, 104, 182			146
San Juan, 400, 382, 341			154
TOTAL 1,570, 896, 1,187			176
PERCENT 100.0, 57.1, 75.6			186

JOB 114-2: COMPLETION CARDS

5" x 3" cards or slips □ ■ 5'/0e

goal B

■ To type 48 wam for 3'/1e.

3-MINUTE TW SKILL DRIVE

Directions: *Spacing—2. Line—60. Tab—5.*

Take a 3-minute TW Pretest; then take up to ten 1-minute TWs until you can type each paragraph within 1 minute without error. Then finish with a 3-minute TW Posttest.

Speed markers are for 3' TW. Circled numbers are 1' goals.

		1'	3'
1	Puerto Rico is an exciting island in the Caribbean Sea	12	
2	about a thousand miles southeast of Miami, just a quick air	24	
3	hop of under two hours. Thirty-five miles wide and about a	36	
4	hundred long, Puerto Rico is about the size of Connecticut.	48	
5	About forty miles east of Puerto Rico are the American	12	60
6	Virgin Islands. These consist of three large islands and a	24	72
7	lot of islets and rocky keys. The three islands have Saint	36	84
8	as part of each name: St. Croix, St. Thomas, and St. John.	48	96
9	All these islands have three things in common. First,	12	108
10	they are vital to the defense of the Panama Canal. Second,	24	120
11	they are superb vacation spots. Third, by drawing tourists	36	132
12	and industry to their shores, they now enjoy a richer life.	48	144

SI 1.47FH

■ 3'/1e

3-MINUTE TW

Spacing—2.
Line—60.
Tab—5.

Speed markers
are for 3' TW.

■ 3'/2e

Acquire a little salt spray from the gulf plus a dozen
sandy beaches, add to it some of the most beautiful scenery
in the country, and blend in a wealth of mineral ores. Now
add cotton, forests, and farms; then top it off with just a
touch of Dixie. We now have a preferred recipe of Alabama.

Maps reveal that the terrain in this state varies much
from north to south. The northern regions of the state are
mostly mountains and plateaus, whereas the southern section
is quite low because of the many river deltas in that area.
Rich, black soil near the rivers has made this region ideal
for farming. ■

Most of the rivers in this state flow toward the gulf,
on the southern coast, but one of the major rivers flows in
a westward direction and then exits to the north. Millions
of dollars have been spent in the past few years to improve
the flow of these rivers. Large dams have been built, and,
as a result, a number of lakes with many miles of shoreline
have been created for the enjoyment of all who adore water.

SI 1.33FE

5-MINUTE TW

Spacing—2.
Line—60.
Tab—5.

Speed markers
are for 5' TW.

■ 5'/3e

West of Alabama is one of the most beautiful states of
all, the state of Mississippi, named after the river of the
same name. The state was the twentieth to be admitted into
the nation. If you could look down on the state from outer
space, you'd know it from its forests in the east, prairies
in central to north sections, and rugged hills in the west.

Long ago tobacco and indigo were thought to be the top
cash crops, and so they were produced for export. However,
within a little while cotton became the top money crop. It
is still big in the delta, but dozens of other parts of the
state also point with justified pride to their cotton crop.

Bauxite, lignite, and sandstone are mined to a limited
extent, but the largest mining efforts have been devoted to
an intensive search for natural gas. Oil and gas fields in
this southern state have produced millions of cubic feet of
gas. There appear to be huge reserves of gas in the middle
of the state, promising some day to make Mississippi a rich
state.

SI 1.38N

JOB 113-1: "REGRETS" LETTER

Workbook 287 □ Body 79 □ SI 1.43N
□ ■ 10'/0e

"Our first letter," says Señor Fernandez, "is to say we are sorry we cannot accommodate a group."

Ms. Rhoda Sillvers, NLA [*Cap initial letters of organization names.*] of Massachusetts, 978 Brewster Road, New Bedford, MA 02701

Dear Ms. Sillvers: Thank you for writing us for reservations for your group for the week of June 12.

I am sorry to tell you that our San Juan motel is booked for that week. We could take care of your group, however, at our Luquillo motel, a beautiful beach resort one hour's drive from San Juan. Enclosed is a booklet about the Luquillo S/S/S.

If you wish us to save rooms at Luquillo, let us know not later than March 23.

[*Use display closing shown on page 246.*]

JOB 113-2: CONFIRMATION LETTER

Workbook 287 □ Body 78 □ SI 1.53FH
□ ■ 10'/0e

"We do have space the following week," says Señor Fernandez, "so we can confirm this convention."

Mr. James F. Mallon, President of the National Writers Association, of 77 New Park Place in Madison, Wisconsin, ZIP 53701

Dear Mr. Mallon: This letter confirms our recent telephone exchange in which I told you that I would reserve 150 rooms for members of your group for the week of June 19.

I am mailing advance registration forms for your members. Those who return them to us will find that they can register in less than a minute when they arrive.

Our banquet manager, Mr. Armando Diaz,

is waiting to hear from you about your needs for luncheons, dinners, and banquets.

[*Use display closing.*]

JOB 113-3: "REGRETS" LETTER

Workbook 289 □ ■ 10'/0e

"I have to turn down another request," says Señor Fernandez. "I think you can do it for me."

We are replying to Dr. Charlotte Thornley, of the American Testing Assn., at 117 Longview Terrace in Tenafly, New Jersey, ZIP 07670. Tell her exactly what was in the first letter except that we suggest she make her reservations at our motel in Arecibo; and of course we will send her a booklet about the Arecibo S/S/S.

JOB 113-4: CANCELLATION-REPLY LETTER

Workbook 289 □ Body 97 □ SI 1.50FH
□ ■ 10'/0e

"Oh, what a disappointment!" says Señor Fernandez. "A 100-room convention canceled their reservations. Please send this reply":

Mr. Howard Stout, President, Illinois Poultry Association, 91 South Adams Street, Joliet, IL 60401. Dear Mr. Stout:

I appreciate your writing to us about the cancellation of your convention. We are, of course, both disappointed and concerned about the bookings. We have recently had inquiries for the week of June 12 that we have had to turn down, since your group had reserved so many rooms. Now we do not know whether we can dispose of them.

In accordance with our written agreement, we will hold your deposit until we know what success we will have in getting some other group to take your place, and then we will make a settlement with you.

[*Use display closing.*]

goal A

■ To type 41 wam for 5'/3e on normal copy.

HOW TO USE THE SPACE BAR

☐ *Tap it quickly with your thumb.*
☐ *Release it instantly.*
☐ *Use it as rapidly as you use any letter key.*
☐ *Don't rest your thumb on it.*

Directions: *Spacing—1. Line—60. Tab—5. Drills—3. Warmup—page 30.*

PRETEST

Take a 5-minute writing on lines 19–36, page 34.

PRACTICE ON TW VOCABULARY

Type each drill three times. Then type lines 1–3 twice more for accuracy gain or lines 4–6 twice more for speed gain.

1 Mississippi southern millions produced Alabama export state 12
2 sandstone justified promising prairies tobacco indigo cubic 12

Accuracy.

3 twentieth beautiful intensive reserves lignite dozens mined 12

|1 |2 |3 |4 |5 |6 |7 |8 |9 |10 |11 |12

Speed.

4 named after river could outer space north hills you'd east, 12
5 west most same name into know from long were cash they crop 12
6 one the was and ago top big but gas oil day all of is if it 12

POSTTEST

Repeat the Pretest 5-minute writing; record your best TW score.

goal B

■ To produce a mailing list from revised copy within 20'/0e.

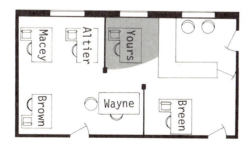

Directions: *Adjust your machine for Job 15-1.*

JOB 15-1: MAILING LIST

Workbook 41 or plain paper, turned sideways ☐ ■ 20'/0e

"Welcome!" exclaims Janice Breen, marketing director for Breen & Burton Service, in Natchez, Mississippi. "I've needed help in updating our dealer data . . . and here you are!"

Giving you the revised dealer list (page 36), Ms. Breen says, "Please retype this. Single-space it, with a blank line after each city. Where we have more than one dealer in a city, list that

city's dealers alphabetically by the names of their stores."

You will use the workbook form for the list; if you do not have it, arrange the list as a table on plain paper.

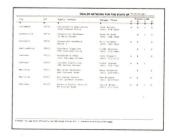

LESSON 112

Directions: *Spacing—1. Tabs 10 and center. Warmup—page 240.*

JOB 112-1: SUBLEASE AGREEMENT

Legal-ruled paper □ **Spacing 1** □ ■ **20′/0e**

"I have two more subleases, like the one you just typed, to be prepared," says Mr. Allumbaugh.

In the first one, the Party of the First Part is Estelle Adams; the Party of the Second Part is Maryanne Ostecky, of 18 Steel River Road, Weirton, West Virginia. The apartment is 12-D, Building 2. Ms. Ostecky is taking it for eight months, beginning April 15, and will pay $250 a month on the 15th of each month.

JOB 112-2: SUBLEASE AGREEMENT

Legal-ruled paper □ **Spacing 1** □ ■ **15′/0e**

"The other one is for a shorter period," says Mr. Allumbaugh, "but it takes as much typing."

In this second one, the Party of the First Part is Reginald Nassau; the Party of the Second

Part is Drue Pele, of 373 Garland Drive in Huntington, West Virginia. The apartment is 9-F, Building 2. Mr. Pele is taking it for eight weeks furnished [*Substitute the word "furnished" for "entirely unfurnished" in the second paragraph.*] beginning a week from next Sunday. He is to pay $100 a week, payable on Friday of each week."

JOB 112-3: COMPLETION CARDS

5″ x 3″ cards or slips □ ■ **5′/0e**

Directions: *Spacing—1. Line—60. Warmup—page 163; then repeat Clinic 13 on page 171.*

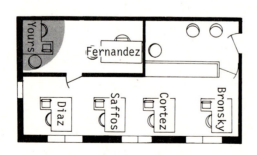

UNIT 29

LESSON 113

Directions: *Spacing—1. Line—60. Warmup—page 240.*

You type for Dino Fernandez, manager of the Sea/Sun/Siesta Motel [also called familiarly the "S/S/S Motel"] in San Juan, Puerto Rico.

Señor Fernandez prefers a special arrangement of the closing lines, like this:

```
                        Cordially yours,

                        SEA/SUN/SIESTA MOTEL


                             Manager
Dino Fernandez/urs
```

City	ZIP	Agency / Address	Manager / Phone	Product Lines A	B	C	D
~~Biloxi~~	~~39533~~	~~Davis Appliances~~ ~~2609 Crestwood Drive~~	~~Wesley Anderson~~ ~~(601) 835-0591~~	~~A~~	~~B~~		~~D~~
Columbus	39701	Christner's Appliances 3549 Almond Drive	Jack Nutter (601) 979-2963	A	B	C	D
Greenville	39~~7~~8 01	Greenville Hardware 12 Main Street	Anne Krisner (601) 188-39~~08~~		B	C	D
Gulfport	39501	Oceanside Hardware Route 2	*Bill Hickman* ~~Robert Winthrope~~ (601) 781-3682	A	B		D
Hattiesburg	39401	Southern Supplies 428 Overlook Drive	Cindy Herrera (601) 333-2480		B	C	D
Jackson	39212	Bradshaw's Shop 1121 Fairway Street	John Stewart (601) 752-7302	A	B		D
Jackson	3~~8~~9 203	Jackson Electrical 788 Dalton Street	*Diane Ingram* ~~James Hunter~~ (601) 752-7302	A	B	C	
Meridian Meridian	39301 39301	*Quickshop Center* *1314 Laramie Street* Meridian Hardware ~~229 Chestnut Drive~~ *680 Forrest Road*	*Pam Brunson* (601) 223-9320 Kaye Galbreth (601) ~~221-4650~~ *220-4451*	A	*B* B		D D
Natchez	39120	Breen & Burton Service 89 Fulton Road	Janice Breen (601) 273-5525	A	B	C	D

LESSON 16

Directions: _Warmup—page 30. Then set your machine for Job 16-1._

JOB 16-1: ALPHABETIC INDEX CARDS

Eight 5″ x 3″ cards or slips of paper □ ■ 10'/0e

"I rely constantly on index cards when writing or phoning our dealers," Ms. Breen says, "and I need a new set. Please make a 5″ x 3″ card for each dealer—except me, of course—on the list. On each card give the dealer's name, name of the store, address, ZIP Code, and—set off separately—the telephone number."

Before you start this job, review the information about index cards at the top of page 37.

The double rule sets off a 1½-inch left margin; the single rule sets off a ½-inch right margin. Typists with electric machines can type the rules with the repeat-underscore key: insert the paper sideways, type a line 9 lines from the top edge, type a second line below it; then reverse the paper and type a single line 3 lines from the top edge. Insert the paper in the normal manner and set the margin stops 2 or 3 spaces inside the lines.

Note that legality depends on content and signatures, not on whether a document is penned or typed, single- or double-spaced, with or without ruled lines. Individual law offices and departments have their own style preferences, like rules for appearance's sake and single spacing to save file-drawer space.

Directions: *Spacing—1. Tabs—10 and center between ruled lines. Type the scripted inserts. Do not type underscores—except for the two signature lines.*

JOB 111-1
(Continued)

SUBLEASE AGREEMENT ↓₃   13

SUBLEASE AGREEMENT MADE this *fifteenth* _____ day of   25
March ____ , 19-- , by and between _____ *Robert L. Bruce* ____ ,   34
Party of the First Part and Sublessor, and *Julian S. Johnson* ,   47
now residing at *12 East Meadow Street, Fairmont, West*   58
Virginia, _____ Party of the Second Part and the Sublessee.   68

The Sublessor hereby subleases to the Sublessee and the Subles-   84
see does hereby take and rent from the Sublessor the premises known as   97
Apartment 2-C _____ , entirely unfurnished, in the building   108
known as Vista Apartments, located at 902 Valley Drive, Charleston, West   122
Virginia, for a term of _____ *six months* _____   129
beginning *on the first day of May, 19--* _____ .   138

The Sublessee hereby covenants and agrees to pay to the subles-   152
sor the rent for each _____ in the amount of *four hundred*   164
dollars ($ *400*), and to pay this amount not later than *the*   175
first day of each month _____ during this sublease term.   186

The Sublessee agrees and covenants not to assign this sublease   200
and not to sublet _____ *Apartment 2-C* _____ of the Vista Apartments   212
or any part thereon without written permission of the Party of the First   226
Part, the Sublessor.   231

The Sublessee agrees and covenants that a reasonable degree of   245
order and quietness will reign for the benefit and enjoyment of the resi-   260
dents of adjoining apartments.   266

The provisions contained in this sublease shall be binding.   280
The terms and provisions of this lease cannot be changed except by writ-   295
ten agreement. ↓₃   298

IN WITNESS WHEREOF the Sublessor and the Sublessee have herein   313
executed this sublease the day and year aforesaid. ↓₂   324

337

3" lines to sign on. *Robert L. Bruce* ____ , SUBLESSOR   *Julian S. Johnson* , SUBLESSEE   350

363
Witness to Signature   Witness to Signature   374

Draft of legal document, prepared on a duplicated form.

Do You Remember?   When typing index cards:

① On line 2, start typing 3 or 4 spaces from the left. Type the last name first. Indicate in parentheses any title other than *Mr.* and *Miss*.

② Leave 1 blank line; then indent 3 or 4 more spaces for the address lines. (Choose 3 or 4 and then keep that alignment.)

③ Leave a blank line and type the telephone number aligned with the address.

```
Breen, Janice (Ms.)  ①

②   Breen & Burton Service
    89 Fulton Road
    Natchez, MS 39120

③   Phone (601) 273-5525
```

Alphabetic file card like this is used in most desk-top address files.

JOB 16-2: GEOGRAPHIC INDEX CARDS

Nine 5″ x 3″ cards or slips of paper □ ■ 10′/0e

"While you're making cards," says Ms. Breen, "please make me a geographic set, too, to send in to our national headquarters. For this set, include a card for Breen & Burton Service."

As shown at the right, a geographic card is filed by its location; lower on the card is the complete address needed for mailings.

```
Mississippi, Natchez 39120

   Breen & Burton Service
   89 Fulton Road
   Natchez, MS 39120

   Phone (601) 273-5525
```

Geographic cards are used for mass mailings.

```
                        August 1, 19--

   NOTICE TO DEALERS:

   Please correct your price list to indicate the following
   price change:
       Cat. Item:   39606V
       Old Price:   $475.00
       New Price:   $519.00
       Effective:   September 15, 19--



                        Janice Breen, Manager
   URS
```

Fill-in postal cards are quick to complete. They have to be addressed too.

JOB 16-3: FILL-IN POSTAL CARDS

Workbook 43 or 5½″ x 3¼″ cards or slips of paper □ ■ 10′/0e

Ms. Breen shows you the adjacent card. "This is the kind of notice we send our dealers when we have a price increase or decrease," she says. "We keep the cards in stock."

You look at the card. Easy.

"Now," she continues, "the reason I'm showing it to you is that I have a price increase on catalog item 4L298W and have to notify the dealers who handle our 'C' product line. The old price is $489.95; effective the 15th of next month, the price will be $524.50. I think there are four dealers—besides Breen & Burton Service—with the 'C' product line (see page 36). Fill in a card for each; address it; get it ready to mail."

Workbook 43 contains four fill-in postal cards for this job. If you do not have them, cut four cards or slips of paper to postal card size (5½ by 3¼ inches) and type each message. Allow maximum space for Ms. Breen's signature. Add your initials.

JOB 16-4: COMPLETION CARDS

Four 5″ x 3″ cards or slips of paper □ ■ 10′/0e

```
JOB 16-3: FILL-IN POSTAL CARDS
1. Prepared by Jerry Vinovenus
2. Proofread with Ernie Jordan
3. Problems: Applied one fill-in card and
   had to make one completely typewritten
   card in its place. Substituting the
   typewritten card took time, but I will
   get the job done in time.
```

At the end of this project, and after all that follow, give your work to your teacher. To each job attach a card (like the one on page 33) telling who typed the work (your name, of course), who helped you proofread it, and what problems—if any—you encountered with the materials or actual production of the assignments.

goal A

■ To type 48 wam for 5'/2e.

5-MINUTE TW SKILL DRIVE

Spacing—2.

Routine:
1. 5' TW.
2. Corrective practice.
3. 5' TW.

Speed markers are for 5' TW. Circled numbers are 1' goals.

■ 5'/2e

Directions: Spacing—1. Line—60.
Tab—5. Warmup—page 240.

If you climb up to the top of a high ridge and stretch out on a 14
big, flat rock, you can take in the whole state of West Virginia in 27
one giant sweep. The warm sunshine creeps between the hills and 40
makes shadows across the hollows with quiet ease. A peek into 53
the hollow below reveals the sight of a cozy home with smoke 65
curling from the patched chimney. A modest barn stands nearby, 78
with a couple of cows and some chickens. Three boys are swing- 90
ing on grapevines as they go toward the creek to fish. It's a 103
peaceful setting and it's quite common in many parts of West 115
Virginia. 117

Look across the valley to the west and you can see the mark of 131
the coal mines, the meandering railroad tracks, and the lines of 144
coal trucks carrying their treasure to waiting consumers. The high 157
smokestacks of the steel mills and the chemical plants puff madly 170
as they show the industrial part of the state. All along the Ohio 184
River, asphalt and cement companies, power plants, and oil 196
depots can be seen. 200

Put on your field glasses and fix your gaze toward the east 213
where remnants of bygone days appear. John Brown made his 225
famous stand at Harpers Ferry. Carefully trimmed landscapes with 238
stately mansions lift their heads high near the city of Charleston. 252
The country's oldest spa is quite near Berkley Springs. Colonial 265
and Civil War relics can be seen throughout the area. Plush 278
resorts bring tourists from all over the nation. Friendly West 290
Virginia has space for both country and city folks. 300

SI 1.37N

goal B

■ To produce a wholly typed legal document on legal-ruled paper.

JOB 111-1: LEGAL DOCUMENT

Legal-ruled plain paper □ **Top margin 2"** □ ■ **20'/0e**

You work for Thomas Allumbaugh, manager of the Vista Apartments in Charleston, West Virginia.

"Bob Bruce is going to sublet his apartment," Mr. Allumbaugh says, "so we have to prepare the document for him and his sublettor to sign."

Mr Allumbaugh gives you the draft shown on page 245.

"Type this on legal-ruled paper, please," he says.

"Legal-ruled" paper is a sheet of 11-, 13-, or 14-inch paper with vertical lines printed, typed, or drawn to set off margin areas.

goal

■ **To use intensive drill to improve basic skill.**

ACTIVITIES	20 MIN.	40 MIN.
Warmup (page 30)	3'	3'
Drive 1 Pretest	4'	4'
Practice 1	9'	9'
Drive 1 Posttest	4'	4'
Drive 2 Pretest	—	5'
Practice 2	—	10'
Drive 2 Posttest	—	5'

DRIVE 1

PRETEST 1

Up reaches, no jumps.

Take two 1-minute timings on lines 1–3. Proofread both; then average the scores.

1 She suggests that he get a separate carriage for the guest. 12
2 He hesitated to hire an old friend first for the ideal job. 24
3 I hope the enclosed idea can hold the guests in the course. 36
   |1 |2 |3 |4 |5 |6 |7 |8 |9 |10 |11 |12

PRACTICE 1

Up reaches, no jumps.

Make four copies. Repeat individual lines for speed gain, or repeat the block of lines for accuracy gain.

4 transport separate variety seemed ideal block clue sent get 12
5 suggested fastened talents gladly makes eager draw hold job 24
6 refreshed enclosed shorten friend meets guest hope hire see 36
7 hesitated carriage measure course first grows neat drop old 48
8 privilege occupied justify rights stack while slip rail its 60

POSTTEST 1

Repeat the Pretest. Score your work and note your improvement.

DRIVE 2

PRETEST 2

Up reaches, few adjacents.

Take three 1-minute timings on lines 9–11. Proofread them; then average the scores.

9   The surprised judge thanked her for getting the desk files. 12
10 Watch just to see who else puts anything on the two floors. 24
11 Thinking people have studied a multitude of needless words. 36
    |1 |2 |3 |4 |5 |6 |7 |8 |9 |10 |11 |12

PRACTICE 2

Up reaches, no adjacents.

Make four copies. Repeat individual lines for speed gain, or repeat each 3-line block of lines for accuracy gain.

12 multitude thinking studied hidden watch think word used old 12
13 surprised needless thanked arises shown noted seem need how 24
14 forwarded invested implied counts meant floor puts just dry 36

15 effective anything closest formed judge files grow else use 12
16 scheduled journals private plenty table shown step loan kit 24
17 physician patients program school total token vary park yes 36

POSTTEST 2

Repeat Pretest 2. Score your work and note your improvement.

2 3 38

Waggoner / Director of Personnel ↓₃ Address: Miss Mary J. Donnelly, 2033 Sweet Briar Road, Lynchburg, VA 24504.

135
145
149

JOB 110-2: GET-WELL LETTER

Workbook 283 or paper trimmed to monarch size ☐ ■ 7'/0e

"That's a good letter!" Mr. Waggoner exclaims. "Think you could paraphrase it for someone else who's been sick?"

This one is Richard Dean, in the Research Department. I just learned the unhappy news today—don't say I called his office, since I didn't. Address: 990 Dale Avenue, Roanoke, Virginia, with a ZIP of 24001.

JOB 110-3: COMPLETION CARDS

5" x 3" cards or slips ☐ ■ 5'/0e

---

goal B

■ **To type 48 wam for 3'/1e.**

Directions: *Spacing—2. Line—60. Tab—5.*

PRETEST

Type this selection for 3 minutes. Your goal is to finish it within 3'/1e.

PRACTICE

Use the 1-minute Piecemeal-Practice routine: Take 1-minute writings, advancing to the next paragraph only when you have mastered a paragraph within 1'/0e.

Spacing 1 for 1' timings; spacing 2 for 3' timings.

Speed counters are for 3' TW. Circled figures are 1' goals.

1 Virginia is big and varied: its forty thousand square   12

2 miles spread from the mountains in the west to the Piedmont   24

3 Plateau in the middle, to the Tidewater at the coast. Near   36

4 the shoreline of Chesapeake Bay are most of the big cities. ①   48

5 From George Washington to Douglas MacArthur, the state   12   60

6 has given our nation great leaders, including among them no   24   72

7 less than eight presidents. The first English colonists in 36   84

8 the nation came to Jamestown and named the colony Virginia. ② 48   96

9 The state has moved from the old, picturesque scene of   12   108

10 lazy plantations into a modern era of big cities and towns, 24   120

11 big and efficient farms, and plants that turn out more than   36   132

12 six billion dollars worth of goods of all kinds every year. ③ 48 144

|₁ |₂ |₃ |₄ |₅ |₆ |₇ |₈ |₉ |₁₀ |₁₁ |₁₂   SI 1.43N

■ **3'/1e**

POSTTEST

Repeat the Pretest. Score your work and note your improvement.

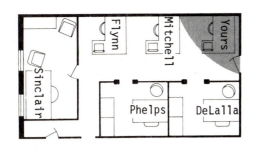

goal A

■ To produce data on printed 5" x 3" filing cards.

Directions: *Spacing—1. Line—60.*
Warmup—page 30; then begin Job 17-1.

JOB 17-1: DATA CARDS

Workbook 45 ☐ ■ 10'/0e

"I am glad you've joined us," says John Phelps, personnel officer. "We need your help in producing a number of data file cards."

He continues, "Here is a copy of the form we fill in and file when an employee leaves us."

```
Crenshaw, Holly Anne                    FINAL
NAME OF INTERVIEWEE                      INTERVIEW
                                         FORM

Clerk-Typist                  Billing
POSITION AT DEPARTURE         DEPARTMENT OR SUPERIOR

7/16/73         8/28/76         8/25/76
DATE EMPLOYED   DATE SEVERED    DATE INTERVIEWED

$100/week       $130/week       Dunn
STARTING SALARY FINAL SALARY    INTERVIEWER
```

"Please fill in similar cards for these persons," Mr. Phelps says, "with this information":

1. Ellen May Drydon, clerk-typist, Marketing Dept., employed 1/22/*this year* at $110/wk, left 9/25/*this year* at $120/wk, interviewed 9/22.

2. Thomas F. Day, stockroom helper, Purchasing Dept., employed 6/17/*last year* at $100/wk, leaving *today* at $105/wk, interviewed *yesterday*.

3. Sue Marie Henry, secretary, Sales Dept., employed 4/15/*last year* at $120 wk, leaving *today* at $150/wk, interviewed *yesterday*.

4. John P. Crane, clerk-typist, Personnel Dept., employed 3/25/*this year* at $120/wk, left *yesterday* at $125/wk, interviewed *yesterday*.

JOB 17-2: DATA CARDS

Workbook 46 ☐ ■ 10'/0e

"Yesterday I interviewed three young women still in school and one man," says Mr. Phelps. "Please type an interview card on each":

1. Alice Ann Monez / 275 Main Street / Elgin, AZ 85611 / phone (602) 835-1354 / (In school) / typing 55 wam/5 min/4e / shorthand 80 wam/3 min/4e / Secretary.

2. James L. Kent / 105 Walnut Street / Miami, AZ 85539 / phone (602) 772-2842 / Unemployed / typing 50 wam/5 min/0e / shorthand (None) / Mail Clerk.

3. Mary Kay Grove / Box 9 / Red Rock, AZ 85245 / phone (602) 246-4832 / (In school) / typing 60 wam/5 min/3e / shorthand 90 wam/3 min/4e / Secretarial.

4. Maria Grove / Box 9 / Red Rock, AZ 85245 / phone (602) 246-4832 / (In school) / typing 72 wam/5 min/3e / shorthand 120 wam/3 min/4e / Secretary.

goals B

■ To produce data on visible-index cards.
■ To type an open table.

Directions: *Adjust your machine for Job 17-3.*

JOB 109-3: RETIREMENT LETTER OF CONGRATULATIONS

Workbook 277 or paper trimmed to monarch size □ Body 89 □ SI 1.46FH □ Line 4″ □ ■ 10′/0e

"Now," says Mr. Waggoner, "I must write to Orman Beck, who is retiring. Use the same letter design, but do not type my name this time. Leave space as though you had typed it, and I'll just sign, since he and I are friends of many years. Ready?"

Dear Orman: I have just noted that you are 18
retiring after twenty-eight years with the 27
company. [*Don't cap "company" in this* 28
kind of reference to one's firm.] What a 30
record! Thank you, Orman, for all you con- 38
tributed to us during those years. 45

   I am sure that your colleagues in Credit 55
[*Capitalize the short form of a department's* ..
name.] have told you how much your ser- 61
vice has been valued, but your friends in 69
Personnel want to add a word about that: 78

All those years you spent in Accounting 86
and then in Credit are deeply appreciated. 94

   So we add our congratulations and our 103
best wishes for a long and healthy retire- 112
ment. 113

   [*closing*] Congratulations again! [*Since the* 120
signer's name and title are omitted, drop ..
8 lines to the inside address.] Mr. Orman D. 129
Beck, Newport Apartments 4B, 7250 Vir- 136
ginia Beach Blvd., Virginia Beach, VA 144
23458. 145

JOB 109-4: RETIREMENT LETTER OF CONGRATULATIONS

Workbook 279 or paper trimmed to monarch size □ ■ 10′/0e

"Please type a paraphrase of that letter for another retiree," says Mr. Waggoner, "ready for my signature."

This one is to Mr. A. M. Rogoff; call him "Dear Arnie" in the salutation. He worked here for 12 years—in Publications, in Advertising, finally in Marketing. Include a reference to his wife Jan. Address: 37B Benns Church Road, Newport News, VA, with a ZIP of 23607.

JOB 110-1: GET-WELL LETTER

Workbook 281 or paper trimmed to monarch size □ Body 97 □ SI 1.41N □ Line 4″ □ ■ 8′/0e

"Next," says Mr. Waggoner, "a get-well letter to one of our veterans. Formal-personal style, of course, this time <u>with</u> name and title."

Dear Miss Donnelly: I called your office 18
today and learned the unhappy news that 26
you have been ill, so I am writing at once 34
to express wishes for a quick and complete 43
recovery. 45

Directions: *Spacing—1. Line—60.*
Warmup—page 240. Editing—capitals.

LESSON 110

   In doing so, I know that I speak for your 54
many friends not only in the Marketing 62
Department but in other departments [*Do* 69
not cap "departments" since it is not a ..
name.] throughout the company. 74

   You are missed, and everyone wonders 83
when you will be back. I hope you will 91
take as long as you need for full recovery, 100
then come back in the full and happy 107
knowledge that your job and your duties 115
await you. [*closing*] Get well, now! ↓₄ James 128

Condado,	Carmen	Maria
LAST NAME	FIRST NAME	MIDDLE NAME OR INITIAL

2. Address: 171 Avenida Marana
Contaro, AZ 85230
3. Telephone: 555-1441
4. Interview date: June 7, 19-- by JD
5. Job title/rank: Secretary 8
6. Starting salary: $150/wk
7. Department: Purchasing
8. Superior: Elfrida Conchise

9. Prior employer: Marana Realty Company, Marana

Condado,	Carmen	Maria
LAST NAME	FIRST NAME	MIDDLE NAME OR INITIAL

TYPIST PLEASE NOTE: THIS SCALE CORRESPONDS TO PICA SPACING. If your machine is elite, use the other side of this card. Set the paper guide so that the scale on your machine corresponds to the spacing on this scale. Set the left margin stop at the first arrow and tab stops at the other arrows. Fold back or remove this stub after typing card.

2. Edward Eagle; 3216 East Uhl Street, Tucson, AZ 85710; phone 525-2272; interview September 18 by JD; junior accountant 6 at $200 a week, accounting dept.; reporting to Stewart Redington; prior work Shell Research, Flagstaff.

3. Merrillee Cordes; 8700 East Kelso, Tucson, AZ 85712; phone 525-8687; interview September 18 by JD; custodian 4 at $125 a week, maintenance; reporting to Enrico Lenher; prior work Painted Rocks Park, Gila Bend.

4. Stephen Goodwin; Box 277, Oracle, AZ 85623; phone 448-8108; interview September 19 by JD; assistant marketing director at $18,000 a year, research dept.; reporting to Kemel Harshaw; prior work Gulf Oil, Yuma.

JOB 17-3: VISIBLE-INDEX CARDS

Workbook 47-48 □ ■ 10'/0e

"Next," says Mr. Phelps, "I'd like you to make visible-index cards for four new employees."

"I beg your pardon," you say, "but I am not familiar with 'visible' index cards."

"Nothing to them." He smiles and shows you a finished card like the one above. "They're like any other data file card except that you type the name an extra time, at the bottom."

1. Mesilia Rincon; 979 San Xavier Street, Sahuarita, AZ 85629; phone 353-7305; interview September 18 by JD; secretary 6 at $140 a week in sales dept.; reporting to Richard Jarvis; no prior employment.

JOB 17-4: OPEN TABLE

Plain paper and 2 carbons □ ■ 10'/0e

Mr. Phelps hands you the table below and says, "This is a list of new employees who joined our staff in September. We are going to have a reception for them on October 16. Please type this with the names in alphabetic order, and make two carbons."

Reception for New Employees		
October 16, 3:30 p.m.			18 / 33
Employee	Department	School or College
Edward Eagle	Accounting	Pima Community College
Harold E. Van Vickle	Payroll	Conchise High School
Carroll Holdbrook	~~Personnel~~ ~~Sales~~	Central High School
Merrillee Cordes	Maintenance	Tucson Senior High School
Cindy Michaels	Marketing	Roosevelt High School
David Dunlap	Sales	Central Arizona College
Mesilia Rincon	~~Sales~~ ~~Receiving~~	Pima Community College
Stephen Goodwin	Research	Eastern Arizona College
Pamela Mehrten	Marketing	Mesa Community College

goal A

■ To produce two letters of congratulations.

JOB 109-1: ANNIVERSARY LETTER OF CONGRATULATIONS

Workbook 273 or paper trimmed to monarch size ☐ Body 110 ☐ SI 1.40N ☐ Line 5″ ☐ ■ 10′/0e

You work as aide to James Waggoner, director of personnel [*Do not cap titles that follow names in sentences.*] in William Hudson Corporation.

"Let's send Jack Stahl a letter of congratulations," says Mr. Waggoner. "Use the formal personal arrangement, please."

JOB 109-2: ANNIVERSARY LETTER OF CONGRATULATIONS

Workbook 275 or paper trimmed to monarch size ☐ Line 5″ ☐ ■ 10′/0e

"I want you to prepare a similar letter to another employee who has an anniversary to be noted," says Mr. Waggoner. "You can make it <u>like</u>, but not an exact copy of, the letter to Mr. Stahl. You know, sort of rewrite it as you go along."

Dear Mr. Stahl: My colleagues and I in the	18
Personnel Department [*Use caps for exact*	22
name of a department.] want to congratu-	25
late you on the fifteenth anniversary of your	34
joining the company and to thank you for	43
those many years of service.	49
Our company is lucky to have persons	57
who, like you, have stuck with us through	66
thick and thin and helped us become the	73
success we believe we are. It is most	82
reassuring to all of us to know that there	91
are veterans like you on whom our future	99
can depend.	102
We hope that your anniversary is a source	111
of pride to you too, and that your friends	120
and family know how highly you are	127
regarded by your colleagues. [*closing*	133
phrase] It is a great day! ↓₄ James Wag-	145
goner / Department of Personnel [*No refer-*	151
ence initials or enclosure note when inside	..
address is shifted to the bottom, where it	..
begins two or three lines below identifica-	..
tion line.] Mr. Jack Stahl, at 191 Grove	158
Avenue in Richmond, VA with ZIP of	161
23220.	162

This letter is to Mr. James Bonsbach, 121 East Hilliard Road, Richmond, VA 23216. The anniversary is his twentieth. That is something!

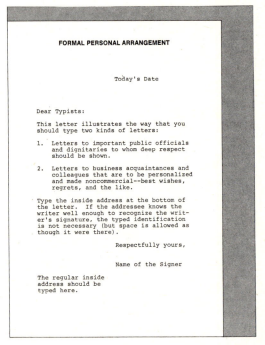

In personal and formal letters, inside address goes at the foot of the page. Illustration is shown on 7¼″ x 10½″ (monarch size) stationery; date is on line 14, with either 4- or 5-inch line.

goals A

■ To produce typed name tags.
■ To produce employee identification cards.

JOB 18-1: TYPED NAME TAGS

Workbook 49 ☐ ■ 10'/0e

"Now," Mr. Phelps continues, "type a name tag for each of the new employees to wear at the reception. Make one for yourself too."

JOB 18-2: TYPED ID CARDS

Workbook 50 ☐ ■ 10'/0e

"There's time to type the ID (identification) card for each new employee too, and I'd like you to take care of that," says Mr. Phelps.

goal B

■ To type 41 wam for 3'/2e.

Directions: *Spacing—1. Line—60. Tab—5.*
Drills—2 or more.

12-SECOND SPRINTS

Four sprints on each line.

1 She said the four girls can swim across the lake with ease. 12
2 Please take one of these big boxes down to the post office. 12
3 May we go to the game with you, or do you have other plans? 12

12" WAM |25 30 35 40 45 50 55 60|

3-MINUTE PIECEMEAL PRACTICE

Circled numbers are 1' goals.

Your goal is to type each paragraph within 1 minute and no errors, all three paragraphs within 3 minutes and 2 errors. Prepare by taking ten 1-minute TWs, repeating each paragraph until you reach the 1-minute goal. Then take a 3-minute TW and attempt to meet that goal.

4   When you think of Arizona, you think of sand and cacti 12
5 and Indians, of cliff dwellings and canyons, of ranches and 24
6 Apaches and Pimas, of Interstate 40, of all the picturesque 36
7 extras in a great state.① 41

8   But think of copper, that precious ore: half the cop- 12 53
9 per produced in this land is from Arizona. Now, think also 24 65
10 of cotton: an enormous portion of the nation's yield comes 36 77
11 from the land of Arizona.② 41 82

12   And think of those quiet colonies of luxury and health 12 94
13 to which such a lot of our senior citizens retire. Now you 24 106
14 see the state as a fine, growing, and important part of our 36 118
15 country--just as it is.③ 41 123

|1 |2 |3 |4 |5 |6 |7 |8 |9 |10 |11 |12   SI 1.42N

The six projects of Part 10 use the following places as their locale:
Unit 28: Virginia, West Virginia
Unit 29: American Caribbean, Other Caribbean
Unit 30: Canadian Border Provinces, Other Provinces

PART 10

Part 10 is like its predecessors in several ways you will recognize and remember:

1. The skill gain expected of you is just 1 more word a minute, making your goal 48 wam for 3 minutes within 1 error and 48 wam for 5 minutes within 2 errors.

2. There are, as usual, six production projects, located in different parts of the hemisphere: Virginia and West Virginia, the Caribbean, and Canada.

3. There is continuous rehearsal of routine letters—the kinds that executives expect their secretaries and other aides to be able to prepare

for them. Review of pertinent language rules continues too. In this part, capitals are the focus.

4. As usual, there are six half-period skill drives and two full-period clinics.

5. You are to correct all errors in production work unless your teacher gives other instructions.

At the start of each practice period, turn to this page for the Warmup. Type three copies of one line from each group below. Vary your selection so that you do not type the same line on any two consecutive days.

SPEED RECALL	1A Andy may pay me for the bicycle if he is paid for the work.	12
	1B The man and the boy had the box and hid it from the police.	24
	1C Pamela may wish to provide them with ham, corn, and turkey.	36
ALPHABET RECALL	2A dot bus fix cow zig vie rug end quo and pay jam lap irk ham	12
	2B king vase true size film copy jade brow hear quit axes dark	24
	2C Lois Jack Fred Inez Abel Trix Hugh Myra Walt Avis Quen Phil	36
NUMBER RECALL	3A The dates to remember are 1910, 1928, 1939, 1947, and 1956.	12
	3B He counted by threes: 3, 6, 9, 12, 15, 18, 21, 24, 27, 30.	24
	3C we 23 24 23 up 70 71 70 it 85 86 85 or 94 95 94 to 59 60 59	36
THINKING WHILE TYPING Insert capitals.	4A i had hickory farm bacon, white leghorn eggs, and wheaties.	12
	4B mr. clinton, the mayor of garden city, is in san francisco.	24
	4C joe put 11 gallons of texaco in his vega in east st. louis.	36

|1 |2 |3 |4 |5 |6 |7 |8 |9 |10 |11 |12

goal A

■ **To type 41 wam for 5'/3e.**

☐ *Feet firmly on the floor.*
☐ *Body a handspan from the machine.*
☐ *Body erect, with both shoulders level.*
☐ *Fingers curled as though pulling a weight.*
☐ *Eyes firmly, unyieldingly on the copy task.*

Directions: *Spacing—1. Line—60. Tab—5. Warmup—page 30; then begin below.*

PRETEST

Type for 5 minutes in a firm effort to type at least 41 wam for 5 minutes within 3 errors.

```
1    If you want to know a state with the oldest of the old    12
2  and the newest of the new, try out New Mexico, where Indian  24
3  and Spanish cultures that are many centuries old lie in the  36
4  shadow of our biggest and newest nuclear and space research  48
5  centers, like Los Alamos and White Sands, built there to be  60
6  near the source from which comes half of America's uranium.  72
7    The state produces a billion dollars a year in mineral    84
8  products; about half the income is from gas and oil.  There  96
9  are dozens of other minerals, including copper, gold, zinc, 108
10 lead, silver, coal, and others.  Another source of money is 120
11 farming; the state built quite a few dams and reservoirs on 132
12 its rivers, producing plenty of water for the fertile soil. 144
13    In New Mexico you can find a desert like the Sahara if   156
14 you go to White Sands, you can see a river like the Nile if 168
15 you go to the Rio Grande, you can cherish the beauty of the 180
16 Rockies if you go to the Sandia Mountains, and in the south 192
17 you can go to the Carlsbad Caverns, the biggest cave in the 204
18 world.                                                       205
   |1   |2   |3   |4   |5   |6   |7   |8   |9   |10  |11  |12   SI 1.38N
```

Speed counters are for 5' TW. Circled figures are 1' goals.

■ **5'/3e.**

PRACTICE ON TW VOCABULARY

Type the designated drills four times each.

Pretest errors	0–1	2–3	4–5	6–+
Drills to type	22–26	21–25	20–24	19–23

For accuracy.

```
19 centuries America's research biggest nuclear uranium newest  12
20 reservoirs cultures minerals cherish centers billion oldest  12
21 producing products; Carlsbad Caverns Spanish dollars dozens  12
22 Mountains including resource Rockies farming produce Grande   12
```

For speed.

```
23 world south river water quite money other about which comes  12
24 find soil dams from half near many like that with want know  12
25 you can see the old try new are for few oil and gas its out  12
26 centers, copper, sands, soil, coal, lead, zinc, gold, them,  12
```

POSTTEST

Repeat the Pretest. Score your work and note your improvement.

goal

■To experience quick cooperation, quick thinking, and quick typing in a work atmosphere.

☐ In Co-Op 9, team up with someone who types about as well as you do. One of you will be Typist A; the other, Typist B.

☐ As in previous Co-Ops, you will be required to communicate in typed form with your classmate in order to obtain information for your projects.

☐ At the conclusion of Co-Op 9, give your teacher all the work you have prepared or received.

CREATIVE CO-OP 9: PREPARING ORIGINAL TABLES

TYPIST A	TYPIST B

1. IDENTIFY SPORTS PERSONALITIES

Type a note to Typist B. List the first names of ten noted sports personalities. Ask Typist B to supply last names to the first names you provided. (*Don't be surprised if the names that Typist B supplies are not the ones you expected.*) Typist B should also indicate in what sport or sporting event each person participates. If you cannot think of ten names, ask Typist B to list both first and last names for those that are missing.

1. IDENTIFY SCREEN PERSONALITIES

Type a note to Typist A. List the first names of ten movie and TV personalities. Ask Typist A to give you a last name for each of the first names you have provided and to identify each person by naming a movie or a TV program or series each person is associated with. [*Do not be surprised if the names that Typist A supplies are not the ones you anticipated.*] If you cannot think of ten names, ask Typist A to provide the missing ones.

2. ANSWER TYPIST B'S INQUIRY

Typist B will be asking you for similar information about movie and TV personalities. Supply as many appropriate last names as you can. If you have no ideas about some names, simply answer "No response"; then provide a complete name for someone else whom you <u>can</u> identify correctly.

2. ANSWER TYPIST A'S INQUIRY

You will be receiving a somewhat similar request from Typist A about sports personalities. Supply as many last names as you can. If you cannot think of an appropriate last name, answer "No response"; then provide the full name of a sports star whom you <u>can</u> identify.

3. PREPARE YOUR TABLE

When you get the names of sports personalities from Typist B, prepare a table. Arrange the names alphabetically in column 1 and the sport or event in column 2. Give the table a title. In the subtitle, indicate that you are the author and Typist B (name him or her) is your consultant.

Give all your work to your teacher.

3. PREPARE YOUR TABLE

When you receive Typist B's memo, prepare and type your table. Arrange names alphabetically in the first column and identify the movie or TV programs in the second. Give your table a title. Indicate in subtitle lines that you are the author and Typist A (name him or her) is your consultant.

Give all your work to your teacher.

You work for Mrs. Judith Wheeler. Yesterday she gave a talk, "Using ZIP Codes," in which she referred to her list of two-letter state abbreviations. This morning, while she is attending company meetings, you receive calls from persons who want a copy of the list. For each caller, prepare a phone message blank.

9:35. Stanley Kendrick, Ponderosa Lumber, U.S. 66, Tijeras, NM 87059, called to say your talk was terrific and could he please have a copy of your list of abbreviations.

10:15. Miss Lauren Bahr, Socorro Realty Company, 1622 Lopez Avenue, Socorro, NM 87801, called to congratulate you on your talk and to ask for a copy of "that list."

10:19. Dexter Hagerman, Alameda Trust, Sandia Street, Alameda, NM 87114, wants you to call him at 525-7000 before 2:45 this afternoon.

10:32. Miss Fran Quivira, Quivira School of Business, Placitas Street, Bernalillo, NM 87004, called to say your talk was "the best we've had all year." Wants the list too.

goal A

■ To produce two letters, each within 10'/0e, using baronial stationery. (5½ by 8½ inches)

JOB 20-1: ACKNOWLEDGMENT LETTER

Workbook 53 □ Body 69 □ SI 1.38N □ ■ 10'/0e

Mrs. Wheeler smiles as you give her the phone messages and says, "I'll be pleased to send them a copy of the list, of course. But two of these people are friends to whom I should write."

You prepare to take dictation.

"The first letter is to Mr. Kendrick."

Dear Stan: I am sorry I missed your tele- 32
phone call, and I thank you for the nice 41
things you said about my talk. 47

I am happy to send you a copy of my list 56
of state abbreviations, but one thing I did 65
not make clear is this: *Display the next* 70
sentence: indent it 5 spaces on each side. ..

The two letters are for use *only* 79
with ZIP Code numbers. *Underscore* 85
"only." ..

I look forward to seeing you at the next 94
meeting of the group. Cordially yours, / 103
Mrs. Judith Wheeler / Training Director / 114
URS / Enclosure 119

JOB 20-2: ACKNOWLEDGMENT LETTER

Workbook 53 □ Body 69 □ SI 1.38N □ ■ 10'/0e

"Next," says Mrs. Wheeler, "send a copy of that same letter to Fran Quivira."

REVIEW JOB 2

☐ Workbook 269 ☐ Body 119 +
subject 20 ☐ Needs 10 commas ☐
SI 1.39N ☐ ■ 10'/0e

Prof. Gerard S. Raleigh, of 3188 University 15
Drive, in Durham, NC 27701. Dear Pro- 23
fessor Raleigh: Re Transmittal of Your Deed 54
I am pleased Professor Raleigh to enclose 64
the deed for the property you have pur- 72
chased at 703 Ninth Street Myrtle Beach 79
South Carolina. Mrs. Edward Fawlkes the 87
woman from whom you purchased the resi- 96

dence wishes you great happiness in your 104
new home. 106

Please note Professor Raleigh that you 116
will need to take this deed to the Horry 124
County registry office in Conway and have 132
the deed recorded. To protect your owner- 140
ship please take care of the deed at once. 149

So I will know that the deed is safely in 159
your hands please sign the enclosed carbon 168
copy of this letter on the indicated line at 177
the bottom and return it to me in the 184
envelope that is enclosed. Yours very truly, 195
Robert N. Snyder [acknowledgment] I here- 205
by acknowledge receipt of the deed from 213
Mrs. Fawlkes [line] Edward W. Kelso [line] 227
Date 235

REVIEW JOB 3: DISPLAY

☐ Workbook 270 or plain paper
☐ ■ 10'/0e

FEDERAL AND STATE HIGHWAYS IN NORTH CAROLINA		page 15
COUNTY Population Seat	FEDERAL HIGHWAYS	STATE HIGHWAYS
WATAGUA 17,530 Boone	221, 321, 421 and Blue Ridge Parkway	194
WAYNE 82,000 Goldsboro	13, 70, 87, 117	55, 102, 111, 222, 581
WILKES 45,300 Wilkes	21, 421	16, 18, 113, 115, 268
WILSON 57,700 Wilson	117, 264, 301	42, 58, 222, 581
YADKIN 22,800 Yadkinville	I-77, 421, 601	67, 268
YANCEY 14,100 Burnsville	19, 19E, 19W and Blue Ridge Parkway	26, 80, 197

goal B

■ To produce a
modification of a
table, with carbons.

JOB 20-3:
OPEN TABLE

Plain paper, carbons
■ 15'/0e

of it to send one to each person who has asked for it, plus one for
yourself if you'd like it."

She continues, "I like my work to look very well typed; so
please *double-space* this table, with an extra blank line after
every 6 entries."

JOB 20-4: COMPLETION CARDS

Four 5″ x 3″ cards or slips of paper
☐ ■ 5'/0e

Giving you the list below, Mrs. Wheeler says, "This is the list of
abbreviations they're asking us for. Please type enough copies

To each page of work, attach a card identifying yourself, your
proofreader, and any problems you encountered.

TWO—LETTER STATE ABBREVIATIONS   20

Including Special Districts ↓3   40

42

AL Alabama	KY Kentucky	OH Ohio	49
AK Alaska	LA Louisiana	OK Oklahoma	58
AZ Arizona	ME Maine	OR Oregon	60
AR Arkansas	MD Maryland	PA Pennsylvania	75
CA California	MA Massachusetts	PR Puerto Rico	86
CO Colorado	MI Michigan	RI Rhode Island	96
			97
CT Connecticut	MN Minnesota	SC South Carolina	107
DE Delaware	MS Mississippi	SD South Dakota	118
DC Dist. of Col.	MO Missouri	TN Tennessee	128
FL Florida	MT Montana	TX Texas	135
GA Georgia	NE Nebraska	UT Utah	143
GU Guam	NV Nevada	VT Vermont	151
			152
HI Hawaii	NH New Hampshire	VA Virginia	161
ID Idaho	NJ New Jersey	VI Virgin Islands	171
IL Illinois	NM New Mexico	WA Washington	180
IN Indiana	NY New York	WV West Virginia	190
IA Iowa	NC North Carolina	WI Wisconsin	199
KS Kansas	ND North Dakota	WY Wyoming	208

These are the official
abbreviations you
should memorize
and use.

CENTER
CHECK →

goal

■ To use intensive
drill to improve
basic skill.

ACTIVITIES	20 MIN.	40 MIN.
Warmup (page 30)	3'	3'
Drive 1 Pretest	4'	4'
Practice 1	9'	9'
Drive 1 Posttest	4'	4'
Drive 2 Pretest	—	5'
Practice 2	—	10'
Drive 2 Posttest	—	5'

CLINIC
4

Directions: *Spacing—1. Line—60.*
Warmup—page 30.

Follow instructions on page 236.

AVOID CLICHES IN YOUR LETTERS

Training Bulletin No. 14

By Ezra Clunes

March 4, 19—

When you compose a letter, your thoughts are more likely to be focused on what you want to say than on the words with which you express it. You draw forth words from some reservoir in the mind, a source that is full not only of some fine words but also of some poor old phrases called cliches.

THE ANCIENT QUILL

Some of the cliches are from a family of old phrases created in the period when correspondence was written slowly, with many flourishes of quill and no fewer flourishes of thought.

Some flourishes, like "yours of the eleventh inst. is at hand" or "thanking you in advance for your generous custom," have both a quaint quality and an odd charm, but such phrases would be rated today as completely insincere, just like that old closing phrase, "Yr Humble and Obedient Servant."

WORD STRETCHERS

Another style of cliche you want to avoid is the kind of wordy phrase we say when we just hate to come right out and say what we mean. We might say "at the present time" instead of "now" or "in the event that" instead of "if." Any such cliche is a funny splash of extra, and empty, wordiness.

If such extra-length phrasing is used often, the writer becomes accustomed to it. The cliches start sounding acceptable, then become habitual—indeed, you can say that of all kinds of cliches. That's their danger. The more one uses them, the less weird they seem to the person who says them.

SO, PLEASE

Let's try to give our letters a modern look: let's use no cliches of any kind. We do not want or need them.

Speed counters are for 5' TW.

Note: "Cliche" is pronounced "Klee-SHAY"; it is normally written with an acute accent over the e: cliché.

■ 5'/2e

REVIEW JOB 1
Follow instructions on page 236.

|1 |2 |3 |4 |5 |6 |7 |8 |9 |10 |11 |12 |13 |14   SI 1.41N

9 9

237

DRIVE 1

PRETEST 1

Take two 1-minute timings on lines 1–4. Proofread both and average the scores.

Up reaches, no doubles.

1 The doctor at the clinic said his dental habits were awful.   12
2 The judge did not deny that his coat model was very choice.   24
3 Karen enjoyed a ride through the park on a very wise horse.   36
4 Somehow his arm flew up and sent the long nail flying away.   48

|1 |2 |3 |4 |5 |6 |7 |8 |9 |10 |11 |12

PRACTICE 1

Make four copies. Repeat individual lines for speed gain if you averaged two or fewer Pretest errors; otherwise, repeat each block of lines for accuracy gain.

Up reaches, no doubles.

5 beneath checked empties instant nations parkway senator leg   12
6 anyhow behind choice clinic dental habits justly praise hit   12
7 front hotel judge liked model named owned plant sharp stick   12

8 bits bolt clip coat deny from gulf high nail sent swim wild   12
9 arm fly hat his how hot its jar job joy kit law lie lot old   12
10 ethic fifth guide horse metal moved parks pride reply stays   12

POSTTEST 1

Repeat Pretest 1. Score your work and note your improvement.

DRIVE 2

PRETEST 2

Take three 1-minute timings on lines 11–14. Proofread them and average the scores.

Up reaches, no inwards.

11 These views are pleasing to those who prefer your colognes.   12
12 The empress did not impress her daughter with her laughter.   24
13 Edmund smiled when he saw three quail sail across the lake.   36
14 Ted Walsh plans to speak to the media about the third game.   48

|1 |2 |3 |4 |5 |6 |7 |8 |9 |10 |11 |12

PRACTICE 2

Make four copies. Repeat individual lines for speed gain if you averaged two or fewer Pretest errors; otherwise, repeat each block of lines for accuracy gain.

Up reaches, no inwards.

15 bigness cologne demands express impress laughed refunds hop   12
16 chairs delays excuse guides lights pencil quotes smiled oil   12
17 civil fixes globe lakes moral quail shook these views while   12

18 coke file hire jury love okay pose ride sail seek task wide   12
19 dry fed him hoe ill jaw led log ran ray saw see ski use way   12
20 drops games holds media noise plans ships speak third wires   12

POSTTEST 2

Repeat Pretest 2. Score your work and note your improvement.

goal B

■ To produce the
second page of a set
of specifications.

JOB 108-2: SPECIFICATIONS, PAGE 2

Workbook 268 or plain paper
☐ ■ 15'/0e

BID SPECIFICATIONS, Page 2 / Mr. Foster   2

N. Harris / March 3, 19--   7

MATERIALS, Continued		..
1 gallon of Dutch Lad paint thinner	$ 10.95	16 / 22
1 roll of 50 foot polyethylene sheeting to protect patio and shrubbery	7.50	30 / 36 / 42
2 replacement brushes @ $7.50	15.00	53
2 roller cover replacements @ $1.98	3.96	59 / 64
1 box of razor blades	1.98	73
1 gallon of Easy-Wipe window cleaner	4.98	80 / 85
25 squares of coarse sandpaper @ $.50	12.50	92 / 97
rental of three extension ladders	30.00	103 / 109
rental of six sections of scaffolding	120.00	116 / 122
rental of coveralls for five painters for 10 days	50.00	129 / 138
rental of electric sanding machine	50.00	145 / 153
TOTAL COST OF MATERIALS	$747.17	163

LABOR: ..

5 painters, each working 8   174

hours a day for 10 days   179

@ $5.00 per hour $2,000.00   188

TOTAL COST OF JOB $2,747.17   197

..

Respectfully submitted,   ..

..

Per Doyle White   211

JOB 108-3: COMPLETION CARDS

5" x 3" cards or slips ☐ ■ 5'/0e

---

goals

■ To produce page 1
of a report, a letter,
and a table, each
within 10'/0e.

Directions: *Review pages 218, 230, and 227.
Editing—insert commas where needed.*

5-MINUTE TIMED WRITING

Plain paper ☐ **Spacing 2** ☐ **Line 50** ☐ **Tab 5**
☐ ■ **47 or more wam/5'/2e**

Using the selection on page 237, take a 5-minute writing to demonstrate that you can type 47 or more words a minute for 5 minutes within 2 errors. Omit all the headings (lines 1–4, 10, 19, and 30). Lines will end even if you use a 50-space line correctly.

REVIEW JOB 1: REPORT, PAGE 1

Plain paper ☐ **Spacing 2** ☐ **Line 6"** ☐ **Tabs 5 and center**
☐ ■ **10'/0e**

Using the selection on page 237, including the headings shown as lines 1–4, 10, 19, and 30, type as much of the material as you should for the *first page of an unbound manuscript.* This will be about 3½ paragraphs. Double-space the work on a 6-inch line of writing.

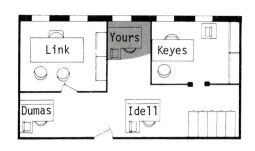

goals A

■ To produce two stock requisitions.
■ To produce two purchase requisitions.

JOB 21-1: STOCK REQUISITIONS

Workbook 57 □ ■ 10'/0e

"Good morning," says Mr. O. D. Link, purchasing manager for the Anchorage offices of Aleutian Allsave grocery chain. "I have some forms I'd like you to fill out for us, please."

Mr. Link continues: "First, please type the following two stock requisitions":

1. For use here in the Purchasing Office, on the third floor, needed by Stella Dumas next Monday:

> 2 reams white mimeograph paper (20 pound)
> 1 dozen packages of correction paper
> 1/2 box company envelopes (No. 10)

2. For use in Inventory Control, second floor, to be delivered to Miss Kenat Chugia by Monday:

> 6 boxes IBM Correctable Film Ribbon (#1136432)
> 2 boxes IBM Lift-Off-Tape (#1136433)
> 1 ream company bond stationery (standard)
> 1 dozen spiral-bound stenographer notebooks

JOB 21-2: PURCHASE REQUISITIONS

Workbook 58 □ ■ 10'/0e

"There are also two purchase requisitions to be prepared," Mr. Link says. "They are both handwritten, but we have to type them in order to have all the copies we need in the right arrangement":

1. Arlene Berkow, head of Transcribing Services on the second floor, wants to replace six old manual typewriters with new IBM 13" Selectric II typewriters, each with a standard 12-pitch Courier element and a 10-pitch Letter Gothic element. She believes that the machines can be obtained from the IBM offices on Seventh Street, here in Anchorage. She wants them "as soon as possible."

2. Roger Shageluk, in Shipping on the first floor, wants to replace 1,200 feet of 8" metal storage shelving with the same quantity of 15" shelving in either metal or wood, whichever is available in Anchorage. He suggests Sutton Contractors' Supplies Company, Boniface Road at 20th Avenue, as a possible supplier. He wants the new shelving "as soon as possible."

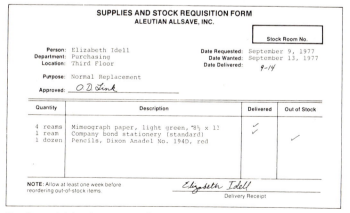

Stock requisition is a request for stationery or other supplies available from the company stockroom.

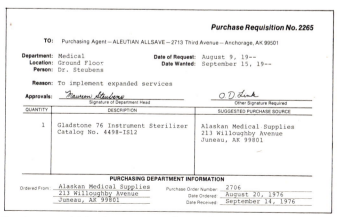

Purchase requisition is a request to the Purchasing Department to buy something from an outside supplier.

Article 4. Payment. Mr. Harris agrees (a) to make a down payment of $100 upon the signing of this Contract, (b) to pay $1,000 upon the end of the fifth full day of work, and (c) to pay the remainder upon the acceptance of the completed job as work

257
265
273
283
291
299

done satisfactorily and according to the Contract. ↓3

308
310

IN WITNESS WHEREOF, the parties hereto have executed this Contract, the third day of March, 19--. [Signature arrangement] ↓3

320
330
333

..

348

```
For Brushes and Rollers, Inc.
```

```
Witness to Signature
```

```
Foster N. Harris ↓3
```

357

371

```
Witness to Signature
```

382

goal A

■ To produce the first page of a two-page set of specifications.

JOB 108-1: SPECIFICATIONS

Workbook 267 or plain paper
☐ Line 6″ ☐ Spacing 1 ☐ ■ 20′/0e

Directions: Spacing—1. Line—60. Warmup—page 215. Then adjust machine for Job 108-1.

"Okay, with the contract ready, let's get the Bid Specifications in shape too," says Mr. Stork. "I hope we're not out of forms!"

BID SPECIFICATIONS

TO: Mr. Foster N. Harris, 820 Cypress Lane, Charlotte, NC 28200, DATE: March 3, 19--

8
18

DESCRIPTION OF JOB:

..

Scrape, sand, and paint a two-story frame house at 820 Cypress Lane, Charlotte, North Carolina. The job includes complete scraping, sanding, and cleaning of surface before painting, one coat of oil-base primer to be applied to all surfaces including shutters and windows and doors, two coats of oil-base regular house and trim paint to be applied to all surfaces except the shutters and doors, one coat of oil-base house and trim semigloss to be applied to shutters and doors. All windows are to be cleaned upon completion of the painting, and the entire area around the house is to be left as it was before painting began. [Later, after

32
41
49
58
67
75
83
91
100
108
117
125
135
142
148

removing paper, fill in the rest of the description area on the form with a "Z" by drawing lines at the top and bottom of the area and then connecting them.]

MATERIALS:

..

The following materials will be purchased by Brushes and Rollers, Inc., to be used on the job:

165
174
175

12 gallons of white oil-base		183
primer Dutch Lad paint		189
@ $12.95 a gallon to be used		195
on all surfaces	$155.40	202
20 gallons of white oil-base		210
regular house and trim type		217
Dutch Lad paint @ $12.95 a		224
gallon to be used on all but		230
shutters and doors	259.00	238
2 gallons of black oil-base		246
regular house and trim semi-		253
gloss Dutch Lad paint		257
@ $12.95 a gallon to be used		264
on shutters and doors	25.90	273

REQUEST FOR QUOTATION
ALEUTIAN ALLSAVE, INC.
2713 Third Avenue — Anchorage, AK 99501

REQUISITION NUMBER MUST APPEAR ON ALL QUOTATIONS

Requisition Number 1783

Date 3/14/--

| QUOTE IN DUPLICATE | X QUOTE IN TRIPLICATE | F.O.B. | Return Your Quotation Not Later Than April 15, 19-- | Required Delivery Date July 1, 19-- |

Alaska Office Supply Company
188 Turnagain Boulevard
Spenard, AK 99503

GENTLEMEN: PLEASE QUOTE US YOUR PRICES ON THE ITEMS SPECIFIED BELOW. ADVISE TERMS OF PAYMENT, SHIPPING POINT, AND SHIPPING DATE. The terms and conditions contained on the reverse side will apply to all purchases. Advise if item not specified below can be purchased in more economical quantity. If so, quote on quantity specified as well as on quantity taking lower price. If any materials included in your quotation are furnished in returnable drums or containers or on returnable reels, etc., kindly advise whether there is an extra charge for same, terms of credit for their return and complete return shipping instructions including proper method of shipment and destination point.

3 Executive desks, 36 x 72 inches, pedestals right and left center drawer, bronze-oak finish, steel construction.

3 Executive desk armchairs, adjustable, to match.

PLEASE REPLY TO THE ATTENTION OF O. D. Link, Purchasing Manager

THIS IS NOT AN ORDER

A request for quotation asks a supplier to reply in writing the price of an item or service.

Purchase Order No. 4901

FROM: Purchasing Agent — ALEUTIAN ALLSAVE — 2713 Third Avenue — Anchorage, AK 99501

To: Anchorage Offices, Inc.
1717 Seventh Avenue
Anchorage, AK 99501

Date: May 1, 1975

Ship Via:

PLEASE SHIP AND BILL US FOR THE GOODS LISTED BELOW. IF FOR ANY REASON YOU CANNOT DELIVER WITHIN 30 DAYS, LET US KNOW AT ONCE. PLEASE REFER TO OUR PURCHASE ORDER NUMBER (ABOVE) IN ALL COMMUNICATIONS

QUANTITY	DESCRIPTION	YOUR CAT. NO.	UNIT PRICE	AMOUNT
3	Executive desks, bronze-oak finish	ED37S	275.00	825.00
3	Executive desk armchairs, same finish	EC37S	135.50	406.50
	Total			1,231.50

NOTE: YOUR BILL TO US SHOULD INDICATE ALL YOUR USUAL DISCOUNTS. PAYMENT WILL BE MADE UPON RECEIPT OF BILL WITH GOODS.

Purchasing Agent

A purchase order is an authorization to buy the items listed at the prices indicated.

---

goal B

■ **To produce requests for quotations.**

JOB 21-3: REQUESTS FOR QUOTATION

Workbook 59–60 ☐ ■ 20'/0e

Mr. Link says, "We often ask competing suppliers to tell us in writing what they would charge. We use a request for quotation form [above], separately typed for each supplier."

Picking up Purchase Requisition 2641, he continues, "Please write to these three firms":

1. Anchorage Construction Co., 2715 Northern Lights Boulevard, Anchorage, AK 99504.

2. Public Building Co., 809 Chugach Way, Spenard, AK 99503.

3. Sand Lake Builders, Inc., International Airport Road, Sand Lake, AK 99505.

"Ask them to tell me, in triplicate, within one month from today, for completion within four months from today, what they would charge for the total cost of materials and labor for installing an all-weather concrete sidewalk, 4 inches thick and 4 feet wide, with suitable de-icing hot-water pipes and hot-water heater and tank for 75 feet along the Third Avenue side of this building."

---

goal A

■ **To produce purchase orders.**

Directions: Spacing—1. Line—60. Warmup—page 30.

JOB 22-1: PURCHASE ORDERS

Workbook 61–62 ☐ ■ 15'/0e

"Okay," says Mr. Link, "Let's do some purchasing! I have three orders ready to send out, so please prepare purchase orders, as follows":

No. 9449: Elmendorf Supplies, Inc. / 800 Whitney Road / Anchorage, AK 99501.

400 3-foot sections of 15″ steel shelving, cat. SS15/3 unit $1.40   560.00

(Continued on next page)

② | 21 | 22

47

**5-MINUTE TW
SKILL DRIVE**

Spacing—2.
Tab—5.

Circled figures
are 1' goals.

■ 2 copies/5'/2e

Take a 5-minute writing (type two copies within 5 minutes and 2 errors). Do corrective practice on awkward passages; then repeat the timed writing.

```
 5        North Carolina is a beautiful state, as its throngs of      12 | 130
 6   tourists will attest:  mountains, plateaus, beaches, ③parks,      24 | 142
 7   memorials, forests--all things good to see.  North Carolina       36 | 154
 8   is also hard at work.  Its textile mills put out more①cloth        48 | 166
 9   than any other mills make.  It produces more wood furniture        60 | 178
10   and bricks than are made elsewhere; it raises and④processes        72 | 190
11   more tobaccos too.  North Carolina throbs with history, for        84 | 202
12   this is the land of Raleigh's lost colony, of Virginia Dare②       96 | 214
13   and James K. Polk, of Kitty Hawk, of the last battle of the       108 | 226
14   Civil War, and of pirate coves among the reefs.⑤                   118 | 235
     |1   |2   |3   |4   |5   |6   |7   |8   |9   |10   |11   |12       SI 1.45N
```

goal B

■ **To produce a
work contract.**

JOB 107-1: CONTRACT

Plain paper ☐ **Line 6″** ☐ **Spacing 1**
☐ **Tabs 10 and center** ☐ ■ **20'/0e**

Reporting to Brushes and Rollers, Inc., a firm of painters, you meet Doyle White, the manager; Dave Stork, the estimator; and Anne Parish, the accountant. Mr. Stork, to whom you report, says, "We have been negotiating for a job painting the house of Foster Harris. Everything is set, and now we put it all in writing. First, the contract for us to do the job."

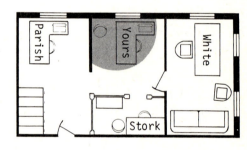

Directions: *Adjust machine for Job 107-1.*

AGREEMENT ↓3

THIS CONTRACT made and concluded   21
this third day of March, 19--, by and be-   29
tween Brushes and Rollers, Inc., of 414   37
Morehead Street, Charlotte, North Carolina,   44
and Foster N. Harris of 820 Cypress Lane,   53
Charlotte, North Carolina.↓3   58

Article 1. Services. Brushes and Rollers,   79
Inc., agrees to provide not fewer than five   88
painters for a period of two weeks (10   95
working days), of eight hours a day, to   104
scrape, sand, and paint the house of Mr.   112
Harris at 820 Cypress Lane.   117

Article 2. Wages. Brushes and Rollers,   136
Inc., agrees to provide painters at the rate   145
of five dollars an hour per employee, not   153
to exceed eighty hours per employee, for   161
the length of time it takes to complete the   170
job.   171

Article 3. Materials. Brushes and   190
Rollers, Inc., agrees to furnish all the ma-   198
terials and to perform all the work speci-   206
fied in the Bid Specifications prepared by   215
Brushes and Rollers on the third day of   223
March, 19--, and appended to this Contract   231
and made a part of this Contract.   239

JOB 22-1: PURCHASE ORDERS

(Continued)

240 8-foot vertical posts, 2″ x 2″ steel, cat. VP2/2, unit $1.60
384.00
72 8-foot vertical end panels, steel, cat. EP15/8, unit $3.30
237.60
Amount   1,181.60
No. 9450: Seward Electric Co. / Blying Sound Road / Seward, AK 99664.
80 4-foot dual tube ceiling fixtures, cat. CF4x2, unit $15.00
1,200.00
160 4-foot dual tube fluorescent lights, cat. DT4, unit $1.50
240.00
Amount   1,440.00

No. 9451: Anchorage Construction Co. / 2715 Northern Lights Boulevard / Anchorage, AK 99504.
1 Replacement of concrete steps at entrance to building, according to specifications in "Plan for Replacing Entrance Steps," cat. ——, unit ——
960.50
Amount   960.50

JOB 22-2: COMPLETION CARDS

5″ x 3″ cards or slips ☐ ■ 5′/0e

> JOB 22-1: STOCK REQUISITIONS
> 1. Prepared by Debbie Struble
> 2. Proofread with Martha Banmark
> 3. No problems, and I like reading and typing about Alaska.

---

goal B

■ **To type 41 or more wam for 3′/2e.**

Directions: *Spacing—1. Line—60 or, with paper turned sideways, 85. Drills—as directed. Tab—5.*

12-SECOND SPRINTS

To accommodate higher speeds, sprints from now on will be arranged as shown here. Each 12-second sprint starts on line 1 and continues on line 2, 3, or 4. To type a full 85-space line, turn the paper sideways.

Each sprint: Four 12″ timings on same sentence.

1   Did you know that Alaska
2   is two and a half times the size of the big state of Texas?   17
3   has more oil than all the rest of the states have together?   17
4   is but two and a half short miles from Russia at one point?   17

12″ WAM: 40   45   50   55   60   65   70   75   80   85

SKILL BLITZ

5   The capital of Alaska is Juneau. The largest place is   12
6   The capital of Alaska is Juneau. The largest place is   24
7   The capital of Alaska is Juneau. The largest place is   36
8   Anchorage. The best known ① city is Fairbanks, a stop on the   48
9   Anchorage. The best known city is Fairbanks, a stop on the   60
10   Anchorage. The best known city is Fairbanks, a stop on the   72
11   polar flights, which is about an equal distance ② from Moscow   84
12   polar flights, which is about an equal distance from Moscow   96
13   polar flights, which is about an equal distance from Moscow   108
14   and Peking and New York.   113
15   and Peking and New York.   118
16   and Peking and New York. ③   123

|1 |2 |3 |4 |5 |6 |7 |8 |9 |10 |11 |12   SI 1.42N

Directions on page 13:
1. 3′ timing.
2. Corrective practice.
3. 3′ timing.

Circled numbers are 1′ goals.

■ 3′/2e

3-MINUTE TW

Take a 3-minute writing on the copy at the top of page 49. Goal: 41 wam for 3 minutes within 2 errors.

Spacing—2.

Speed markers are
for 5' TW.
Circled numbers
are 1' goals.

■ 5'/2e

1 Paint a picture of a peaceful coast with sandy beaches along   13
2 which lies a gracious old port depicting history from the Old   26
3 South. Work in the hues of the formal gardens with magnolias.   38
4 Add green for the forests and eerie gray for an old swamp. Paint   52
5 in some bright dabs for a famous dance of the twenties called the   65
6 Charleston. Save a corner for some of the special plants of the   78
7 state such as the gardenia and the poinciana and the indigo, from   91
8 which a dye can be made. This is the Low Country of South   103
9 Carolina.   105

10 Now let's start painting a second canvas, for folks in South   118
11 Carolina have two very different regions within their state. Let us   132
12 brush on rolling green hills and mix in some azure blue moun-   144
13 tains with crystal clear streams for lots of waterpower. And add   157
14 the fast growth of new industry, along with the continued growth   170
15 of the textile mills. Add a blue spot for the atomic energy plant   184
16 on the Savannah River, and work in the white of cotton and the   196
17 green of tobacco. Look well at the Up Country of South Carolina.   209
18 Set your work in gold befitting the eighth colony of the first   222
19 thirteen, and note how the pride of the Old South shines through.   235

|1 |2 |3 |4 |5 |6 |7 |8 |9 |10 |11 |12 |13 |14   SI 1.33FE

goal A

■ To type 47 wam
for 5'/2e.

LESSON
07

Directions: *Spacing—1. Line—60.*
Warmup—below.

WARMUP, PLUS

Untangle line 2.

Type lines 1–4 three times each; then take four 12-second sprints either on lines 1
and 2 (for speed gain) or on lines 3 and 4 (for accuracy gain).

1 Why in the world does it take so long to write us a letter?   12
2 What takes long so is out figuring just what is one to say.   12
3 The Zanzibar Express was jolting us four but moved quickly.   12
4 we 23 24 25 up 70 71 72 to 59 60 61 or 94 95 96 it 85 86 87   12

12" WAM: 25   30   35   40   45   50   55   60

9 106 107   233

Spacing—2.
Line—60.
Tab—5.

Speed markers
are for 3' TW.

1　　　　Alaska sits up there at the top of the world, watching　12
2　the three biggest nations in the world watch each other and　24
3　probe each other with radar beams. The same radars keep an　36
4　eye on the passenger planes that jet along the polar skies.　48
5　They keep an eye, too, on the planes that serve the cities,　60
6　camps, and diggings of Alaska; in many parts of the state a　72
7　plane is just about the only way you can get in or get out.　84
8　　　　Planes are vital to Alaska, just as Alaska is vital to　96
9　planes, but trucks and ships are important, too, since they　108
10　bring in nine-tenths of the food, goods, and amenities that　120

■ 3'/2e

11　Alaskans need. ■　123
12　　　　Alaska pays for its food, goods, and amenities in gold　135
13　and oil, in salmon and lumber, in crab and furs––the minks,　147
14　beaver, otter, fox, and so on, for which many buyers in the　159
15　other states ask as eagerly as buyers of power beg for oil.　171
16　But Alaska also pays in two other ways: in the inspiration　183
17　which Alaska gives all who yearn for frontier opportunities　195
18　and in the watchful protection that the state gives us all.　207

|1　|2　|3　|4　|5　|6　|7　|8　|9　|10　|11　|12　　　SI 1.34FE

Spacing—2.
Line—60.
Tab—5.

Speed markers
are for 5' TW.

19　　　　In the middle of the Pacific Ocean is a set of jewels,　12　219
20　called the Hawaiian Islands, that are incredibly beautiful.　24　231
21　If you have been there, you know how lovely are the people,　36　243
22　the beaches, the flora, the sunshine spirit; and if you are　48　255
23　a stranger to this paradise, you cannot realize the beauty.　60　267
24　　　　The island group is a chain of mountains, craters, and　72　279
25　coral reefs, ranging from towering volcanic peaks to lonely　84　291
26　little islets that are hidden at high tide. The long chain　96　303
27　stretches on and on for sixteen hundred miles, but the main　108　315
28　group consists of four large islands, four little ones, and　120　327
29　about twenty very small ones.　126　333
30　　　　The magic element in Hawaii is its growing season: it　138　345
31　never quits. Crops are planted on schedules that allow new　150　357
32　pickings and harvesting all year round. Only about a tenth　162　369
33　of the land can be farmed, but the earth is so fertile that　174　381
34　any crop in the world can be grown in Hawaii.　183　390
35　　　　So all year round the visitors come to Hawaii to enjoy　195　402
36　the sun, the sights, the beaches, and the flowers.　205　412

■ 5'/3e

|1　|2　|3　|4　|5　|6　|7　|8　|9　|10　|11　|12　　　SI 1.41N

JOB 106-1: LEGAL LETTER

Workbook 265 □ Body 178 + 60 extras
□ SI 1.43N □ ■ 15'/0e

Directions: *Spacing—1. Line—60.*
Warmup—page 215; then adjust machine for
Job 106-1: Spacing—1. Line—6". Tabs—5 and center.

"Now I want to write to a witness to get her to come in and give us a sworn statement," Mr. Snyder says.

"A deposition?" you ask.

"Right, a deposition," he replies.

Mrs. Martha N. Herbst, of 9945 Peach Grove 15
in Charleston, SC 29400. Dear Mrs. Herbst: 25
Re Request for Deposition 51

It is our understanding that you were 60
present in the office of Dr. Jeffery Jenks 68
when Mrs. Melvin Corbin was treated for a 77
back injury. Your testimony in this matter 85
may become important. Rather than require 94
your attendance in court, however, we may 102
be able to take a sworn statement (a deposi- 111
tion) from you in our office if you are 120
willing to give it. 124

You would come to our office at a time 133
when a court reporter and the lawyers for 141
both sides are present. You would be asked 150
to answer the following questions: 157

Q1. Were you present when Mrs. Corbin 166
was treated? 168

Q2. Who treated Mrs. Corbin? 176

Q3. What did Mrs. Corbin say to the 184
doctor? 186

Q4. What treatment did you see Dr. Jenks 196
give her? 198

The court reporter would record all the 207
questions and answers and then prepare the 215
written deposition for you to sign. The 223
statement then becomes testimony that can 232
be used in court. 235

Please call this office some time during 245
the next week to make an appointment for 253
us to take the deposition. Yours very truly, 265
Robert N. Snyder, urs 275

JOB 106-2: COMPLETION CARDS

5" x 3" cards or slips □ ■ 5'/0e

JOB 105-5: INQUIRY LETTER
1. Typed by Steven Rosenberg
2. Proofread with Lorraine Quincy
3. No problems in producing this job.

Directions: *Spacing—1. Line—60. Tab—5.*

1 The state of South Carolina
2   was the first to secede from the Union in the Civil War.   17
3   is the site of Fort Sumter, where that war really began.   17
4   was also one of the colonies in the American Revolution.   17

12" WAM: 45 50 55 60 65 70 75 80 85

Take a 5-minute writing on the selection at the top of page 233. Do corrective drill practice on awkward passages, and then repeat the 5-minute writing.

■ To type 41 wam for 5'/3e on normal copy.

CHECK YOUR WRISTS

☐ *Low (almost touch machine).*
☐ *Close (thumbs almost touch).*
☐ *Flat (backs of hands are level).*
☐ *Angled (heel lower than tips).*
☐ *Motionless (no bounce, no flourish).*

Directions: *Spacing—1. Line—60. Tab—5. Warmup—page 30; then start Pretest.*

PRETEST
PRACTICE ON TW
VOCABULARY

Take a 5-minute writing on lines 19–36, page 49. Goal: 41 wam/5'/3e.

Type, four times each, the drill lines indicated in this guide table.

Pretest errors	0–2	3–4	5–6	7–+
Type lines	4–8	3–7	2–6	1–5

For accuracy.

1 mountains, paradise, Hawaiian stranger Pacific jewels, come 12
2 incredibly beautiful Islands, craters, realize fertile lone 12
3 harvesting schedules sunshine volcanic sixteen hundred stop 12
4 stretches, towering, beaches, consists picking flowers reef 12

For speed.

5 hidden called middle lonely little islets lovely people can 12
6 enjoy round grown world earth tenth allow quits never crops 12
7 that have been know from high tide long main four very ones 12
8 only land crop year set are you how but the one any two sun 12

POSTTEST

Repeat the Pretest. Score your work and note your improvement.

■ To produce informal letters on personal stationery.

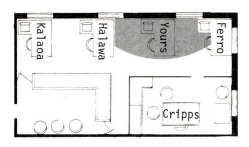

Directions: *Begin Job 23-1 below.*

JOB 23-1: INFORMAL LETTERS

Workbook 63–66 ☐ Body 130 ☐ SI 1.22E
☐ ■ 20'/0e

You work for Don Cripps in the Cripps-Kalaoa public relations firm. You meet Chris Ferro, Bill Halawa, and Sue Kalaoa, and then you return to Mr. Cripps. He says, "I have an informal letter that I'd like you to type on my personal notepaper. You will type it three times to send to three persons":

1. Mr. Edward T. Chin / Honolulu Herald / ..
3217 Kapiolani Boulevard / Honolulu, HI ..
96814 / Ted, ..

Do you recognize the enclosed page 7
of work? *Paragraph.* It is a copy of a 12
mimeographed page that I found in the file 21
cabinet I was given when I began to work 29
here. No one in this office knows where it 38
came from or who wrote it. Do you know? 46
Paragraph. I have checked the statistics 52
with those in a new almanac and find that 61
they are right. I want to use the page in 69

(Continued on next page)

John Foster Sons & Associates, at 22400 Wolfton Street in Orangeburg, South Carolina 29115. Ladies and Gentlemen and so on. In the body, be sure to substitute "Orangeburg" for "Spartanburg"; otherwise it's the same letter.

JOB 105-3: INQUIRY LETTER

Workbook 261 □ **Body 80 + 20 subject**
□ **SI 1.43N** □ ■ **6'/0e**

Mr. Snyder continues, "We must find the two nephews too. So we'll write the same letter to this law firm":

Martin, Bell & Associates, at 2940 Bellingham Avenue in Van Wyck, SC 29744. Ladies and Gentleman and so on. In the second paragraph, make it "for two nephews, John T. Linton and Barry P. Linton, both of whom lived in Van Wyck at one time." Then continue with the original letter.

goal B

■ **To produce three similar letters within 20'/0e.**

JOB 105-4: INQUIRY LETTER

Workbook 261 □ **Body 89 + 20 subject**
□ **SI 1.30FE** □ ■ **7'/0e**

Mr. Snyder says, "Now I must write to some court reporters to find who can give me a day or two for taking depositions. This is the first one."

Miss Sally N. Uthman, at 4515 Magnolia	14
Street in Charleston, SC 29404. Dear Sally:	23
Re Court Reporting for Us	49
I am writing because I have not been able	59
to reach you on the phone. We will have	67
several depositions to be taken in the next	76
few weeks, [*comma before conjunction in a*	78
compound sentence] and we hope you	81
might be free to serve as our reporter for	90
them.	91
The appointments would be for mornings,	100
which means that you would have the rest	108
of the day in which to transcribe notes.	117
Please phone me or write me soon to let	126
me know what days between now and, say,	134
[*interrupting expression*] April 15 you	137
would be able to help us. Cordially yours,	147
Robert N. Snyder, urs	156

JOB 105-5: INQUIRY LETTER

Workbook 263 □ **Body 91 + 20 subject**
□ **SI 1.24E** □ ■ **6'/0e**

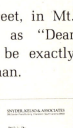

"I want to send that same message to another court reporter," says Mr. Snyder.

Mr. Roux F. Lake, at 798 Myrtle Street, in Mt. Pleasant, SC 29464. Address him as "Dear Roux." The body of the letter will be exactly the same as the one for Sally Uthman.

JOB 105-6: INQUIRY LETTER

Workbook 263 □ **Body 89 + 20 subject**
□ **SI 1.28FE** □ ■ **6'/0e**

"There is one more reporter to whom I want to write for afternoon depositions."

Mrs. Pauline T. Dawkins, of Inlet Drive, at Isle of Palms, SC 29451. She has worked for me many times before, so she's "Dear Pauline."

Be sure to change the wording of the second paragraph. Make it: "The appointments would be for afternoons, which means that you would have a day and a half in which to transcribe the notes."

something I am preparing for the state, but 78
of course I want to get permission to do so 87
if I can find out from whom to get it. *Para-* 95
graph. Because of its professional style, it 103
seems to me that it is a typed version of 111
something from a magazine or paper. *Display* 118
in complimentary closing position: Can you 120
help me? *Don't forget:* Enclosure 124

2. Same letter to Mr. James S. Keokea /
Hilo Island Enterprise / 290 Onomea Drive /
Papaikou, HI 96781. Start it "Jim."
3. Same letter to Mr. Kesini McKeogh /
Maui New Press / 362 Waikapu Road /
Wailuku, HI 96793 / Start it "Kess."

*Note: The addresses are used only on
the envelopes, not on the informal letters.*

goal A

■ **To produce
three copies of a
display table.**

LESSON 24

Directions: *Spacing—1. Line—60. Warmup page 30,
then begin Job 24-1.*

JOB 24-1: DISPLAY TABLE

Plain paper and 2 carbons □ ■ 20′/0e

"Next," says Mr. Cripps after checking the notes you typed for
him, "we have to prepare the Fact Sheet that is the enclosure."

Giving you the fact sheet (next page), he adds, "We'll need three
copies, of course."

You study it: a fairly simple copy-centering problem to be
typed on a 60-space line. To make three copies, you will need
an original copy and two carbon copies.

goal B

■ **To relay telephone
messages via an
unfamiliar message
blank.**

JOB 24-2: PHONE MESSAGES

Workbook 65–67 □ ■ 15′/0e

1. Message for Donald Cripps, taken by you
today at 11:35, from Mrs. Kapiaua Williams,
foreman at Honolulu Printing (484-3300):
If you want all handbook proofs at one time,
they will be delivered on Wednesday of next
week; but you could have the first 40 now.
Action: If you want the first 40, phone her.

Directions: *Adjust your machine for Job 24-2.*

2. Message for Donald Cripps, taken by you at 1:40, from Harold
Van Vickle, Honolulu manager for Superior Publications
(484-8209), who wants to lunch with you next Monday if possible. *Action:* Please phone him to confirm engagement.

3. Message for Susan Kalaoa, taken by you at 1:45, from Ellen
Waiawa, from the airport to say thanks for a fine time in Honolulu. She can be reached at her new address: 717 Kapaa Village,
Lihue, HI 96766. *Action:* Let her know when she is to start "the
book."

JOB 24-3: COMPLETION CARDS

5″ x 3″ cards or slips □ ■5′/0e

PRACTICE 2

Type drills twice; then repeat twice more those for the harder character.

Apostrophe drill.

```
25  visitor's problem's title's panel's widow's lemon's giant's    12
26  auditor's memento's shelf's ivory's field's audit's wales's     24
27  antique's element's graph's proof's juror's badge's right's     36
28  banquet's surname's front's fight's vixen's token's clock's     48
29  speaker's luggage's wagon's habit's zebra's grape's stage's     60
```

Colon drill and space bar drill.

```
30  turkey:  handle:  eighth:  panels:  social:  profit:  corn:    12
31  signal:  island:  chapel:  handle:  formal:  height:  than:    24
32  drinks:  ethics:  scores:  tables:  candid:  thanks:  tank:    36
33  basics:  habits:  enable:  inland:  vacant:  topics:  that:    48
34  almost:  employ:  events:  mother:  intent:  source:  cope:    60
```

POSTTEST 2

Repeat Pretest 2, score your work, and note your improvement.

goal A

■ To produce three similar letters within 20'/0e.

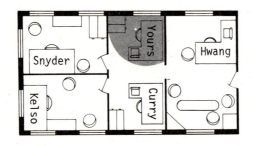

Directions: *Spacing—1. Line—60. Warmup—page 215. Editing—commas.*

JOB 105-1: INQUIRY LETTER

Workbook 259 ☐ **Body 75 + 20 subject** ☐ **SI 1.43N** ☐ ■ **7'/0e**

You are secretary to Robert N. Snyder, of the law firm of Snyder, Kelso & Associates. Mr. Snyder comments: "I have several letters for you to type—we must track down some missing heirs. By the way, I like my letters to be full-blocked" (no indentions—every line starts at the left margin).

Froesch and Froesch, Inc., at 3711 Boiling   15
Springs Road, in Spartanburg, SC 29303.   22
Ladies and Gentlemen: [*Be sure to under-   27
score the following subject line.*] Re Bessie   45
L. Linton Estate   55

We are trying to locate a number of de-   63
scendants of Bessie L. Linton, whose estate   72
is being probated.   76

We are searching in particular for a   84
niece, Mrs. Sue Ann Kinman nee [*under-   92
score "nee"*] Linton, who lived in Spartan-   97
burg and in nearby Greer at one time but   105
whose present address is not known to us.   114
We are writing to ask whether you know   122
her or where she lives.   127

We shall be grateful for any help that   136
you may be able to give us.   141

Yours truly, Robert N. Snyder, urs   155

JOB 105-2: INQUIRY LETTER

Workbook 259 ☐ **Body 75 + 20 subject**
☐ **SI 1.45N** ☐ ■ **6'/0e**

"I know that Mrs. Kinman lived in Orange-burg at one time too, so let's send the same letter to another law firm."

FACT SHEET ABOUT HAWAIIAN GEOGRAPHY

"What Hawaiians Should Be Able to Tell Visitors"

Principal Islands	Hawaii (largest), Kahoolawe (it is uninhabited), Kauai, Lanai, Maui, Molokai, Nihau, Oahu.	23 24 55 67 80 87 93
Area and Rank	Area is 6,450 square miles, making the state 47th; smaller states are Connecticut, Delaware, Rhode Island.	105 113 121
Archipelago	More than 150 volcanic mountains, craters, and reefs stretch northwest to southeast 1,600 miles across the mid-Pacific Ocean.	132 140 149 154
State Capital	Honolulu, on the island of Oahu.	165
Temperature Range	Honolulu: 57° to 88°.	175
Rainfall	Varies from 400 inches a year at top of Waialeale (mountain) to 24 inches a year at the Honolulu airport.	186 194 202
Highest Peak	Mauna Kea (volcano) on island of Hawaii, 13,796 feet.	213 218
Highest Lake	Lake Waiau, on Mauna Kea, 13,020 feet (highest lake in the United States).	230 239
Southernmost Point	Ka Lae ("South Cape") on island of Hawaii is the southernmost point in the United States.	252 260 265
Principal Industries	Defense, tourism, and agriculture.	278
Principal Crops	Sugar is first, pineapples second.	290 302

goals

- To type 41 or more wam for 5'/3e.
- To produce 5" x 3" fill-in cards, visible-index cards, postal cards, and a ruled table.

REVIEW 2

Directions: *Spacing—1. Line—60. Tab—5.*
Warmup—page 30; then start page 53.

■ **goal**

■ To improve control
of punctuation keys
and space bar.

ACTIVITIES	20 MIN.	40 MIN.
Warmup (page 215)	3'	3'
Pretest 1	5'	5'
Practice 1	7'	7'
Posttest 1	5'	5'
Pretest 2	—	5'
Practice 2	—	10'
Posttest 2	—	5'

Directions: Spacing—1. Line—60. Tab—5.
Warmup—page 215.

DRIVE 1

PRETEST 1

To find whether commas or semicolons are harder for you, take a 2-minute timing
on lines 1–4, then a 2-minute timing on lines 5–8, and compare scores.

Stress on comma.

1	He paid the city, town, and lake firms for a right to fish.	12
2	They may make a big profit with the corn, hay, and turkeys.	24
3	Blanche may own title to the land, lake, and island by May.	36
4	I think we should have meat, potatoes, and milk for dinner.	48

|1 |2 |3 |4 |5 |6 |7 |8 |9 |10 |11 |12

Stress on semicolon.

5	The chairman got the audit form; the city auditor signs it.	12
6	Their big problems may end; their firm is busy with panels.	24
7	Rodney pays for the land work; they pay for the audit work.	36
8	It is now time for us to go; it is not time for them to go.	48

PRACTICE 1

Type drills twice; then repeat twice more those for the harder character.

Comma drill.

9	maps, girl, make, firm, kept, busy, half, snap, held, when,	12
10	pens, turn, odor, worn, name, they, pays, them, kept, such,	24
11	have, paid, wish, form, land, lake, duty, down, oaks, gown,	36
12	held, busy, with, envy, they, kept, snap, from, sign, town,	48

Semicolon drill.

13	down; jamb; wish; name; them; hard; such; paid; form; make;	12
14	city; paid; fish; maps; they; land; also; kept; coal; lame;	24
15	their; angle; right; gland; chair; laugh; lamb; tidy; bowl;	36
16	ivory; slept; panel; girls; turns; fight; melt; idle; slay;	48

POSTTEST 1

Repeat the Pretest, score your work, and note your improvement.

DRIVE 2

PRETEST 2

To find whether apostrophes or colons are harder for you, take a 2-minute timing
on lines 17–20, then a 2-minute timing on lines 21–24, and compare scores.

Stress on apostrophe.

17	It's their turn to cut the neighbor's field of corn or hay.	12
18	Lena's firm may make a big profit with the auditor's forms.	24
19	Bob's profit with the corn may go to aid the widow's girls.	36
20	A town's citizens voted not to approve the board's request.	48

|1 |2 |3 |4 |5 |6 |7 |8 |9 |10 |11 |12

Stress on colon.

21	The chairman may do it: he may handle their work problems.	12
22	Their problem is authentic: they did sign for eight gowns.	24
23	Their profit is big: they paid naught for the cork panels.	36
24	The prize was treasured: it will be a trip to the Bahamas.	48

Take a 5-minute timing on this selection. Minimum goal: 41 wam/3e.

1	When we opened our new office on West Third Street, we	12
2	interviewed a large number of job applicants. Three of the	24
3	ones we chose are described below.	31
4	The first is Rose Ann Parr, of 105 Mentor Lane, as our	43
5	clerk–typist. Right now she is a typist for Park Bros. On	55
6	her test, she typed 50 words a minute for 5 minutes with no	67
7	errors, which is the top score anyone has made on the test.	79
8	The second is Steve O. Quinn, of 1300 Fidor Road, whom	91
9	we have hired as a junior accountant. He works for Fairley	103
10	and Dixon, the famous building firm. Steve took the typing	115
11	test even though he was not required to do so; he typed for	127
12	5 minutes at 55 words a minute, with just 5 errors. He did	139
13	not undertake the shorthand test.	146
14	The third is Irene T. Sanchez, of 284 Parker Road, our	158
15	new secretary. She is a school secretary at the Roger High	170
16	School right now. Miss Sanchez scored 60 words a minute on	182
17	her typing test, with only 2 errors in 5 minutes. She took	194
18	dictation at 100 for 3 minutes, transcribed perfectly.	205
19	These three persons do not know that they have won the	217
20	jobs, and one of the first things we must do is notify them	229
21	so that they can give their present employers the customary	241
22	two weeks' notice that they will be leaving.	250

SI 1.30FE

REVIEW JOB 1: 5″ X 3″ DATA CARD

Workbook 69 ☐ ■ 10'/0e

Fill in three of the four 5″ x 3″ data cards in the workbook from the information in the TW selection above. You are the interviewer. The fourth card on the workbook page is a spare you can use if you spoil one of the other cards. On any line for which you do not have the necessary information, type N/A (meaning that the information is "not available"). For the addresses, use the indicated street addresses and the name of your community, your state, your ZIP Code, and your telephone number. Use today's date.

POTENTIAL EMPLOYEE INTERVIEW FORM			
Acosta, Eileen M.			
LAST NAME FIRST NAME INITIAL			
75 Snyder Avenue	Denville	NJ	07834
STREET	CITY	STATE	ZIP
931-1762		Atlas Corp.	
TELEPHONE		PRESENT EMPLOYER	
72 wam, 5 min, 0e		120 wam, 3 min, 0e	
TYPING TEST SCORE		SHORTHAND TEST SCORE	
Secretary		Ruth A. Jevon	10/16/--
POSITION DESIRED		INTERVIEWER	DATE

2 ◢2

JOB 104-1: LETTER

Workbook 255 ☐ Body long ☐ SI 1.39N ☐ ■ 20'/0e

Miss Hall says, "While I put together the Highway Commission report, could you take a letter for Mr. Swanson?" You say you will be glad to.

"Good. There will be four things to note as you transcribe the letter," she says. "First, we line up the date with the right margin. Second, we indent paragraphs 5 spaces. Third, we center and underscore any subject line. Fourth, we always use a company signature line."

Then Mr. Swanson dictates:

This is to Mr. George T. Redpath, of the   12
Bismarck Hardware Company at 2402 East   20
Main Street, Bismarck, ND 58501. Dear Mr.   29
Redpath: Subject: January Audit   49

I have completed an audit of your books   65
for the month of January and can report to   74
you that you have begun the new year with   82
a very fine profit. It is the best month on   92
record.   93

A comparison of the figures for each of   103
the past three months shows that the im-   111
provement you began in November is con-   118
tinuing and is increasing. Here are the   127
summary figures: [*Arrange the data in four*   130
columns with leaders between the first and
second columns. Use "November," "Decem-

ber," and "January" as headings for the
second, third, and fourth columns.]

Net Sales . . . November $15,650.00 . . .   149
December $19,250.50 . . . January $25,675.00   157
Cost of Goods Sold . . . November   162
$9,225.00 . . . December 11,640.50 . . .   167
January 13,706.00   176
Gross Profit . . . November $6,425.00 . . .   185
December $7,610.00 . . . January $11,969.00   192
Operating Expenses . . . November   203
4,275.00 . . . December 4,809.50 . . . Janu-   213
ary 4,680.75   221
Net Income . . . November $2,150.00 . . .   232
December $2,800.50 . . . January $6,289.25   244
[*Close each money column with a double*
underscore.]

There may be many ways to account for   262
the big increase in sales in January Mr.   270
Redpath but it looks to me as though the   279
special $750 advertising campaign you ran   288
turned out to be very effective. I do not   296
know how soon you can repeat that sort of   304
drive for sales but it certainly has paid off   313
for January. / Cordially yours, / [*our name*   324
in all caps] SWANSON FINANCE & RE-   332
SEARCH / T. L. Swanson, President / urs   345

goal B

■ To produce two memos on forms within 15'/0e.

JOBS 104-2 AND 104-3: MEMOS WITH FINANCIAL STATEMENT

Workbook 257 ☐ Supply 3 commas ☐ ■ 8'/0e

Mr. Swanson says, "That financial statement is so good that I am going to share it with two friends. Please use my personal memo form."

One copy is to Mr. Otis Fitzgerald, whose address, which you need for the envelope, not the memo, is 2515 Olson Drive, Grand Forks, ND 58201. The other is to Gary W. Lundberg (I call him "Gary," of course) at 711 Sioux Hill, Fargo, ND 58102. Subject is "Power of Advertising," and the message is:

Otis (or Gary) when I mentioned to you last week that some businesses are able to turn themselves around I had in mind figures like these from one of my clients:

[*Insert the six-line financial statement from the letter, please.*]

Part of the improvement came from careful control of inventory but another part came from a good advertising campaign. / TLS / urs

JOB 104-4: COMPLETION CARDS

5" x 3" cards or slips ☐ ■ 5'/0e

REVIEW JOB 2: VISIBLE-INDEX CARDS

Workbook 71-72 □ ■ 10'/0e

Fill in three of the four visible-index cards in the workbook from the information on the cards you typed in Review Job 1 and the table at the foot of this page. In the addresses, use the name of your community and state and your ZIP Code number. For "Department," indicate "West Third Street Office." For any information not available to you, type N/A on the card. The spare workbook card is for your use if you spoil one of your cards. Thelma L. Edwards is the supervisor; you are the interviewer, so use your initials at the date (today's) on line 5.

Lebron,	Joseph	A.
LAST NAME	FIRST NAME	MIDDLE NAME OR INITIAL

2. Address: 56 Second Street
Garden City, NY 11530
3. Telephone: N/A
4. Interview date: October 4, 19-- by RAJ
5. Job title/rank: Editorial Assistant
6. Starting salary: $165/wk
7. Department: West Third Street Office
8. Superior: Thelma L. Edwards

9. Prior employer: Wilson Dictionary Company

LAST NAME	FIRST NAME	MIDDLE NAME OR INITIAL
Lebron,	Joseph	A.

10   20   30   40

TYPIST PLEASE NOTE: THIS SCALE CORRESPONDS TO PICA SPACING. If your machine is elite, use the other side of this card. Set the paper guide so that the scale on your machine corresponds to the spacing on this scale. Set the left margin stop at the first arrow and tab stops at the other arrows. Fold back or remove this stub after typing card.

Don't forget the bottom line on visible-index cards.

REVIEW JOB 3: FILL-IN POSTAL CARDS

Workbook 70 □ ■ 10'/0e

Use the data on the three cards you typed in Review Job 2 to fill in three of the four workbook postal cards. Indicate that the employee is to start working three weeks from next Monday (check that date to be sure you have it right).

EMPLOYMENT NOTICE

Date: August 19, 19--

Miss Theresa Alfredez

We are pleased to confirm your employment and to ask you to report for duty as follows:

Date to Report: September 15 at 8:30 a.m.
Place to Report: Carlton Building

PERSONNEL DEPARTMENT
The Stevenson Agencies, Inc.

urs

Begin the name at the start of the line.

REVIEW JOB 4: RULED TABLE

Plain paper □ Spacing 2 □ ■ 10'/0e

OPENING STAFF
West Third Street Office

Employee	Position	Salary	
			10
			27
Employee	Position	Salary	39
			47
			59
Thelma L. Edwards	Manager	$325/WK	68
Duanne C. Clark	Asst. Manager	225/WK	77
Steve O. Quinn	Accountant	200/WK	86
Irene J. Sanchez	Secretary	170/WK	95
Rose Ann Parr	Clerk-Typist	150/WK	103
			116
Total Salary	. . .	$1,070/WK	123
			135

RECOMMENDATIONS OF THE NORTH DAKOTA HIGHWAY IMPROVEMENT COMMISSION

County Population Seat	Estimated Expense	Recommended Improvements	Estimated Months Required
Towner 5,750 Cando	$1,500,000	Modernize and resurface State Highway 17, including interchange with U.S. 281 at Cando.	4 to 5
Traill 10,583 Hillsboro	$ 250,000	_Reconstruct_ ~~Construct new~~ bridge where State Highway 18 crosses Elm River south of Mayville, including reinforcement of (banks ~~of the~~ river).	5
Walsh 18,055 Grafton	$ 240,000 225,000	Construct new bridge where U.S. 81 crosses Forest River near Minto. Remodel present bridge where U.S. 81 crosses Park River near Grafton.	6 3 to 4
Ward 47,598 Minot	$ 175,000	Repair and modernize bridge on U.S. 52 where it crosses Des Lacs river, _north of Coulee._	3 to 4
Wells 9,500 Fessenden	$ 50,000	_Restore retaining walls along Pipestem River between Dover and Heaton._	2 to 3
Williams 22,750 Williston	$ 100,000 125,000	_Modernize_ Mod public ~~boat~~ marina and access roads along Little Muddy River, 1 mile north of Williston. ~~Also,~~ repair and resurface unnumbered county road south from Wilrose to Ray (junction with U.S. 2).	3 1 to 2

Continuous pages of data: horizontal rules, with 1 blank space above and 1 blank space below, separate the sections; vertical rules, with 2 or 3 spaces before and after them, separate the columns.

goal A

■ To produce a letter with a financial statement in 20'/0e.

Directions: _Spacing—1. Line—60. Warmup—page 215. Editing—check for commas._

goal

■ **To experience creative thinking, accurate typing, and cooperation in a work atmosphere.**

☐ *You and a teammate are Typist A and Typist B.*

☐ *You are members of the Arrangements Committee for The Mississippi Club, 222 Raworth Avenue, Natchez, Mississippi 39120.*

☐ *You are to prepare membership cards and certificates for new members. They are the first eight names listed on page 36. Unfortunately, all the cards and certificates are used up, so the two of you will have to create temporary new ones.*

☐ *Give a copy of all your work to your teacher.*

CREATIVE CO-OP 2: "MINI-TASKS" FOR A MEMBERSHIP MEETING

TYPIST A

You are responsible for four new members: Nutter, Krisner, Hickman, and Herrera.

1. Tell Typist B in writing (note or card) that you will prepare the membership *cards* for all eight persons if Typist B will prepare the membership *certificates* for the members.

> November 12, 19--
>
> David,
>
> Our supply of membership cards and certificates has been exhausted, and it appears that we will have to design some new ones for this year's initiation.
>
> I will prepare the cards if you will work on the certificates. With both of us working on this project, we should be able to finish it in time for our initiation.
>
> Sue

2. Design a wallet-size membership card. It must not be larger than 3½" x 2". Use both sides only if you must. Provide (a) the club's name and address, (b) the fact that the card *is* a membership card, and (c) a place to fill in the name and address of the member.

THE MISSISSIPPI CLUB

222 Raworth Avenue
Natchez, Mississippi 39120

M E M B E R S H I P   C A R D

JANICE BREEN
Name of Member

NATCHEZ   MISSISSIPPI   39120
City   State   ZIP

---

3. Make eight such cards. Send four of them to Typist B, along with a note saying that (a) you are waiting for the certificates, if in fact you are; and/or (b) here are four membership cards for the four persons for whom Typist B is responsible. Remind Typist B to fill in the names and addresses.

> November 18, 19--
>
> David,
>
> Here are four copies of the membership cards I designed. Be sure to fill in the information pertaining to each of the four new members for whom you are responsible.
>
> When I receive the membership certificates from you, I will fill them in with information pertaining to the four new members for whom I am responsible.
>
> Sue

4. Fill in the four cards for your people.

5. When you receive the certificates from Typist B, fill them in for your people.

6. Write a note to the secretary of the club (your teacher) to transmit the cards and certificates for your four new members.

TYPIST B

You are responsible for four new members: Stewart, Ingram, Brunson, and Galbreth.

1. Inform Typist A (by typing a note or card) that you are designing the membership *certificates*. Ask Typist A to design the membership *cards*.

> November 12, 19--
>
> Sue,
>
> We used the last of our membership cards and certificates during the last initiation. It looks like we will have to design some new ones for this year's initiation.
>
> So that we can finish both items before then, I think each of us should work on a separate task. I'll design the certificates if you will work on the cards.
>
> David

2. Design the membership certificate. It must not be larger than 8½" x 5½". The following items must appear on the certificate: (a) the club's name and address, (b) the fact that it *is* a certificate of membership, and (c) a place to fill in the name and address of the member.

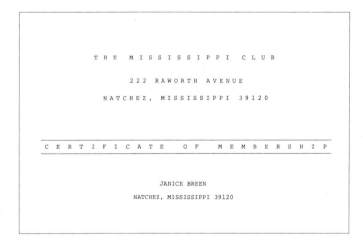

THE MISSISSIPPI CLUB

222 RAWORTH AVENUE

NATCHEZ, MISSISSIPPI 39120

C E R T I F I C A T E   O F   M E M B E R S H I P

JANICE BREEN
NATCHEZ, MISSISSIPPI 39120

3. Make eight certificates. Send four to Typist A with a note saying that (a) here are four certificates for the members for whom Typist A is responsible (remind Typist A to fill in names and addresses and (b) you are waiting for the membership cards (if in fact you are).

> November 18, 19--
>
> Sue,
>
> These four membership certificates should be completed by adding information pertaining to the four members for whom you are responsible.
>
> When you send me the membership cards, I will complete them by adding information pertaining to the members for whom I am responsible.
>
> David

4. Fill in four certificates for your people.

5. When Typist A sends you the cards, fill them in for your people.

6. Write a note to the secretary of the club (your teacher) to transmit the cards and certificates for your four new members.

Take up to ten 1-minute timings until you can type each paragraph within 1 minute without error. Then take a 5-minute timing to achieve 47 wam/5'/2e.

1	North Dakota is at the top center of the United States		12
2	and in the exact center of North America; every map attests		24
3	to the first fact, and there is a stone monument near Rugby		36
4	(in Pierce County) which testifies to the second fact. ①		47
5	There are some mountains and some valleys, but most of	12	59
6	the state is a quiet prairie that goes on to the horizon on	24	71
7	all sides, carpeted in windswept fields of wheat and barley	36	83
8	and other grains. There are also sugar beets and hay. ②	47	94
9	So North Dakota is farming, and its cities are centers	12	106
10	for processing and shipping the products of the fields. In	24	118
11	Bismarck, Grand Forks, Minot, and other cities, the tallest	36	130
12	buildings are grain silos, jutting up like skyscrapers. ③	47	141
13	The first settlers were fur trappers and traders; they	12	153
14	were followed by farmers and ranchers who built their towns	24	165
15	and schoolhouses, erected churches, turned the soil and ran	36	177
16	up their herds, and brought prosperity to the prairies. ④	47	188
17	North Dakota matters to all Americans because it is an	12	200
18	awesome shield to the nation. Giant air bases and networks	24	212
19	of radar are centered here, and huge missiles crouch in the	36	224
20	sunken silos, a deterrent guard for the western world. 47⑤	47	235

Speed markers are for 5' TW. Circled numbers are 1' goals.

■ 5'/0e

|1 |2 |3 |4 |5 |6 |7 |8 |9 |10 |11 |12   SI 1.42N

goal B

■ To produce a block display of data.

JOB 103-1: BLOCK DISPLAY

Plain paper ☐ ■ 20'/0e

You work for Mr. T. L. Swanson, who heads his own management-consultant firm.

"Right now," says Miss Hall, his secretary, "we are finishing a big project we undertook for the Highway Improvement Commission."

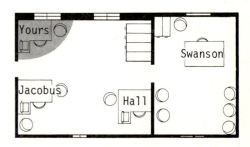

Directions: *Adjust machine for Job 103-1.*

Giving you the draft on the next page, Miss Hall says, "Please type this page 8. When I did pages 1 through 7, I used 1-inch margins all around, with the paper turned sideways. Maybe you can do that too, please?"

(Continued on next page)

PART 3

Part 3 continues in the pattern that should now be familiar to you:

1. Each unit includes two work-experience projects, separated by two short skill drives and followed by a skill clinic.

2. Each work-experience project contains about an hour's business typing.

3. Each project, presented in narrative form, takes place in a different state.

Unless your teacher specifies otherwise, you are to correct any errors you may make in your production assignments. Corrections must be expertly done—almost undetectable.

4. At the start of each practice period, turn to this page and type the Warmup: From each set of sentences below, select one sentence and type it four or more times.

You will practice typing checks, receipts, fill-in forms, payroll papers, and business financial statements, along with some letters, tables, and reports. You will increase your speed by 1 word a minute, to 42, in Part 3.

SPEED RECALL	1A When did she go to the man and pay for the Oak Lake island?	12
	1B I am to go to work for the audit firm by the eighth of May.	24
	1C If the eight men do the work right, they may make a profit.	36
ALPHABET RECALL	2A Vic quickly mixed grape juice with the frozen strawberries.	12
	2B Paul reviewed the subject before giving Kay and Max a quiz.	24
	2C Jack quietly gave some of his prize boxes to the dog owner.	36
NUMBER REVIEW	3A They found invoices 10, 28, 39, 47, and 56 in the corridor.	12
	3B Type page 10 or 28, page 39 or 47, and then page 56 or 100.	24
	3C They traveled on flights 10, 28, and 39. We had 47 and 56.	36
THINKING WHILE TYPING Edit these lines.	4A D--r S-r: Pl--s- l-t -s kn-w wh-n w- m-y -xp-ct th- -rd-r.	12
	4B Fr--nd, b-l--v- m- wh-n - s-y - r--ll- w-nt t- b- - h-lp-r.	24
	4C B-b d--sn't r--l-z- th-t th- -rd-r w-ll b- d-l-y-d s- l-ng.	36

|1 |2 |3 |4 |5 |6 |7 |8 |9 |10 |11 |12

30-SECOND SPRINTS

Three copies or three 30" TWs. Goal: 60+ wam.

5-MINUTE SKILL BLITZ

Circled numbers are 1' goals.

Routine:
5' writing.
5' corrective practice.
5' writing.

■ 5'/2e

Directions: *Spacing—1. Line—60. Tab—5.*

```
     01    03    05    07    09    11    13    15    17    19    21    23
 1  South Dakota is divided down the middle, north to south, by    12
     25    27    29    31    33    35    37    39    41    43    45    47
 2  the Missouri River.  East of the river is excellent farming     24
     49    51    53    55    57    59    61    63    65    67    69    71
 3  country, west of the river is a vast cattle range, so it is     36
     73    75    77    79    81    83    85    87    89    91    93    95
 4  natural for meat and grain to be the state's money harvest.     48

 5      The state of South Dakota has a unique feeling for one      12
 6      The state of South Dakota has a unique feeling for one      24
 7      The state of South Dakota has a unique feeling for one      36

 8  of the famous pony soldiers, George A. Custer.   Mention his    48
 9  of the famous pony soldiers, George A. Custer.   Mention his    60
10  of the famous pony soldiers, George A. Custer.   Mention his    72

11  name to most people, and they journalize on his last battle    84
12  name to most people, and they journalize on his last battle    96
13  name to most people, and they journalize on his last battle   108

14  with the Indians; but speak of him in South Dakota, and his   120
15  with the Indians; but speak of him in South Dakota, and his   132
16  with the Indians; but speak of him in South Dakota, and his   144

17  name is cheered, for it was one of his expeditions into the   156
18  name is cheered, for it was one of his expeditions into the   168
19  name is cheered, for it was one of his expeditions into the   180

20  Black Hills that found gold and began a gold rush.   That is   192
21  Black Hills that found gold and began a gold rush.   That is   204
22  Black Hills that found gold and began a gold rush.   That is   216

23  why they named a town for him.                                222
24  why they named a town for him.                                229
25  why they named a town for him.                                235
    |1  |2  |3  |4  |5  |6  |7  |8  |9  |10  |11  |12      SI 1.28FE
```

TO CUT DOWN ON ERRORS

□ *Push for smoothness, not speed.*
□ *Sit erect, shoulders level.*
□ *Sit back in chair, feet on floor.*
□ *Type with fingers, not wrists.*
□ *Type with fingers, not arms.*
□ *Keep eyes on the copy.*

LESSON **03**

Directions: *Spacing—1. Line—60. Tab—5.*
Warmup—page 215.

goal A

■ To type 47 wam for 5'/2e.

9 102 103

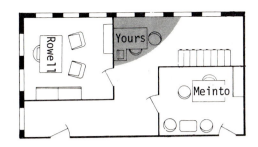

goal A

■ To type receipts on a printed form.

Directions: *Spacing—1. Line—60. Tab—5. Warmup—page 56; then begin Job 25-1.*

JOB 25-1: RECEIPTS

Workbook 73 or 8½″ by 2″ slips of paper □ ■ 20′/0e

David J. Meinto, head of the treasurer's office at Healy-Marlowe, welcomes you to the staff and gives you your first assignment. "Help our cashier," he says, "by typing out receipts for $5 supper money, ready for these people to sign when they are paid":

Doris Rubin, Denise Esposito, Joe Wallace, Jim Gray, Jerry Stoner, Gloria Rowell, Charles Brader, June Klos.

August 19, **19** --

Received *from* Healy-Marlowe, Inc.

Twelve dollars and no/100 - - - - - - - **Dollars**

Taxi fares for delivering rush packages

Irving K. Schwartz
Irving K. Schwartz

$ 12.00

Receipts are usually typed on printed forms.

August 19, 19--

I acknowledge receipt from Healy-Marlowe, Inc.,
the sum of Twelve Dollars ($12.00) issued to
me for taxi fares for delivering rush package.

Irving K. Schwartz
Irving K. Schwartz

$12.00

Receipts can be typed on memo slips too.

---

goal B

■ To type checks on printed forms.

JOB 25-2: CHECKS

Workbook 74-75 □ ■ 20′/0e

"Next," says Mr. Meinto when you finish the receipts, "I have okayed the payment of some bills. Please prepare checks for the following":

Directions: *Adjust your machine for Job 25-2.*

HEALY-MARLOWE, INC.
12 Connecticut Boulevard
Hartford, CT 06108   51-525/111

September 1, 19 -- No. 5

PAY
TO THE
ORDER OF Hartford Trucking Company - - - - - - - - - $22.50

Twenty-two and 50/100 - - - - - - - - - - - - - - - - - DOLLARS

CONNECTICUT TRUST COMPANY
NEW HAVEN, CONNECTICUT

HEALY-MARLOWE, INC.

Memo Invoice 9-14CS   *David J. Meinto*
⑈ 0⑈⑈⑈-0525⑈   ⑈9⑈59⑈52⑈6⑈   AUTHORIZED SIGNATURE

Type a check so that it cannot be altered. On "memo" line, indicate in a word or two what check was for.

21. Felton Fibre Company, $75, for binders in which to keep departmental records.
22. Jerry Stoner, $100, freelance report.
23. Connecticut Tire Company, $1,574.75, for tire replacement on our trucks.
24. Trumbull Hardware Company, $18.50, repairs on lawn mower used by Building Maintenance.

25. Mrs. Freda Hawn, $16, refund.
26. Miss Faith Cheshire, $225, settlement in accident liability.
27. University of Connecticut, $297, tuition for employee June Klos.
28. Waterbury Electricians, $78.80, for Invoice 823-77.

JOB 101-4: LETTER

Workbook 251 ☐ **Body 132 + 18 PS**
☐ **SI 1.36N** ☐ ■ **10'/0e**

"The last copy of the letter goes to a very distinguished woman to whom we show great respect. Use "Miss" and her last name only!"

Miss Lou Ann Melligard, 451 Main Street, in Groton, South Dakota 57401. Dear Miss

Melligard:

[*Since you will use "Miss Melligard" throughout, back up the complimentary closing enough to accommodate that name there too.*]

[*Change the third sentence to this.*] When Bill Blucas said he thought that you had had a fire at the store, I thought I should write to you once more in case my earlier letter had missed you.

[*Postscript without "PS."*] I have an idea: could you come early enough to have lunch with me before the meeting starts?

■ **To design and produce a special notice.**

JOB 102-1: NOTICE

Plain paper ☐ **SI 1.45N**
☐ **4 copies** ☐ ■ **15'/0e**

"We must enclose a copy of the February 10 notice in each letter," says Ms. Davis. "All I have is this printed one. Please copy it."

Directions: *Spacing—1. Line—60. Warmup—page 215. Then begin Job 102-1.*

JOB 102-2: COMPLETION CARDS

5" x 3" card or slip ☐ ■ **5'/0e**

JOB 102-1: NOTICE
1. Typed by Chris Sampson
2. Proofread with Karen Gillespie
3. There ought to be some way to estimate how much space an unarranged notice like this will take other than typing it once to find out and then have to make it final and attractive.

February 10, 19--

NOTICE TO MEMBERS OF THE
BOARD OF DIRECTORS OF
THE ABERDEEN CO-OP:

A special meeting of the Board of Directors of The Aberdeen Co-op will be held at two o'clock, Friday, March 3, at the Elks Club, Willard Street, Aberdeen, South Dakota.

The primary purpose of the meeting is to elect a new treasurer to replace Miss Mildred Swenson, who resigned because she and her family are moving away.

A second purpose of the meeting is to discuss the report of the Sales Manager, who recommends that we open outlets in Yankton and either Belle Fourche or Rapid City. If we decide to do so, we might save a great deal of money on store leases by acting in time to contract for the space before May 1.

Because of the urgency of the first purpose and the importance of the second, all members of the Board are urged to make a special effort to attend the March 3 meeting.

VIRGIL BIXTON, Secretary

goal A

■ To produce voucher checks.

Directions: *Spacing—1. Line—60. Tab—5.*
Warmup—page 56; then begin Job 26-1.

JOB 26-1: VOUCHER CHECKS

Workbook 76 ☐ ■ **15′/0e**

"I need two voucher checks," says Mr. Meinto. "First, retype this one (at right), changing the amount from $150 to $250. Then, as Check No. V8, type a similar one for $250 for Dr. Richard Loomis / University of Connecticut / Storrs, CT 06268."

Voucher Check. The top half is like any other check. The bottom half gives the reason for the check and the payee's address (note guides).

JOB 26-2: COMPLETION CARDS

5″ x 3″ cards or slips of paper ☐ ■ **5′/0e**

HEALY-MARLOWE, INC.
12 Connecticut Boulevard
Hartford, CT 06108

51-525 / 111

October 6, 19 -- No V7

PAY TO THE ORDER OF Dr. Stewart Atwells - - - - - - - - - - - - - $150.00

One hundred fifty and no/100 - - - - - - - - - - - - - - DOLLARS

CONNECTICUT TRUST COMPANY
NEW HAVEN, CONNECTICUT

HEALY-MARLOWE, INC.

Memo Conference Gratuity

AUTHORIZED SIGNATURE

⑆0111⑁0525⑈ 19⑆59⑆5216⑆

DETACH AND RETAIN THIS STATEMENT • The attached check is in payment of items described below. If not correct, notify us promptly

This check is in payment of your expense and gratuity fee for your participation in our staff conference.

┌   ┐
Dr. Stewart Atwells
Brown University
400 Waterman Street
Providence, RI 02910
└   ┘

---

goal B

■ To type 42 wam for 3′/2e.

3-MINUTE PIECEMEAL PRACTICE

Circled numbers are 1′ goals.

Directions: *Spacing—1. Line—60. Tab—5.*

Read the copy, and practice any words that look difficult. Then use the three paragraphs for piecemeal practice as described on page 41.

```
1    Connecticut is a blend of picturesque villages, cities      12
2  full of factories, and nets of highways that crisscross the   24
3  state.  The horizon is jagged with trees, steeples, and the   36
4  smokestacks of busy factories.①                               42

5    The state is one of the smallest, but it is one of the   12  54
6  most productive.  Its manufactured goods are worth at least  24  66
7  six billion a year and include such things as nuclear subs,  36  78
8  jet engines, and fine cutlery.②                              42  84

9    The state has a firm place in our history.  It was one   12  96
10 of the colonies, was in the War of Independence, and in the  24  108
11 days of sailing ships was home port to thousands of sailors  36  120
12 on Yankee clippers or whalers.③                              42  126
   |1   |2   |3   |4   |5   |6   |7   |8   |9   |10  |11  |12      SI 1.41N
```

3-MINUTE TW ON NEW COPY

Turn to lines 1–16 at the top of the next page and, without advance practice, take a 3-minute writing. Goal: 42 wam for 3 minutes within 2 errors.

Ms. Davis continues, "I will dictate the first letter to you; after that, you can use the same letter to the others with just minor changes."

This letter is to Mr. James L. Thomas, at Rural Route 1, in Redfield, SD 57469.　12　19

Dear Jim: Did you receive our letter about the special Board meeting next week?　30　37

You are one of the few Board members from whom we have not heard, Jim. [*Note comma before name in direct address.*] Because I knew you and your family were away on vacation but might be back in time, I thought I should write to you once more.　46　53　..　61　68　77　78

It is especially important that you attend the meeting because we are going to elect a new treasurer to replace Mildred Swenson. We shall miss her a great deal, Jim, [*commas before and after name in direct address*] but we must elect her replacement now.　88　97　105　113　..　119　120

Because our Board room is being repainted, we will hold the special meeting　128　137

at the Elks Club on Willard Street. It will begin at two o'clock and should be over not later than four o'clock. [*Type the next sentence as a complimentary closing; it includes a comma before a name in direct address.*] Be sure to attend, Jim! / Hester Davis, President / urs [*Arrange the enclosure note in two lines.*] Enclosure: Official/Notice of Meeting　146　154　160　..　..　172　177　183　185

JOB 101-2: LETTER

Workbook 247 □ **Body 135** □ **SI 1.35N** □ ■ **10'/0e**

"The next letter," says Ms. Davis, "is exactly the same except for the name and address, the name that recurs in the letter, and the third sentence.

The name and address are Mrs. Mary Forman, at Forman Hardware Company, 3131 LaCrosse Street, Watertown, South Dakota 57201. Dear Mary: [*Use "Mary" throughout.*]

[*Change the third sentence to this.*] When I heard that Stan had been in and out of the hospital lately, I thought you might have missed my letter and so I should write to you again. Hope Stan is a lot better!

JOB 101-3: LETTER

Workbook 249 □ **Body 125 + 27 PS** □ **SI 1.36N** □ ■ **10'/0e**

Send the same letter [*Job 101-1*] to Mr. William F. Blucas, at 351 Haven Street, Mitchell, SD 57301. Dear Bill: [*Use "Bill" throughout.*]

Directions: *Adjust machine for Job 101-3.*

[*Change the third sentence to this.*] When I could not reach you on the telephone, I thought I should write to you once more in case my earlier letter had missed you.

[*Add the following as a postscript; do not use the letters "PS."*] I have an idea: Bill [*Need a comma after "Bill"?*] could you pick up Jim Thomas as you drive through Redfield? He isn't feeling so well and would probably appreciate a lift.

3-MINUTE TW

Spacing—2.
Line—60.
Tab—5.

Speed markers
are for 3' TW.

■ 3'/2e

1　　　Rhode Island is our smallest state, but its people are　12
2　among the most progressive--there is a statue of "The Inde-　24
3　pendent Man" on top of the dome of the state capitol. This　36
4　is a reminder that Rhode Island had declared itself free of　48
5　England two months before the other colonies did.　58
6　　　Smallest state it may be, but it has the longest name:　70
7　State of Rhode Island and Providence Plantations. There is　82
8　a Rhode Island in Narragansett Bay, but the state itself is　94
9　not an island. Much of it, other than the lowland sections　106
10　around the Bay, is forest land and farmland on that plateau　118
11　which makes up most of New England.　125
12　　　It is in the lowlands, from Newport to Pawtucket, how-　137
13　ever, that the bulk of the people live and work. Along the　149
14　bayside shores are giant factories where textiles, jewelry,　161
15　and metal products like tools and engines are made and huge　173
16　docks from which they are shipped.　180

|1　|2　|3　|4　|5　|6　|7　|8　|9　|10　|11　|12　　SI 1.39N

5-MINUTE TW

Spacing—2.
Line—60.
Tab—5.

Speed markers are
for 5' TW.

■ 5'/3e

17　　　Half the folks in New England live in the Commonwealth　12　192
18　of Massachusetts--five million of them in all. Four out of　24　204
19　five live in the cities, a fact that explains why the state　36　216
20　is forty-fifth in size but ninth in people.　45　225
21　　　Massachusetts is blessed with rivers to provide trans-　57　237
22　portation and water power. All its life the state has been　69　249
23　a manufacturing center, and today it makes more wool cloth,　81　261
24　more machines that work with electric power, and more shoes　93　273
25　and other leather products than does any other state. And,　105　285
26　for the sake of the record, it is first in cranberries too!　117　297
27　　　But mention of Massachusetts to most people leads them　129　309
28　to think not of factories but of Paul Revere, of Minutemen,　141　321
29　a feast of turkey at Thanksgiving, and the like. Massachu-　153　333
30　setts is so endowed in history that it means history to us.　165　345
31　　　The next time you look at a map of the state, note how　177　357
32　Cape Cod resembles an arm, bent at the elbow. To the eager　189　369
33　thousands the world round who would like to immigrate, that　201　381
34　arm seems to be waving and beckoning to them.　210　390

|1　|2　|3　|4　|5　|6　|7　|8　|9　|10　|11　|12　　SI 1.38N

Are consecutive finger motions or proximate motions harder? To find out, take two or three 1-minute timings on lines 1–4 and average your scores. Do the same on lines 5–8.

Stress consecutive finger motions.

1 Cecile just decided to deduct the old music from her taxes. 12
2 Ola just loves to ski or swim on holidays in the mountains. 24
3 Dee declined the grant because she received free schooling. 36
4 The dents in the desk were made by the students in science. 48
|1 |2 |3 |4 |5 |6 |7 |8 |9 |10 |11 |12

Stress proximate finger motions.

5 William plans to apply for a legal hearing in a few months. 12
6 Jill began to climb the cliff seven times before making it. 24
7 Howard will send his books before going to military school. 36
8 Dru drove a car over a drastic course that was quite hilly. 48

PRACTICE

Type drills for the harder motion three to six times; the others, two to four times.

Consecutives.

9 sw swing sweet swell switch swivel swollen sweater swimming 12
10 ki kinds kings kinks kindly killed kindest kitchen kindness 24
11 ce cease cedar ceded center cement certify certain ceilings 36
12 lo loans local locks losses lovely located locally location 48
|1 |2 |3 |4 |5 |6 |7 |8 |9 |10 |11 |12

Proximates.

13 aw award awful awake awhile awaken awfully awkward awarding 12
14 hi hilly hinge hints hinges higher highway himself highways 24
15 fe fears feels fewer fences feeler fearing fencing feelings 36
16 li limit lists lives lining limits listing linings lifetime 48

POSTTEST

Repeat the Pretest completely. Score your work and note your improvement.

goal A

■ To produce two similar letters within 20'/0e.

JOB 101-1: LETTER

Workbook 245 □ **Body 125** □ **SI 1.36N** □ ■ **10'/0e**

UNIT 26

LESSON 101

Directions: Spacing—1. Line—60. Warmup—page 215. Editing—commas with names in direct address.

"Welcome to the Aberdeen Co-op!" exclaims Mrs. Georgia Deeg, the office manager. She presents you to Virgil Bixton, secretary of the corporation; to Mildred Swenson, who is leaving at the end of this week; and to Hester Davis, president of the co-operative. Your first assignments are to type for Ms. Davis.

"You heard that Miss Swenson is leaving?" asks Ms. Davis. "Well, she is our treasurer; so we must have a special meeting of the Board of Directors to elect her replacement. We sent out notices two weeks ago, but we still have not heard from four directors, so we must write to them about attending the meeting."

222

goal A

■ **To type at least 42 wam for 5'/3e.**

KEEP YOURSELF RELAXED

☐ *Shoulders level.*
☐ *Elbows limp, hanging loose.*
☐ *Wrists fixed, motionless.*

Directions: *Spacing—1. Line—60. Tab—5.*
Warmup—page 56; then start Pretest.

PRETEST
PRACTICE ON
TW VOCABULARY

Take a 5-minute writing on lines 17–34, page 59. Goal: 42 wam 5'/3e.

Type, four times each, the drill lines indicated in this guide table.

Pretest errors	0–2	3–4	5–6	7–+
Type lines	4–8	3–7	2–6	1–5

For accuracy.

1 transportation Minutemen, beckoning electric England people   12
2 manufacturing cranberries resembles machines leather rivers   12
3 Massachusetts forty-fifth thousands products history turkey   12
4 Commonwealth Thanksgiving immigrate explains cities, waving   12

For speed.

5 ninth blast water power cloth leads think feast elbow eager   12
6 half size next time more wool than does work with most sake   12
7 all out why and set its has any for too not but map how arm   12
8 of them of five in size to most to them to the in all to be   12

POSTTEST

Repeat the Pretest. Score your work and note your improvement.

goal B

■ **To produce a ruled table from incomplete data.**

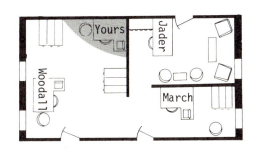

Directions: *Begin Job 27-1 below.*

JOB 27-1: REPORT WITH TABLE

Plain paper ☐ ■ **20'/0e**

Mr. Mark Jader, statistician at The Massachusetts Corporation, shows you to your desk. When you are ready, he says, "I have a report with a table for you to type in the standard arrangement for a business report":

Title on Line 9: WHO OWNS OUR COMPANY?   15

Subtitle lines: A Special Report by / The   32
Finance Committee / Mark Jader, Chairman   61

BACKGROUND This report has been   71
requested by the Board of Directors. The   79
committee is indebted to the Secretary of   87
the corporation for making the records open   96
to us.   98

PRESENT OWNERS As of January of this   107
year, the owners of common stock of the   115
corporation were grouped as follows: *In*   123
this table, leave 6 spaces between columns.

JOB 100-1: OPEN TABLE

Plain paper □ ■ 10'/0e

"Next," says Dr. Urban, as he gives you the clipping below, "convert this information into a table for me."

"What should it be entitled?" you ask.

"Oh, I think 'Principal Indian Nations of the Eastern Woodland Groups' would do it. That's long, but put it in two lines."

EASTERN WOODLAND GROUPS
Principal Indian Nations. The principal Indian nations of the Eastern Woodland Group are:

Abnaki	Chocktaw	Massachuset	Pequot
Algonquin	Cree	Menominee	Potawatomi
Beothuk	Creek	Miami	Powhatan
Caddo	Delaware	Micmac	Sauk-Fox
Calusa	Erie	Montagnais	Shawnee
Catawba	Huron	Naskapi	Timucua
Cherokee	Illinois	Ojibwa	Winnebago
Chickasaw	Iroquois	Ottawa	

JOB 100-2: OPEN LISTING

Plain paper □ ■ 10'/0e

Dr. Urban gives you the clipping below. "Could you make a listing of the Iroquois tribes for me?"

Make it attractive.

THE IROQUOIS NATION
The Six Tribes. As readers of Cooper's *Last of the Mohicans* know, the New York Iroquois figured prominently in colonial American history. There were six tribes in the Iroquois federation: Cayuga, Mohawk, Oneida, Onondaga, Seneca, and Tuscarora.

---

goal B

■ To produce a composite display of two tables within 15'/0e.

JOB 100-3: TABLE DISPLAY

Plain paper □ ■ 15'/0e

"I am going to need both those tables [*Jobs 100-1 and 100-2*] for my meeting on March 1," says Dr. Urban. "Please figure some attractive way to put them both on the same sheet of paper, ready for me to have duplicated."

Think about it: the smaller table, which should go at the top, takes 16 lines; the bigger one, 20 lines: so $66 - 36 = 30$ lines left over. This might be divided into 10 lines top margin, 10 between tables, 10 bottom margin.

Job 100-4: COMPLETION CARDS

5" x 3" cards or slips □ ■ 5'/0e

---

goal A

■ To find which of two motions is harder; then to practice them both proportionately to increase skill.

ACTIVITIES	20 MIN.	40 MIN.
Warmup, page 215	3'	5'
4 Pretest 1-minute TWs	5'	—
6 Pretest 1-minute TWs	—	10'
Practice drills, 3 times	7'	—
Practice drills, 6 times	—	15'
Repeat the Pretest	5'	10'

CLINIC 17

Directions: *Spacing—1. Line—60. Warmup—page 215. Timetable—see adjacent box.*

Group	Number	Percent	
Individuals	13,000	35.5	139 / 149
Institutions	8,900	24.4	157
Security dealers	2,300	6.3	166
Foreign holders	9,700	26.6	174
All others	2,600	7.2	187
TOTAL	36,500	100.0	194

These figures can be roundly summarized as "one-third of the owners are individuals, a fourth are institutions, and another fourth are foreign holders."

TREND This committee was able to obtain similar data for 1965. These figures show that individuals have decreased from 78.3 percent in 1965 to 35.5 percent today, while institutions increased from 9.3 percent in 1965 to 24.4 percent today, and—this will amaze you—foreign holders have increased from 0.8 percent in 1965 to 26.6 percent today.

A complete table of all data is appended to this report.

THE COMMITTEE

Today's date

---

goal A

■ To produce a ruled table on a page turned sideways.

JOB 28-1: RULED TABLE

Plain paper ☐ ■ 20'/0e

Directions: *Spacing—1. Line—60. Tab—5. Warmup—page 56; then begin Job 28-1.*

LESSON 28

"Next," says Mr. Jader, "I need an updated copy of this table about the stock ownership of our company. Please turn the paper sideways."

There are 51 lines on a standard sheet turned sideways.

STOCK OWNERSHIP OF THE MASSACHUSETTS CORPORATION

	January 31, 1965		January 31, 1975		This Year	
	Holders	Percent	Holders	Percent	Holders	Percent
Individuals:						
Men	3,600	23.8	4,200	19.4	~~4,600~~ 4,800	~~13.7~~ 13.1
Women	4,300	28.4	4,900	22.7	~~5,200~~ 5,300	~~15.6~~ 14.5
Jointly held ...	3,950	26.1	3,400	15.7	~~3,100~~ 2,900	~~9.3~~ 7.9
Institutions	1,400	9.3	3,600	16.6	~~8,500~~ 8,900	~~25.4~~ 24.4
Security dealers	450	3.0	500	2.3	~~1,800~~ 2,300	~~5.4~~ 6.3
Foreign holders	120	0.8	3,200	14.9	~~7,800~~ 9,700	~~23.3~~ 26.6
All others	1,300	8.6	1,800	8.4	~~2,400~~ 2,600	~~7.3~~ 7.2
TOTALS	15,120	100.0	21,600	100.0	~~33,400~~ 36,500	100.0

goal B
■ To produce a
two-page speech
within 20'/0e.

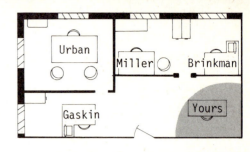

JOB 99-1: SPEECH

Plain paper ☐ ■ 20'/0e

You are departmental secretary at Syracuse University for Dr. Thomas E. Urban and Professors Gary L. Miller and William E. Brinkman.

"First thing," says Dr. Urban, "is to get me ready for a state meeting on March 1. Please make me a typed copy of what I will say as the chairman of a panel on New York State Indians."

A "speech" is typed with spacing 3, line 50, tab 5, and standard manuscript top and bottom margins.

<table>
<tr><td>Panel Discussion</td><td>12</td></tr>
<tr><td>The Role of the Indian in New York State</td><td>38</td></tr>
<tr><td>March 1, 19--</td><td>48</td></tr>
</table>

Good afternoon, ladies and gentlemen. I am Thomas Urban, chairman of today's panel on "The Role of the Indian in New York State." — 59, 67, 75, 76

I. INTRODUCTIONS — 89

The other two panel participants are: — 98

First, from Oneida Community College, in Rome, New York, Professor Alice T. Stanwix. — 107, 114, 116

Second, from the College of Oneonta, in Oneonta, New York, Dr. Lawrence Coulter. — 125, 133

II. OVERVIEW — 143

Our topic involves two questions: — 151

(Slide 1) — 159

First, "How is the New York Indian faring on the seven state Indian reservations?" — 168, 177

(Slide 2) — 202

Second, "How is the New York Indian faring outside the state Indian reservations?" — 210, 220

(Back to Slide 1) — 232

To open the first topic, our speaker is Professor Stanwix. With more than twenty years' experience on state Indian commissions, she is well qualified to discuss the reservation question. Miss Stanwix. — 244, 249, 257, 266, 273

[*Type a line of periods across the page to indicate someone else is speaking.*] — ..

.... — 283

Thank you very much, Miss Stanwix. — 291

(Advance to Slide 2) — 306

Dr. Coulter will open the discussion on this second topic. A specialist in helping Indians find off-reservation jobs, Dr. Coulter, too, knows what he is talking about. Dr. Coulter. — 315, 324, 333, 342, 343

.... — 354

Thank you very much, Dr. Coulter. — 361

goal A
■ To produce two
tables from
unarranged data,
each within 10'/0e.

LESSON **100**

JOB 28-2: REVISED TABLE

Plain paper ☐ ■ 15'/0e

"I found this clipping in a magazine," says Mr. Jader, giving you the table in the next column. "To be really useful, it should be arranged alphabetically. So, please rearrange it into alphabetic sequence, with the name of the harbor in the first column, the rank in the second, and the tonnage last. Thanks a lot."

JOB 28-3: COMPLETION CARDS

5" x 3" cards or slips of paper ☐ ■ 5'/0e

Prepare completion cards for the jobs you've just finished.

Commerce at Principal New England Ports (Figures are tons of 2,000 pounds.)		
Rank	Harbor	Tonnage
1	Portland, Maine	27,237,553
2	Boston, Mass.	22,610,760
3	New Haven, Conn.	11,297,138
4	Providence, R.I.	9,471,235
5	Fall River, Mass.	3,541,631
6	Bridgeport, Conn.	3,426,096
7	Portsmouth, N.H.	1,833,373
8	Salem, Mass.	1,486,468
9	New London, Conn.	1,431,458
10	Searsport, Maine	1,154,030
11	Norwalk, Conn.	1,106,521
12	Stamford, Conn.	937,967
13	New Bedford, Mass.	658,657
14	Beverly, Mass.	228,863
15	Gloucester, Mass.	204,326

26
48
59
65
76
83
91
98
106
114
122
130
137
145
153
160
168
176
183
191
202

---

goal

■ To use intensive drill to improve basic skill.

ACTIVITIES	20 MIN.	40 MIN.
Warmup, page 56	3'	3'
Drive 1 Pretest	4'	4'
Drive 1 Practice	9'	9'
Drive 1 Posttest	4'	4'
Drive 2 Pretest	—	5'
Drive 2 Practice	—	10'
Drive 2 Posttest	—	5'

Directions: *Spacing—1. Line—60. Warmup—page 56; then begin Drive 1.*

DRIVE 1

PRETEST 1

Left-hand accent.

Take two 1-minute writings on lines 1–3. Proofread both and average the scores.

1 Barbara was last seen at the new dress sale late last week. 12
2 Ada stated she had traded the car off after it was wrecked. 24
3 Gerald prefers trees that have very few leaves or branches. 36

|1 |2 |3 |4 |5 |6 |7 |8 |9 |10 |11 |12

PRACTICE 1

Type four copies of each line (for speed gain) or four copies of the whole block of lines (for accuracy gain).

Left-hand accent.

4 possess wrecked assets leaves trades trees state weeks last 12
5 cashier prefers leased lesson branch dress after seems cash 24
6 lessons dresses stated retain horses bases taxes farms cars 36
7 between pleases assure tassel passes tease refer meets wash 48
8 sixteen referee pretty letter masses meter sewer cases fast 60

POSTTEST 1

Repeat the Pretest. Proofread, average your scores, and note your improvement.

goal A

■ To type 47 wam for 5'/2e.

Directions: Spacing—1. Line—60. Tab—5.
Warmup—page 215.

PRETEST
Spacing—2.

Take a 5-minute timing. Score your work and jot down your scores.

1 When the United States became a republic a little over two   13
2 centuries ago, New York was fifth in population. About thirty   25
3 years later it had moved up to first place, which it held for 150   39
4 years. The 1970 census showed that California had moved to first   52
5 place by more than a million and a half. Today New York State   64
6 has approximately 18 million citizens.   72

7 New York ranks first in manufacturing, for it is first in the   85
8 number of plants, employment, size of payrolls, plus the value of   99
9 what is made. It leads other states in retail and service trades. It   113
10 is the national center of commerce, finance, communication, and   126
11 foreign trade. With harbors on both the Atlantic Ocean and the   138
12 Great Lakes, connected by a canal through the state, it is of   151
13 course first in shipping.   156

14 New York is the shape of a great funnel, tilted just a little bit   170
15 toward the west, with Long Island serving as the flexible nozzle   183
16 that runs out to sea. It is mountainous in the north and east and,   197
17 because of glaciers in the Ice Age, level in the center and west   210
18 and rolling in the south. All this variety in terrains means that   223

■ 5'/2e   19 New York has everything from ski slopes to sandy beaches.   235

|1 |2 |3 |4 |5 |6 |7 |8 |9 |10 |11 |12 |13 |14   SI 1.40N

Speed markers are for 5' TW. Circled numbers are 1' goals.

PRACTICE
Spacing—1.

Type three times each the lines indicated in this chart.

Errors in Pretest	0–1	2–3	4–5	6–+
Lines to practice	20–24	21–25	22–26	23–27

Speed phrases.   20 for it is, held for, has made, is made, is the, or of, or a   12
21 it is the, it is of, both the, of what, in the, and a, to a   24
22 more than, when the, plus the, size of, it had, up to, of a   36
23 ranks first place fifth state great shape level north sandy   48

Accuracy.   24 approximately employment republic glaciers funnel when they   12
25 manufacturing California payrolls terrains tilted runs 1970   24
26 communication population commerce flexible nozzle show that   36
27 mountainous everything different centuries retail north 150   48

POSTTEST   Repeat the Pretest. Score your work and note your improvement.

PRETEST 2

Take three 1-minute timings on lines 9–11. Proofread all; then average scores.

Up-reach accent.

9 Joseph decided to start a charity drive for their highways. 12
10 Ralph hired those fellows to take his stock to the station. 24
11 Phil would like to take his staff to see the newest chairs. 36
|1 |2 |3 |4 |5 |6 |7 |8 |9 |10 |11 |12

PRACTICE 2

Type four copies of each line (for speed gain) or four copies of each block of lines (for accuracy gain).

12 boarded watches hiring drapes arches staff photo raise jobs 12

Up-reach accent.

13 railway suggest raises waists hinges fears heirs lists fail 24
14 airways hauling states steady useful tales polls allow bulb 36

15 legends oranges praise search upward jiffy wards debts help 12
16 highest studies offset orphan selves tests roses those uses 24
17 applies airmail worked target oldest lying ethic fifty play 36

POSTTEST 2

Repeat Pretest 2. Score your work and note your improvement.

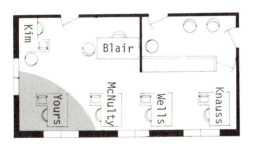

goal A

■ To produce invoices with two addresses and other special features.

Directions: *Spacing—1. Line—60. Warmup—page 56; then begin Job 29-1.*

JOB 29-1: INVOICES WITH TWO ADDRESSES
Workbook 77–78 □ ■ Each 5'/0e

"Welcome to the Billing Department," says Dave Blair, "for we certainly need help! We're filling orders to three Illinois high schools. Note that there are two addresses on each—that of the school to which the goods are shipped and that of the Board of Education offices to which the bill is sent. Ready?"

No. 6171: Ship to Eisenhower High School / 1200 South 16 Street / Decatur, IL 62521 / Bill to Administrative Offices / Decatur School District 61 / 101 West Cerro Gordo / Decatur, IL 62523 / via Parcel Delivery Service / 24 Regulation Type F Basketballs @ 4.90 = 117.60 / 12 Regulation Type L Basketballs @ 2.75 = 33.00 / Total = 150.60 / Delivery Charges = 4.00 / TOTAL AMOUNT DUE = 154.60.

No. 6172: Ship to East High School / 2601 Dempster Street / Park Ridge, IL 60068 / Bill to Administrative Office / Maine Township School District 207 / Park Ridge, IL 60068 / via Parcel

Standard invoice form with two addresses.

photograph and a brief summary of your
career. / Cordially yours, / Sally W. Poff /
Managing Editor [*Omit reference initials; in
their position type the adjacent display to
give Mr. Oppenheim a place to sign the
agreement and to date it.*]

205
218
222
..
..
253

```
                                          Sally W. Poff
                                          Managing Editor ↓2

      I hereby accept the agreement
      stated in this letter. ↓2

      ─────────────────────────────────
      Albert V. Oppenheim ↓2

      ─────────────────────────────────
      Date
```

One of many kinds of approval lines.

goal B

■ **To type 47 wam for 5′/2e.**

5-MINUTE PIECEMEAL PRACTICE

Spacing 1 for 1′ TWs; spacing 2 for 5′ TW.

Speed markers are for 5′ TW. Circled numbers are 1′ goals.

■ **5′/2e**

Directions: *Spacing—1. Line—60. Tab—5.
Begin the Piecemeal timings at once.*

Take up to ten 1-minute timings, advancing from one paragraph to the next only
when you complete it within 1 minute and no errors. When all paragraphs have
been mastered, take a 5-minute writing over all. Goal: Type the entire writing
within 5′/2e.

```
 1        New York City stands as a giant with a dozen faces and        12
 2   open arms as it greets the millions of tourists who come to        24
 3   it each year, shelters the seven other millions who live in        36
 4   the city, and gives work to more millions of commuters.        47

 5        For the tourists, the city has limitless places to see    12 | 59
 6   and things to do.  It is a gourmet's heaven.  It's the main    24 | 71
 7   stem of art, ballet, music, the theater.  It is the world's   36 | 83
 8   biggest shopping center for anything you care to name.        47 | 94

 9        New York City has buildings so big that they disappear   12 | 106
10   into the clouds on a cloudy day, and there are more of them   24 | 118
11   than you will see in any other one place in the world.  Oh,   36 | 130
12   it is huge, so huge it even has walking traffic jams.         47 | 141

13        It may also be the hardest-working place in the world.   12 | 153
14   It has more tonnage in its harbor, more planes on its three   24 | 165
15   huge airfields, more offices with good jobs, and more girls   36 | 177
16   and boys in classrooms than anywhere else in the world.       47 | 188

17        But best of all, regardless of its extra size, the Big   12 | 200
18   Apple (as it calls itself) has a spirit like no place else:   24 | 212
19   It has done everything, it can do anything, and like a tall   36 | 224
20   lady with a torch in the harbor, it welcomes everyone.        47 | 235
   |1   |2   |3   |4   |5   |6   |7   |8   |9   |10  |11  |12       SI 1.34FE
```

Delivery Service / 12 Regulation Type F Basketballs @ 4.90 = 58.80 / 12 Regulation Type L Basketballs @ 2.75 = 33.00 / 2 Type W Hoops @ 5.00 = 10.00 / Total 101.80 / Delivery = 3.50 / TOTAL AMOUNT DUE 105.30.

No. 6173: Ship to Lanphier High School / 1200 North 11 Street / Springfield, IL 62702 / Bill to Administrative Offices / Springfield School District 186 / 1900 West Monroe Street / Springfield, IL 62674 / via Your Truck Pickup / 12 Type W Hoops @ 5.00 = 60.00 / 6 Type K Hoops at 5.25 = 31.50 / TOTAL AMOUNT DUE 91.50.

No. 6174: Ship to Employee Relations Department / Foster & Curry, Inc. / 1520 Montague Street / Rockford, IL 61102 / Bill to same [*type the word "same" in the "Bill to" section*] via Parcel Delivery Service / 2 Regulation Type L Basketballs @ 2.75 = 5.50 / 2 Regulation Type P Basketballs @ 2.00 = 4.00 / 1 Type W Hoop @ 5.00 = 5.00 / Total = 14.50 / 5% sales tax = .73 / Delivery Charges = 1.25 / TOTAL AMOUNT DUE 16.48. [*Note: Sales tax chargeable to all customers except nonprofit institutions (like schools).*]

goal B

■ To produce credit memos.

JOB 29-2: CREDIT MEMOS

Workbook 79–80 □ ■ Each 5'/0e

"Thank you," says Mr. Blair when you give him the invoices you typed. "Now I have some credit memos to rush out. Please take care of these":

No. 843: Williams and Finch, Inc. / 181 Danvers Street / Normal, IL 61761 / Account credited for 6 Regulation Type F Basketballs, damaged in transit, @ 4.90 = 29.40 / 1 Basketball Inflation Pump and Needle, not ordered, @ 3.75 = 3.75 / 5% sales tax refund on the above = 1.65 / Transportation refund on the above = 3.45 / TOTAL AMOUNT CREDITED = 38.25.

No. 844: Administrative Office / Peoria School District 150 / 3202 North Wisconsin Street / Peoria, IL 61603 / Account credited for 7 Regulation Type L Basketballs, returned from Richwoods High School as credit on Invoice No. 5890, @ 2.75 = 19.25 / 2 Type W Hoops, damaged in transit, @ 5.00 = 10.00 / Transportation refund on the above = 2.60 / TOTAL AMOUNT CREDITED = 31.85.

No. 845: Mr. Wayne Williams / Young and Cartell Inc. / 879 Second Street / Moline, IL 61265 / Account credited for 4 Laminated Backboards, with Mounting Rods, not suitable for customer's purpose, @ 15.50 = 62.00 / 5% sales

Directions: *Adjust your typewriter for Job 29-2 and begin it.*

tax refund on the above = 3.10 / Note: No transportation refund on above, by agreement with the customer. TOTAL AMOUNT CREDITED = 65.10.

No. 846: Administrative Office / Maine Township School District 207 / 1111 Dee Road / Park Ridge, IL 60068 / Account credited for 2 Regulation Type L Basketballs, returned from West High School as uninflatable, @ 2.75 = 5.50 / 3 Regulation Type F Basketballs, returned from East High School as inventory reduction, @ 4.90 = 14.70 / Transportation refund on first item only = 1.85 / TOTAL AMOUNT CREDITED = 22.05.

	LOG 530 E. Washington Street Springfield, Il. 62701	Credit Memorandum	
	LINCOLNLAND SPORTING GOODS COMPANY		No. 843

TO: Williams and Finch, Inc.
181 Danvers Street
Normal, IL 61761

DATE: October 8, 19--

Your Account has been Credited as follows

QUANTITY	DESCRIPTION	UNIT PRICE	AMOUNT
6	Regulation Type F Basketballs, damaged in transit	4.90	29.40
1	Basketball Inflation Pump and Needle, not ordered	3.75	3.75
	5% Sales tax refund on the above		1.65
	Transportation refund on the above		3.45
	TOTAL AMOUNT CREDITED		38.25

Standard form for a credit memorandum.

[*interrupting expression*] that we have decided to send a letter of agreement to Mr. 67
Oppenheim and to use his article in the 75
June issue. You see, [*introductory expression*] we are following your advice. 85

We have hired another person, [*insert 92
your name*], [*appositive*] to work on special 98
projects. You will be pleased, I know, 107
[*interrupting expression*] with the new work 110
loads. [*complimentary closing*] Get well 116
quickly! / Sally W. Poff [*no title*] / urs 126

JOB 97-4: THANK-YOU LETTER

Workbook 241 □ **Body 91** □ **SI 1.40N**
□ **Insert 6 commas** □ ■ **10'/0e**

"Oh," says Miss Poff, "here's another thank-you note I meant to dictate earlier."

goal A

■ To produce a letter
with an acceptance
line within 15'/0e.

JOB 98-1: LETTER WITH RETURN
APPROVAL LINE

Workbook 243 □ **Body 164 + 80**
display □ **SI 1.47FH** □ **Insert 14**
commas □ ■ **15'/0e**

"Now for our regular editorial mail," says Miss Poff, "starting with a letter of agreement."

Mr. Albert V. Oppenheim / 1965-A LaFay- 15
ette Avenue / The Bronx, NY 10473 / 22

Dear Mr. Oppenheim: We are very happy 32
I am pleased to tell you that we can once 41
more feature one of your fine articles. This 50
one "Tailoring With Stripes" will have 59
great appeal to our subscribers. We try to 67
maintain a balance of articles on all aspects 78
of sewing in each issue as you know and 87
this one by you will complete our plans 96
for the June issue. 97

Mr. and Mrs. Albert Teel / 645 Ocean Park- 15
way / Brooklyn, NY 11230 / Dear Teels: / 26

Thank you very much indeed for sending 35
me the clipping from the San Francisco 48
Chronicle. I had no idea our magazine 60
was being quoted of course and I admit that 69
I am pleased we were so honored. [*Did you 76
insert the four commas needed so far?*]

It was very kind of you to go to so much 85
trouble for us, and I am very grateful to 93
you. I am sending you as a token of my 101
appreciation two tickets to the fashion show 110
we shall sponsor on March 15. I do hope 119
you will attend and let me meet you. [*Did 126
you add the two extra commas this paragraph needs?*]

Cordially yours / Sally W. Poff / Managing 141
Editor / urs / Enclosures: / 2 tickets [*Always 148
identify valuable enclosures.*]

We would like to feature your picture and 105
a brief review of your career on the edito- 114
rial page in the front of the issue. In addi- 123
tion we will display the title of the article 132
on the cover. We will in other words really 142
feature the article. 146

If you agree to these stipulations Mr. 154
Oppenheim we will pay you $200 within 163
six weeks of the month of issue. 170

To indicate your agreement will you 178
please sign the original of this letter and 187
return it to us. Please send us also a recent 197

goal A

■ To produce statements of account.

Directions: *Spacing—1. Line—60.*
Warmup—page 56; then adjust your machine
for Job 30-1.

JOB 30-1: MONTHLY STATEMENTS

Workbook 81–82 ☐ ■ **Each 5'/0e**

1. Mason, Graham, and Sons / 181 Andrews Avenue / Joliet, IL 60436 / Sept. 1 Brought Forward (Balance) 0.00 / Sept. 4 Invoice 5477 (Charges) 195.50 (Balance) 195.50 / Sept. 7 Invoice 5639 (Charges) 422.60 (Balance) 618.10 / Sept. 16 Payment on Account (Credits) 700.00 (Balance) +81.90 / Sept. 24 Invoice 5721 (Charges) 125.00 (Balance) 43.10 / Sept. 30 AMOUNT NOW DUE = (Balance) 43.10.

2. Williams and Finch, Inc. / 676 Carston Avenue / Normal, IL 61761 / Sept. 1 Brought Forward (Balance) 15.85 / Sept. 10 Payment on Account (Credits) 15.85 (Balance) 0.00 / Sept. 21 Invoice 5339 (Charges) 176.50 (Balance) 176.50 / Sept. 24 Credit Memorandum 794 (Credits) 18.75 (Balance) 157.75 / Sept. 27 Payment on Account (Credits) 100.00 (Balance) 57.75 / AMOUNT NOW DUE = (Balance) 57.75.

3. Administrative Offices / Peoria School District 150 / 3202 North Wisconsin Street / Peoria, IL 61603 / Sept. 1 Brought Forward (Balance) 0.00 / Sept. 3 Invoice 5401 (Charges) 56.50 (Balance) 56.50 / Sept. 12 Payment on Account (Credits) 56.45 (Balance) 0.05 / Sept. 22 Invoice 5557 (Charges) 164.23 (Balance) 164.28 / Sept. 30 AMOUNT NOW DUE (Balance) 164.28.

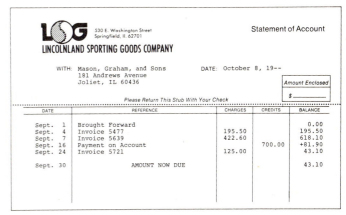

A statement is a history of transactions.

JOB 30-2: COMPLETION CARDS

5" x 3" cards ☐ ■ **5'/0e**

goal B

■ To type 42 or more wam for 5'/3e on hard copy.

Directions: *Spacing—1. Line—60. Tab—5.*
See Sprint directions on page 48.

12-SECOND SPRINTS

Take four 12-second sprints on each of the three complete sentences.

1 Chicago is the place where the
2   airport has far more planes in and out than any other. 17
3   name of the city is an Indian word meaning wild onion. 17
4   city was wiped out in the biggest fire in our history. 17

12" WAM: 40 45 50 55 60 65 70 75 80 85

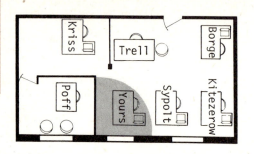

goal A

■ To produce two letters within 20'/0e.

Directions: *Spacing—1. Line—60. Warmup—page 215. Editing—commas. WB—237–238.*

JOB 97-1: THANK-YOU LETTER

Workbook 239 □ **Body 75** □ **SI 1.35N** □ ■ **7'/0e**

You report to Miss Sally W. Poff, the managing editor of *Plaids and Stripes*, a magazine for "do-it-yourself" persons who like to sew. Miss Poff introduces you to your colleagues, then says:

"I have a number of short thank-you notes to get out, and I'll appreciate your doing them for me. Let me dictate."

Mr. Brandon A. Latta / 251 St. Luke's Place /	15
Jackson Heights, NY 11372 /	20
Dear Mr. Latta: Thank you very much, my	31
friend, [*commas for direct address*] for that	34
beautiful book of 1880 dress patterns. I	43
found it fascinating, as you must have	50
known I would [*comma before afterthought*]. And by the way, [*introductory*	53
phrase] I marvel that the book is in such	57
fine condition.	64
	67
It is a real treasure; accordingly, [*introductory expression*] it is being placed in	75
the showcase where our guests will be able	80
to see it.	89
	91
I am very grateful to you for sending it	100
to me, of course [*afterthought*]. Cordially	108

yours, / Sally W. Poff / Managing Editor / URS
     120
     122

JOB 97-2: THANK-YOU LETTER

Workbook 239 □ **Body 69** □ **SI 1.49FH** □ ■ **10'/0e**

"The second one is to a woman who gave me an interview that I will write up later," says Miss Poff. "I want to thank her."

Ms. Gertrude J. Kinsey / President, The	15
Women's Bank / 1800 Avenue of the Americas / New York, NY 10020 / Dear Ms.	22
Kinsey: /	30
	31
Thank you for the interview that you	40
gave me so generously yesterday. It was	48
more than a pleasure to meet you, and all	56
you told me about your life and the bank	65
was, of course, [*interrupting expression*]	68
most interesting.	71
As soon as the article is ready, I will	80
send it to you for corrections and/or approval. I will also send you, as you	89
requested, [*interrupting expression*] a copy	96
of our magazine.	100
	103
Cordially yours, and so on, as usual.	121

goal B

■ To produce two letters within 20'/0e.

JOB 97-3: GET-WELL LETTER

Workbook 241 □ **Body 85** □ **SI 1.29FE** □ ■ **10'/0e**

"The next letter is a 'hurry-back' one to one of our staff members. Let me dictate":

Ms. Serene Kitzerow / 210 West 90 Street /	15
New York, NY 10024 / Dear Serene: /	22
This is just a quick note, obviously,	31
[*interrupting expression*] to let you know	34
that we miss you and hope you will soon	43
be back with us.	46
You will be pleased to know, I am sure,	55

SKILL BLITZ

Directions on
page 13:
1. 3' timing.
2. Corrective
practice.
3. 3' timing.

Circled numbers
are 1' goals.

5	Chicago is the capital of Middle America, not just be—	12
6	Chicago is the capital of Middle America, not just be—	24
7	Chicago is the capital of Middle America, not just be—	36
8	cause it's near the population ① center but rather because it	48
9	cause it's near the population center but rather because it	60
10	cause it's near the population center but rather because it	72
11	is the hub of rail and air and highway transportation and a ②	84
12	is the hub of rail and air and highway transportation and a	96
13	is the hub of rail and air and highway transportation and a	108
14	center for distributing goods.	114
15	center for distributing goods.	120
16	center for distributing goods. ③	126

■ 3'/2e

|1 |2 |3 |4 |5 |6 |7 |8 |9 |10 |11 |12   SI 1.64H

17	You probably know that Illinois, with its endless long	12
18	plains of rich soil, is one of the top states in farm goods	24
19	like corn and meat, but many do not realize that it's a top	36
20	state in manufacturing and also in mining.	45
21	The state has a lot of coal mines and oil fields; they	57
22	provide power for the steel mills and factories. The state	69
23	has access both to the Great Lakes and to the central river	81
24	system of the nation; it is not hard to get its products to	93
25	market, for the state is crossed by rail lines and highways	105
26	and air routes too. It is no wonder that the state has for	117
27	its nickname the words "The Inland Empire."	126

■ 3'/2e

|1 |2 |3 |4 |5 |6 |7 |8 |9 |10 |11 |12   SI 1.26FE

KEEP YOUR EYES ON THE COPY

☐ *When you return the carriage or carrier.*
☐ *When you wonder whether you made an error.*
☐ *When you come to a number or rarely used*
 alphabet letter.

LESSON
31

Directions: *Spacing—1. Line—60. Tab—5.*

Type each line three times; then take 12" sprints on lines 1 and 2 if your major need
is for more speed or on lines 3 and 4 if your major need is for greater accuracy.

1	Indiana is known as the Hoosier State, but do you know why?	12
2	we drove through fort wayne, indianapolis, and terre haute.	12
3	The squads of Wexfork police jumped in to seize everything.	12
4	The kilometer markings: 10 km, 28 km, 39 km, 47 km, 56 km.	12

12" WAM: 25   30   35   40   45   50   55   60

The six projects of Part 9 use as their locale:

Unit 25: New York City, New York State

Unit 26: South Dakota, North Dakota

Unit 27: South Carolina, North Carolina

PART 9

Part 9 is like its predecessors in several ways you will recognize and like:

1. The skill gain expected of you is, as usual, just 1 more word a minute. The goal is now 47 wam for 3 minutes within 1 error and 47 wam for 5 minutes within 2 errors.

2. There are six production projects, as usual, located in different parts of the country—in New York City and New York State, in the Dakotas, in the Carolinas.

3. There is heavy emphasis on correspondence, especially on "how do you say it?" letters,

that is, what to say in a congratulatory letter, a thank-you letter, a get-well-soon letter, and so on. You will continue the language-rules review, too.

4. There are, as usual, six half-period skill drives and two full-period clinics.

5. You will correct all errors in production work unless your teacher directs you to do otherwise.

At the start of each practice period, turn to this page to warm up. Type three copies of one sentence from each group below.

SPEED RECALL	1A Their firm is paid to paint half the signs for those towns.	12
	1B The men may fix their antique auto and go downtown with it.	24
	1C If they pay me for the emblem, I may make it to the social.	36
ALPHABET RECALL	2A Francis and Max proved quite lucky with the big jazz bands.	12
	2B Pam found Vi was right: Jack was being quite lazy and lax.	24
	2C Five wizards jumped very quickly into the box on the stage.	36
NUMBER RECALL	3A Type 1 and 2 and 3 and 4 and 5 and 6 and 7 and 8, 9, or 10.	12
	3B The 10 men lived 28 days at 3947 North Cory Street for $56.	24
	3C The prefix 789 replaces 234, so my new listing is 789-0561.	36
THINKING WHILE TYPING Insert capitals.	4A mr. edward c. jones joined smith & smythe, inc., last june.	12
	4B jo anne invited sue ellen to visit kay at easter in denver.	24
	4C bob and i saw tom scott with my friends mr. and mrs. clark.	36

|1 |2 |3 |4 |5 |6 |7 |8 |9 |10 |11 |12

9

Type each line twice; then repeat lines 5–8 twice more if your major need is for more speed or lines 9–12 if your major need is for greater accuracy.

For speed.

5 return chiefs Little Turtle almost expect Wabash amazed our   12
6 giant steel mills along shore dunes maize labor plant cover   12
7 whom once kept that have come clad grow corn eggs hogs coal   12
8 the for was and two who out are now big one all to, is, or,   12

For accuracy.

9 playground Michigan Tecumseh plateaus excited Indiana major   12
10 industrial scratched bonanza; caverns ancient forests worth   12
11 quarrying factories settlers southern workers factory dairy   12
12 startling including dwindled although Indians dollars saves   12

5-MINUTE TW

13   If the ancient Indians for whom Indiana was named were   12
14 to return (including Tecumseh and Little Turtle, two chiefs   24
15 who almost kept the settlers out), they would be amazed and   36
16 excited by the changes that have come about in their lands.   48

Speed markers are for 5′ TW.

17   The forests have dwindled, of course, although a sixth   60
18 of the state is still clad in trees. The little plots that   72
19 Indians scratched to grow maize are now big farms that pro—   84
20 duce billions of dollars' worth of corn along with the eggs   96
21 and hogs and dairy goods that you expect of farms. The old   108
22 caverns of the southern plateau are still there, of course,   120
23 but the caves in the hills by the Wabash turned out to be a   132
24 coal bonanza; mining is a major thing now, as is quarrying.   144
25   Even more startling to the Indians would be the plants   156
26 and factories that cover the state. More than one—third of   168
27 all the workers in the state labor in a mill, a factory, or   180
28 an industrial plant. What was once an Indian playground in   192
29 the dunes along the Lake Michigan shore now boasts the city   204

■ **5′/3e**

30 of Gary and giant steel mills.   210

|1 |2 |3 |4 |5 |6 |7 |8 |9 |10 |11 |12   SI 1.35N

goal B

■ To produce a ruled table from a revised draft.

JOB 31-1: RULED TABLE

☐ ■ **20′/0e**

Your employer is Miss Phyllis Gold, sales manager of Kester-Armstrong. She greets you and then says: "It's the end of the quarter and time to compare the performances of our branch stores. Please type this for me as a starter." She gives you the draft on the next page.

goal

■ **To experience creative thinking, accurate typing, and cooperation in a work atmosphere.**

☐ *You and a classmate are Typist A and Typist B.*

☐ *You are members of the Planning Committee for the Freedom Insurance Company of Austin, Texas [see page 155].*

☐ *You are to prepare a Certificate of Achievement (for sales over $90,000) and an Honorable Mention Award (for sales over $50,000) to be awarded to the salespersons on page 155. (Note: Sharon Brown's name was left off the list—she sold $53,250 worth of insurance.)*

☐ *Give a copy of all your work to your teacher.*

CREATIVE CO-OP 8: FORMS DESIGN

TYPIST A

You are to prepare the Certificate of Achievement. You are responsible for seeing that Cyrus, Gaston, Mancini, and Stevens receive the appropriate certificates.

1. Inform Typist B, by a note, that you will design the Certificate of Achievement if Typist B will prepare the other one—the Honorable Mention Award.

2. Design the certificate on an 8½" x 11" sheet (turned sideways). Design a border for it and include the following on the certificate: (a) name of the certificate; (b) the name of the company, its city and state; (c) a line on which to type the recipient's name; and (d) an

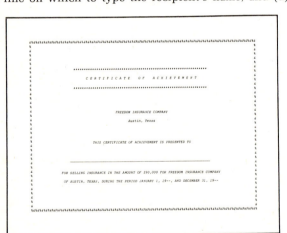

indication that the certificate is awarded for selling $90,000 worth of insurance in the last calendar year.

3. Make four of these certificates. Keep and fill in two of them; send the other two to Typist B. Ask for two Honorable Mention certificates.

4. Complete the other two certificates. Transmit all four to your teacher with a note that tells what they are.

TYPIST B

You are to prepare the Honorable Mention Award. You are responsible for seeing that Allgor, Lopez, Smith, and Brown receive the appropriate certificates.

1. Write to Typist A to say that you will design the Honorable Mention Award if Typist A will design the Certificate of Achievement. Make it a short note.

2. Design the certificate on an 8½" x 11" sheet (turned sideways). Design a border for it and include the following on the certificate: (a) name of the certificate; (b) the name of the company, its city and state; (c) a line on which to type the recipient's name; and (d) an indication that

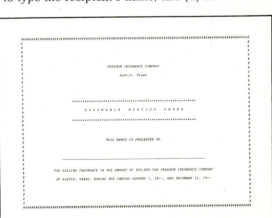

the certificate is awarded for selling $50,000 worth of insurance in the last calendar year.

3. Make four of these certificates. Keep and fill in two of them; send the others to Typist A and ask for two Certificates of Achievement.

4. Complete the other two certificates. Transmit all four to your teacher with a note that tells what the certificates are.

6
26
44
63
71
83
102
117
133
148
162
177
190
208

JOB 31-1: TABLE
Paper sideways

Table 1

ANALYSIS OF SALES PERFORMANCE

<u>Second</u> Quarter of This Year

Considerations	South Bend	Fort Wayne	Terre Haute	New Albany
Sales goal	40,000	50,000	42,500	37,500
Actual sales	36,500	44,000	38,500	36,000
Performance percentage	91.2%	88.0%	90.6%	96.0%
Rank in performance percentage	2	4	3	1
Sales increase over last year	+4,500	+3,500	+4,000	+3,000
Rank in sales increase	1	3	2	4

goal A

■ To produce a ruled table from a revised draft.

JOB 32-1: RULED TABLE

☐ ■ 15′/0e

LESSON **32**

Directions: *Spacing—1. Line—60. Warmup—page 56; then begin Job 32-1.*

"This is the other table I need," says Miss Gold about the table below. "When you have it done, let me know so we can prepare the report that I always have to make to send along with the tables."

Table 2

ANALYSIS OF OPERATIONS

<u>Second</u> Quarter of This Year

Considerations	South Bend	Fort Wayne	Terre Haute	New Albany
Gross income from sales	36,500	44,000	38,500	36,000
Less direct costs and expenses:				
Salary and commissions	13,500	15,000	14,000	16,000
Cost of merchandise sold	10,950	13,200	9,625	10,080
Plant operation	3,000	4,000	3,500	3,500
Advertising and promotion	2,100	3,620	3,675	2,880
Net income	6,950	8,180	7,700	3,540
Earnings rank	3	1	2	4
Net as a percent of gross sales	19.0%	18.6%	20.0%	9.8%
Rank of net percent of sales	2	3	1	4

6
22
40
58
66
79
97
113
120
135
150
166
182
198
211
226
240
258

3 | 31 | 32

REVIEW JOB 1: PAGE OF BID SPECIFICATIONS

Plain paper □ **Spacing 1** □ **Body 2** □ **Top margin 2″**
□ **Line 6″** □ **Tabs 10 and center** □ ■ **15′/0e**

Using the material on page 212 (including lines 1, 7, and 19), type as much as you would on the first page of a set of specifications. Heading:

BID SPECIFICATIONS

For the Construction of a Swimming Pool

On the Property Located at

14 Maple Valley Road

City of Renton

King County

State of Washington

REVIEW JOB 2: PERMIT FORM

Workbook 235 □ ■ **10′/0e**

Using the following information, prepare an application for a building permit for construction of a swimming pool:

This is for Benjamin T. Edwards, 14 Maple Valley Road, Renton, WA 98055. Phone: 830-5155. Lot number is 217 in Block 87N. Faustin Yorke, Jr., is designer; his license number is ArLi 3771 and his phone number is 831-1100. There is no engineer. The contractor is Curtis & Weeber, whose license number is CeLi 0925 and whose phone is 839-9473. The project is a swimming pool; this is described as "30x20 8to2 swimming pool in rear yard (south side of dwelling) with protective chain-link fence." The construction is considered an addition to the residence, worth $5,200.

REVIEW JOB 3: LETTER

Workbook 236 □ **Body 67** □ **SI 1.37N** □ ■ **8′/0e**

Write the following letter to Mr. Edwards for Mr. Yorke's signature.

Enclosed please find the application form for the building permit we must have for building the swimming pool at your home.

Please sign the form on the indicated line at the foot of the page and then return the form to me.

I will see that it is processed so that we can be sure to have the permit before we are ready to start the construction. Cordially yours, [*notations?*]

REVIEW JOB 4: RULED TABLE

Plain paper □ **Spacing 2** □ ■ **10′/0e**

CONSTRUCTION SCHEDULE

Date	Activities	Responsibility
April 15	Obtain building permit	Yorke
May 1	Contract with Curtis & Weeber	Edwards
7	Complete architectural drawings	Yorke
15	Begin excavation	C & W
22	Begin setting up forms	C & W
28	Install and check drains	C & W
31	Pour concrete	C & W
June 6	Set tiles	C & W
13	Test for watertightness	all
16	City occupancy inspection	Edwards
20	Restore landscape	C & W
July 1	Settle all expenses and bills	Edwards

JOB 32-2: BUSINESS REPORT

□ Plain paper □ Review
page 20 □ ■ 15'/0e

SALES REPORT FOR THE SECOND QUAR- 23
TER / Submitted to Members / Of the 52
Executive Committee / By Phyllis Gold / 68
Sales Manager / SALES ARE UP / In the 85
months of April, May, and June our four 94
stores sold $155,000 worth of merchandise, 102
which is 91% of the $170,000 that we 110
had budgeted. The $155,000 is $15,000 117
over the first quarter's sales and $22,500 125
ahead of last year's sales during the same 134
period. We believe we will continue to 142
improve. 144

RESULTS ARE SPOTTY / Some stores did 153
better than others. 157

Table 1 shows that the New Albany store 166
came closer to making budget than did any 174

of the others, while the Fort Wayne store 183
turned in the greatest volume of sales (as 191
it usually does). 195

Table 1 also shows that the South Bend 204
store had the biggest increase in sales over 213
the second quarter last year. It is note- 221
worthy that each of the stores improved 229
over last year. 233

Table 2 shows that the Fort Wayne store 242
returned the greatest amount of profit 249
(again, as usual), but that the Terre Haute 258
store returned the greatest percentage of 267
profit: 20.0%! The South Bend store, with 276
19.0% profit, was a close second. 283

THINGS WE'LL WATCH FOR / 288

1. How to help South Bend increase its 297
volume sharply. 300

2. How to budget Fort Wayne more pre- 308
cisely. 311

3. What Terre Haute does to maintain its 321
remarkable score. 324

4. What New Albany has to do to clear 333
more net profit. 336

JOB 32-3: COMPLETION CARDS

5" x 3" cards or slips □ ■ 5'/0e

ACTIVITIES	20 MIN.	40 MIN.
Warmup, page 56	3'	3'
Pretest (four 1' TWs)	5'	—
Pretest (four 2' TWs)	—	10'
Practice (lines—3)	7'	—
Practice (lines—6)	—	17'
Posttest (repeat Pretest)	5'	10'

CLINIC
6

Directions: *Spacing—1. Line—60. Tab—5.
Warmup—page 56; then begin the Pretest.*

PRETEST

**Weighted with
doubles and down
reaches.**

Take two timings on each paragraph (lines 1–4 and 5–8) and average your scores.
(See schedule.)

```
1     The common ant is small and labors within a scale that   12
2  seems little to most.  To the ant a little seems like a lot   24
3  and three feet a long jaunt.  An average ant is very active   36
4  and packs a vast supply of goods all day and all week long.   48
   |1   |2   |3   |4   |5   |6   |7   |8   |9   |10  |11  |12
```

(Continued on next page)

goals

- To type 46 or more wam for 5' within 2e.
- To produce a page of specifications, a form, a letter, a ruled table.

Directions: Spacing—1. Line—60. Warmup—page 190; then begin the review.

5-MINUTE WRITING

Spacing—2.
Line—60.
Tab—5.
Omit lines 1, 7, 19.

Speed markers are for 5' TW.

GENERAL

2 The requirements of the Department of Building Permits and 13

3 Inspection of the City of Renton are to be fulfilled in all regards, 27

4 including the requirements as to the materials used, the proce- 39

5 dures followed in the construction plan, the provisions for safety, 53

6 adherence to zoning laws, and so on. 60

EXCAVATION

8 The contractor will be responsible for lifting and for conserving 74

9 the topsoil at the place of excavation. He will be responsible for 88

10 removing the dirt that is excavated, and he is to have the dirt 101

11 removed as quietly as possible, with as little disturbance of the 114

12 present lawns as possible. 119

13 When the work is done, the contractor will restore all lawns, 132

14 shrubs, bushes, and soil to their present state. 142

15 The contractor will excavate completely but only as is directed 156

16 in the plan of the architect, no more and no less. Where the 168

17 excavation comes close to the roots of the trees, care will be 181

18 taken to protect them when possible. 188

CONSTRUCTION

20 The contractor will be responsible for the building of all con- 202

21 crete forms, for the installation of drains, for the placement of 215

22 steel rods used for reinforcement, and for the pouring of all of the 228

23 concrete. ■ 230

24 When the concrete has set, the contractor will surface the walls 244

25 and bottom of the pool with permanent tile of the design and 256

26 quality indicated in the plans of the architect. Both drains will be 270

27 capped with screened lids of the design and quality indicated in 283

28 the plans of the architect. These tiles and lids are to be provided 296

29 by the contractor. 300

SI 1.50FH

- 5'/2e

5 Each anthill will have capacity for a full family even 12
6 though it looks like only a pile of loose dirt. It carries 24
7 a group of rooms and tunnels at several levels. Each queen 36
8 soon produces a brood of willing workers to carry out dirt. 48

|1 |2 |3 |4 |5 |6 |7 |8 |9 |10 |11 |12

PRACTICE

Repeat each drill three or six times (see schedule, page 69). Repeat individual lines for a speed gain or repeat groups of lines for an accuracy gain.

For speed.

Accent doubles, de-emphasize adjacent keys.

9   allowing tunnels common supply annual bluff cooks full feel 12
10 attitude connect allied affair school malls books week toll 24
11 attorney billing lesson appeal affect tolls carry seem door 36
12 dropping connect choose proofs canned heels polls cool seem 12
13 commutes calling button billed chills affix calls been nook 24
14 applying channel collar called cannot bells apply book ball 36

|1 |2 |3 |4 |5 |6 |7 |8 |9 |10 |11 |12

For accuracy.

Accent downs, de-emphasize left-hand runs.

15 inquired capable baking avoids scenic above links came pale 12
16 skimmers blanket bottle scheme firmly plant about balk sale 24
17 behavior capital thanks vainly values rices knife wove bank 36
18 chemical knowing valley banana campus coach flank able vain 12
19 capacity schemes caught enable paving candy think acme came 24
20 mailable banking drinks bakery almost above banks main sink 36

POSTTEST

Repeat the Pretest. Score your work and note your improvement.

goal A

■ To prepare a payroll register.

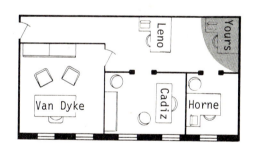

Directions: *Spacing—1. Line—60.*
Warmup—page 56; then begin Job 33-1.

JOB 33-1: PAYROLL REGISTER (FORM)

Workbook 85 □ ■ 20'/0e

In the accounting department of a huge lumber company, Arkansas Big Trees, Inc., you meet the senior accountant, Arthur Van Dyke, and his staff. You are asked to work with Mrs. Annemarie Horne, who is in charge of the payroll operation.

She smiles and says, "You've arrived just in time to help with this week's payroll."

She shows you the draft for a payroll register [top, page 71]

and comments, "This is the register from Shipping, which just got here. Please type it on a clean form [workbook 85] in the style shown by the typing in line 1. Note that it is not

easy to make the figures fit in the small spaces, but you can do it if you control the carriage or carrier with half spacing."

3   33

DEPT. USE ONLY		
APPV'D BY		
ZONING		
FIRE ZONE		
LOT SIZE		
ALLEY		
BLDG SETBACK		
AFFIDAVITS		
FILE WITH		

JOB ADDRESS
3217 Snohomish Street

LEGAL DESCR. LOT 867 BLK 23-C SUBDIVISION OR TRACT Park 90

OWNER'S NAME Eugene A. Lowell PHONE 839-4628

OWNER'S ADDRESS 3217 Snohomish Street Bellevue WA ZIP 98201

ARCHITECT OR DESIGNER Faustin Yorke, Jr. LIC. NO. ArLi 3771 PHONE 831-1100

ENGINEER n/a LIC. NO. PHONE

CONTRACTOR Perkins & Reigel, Inc. LIC. NO. CoLi 0019 PHONE 837-7069

USE OF BUILDING PROPOSED Fireplace in residence EXISTING None

DESCRIBE WORK Fireplace and hearth, interior of dwelling

CLASS OF WORK NEW ☐ ALTERATION ☒ MOVE ☐
ADDITION ☐ DEMOLISH ☐ CHANGE OF OCCUPANCY ☐

VALUATION about $1,400

Do not write below this line; departmental use only.

JOB 96-2: FILL-IN BUILDING PERMIT FORM

Workbook 231 ☐ ■ 10'/0e

Mr. Yorke continues, "Please let me dictate the information for another form we must do."

This application is for Carl F. Stoller, 338 Eighth Street, Bremerton, WA 98310, whose phone is 834-2212. The lot number is 12/43; there is no block number, so the block entry is N/A [*not applicable*]; it is in the Bridge Park subdivision.

I'm the designer, there is no engineer, and the contractor is Cole Bros., whose license number is 2844 and whose phone number is 836-9099.

The job is to build a carport, and the description is "Construct three-pole carport on north side of building with 25' driveway from the street to the carport." This construction is, of course, an addition to the dwelling. The valuation is about $2,500.

JOBS 96-3 AND 96-4: LETTERS

Workbook 233 ☐ ■ 15'/0e

"Now we must get the two owners, Mr. Lowell and Mr. Stoller, to sign the applications for building permits," says Mr. Yorke. "It is not convenient for them to come in to this office."

Mr. Yorke continues, "Well, we will just have to use the

mail. Please compose a letter to each owner for me to sign. Tell him that we are enclosing the application for the building permit, that he is to sign it on the indicated line at the foot of the page, and that we ask him to send the form back to us for processing in his behalf."

The names and addresses are on the forms (96-1 and 96-2).

JOB 96-5: COMPLETION CARDS

5" x 3" cards or slips ☐ ■ 5'/0e

PAYROLL REGISTER

For the Week Beginning **October 9,** 19 __ and Ending **October 15,** 19 __ Paid **October 18,** 19 __

	EMPLOYEE DATA				EARNINGS			DEDUCTIONS					NET PAY		
NO.	NAME	MARITAL STATUS	EXEMP.	HOURS	REGULAR	OVERTIME	TOTAL	INCOME TAX	FICA TAX	INSURANCE PREMIUMS	UNION DUES	OTHER	TOTAL	AMOUNT	CK. NO.
1	Mary Ann Morris	M	4	40	212 00		212 00	20 40	12 40	3 00	2 00		37 80	174 20	
2	Ronald Nelson	M	3	45	160 00	30 00	190 00	19 30	11 12	3 00	2 00		35 42	154 58	
3	Rachel Porter	S	1	42	160 00	12 00	172 00	26 80	10 06	3 00	2 00		41 86	130 14	
4	Andrew Purdom	S	1	40	200 00		200 00	33 50	11 70	3 00	2 00		50 20	149 80	
5	William Rand	M	3	40	200 00		200 00	21 30	11 70	3 00	2 00		38 00	162 00	

Standard payroll register requires careful positioning of figures within the indicated areas.

JOB 33-2: PAYROLL VOUCHER CHECKS

Workbook 86–88 ☐ ■ **20′/0e**

"Next," says Mrs. Horne, "Please type the payroll check for each of the five employees on the payroll register. Number them 1028A, 1028B, and so on. Use October 18 as the 'date paid.'"

The illustration at the right shows how your first check will look. Insert figures carefully.

Most interesting of all forms: a paycheck.

LESSON **34**

Directions: *Spacing—1. Line—60. Warmup—page 56.*

JOB 34-1: TRANSMITTAL NOTES

Workbook 85 ☐ ■ **15′/0e.**

"We have to get these paychecks signed right away," says Mrs. Horne, "so we need to prepare two informal notes: one to accompany the checks to Mr. Van Dyke and tell *him* why they are late; and one for him to use in sending the checks to the man who will sign them, Mr. Carsons, the treasurer. Let's prepare the two memos."

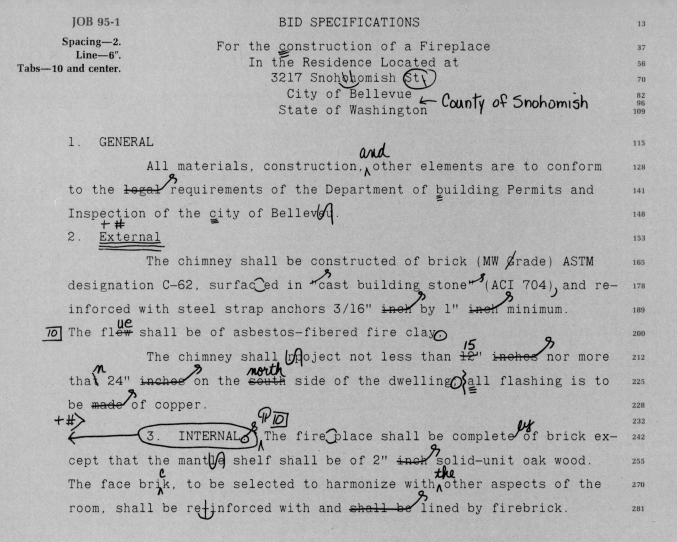

Spacing—2.
Line—6".
Tabs—10 and center.

For the construction of a Fireplace   37
In the Residence Located at   56
3217 Snohomish St   70
City of Bellevue   82
State of Washington   ← *County of Snohomish*   96
   109

1.   GENERAL   115

All materials, construction, *and* other elements are to conform   128

to the ~~legal~~ requirements of the Department of building Permits and   141

Inspection of the city of Bellevue.   148

2.   External   153

The chimney shall be constructed of brick (MW grade) ASTM   165

designation C-62, surfaced in cast building stone (ACI 704), and re-   178

inforced with steel strap anchors 3/16" ~~inch~~ by 1" ~~inch~~ minimum.   189

The flew *ue* shall be of asbestos-fibered fire clay.   200

The chimney shall project not less than ~~12"~~ *15* ~~inches~~ nor more   212

than 24" ~~inches~~ on the ~~south~~ *north* side of the dwelling. all flashing is to   225

be ~~made~~ of copper.   228
   232

3.   INTERNAL   The fireplace shall be complete*ly* of brick ex-   242

cept that the mantle shelf shall be of 2" ~~inch~~ solid-unit oak wood.   255

The face brik, *c* to be selected to harmonize with *the* other aspects of the   270

room, shall be reinforced with and ~~shall be~~ lined by firebrick.   281

JOBS 96-1: FILL-IN FORM

Workbook 229 □ ■ 10'/0e

Mr. Yorke gives you the form at the top of page 211 and says, "Please type this for me. Do not type on the lines; type midway between them."

Directions: *Spacing—1. Line—60.*
Warmup—page 190. Then begin Job 96-1.

Pointing to the tiny guide words, he adds, "Note that the guide words are for the spaces below them, not above them."

Memo 1: To Arthur Van Dyke, Accounting / Here are the last of the payroll checks for the week, ready for Mr. Carsons to sign.

I am sorry that the checks are so late, but we were held up more than a day by Shipping. The payroll clerk in that department is on vacation, and the substitute was ill and therefore absent. I had to have Miss Leno go down there and assemble the necessary data.

I hope that there will be no difficulty in getting the signature. / CH

Memo 2: To Everett T. Carsons, Treasurer / Here are the final payroll checks for the week, ready for your signature.

The unusual delay of one day was caused by the absence of the employee in charge of the Shipping Department's payroll records. It took a bit of doing, but one of our staff went to the rescue.

If you will let us know when you have finished signing the checks, I'll have someone come up to get them and route them to the persons who are waiting for them. / AVD

JOB 34-2: COMPLETION CARDS

5″ x 3″ cards or slips ☐ ■ 5′/0e

JOB 33-1: PAYROLL REGISTER
1. Typed by Priscilla Fontaine
2. Proofread with Audrey Farber
3. This job would have been a lot easier if I had been using an elite typewriter instead of a pica one.

goal B

■ To type 42 wam for 3′/2e.

Directions: Spacing—1. Line—60. Tab—5.

12-SECOND SPRINTS

Four sprints on each sentence.

1 You should know that Arkansas
2 raises more than one million bales of cotton per year. 17
3 produces most of the bauxite that is mined in America. 17
4 is the only state that really has a real diamond mine. 17

12″ WAM: 35 40 45 50 55 60 65 70 75 80 85

3-MINUTE PIECEMEAL PRACTICE

Take ten 1-minute TWs, working on each paragraph until you type it in 1 minute with no errors. Then take a 3-minute writing with a goal of 42 wam with only 2 errors.

Spacing 1 for 1′ timings; spacing 2 for 3′ timing.

Circled figures are 1′ goals.

5 For a long time Arkansas has been a farming state, but 12
6 an exciting program of river improvement, to control floods 24
7 and to provide navigation, has recently caused great growth 36
8 in industry and in employment.① 42

9 Oil has been found in many parts of this big state, so 12 | 54
10 that refining and transporting the oil is now big business. 24 | 66
11 The Ozark Plateau, with mountains and lakes and forests, is 36 | 78
12 host to millions of tourists.② 42 | 84

13 One of the unique things about Arkansas is its thermal 12 | 96
14 springs. There are nearly fifty of them in a cluster, just 24 | 108
15 a few miles from the edge of the Ozarks; they are the heart 36 | 120
16 of a beautiful national park.③ 42 | 126

■ 3′/2e

1 2 3 4 5 6 7 8 9 10 11 12   SI 1.41N

3   34   72

9   northwest electric roaring through zigzags bright river jut   12
10   seaport, twisting erected, islands raging, along about it's   24
11   millions plateaus industry variety mighty cities major, few   36
12   products aircraft research ranges, between other goods name   48

POSTTEST

Repeat the Pretest timed writing, score your work, and note your improvement.

TW SELECTION

Spacing—2.

13   The state of Washington is the northwest corner of the United   13
14   States, and it's a rugged place. Mountains jut into the horizon on   27
15   all sides; roaring rivers dash through deep, jagged gorges and   38
16   coulees; and the sea itself has pushed in deep bays at a dozen   51
17   sites along the rough and ready coast.   60

18   The biggest of the gulfs is Puget Sound, which is full of islands   74
19   and lined with bays and major cities like Tacoma and Seattle and   86
20   Kent, to name a few. Seattle is a seaport, one of the biggest and   99
21   best on the West Coast; and millions of tons of wood products,   112
22   foods, aircraft and missiles, and a wide variety of other goods   125
23   steam out from it each month.   132

24   The rest of the state is full of plateaus and mountain ranges.   145
25   Twisting between them are rivers that race through deep, green   157
26   valleys. The rivers are feeders to the mighty, raging Columbia,   170
27   which zigzags through the middle and along the bottom of the   182
28   state. There are so many rough rivers in the state that about   195
29   ninety dams had to be erected to quell them; as a result there is   208
30   all the electric power one could want for research and industry,   221
31   so the future of Washington is bright.   230

Speed markers are for 5' TW. Circled numbers are 1' goals.

■ 5'/2e

|1 |2 |3 |4 |5 |6 |7 |8 |9 |10 |11 |12 |13 |14   SI 1.37N

goal B

■ To produce a page of specifications.

JOB 95-1: SPECIFICATIONS

Plain paper ☐   ■ 15'/0e

Faustin Yorke, Jr., architect and builder, gives you the revised work on page 210 and says, "Please retype this first page of the specifications for Gene Lowell's fireplace." Then he adds, "I hope you can read all the corrections."

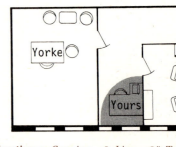

Directions: *Spacing—2. Line—6". Tabs—10 and center. Begin Job 95-1.*

Directions: *Spacing—1. Line—60. Tab—5. Warmup—page 56; then begin the Pretest.*

PRETEST

Type for 5 minutes in a firm effort to type at least 42 wam within 3 errors.

```
 1          Louisiana means romantic things to most people:  Mardi     12
 2     Gras days with dancing in the streets, Dixieland jazz along      24
 3     Canal Street, cotton bales on the levee, fierce pirates and      36
 4     sailing ships lurking in the bayous, and other such dreams.      48
 5     But there is another side, a serious one, to Louisiana too.      60
 6          The state has fertile soil, huge mineral deposits both      72
 7     inland and offshore, as well as so many miles of waterways.      84
 8     From the soil come the nation's biggest crops of cane syrup      96
 9     and sweet potatoes, as well as notable harvests of rice and     108
10     cotton and soybeans and corn.  From the minerals come first     120
11     place in salt and sulphur and second in oil and natural gas     132
12     (much of these from offshore drilling).  From that waterway     144
13     system comes easy transport for people and products, so all     156
14     kinds of industry are attracted to many parts of the state.     168
15          The income of the state is about ten billion dollars a     180
16     year.  Half of this is from minerals alone.  The whole fish     192
17     industry, including those famed shrimp, earns merely half a     204
18     percent of that annual income.                                  210
```

SI 1.44N

Speed counters are for 5' TW. Circled figures are 1' goals.

■ **5'/3e**

PRACTICE ON TW VOCABULARY

Type the designated drills four times each.

Pretest errors	0–1	2–3	4–5	6–+
Drills to type	22–26	21–25	20–24	19–23

Accuracy.

```
19     Louisiana potatoes, products, dancing sailing natural state     12
20     Dixieland transport industry, pirates lurking biggest parts     24
21     thousands drilling) romantic minerals harvest billion kinds     36
22     attracted including deposits soybeans sulphur dollars whole     48
```

Speed.

```
23     things cotton dreams inland second people annual income six     12
24     sweet Mardi bales shore syrup first place famed levee miles     24
25     days jazz also very soil ways rice crop corn salt year fish     36
26     and for the gas all oil any ago are to in is of or if on an     48
```

POSTTEST

Repeat the Pretest. Score your work and note your improvement.

Directions: Spacing—1. Line—60. Tab—5.

1 The beautiful state of Oregon
2   has so many beavers that it is named the Beaver State.   17
3   is the source of all the nickel that America produces.   17
4   enjoys the biggest salmon industry in the whole world.   17

12" WAM: 45   50   55   60   65   70   75   80   85

Take 1-minute timings (maximum, 10) until each paragraph is typed within a minute without error; then copy all three paragraphs within 3 minutes and 1 error.

5   The beautiful state of Oregon, in the northwest corner   12
6   of the nation, has a low range of mountains along the coast   24
7   and a high range about a hundred miles in. Between the two   36
8   is one of the loveliest valleys you will ever see. ①   46

9   The valley is always green because the rain clouds can   12 | 58
10 get over the first mountain range but have to drop the rain   24 | 70
11 to clear the second; showers are therefore frequent, so the 36 | 82
12 state leads the nation in many kinds of produce. ②   46 | 92

13   Oregon ranks first in mint, cranberries, filbert nuts, 12 | 104
14 lily bulbs, and many vegetables. The state has the biggest 24 | 116
15 reserve of standing timber, too, and so many dams for power 36 | 128
16 that processing wood is quite a sizable industry. ③   46 | 138

|1 |2 |3 |4 |5 |6 |7 |8 |9 |10 |11 |12   SI 1.39N

LESSON 95

Directions: Spacing—1. Line—60. Tab—5.
Warmup—page 190.

Take a 5-minute writing on the TW selection on the next page, lines 13–31.

Type two times each the lines indicated in this chart.

Errors in Pretest	0–1	2–3	4–5	6–+
Lines to practice	1–9	2–10	3–11	4–12

1 corner rugged jagged gorges pushed rivers ninety future one   12
2 place dozen sites along rough coast quell gulfs rough major   24
3 want dams that race full rest them wise best each tons bays   36
4 into the all the and the is the of the on the to the in the   48

5 Washington Columbia United States There Coast Kent This Few   12
6 Mountains Twisting Seattle Tacoma Puget Sound West They The   24

7 missiles Seattle between valleys rugged jagged quell, foods   12
8 millions coulees biggest feeders middle bottom goods, green   24

(Continued on next page)

JOB 35-1: RULED TABLE

Plain paper □ ■ 15′/0e

Directions: *Adjust the machine for Job 35-1.*

"I've been told that you are great with tabulations," says William F. Hrudicka, assistant vice president for research and development at The Math Store, Inc. "Well, here is a table for you to get started on." He hands you the handwritten draft shown below.

Average Monthly Operation
The Math Store, Inc.

City	Revenue	Gross Profit	Net Profit
Baton Rouge	$ 42,614	$ 14,728	$ 5,673
Monroe	36,179	10,775	4,851
New Orleans 1	57,025	21,455	8,115
New Orleans 2	52,666	17,673	6,790
Shreveport	40,860	13,280	5,251
Totals	$229,344	$ 77,911	$ 30,680
Percent of Revenue	100.00%	33.97%	13.38%

17
31
45
56
69
80
89
100
111
121
134
144
155
169

JOB 36-1: RULED TABLE

Plain paper □ ■ 15′/0e

LESSON 36

Directions: *Spacing—1. Line—60. Warmup—page 56; then adjust machine for Job 36-1.*

"Thank you," Mr. Hrudicka says as you give him the first table. "Here is another one [top of next page]. My last secretary often had trouble positioning dollar signs. I mention this because they are rather tricky in this table, and I thought I should alert you to them."

Mr. Lowe will arrive late on Monday, 57
March 5; so we ask that his room be 66
held for him. Payment for the room is 74
guaranteed by this company. 79

Please send us a confirmation that we 88
may give to Mr. Lowe for his presenta- 95
tion when he arrives at the Inn. / Thank 105
you for your help. / THE OPENHEARTH 114
and so on. 132

JOB 93-4: RESERVATION LETTER

Workbook 225 □ ■ 10'/0e

"Now," says Miss Hood, "make a
similar request for Dick C. Frame at
the Winema Motor Hotel at 1111
Main Street, Klamath Falls, OR
97601."

JOB 94-1: RESERVATION LETTER

Workbook 227 □ **Body 85 + company
signature** □ **SI 1.38N** □ ■ 5'/0e

Miss Hood says, "Write to the Country Squire Motel, Interstate 5,
Eugene, Oregon 97403, asking for
rooms for both men on Tuesday and
Wednesday. Use the same letter you
used before for the two men." (That
was Job 93-1.)

JOBS 94-2 AND 94-3: SCHEDULES

Plain Paper □ ■ 10'/0e

Giving you the adjacent list, Miss
Hood says, "Here is a summary for
Mr. Lowe. Please type it for him with
a copy for our file. Then type a similar list for Mr. Frame. It will be the
same except for Monday, March 5,
when he is in Klamath Falls."

JOB 94-4: COMPLETION CARDS

5" x 3" cards or slips □ ■ 5'/0e

Directions: *Spacing—1. Line—60.
Warmup—page 190. Then begin Job 94-1.*

RESERVATIONS REQUEST_ED_

For John F. Lowe

March 1	Thursday	
March 2	Friday	_2#_

_1#_ Umatilla Wayside Inn
Interstate 80 North
Pendleton, OR 97801

March 3 Saturday
March 4 Sunday

Sheraton Lodge
Route U.S. 20
Vale, OR 97918

March 5 Monday

The Inn of the seventh Mountain
Cascades Lakes Highway
Bend, OR ~~97918~~ _97701_

March 6 Tuesday
March 7 Wednesday

_1#_ Country Squire Motel
Interstate 5
Eugene, OR 97403

Estimated Monthly Operation
For Five Additional Outlets *

City	Revenue	Gross Profit	Net Profit
Alexandria	$ 36,000	$ 12,200	$ 5,600
Lafayette	20,000	6,800	2,700
Lake Charles	32,000	10,800	4,300
Natchitoches	18,000	6,100	2,400
Ruston	22,000	7,500	2,900
Monthly Totals	$128,000	$ 43,400	$ 17,900
Annual Totals	$1,536,000	$520,800	$214,800

*Constructed from (a) on-site estimates and (b) projection of financial ratios in the present outlets.

18
37
50
61
74
85
96
107
118
127
140
152
164
177
189
197

goal B

■ **To produce a long letter with technical data.**

JOB 36-2: LETTER

Workbook 89 □ ■ 15'/0e

THE MATH STORE, INC.

"Now that you have prepared those two tables for me," says Mr. Hrudicka, "let's prepare the letter they are to be enclosed with":

Mr. Harold T. Benchley / Arke, Benchley, and Young / 721 Winbourne Street / Baton Rouge, LA 70805 / Dear Mr. Benchley: / — 16, 23, 31

I am sorry that the papers I gave you last week did not have all the data you need, and I am pleased to send it now. — 41, 49, 56

To get the data that would help our management decide whether to enlarge our chain of Math Stores, I made a study of the sales and profits in our present stores. The figures appear in the "Average Monthly Operation" table that is enclosed. — 64, 72, 80, 89, 98, 105

Then I visited nine cities in the state. In each I conferred with merchants, viewed — 115, 123

their financial statements, sought advice, and in due time made estimates of what a store ought to be able to sell each month in each town. Five of these were so good they appear in the "Estimated" table also enclosed. — 132, 140, 149, 158, 165, 167

In the second table, I applied to the sales figures the same percents for profit that I found in the study of the present stores: 33.9% of sales for gross profit, 13.97% for net. If the stores are added and my projections hold true, then: — 177, 186, 195, 203, 211, 217

1. Sales will increase 55.81%, to $4,288,000. — 225, 227

2. Gross profits will increase 55.70%, to $1,455,700. — 236, 239

3. Net profits will increase 66.19%, to $512,000. — 247, 249

Please let me know if you need other details or information. / Sincerely yours, / William F. Hrudicka / Research and Development / urs / 2 Enclosures — 258, 268, 280, 285

JOB 36-3: COMPLETION CARDS

5" x 3" cards or slips □ ■ 5'/0e

JOB 35-1: RULED TABLE
1. Typed by Eric Archer
2. Proofread with Stephanie Wise
3. No problems in producing this job.

goal A

■ **To produce two reservations letters within 20'/0e.**

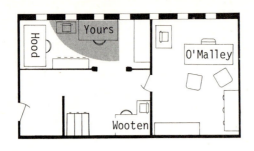

JOB 93-1: RESERVATION LETTER

Workbook 219 □ **Body 85 + company signature** □ **SI 1.38N** □ ■ **10'/0e**

You assist Susan T. Hood in the Sales Department of the Openhearth Corporation. She says, "We must request reservations for two executives who are about to make a fast visit to our offices all over the state."

She dictates:

Reservations Manager / Umatilla Wayside Inn / Interstate 80 North / Pendleton, OR 97801 /   16   23   24

Dear Madam or Sir: Please reserve single rooms for two of our men, Mr. John F. Lowe and Mr. Dick C. Frame, [*note commas with appositives*] for the nights of Thursday and Friday, March 1 and 2 [*note comma in date*].   35   42   48   51   59   ..

The men will arrive late on Thursday, March 1, [*note commas*] and so we ask that their rooms be held for them. Payment for   68   73   82

both rooms is guaranteed by this company.   91

Since each man will be driving his own car, the two will arrive separately. Please send us, therefore, [*commas around interrupting word*] two confirmations—one in the name of each man.   100   109   112   118   122

[*Type the following words as a complimentary closing.*] Thank you for your help. / THE OPENHEARTH CORPORATION / Susan T. Hood / Sales Department / urs / cc Mr. Lowe / cc Mr. Frame   ..   129   137   150   155

JOB 93-2: RESERVATION LETTER

Workbook 221 □ **Body 85 + company signature** □ **SI 1.38N** □ ■ **10'/0e**

Miss Hood continues, "Please type the next reservation letter, making whatever changes are necessary."

Both men want to spend the next two nights, Saturday and Sunday, March 3 and 4, at the Sheraton Lodge on Route U.S. 20 in Vale, Oregon 97918. They will drive separately.

goal B

■ **To produce two reservations letters within 20'/0e.**

JOB 93-3: RESERVATION LETTER

Workbook 223 □ **Body 67 + company signature** □ **SI 1.35N** □ ■ **10'/0e**

"The next night," says Miss Hood, "is Monday, March 5. Mr. Lowe and Mr. Frame will stay in different cities that night."

Reservations Manager / The Inn of the Seventh Mountain / Cascades Lake Highway / Bend, Oregon 97701 / Dear Madam or Sir: /   15   23   30   31

Please reserve a single room for Mr. John F. Lowe for the night of Monday, March 5.   41   49

goals

■ To type at least 42 wam for 5'/3e.
■ To produce a full-page memorandum.
■ To produce a financial statement.
■ To produce two voucher checks.

Directions: *Spacing—1. Line—60.*
Warmup—page 56; then begin the timed writing.

5-MINUTE TW

Spacing—2.
Tab—10.
Line—60.

Speed markers are for 5' TW.

■ 5'/3e

Take a 5-minute writing. Note that paragraphs are to be indented 10 spaces.

```
1        When we finished the meeting at which we reviewed      11
2   plans for the best use of the equipment in the graphic arts  23
3   lab, I promised to summarize the procedures on which we all   35
4   concurred.  This is intended as that summary.  I ask you to   47
5   read and review these comments with thought, so that at our   59
6   next meeting we may amend them as necessary, and then adopt   71
7   them as a basis for a trial run of, say, one or two months.   83
8        First, we said that each department will pick out       94
9   its best typist for this purpose and send him or her to the  106
10  lab for training in the operation of all basic equipment or  118
11  of whatever special machines have in the past been the ones  130
12  most frequently used for the production of that department.  142
13       Second, we said that the lab staff would help out      153
14  when a department has a production job too complex for that  165
15  department's typist.  The department will try to allow four  177
16  or five days for the lab staff to do the work, not that the  189
17  job would require that much time but simply to permit us to  201
18  minimize conflicts by a careful schedule for the equipment.  213
19       I believe that these two points are the ones that      224
20  we resolved at the meeting, and I hope I have expressed the  236
21  two points clearly.  I want to add that I am very grateful,  248
22  indeed, for the cooperative attitude which each of you has.  260
   | 1 | 2 | 3 | 4 | 5 | 6 | 7 | 8 | 9 | 10 | 11 | 12 |   SI 1.35N
```

goal

■ To increase your
mastery in using
quotation marks and
colons.

ACTIVITIES	20 MIN.	40 MIN.
Warmup (page 190)	*3 '*	*3 '*
Drive 1 Pretest	*5 '*	*5 '*
Drive 1 Practice	*7 '*	*7 '*
Drive 1 Posttest	*5 '*	*5 '*
Drive 2 Pretest	*—*	*5 '*
Drive 2 Practice	*—*	*10 '*
Drive 2 Posttest	*—*	*5 '*

Directions: *Spacing—1. Line—60.*
Warmup—page 190.

DRIVE 1

PRETEST 1

**Stressing the
quotation mark.**

Take two 2-minute timings on lines 1–4; proofread both and average the scores.

```
1  The downtown cycle element did "dig" the eighty rock disks.   12
2  The formal gowns may be a "wow" for the visit by the panel.   24
3  The visible signal by the big lake is a "gem" of a problem.   36
4  David said "yes" when we asked him to drive the bus for us.   48
   |1   |2   |3   |4   |5   |6   |7   |8   |9   |10  |11  |12
```

PRACTICE 1

Make four copies of each drill line.

```
5  "the" "hay" "and" "men" "for" "pan" "but" "own" "fix" "may"   12
6  "mat" "vat" "ham" "pat" "tab" "van" "war" "add" "bag" "cab"   24
7  "palm" "past" "load" "leap" "name" "mark" "hot" "sea" "fad"   36
8  "loan" "feel" "bale" "dart" "gaze" "bake" "pal" "act" "cat"   48
```

POSTTEST 1

Repeat the Pretest. Score your work and note your improvement.

DRIVE 2

PRETEST 2

Take two 1-minute timings on lines 9–11 and average the scores. Similarly, take two 1-minute timings on lines 12–14 and average the scores. Compare the two averages.

Stress on right hand.

```
9   It is their opinion that Jimmy will join the union at noon.   12
10  Phyllis knows her pumpkins will soon look like they should.   24
11  Phillip enjoys looking at and collecting only common coins.   36
    |1   |2   |3   |4   |5   |6   |7   |8   |9   |10  |11  |12
```

**Stress on
adjacent keys.**

```
12  Cheri hopes to open her sweater shop after her buying trip.   12
13  Everett was asked to serve as foreman for the jewelry shop.   24
14  An old sailor went to a newer school on a different street.   36
```

PRACTICE 2

Type each line three times; then repeat three more times either lines 15–17 (if you scored lower on lines 9–11 than you did on lines 12–14) or lines 18–20.

Stress on right hand.

```
15  jolly imply phylon minimum million homonym opinion nonunion   12
16  poppy hilly onion pupil pulpy nylon milky phony plump lumpy   24
17  hill pink hook pool moon noon join milk mill upon look junk   36
```

**Stress on
adjacent keys.**

```
18  threw unsaid fireman require superiors therewith assortment   12
19  bonds class clerk forth funds jewel mower poems prior renew   24
20  asks bore dope ends here open mere port rope sash suit pass   36
```

POSTTEST 2

Repeat the Pretest. Score your work and note your improvement.

```
                interoffice memorandum
To  All Department Heads

From  Stewart Kennard

Date  October 10, 19--

Subject  Use of the Graphic Arts Lab
```

Interoffice memo on a printed form.

```
            INTEROFFICE MEMORANDUM

     To       All Department Heads
     From     Stewart Kennard
     Date     October 10, 19--
     Subject  Use of the Graphic Arts Lab
```

Interoffice memo on plain paper.

REVIEW JOB 1: INTEROFFICE MEMORANDUM

Workbook 91 or plain paper ☐ ■ 10'/0e

Type the timed-writing selection on page 76 as an *Interoffice Memorandum* to *All Department Heads*, from *Stewart Kennard*, date with *today's date*, on the subject of *Use of the Graphic Arts Lab*. Use the printed form on Workbook 91 if you have it; otherwise, use plain paper. Use single spacing. Do not indent the paragraphs.

REVIEW JOB 2: FINANCIAL STATEMENT

Plain paper ☐ **Space as shown** ☐ ■ 15'/0e

Center the following statement on a sheet of plain paper turned sideways (you will have 51 lines of space) and with the table spread out to 80 spaces (it is shown here on 78 spaces). Make all the indicated corrections.

Strong Brothers, Inc.

CONSOLIDATED STATEMENT OF OPERATIONS

For ~~Three~~ *Two* Months Ended ~~November~~ *September* 30, 19 —

	Summary, Items	This Year	Last Year
	Net Sales (in thousands of dollars)	$ 30,183	$26,297
	Net earnings (in thousands of dollars)	$ 1,471	$ 1,150
CENTER CHECK →	Ratio of Net Earnings to Sales, adjusted to reflect a stock split paid in the form of a 33 1/3% stock dividend last January	4.9%	4.4%
	Earnings Per Share (in dollars)	$ 0.30	$ 0.23
	Cash Dividends Per Share (in Dollars)	$ 0.30	$ 0.30
	Book Value Per Share (in dollars)	$ 16.28	$ 16.90
	Net Working Capital (in thousands of dollars) ...	$53,289	$54,403
	Current Ratio	6.0/ 1	5.8 / 1

REVIEW JOB 3: VOUCHER CHECKS

Workbook 92 ☐ ■ 5'/0e

Prepare two voucher checks, each for $100 for expenses at the September 12 conference. Address them to (1) Dr. Erna McKenney / 175 Roselawn Avenue / Mt. Lebanon, PA 15128; and (2) Mr. John F. Cooke / 138 Duquesne Road / Munhall, PA 15120.

JOB 92-1: BOXED TABLE

(Continued)

"Each director was asked to indicate a first, second, and third choice. Then I got 'weighted' scores by giving 3 points for a first choice, 2 for a second, and 1 for a third."

He points to the Abilene row.

"Abilene, for example, got 12 firsts (36 points), 19 seconds (38 points), and 12 thirds (12 points) for a total of 86 points."

"What city won?" you ask.

"Looks like Midland," he says, "with 137."

You ask, "I suppose you want the table arranged by the weighted scores? With Midland first, Fort Worth second, and so on?"

"That's a good idea," he says. "Thanks."

You continue, "And with more space, the *standard* space, between columns?"

"Right. Make it attractive!"

VOTE ON CORPORATE HEADQUARTERS LOCATION

City	Mentions			Weighted Score
	1	2	3	
Abilene	12	19	12	86
Amarillo	15	8	12	73
Austin	18	14	28	110
Dallas	22	24	18	134
El Paso	18	21	16	112
Fort Worth	25	20	21	136
Lubbock	9	22	24	95
Midland	31	14	16	137
San Antonio	10	17	13	77
Total	160	160	160	. . .

goal B

■ To arrange and produce an agenda within 15'/0e.

JOB 92-2: AGENDA

Plain paper □ ■ 15'/0e

"I wish my handwriting was clearer," apologizes Mr. Acuna as he gives you the handwritten copy below. "Please type this in whatever is the standard, attractive arrangement—with a couple of horizontal lines to dress it up a bit."

JOB 92-3: COMPLETION CARDS

5" x 3" cards or slips □ ■ 5'/0e

Board of Directors of the — AGENDA Of the Special Meeting of the Pan-Texas Beef Corporation (insert date — first Friday of next month)

1. Report (Minutes) of the Secretary
2. Report of the Treasurer
3. Report of the President
4. Report of the Committee to Select a Site for the New Corporate Headquarters Building
5. Action on Corporate Headquarters Site
6. Report of the Committee on Irrigation of the Six Ranches
7. Action on the Irrigation Proposal
8. Appointments of Nominations Committee
9. Such Other Business as may Come Before the Board of Directors

goal

■ **To experience creative thinking, accurate typing, and cooperation when typing financial statements.**

□ *You and another student typist are Typist North and Typist South, managers of the northern and southern halves of Louisiana Servicom, Inc.*

□ *You are to assemble data for the general manager to use at the next stockholders' meeting. He wants (1) an Income and Expense Report and (2) an Expense Analysis Report combining both halves.*

□ *You and your fellow typist are to create and combine the data and then prepare the reports.*

CREATIVE CO-OP 3: DEVELOPING FINANCIAL TABLES

TYPIST NORTH

1. Without writing in the book, prepare these data for your half of the firm (make up the missing figures to total $43,000 and $14,000):

Income from January sales .... _____
Income from February sales .... _____
Income from March sales .... _____
   Total income **$43,000**

Expenses, insurance .... _____
Expenses, salaries .... _____
Expenses, utilities .... _____
Expenses, miscellaneous .... _____
   Total expenses **$14,000**

2. Type a copy of your data and send it to Typist South, along with a note (1) asking for similar data about Servicom South and (2) saying that you will prepare the Income and Expense Report if Typist South will do the Expense Analysis Report.

3. Combine the northern and southern data; then prepare for Louisiana Servicom, Inc. / Income and Expense Report / For the Quarter Ended March 31, 19--.

Use these guidelines:

a. Double-space the heading lines. Single-space other lines except for blank lines: 2 after the heading, 1 between sections of the report.

b. List the sales income for each month and list each kind of expense.

c. Subtract expenses from sales income to get the Net Income figure.

4. Show all your work to your teacher.

TYPIST SOUTH

1. Without writing in the book, prepare these data for your half of the firm (make up the missing figures to total $26,000 and $8,000):

Income from January sales .... _____
Income from February sales .... _____
Income from March sales .... _____
   Total income **$26,000**

Expenses, insurance .... _____
Expenses, salaries .... _____
Expenses, utilities .... _____
Expenses, miscellaneous .... _____
   Total expenses .... **$ 8,000**

2. Type a copy of your data and send it to Typist North, along with a note (1) asking for similar data about Servicom North and (2) saying that you will prepare the Expense Analysis Report if Typist North will prepare the Income and Expense Report.

3. Combine the northern and southern data; then prepare for Louisiana Servicom, Inc. / Expense Analysis Report / For the Quarter Ended March 31, 19--.

Use these guidelines:

a. Double-space the whole report. Leave 2 blank lines below the 3-line heading.

b. Arrange the data in four columns: Expense Item, North, South, Total. Be sure to double-check your figures, including a total figure for each column, so that the cross totals check at the bottom right.

4. Show all your work to your teacher.

goal B

■ To revise and produce a ruled table in 20'/0e.

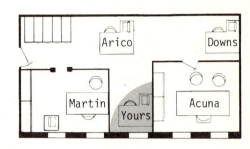

JOB 91-1: RULED TABLE

Plain paper □ ■ **20'/0e**

You work for Antonio Acuna, corporate treasurer for the Pan-Texas Beef Corporation.

"In preparation for a special meeting of the Board of Directors which we will hold in about two weeks," he says, "I'm getting some figures together, and I want you to type them."

Giving you the clipping at the right, he continues, "This is from our last annual report. Please type it, making three changes. First, delete the asterisk in the title and delete the footnote. Second, insert the word 'County' under each of the ranch names—'Culberson County,' 'Hartley County,' and so on. Third, insert the word 'Acres' after each of the quantities, making it '18,000 acres,' '20,000 acres,' '12,500 acres,' '17,500 acres,' and so on."

"That will enlarge the table a good deal," you observe, "both wider and longer."

"Right!" he says. "Just what I want."

	USABLE GRAZING LAND* Of the Pan-Texas Beef Corporation		
Ranch	Before Irrigation	After Irrigation	Increase
No. 1 Culberson	18,000	20,000	11.1%
No. 2 Hartley	12,500	17,600	40.8%
No. 3 Motley	9,800	13,000	32.7%
No. 4 Nolan	24,200	28,700	18.6%
No. 5 Duval	13,000	18,200	40.0%
No. 6 Coryel	13,600	19,500	43.4%
TOTAL	91,100	117,000	28.4%

*Expressed in acres.

goal A

■ To revise and produce a boxed table in 20'/0e.

JOB 92-1: BOXED TABLE

Plain paper □ ■ **20'/0e**

"The next job is a little more complex," says Mr. Acuna as he gives you the table at the top of page 204. "It might be easier to do if you know what it is for. You see, we are going to build a new corporate headquarters building, and we took a vote among the 160 directors to see in which city they preferred the new building to be constructed."

He points at the middle three columns.

(Continued on next page)

8 | **91** **92**

The six projects of Part 4 use the following states as their locale:

Unit 10: Maryland, Delaware, and Washington, D.C.

Unit 11: Iowa, Missouri

Unit 12: California

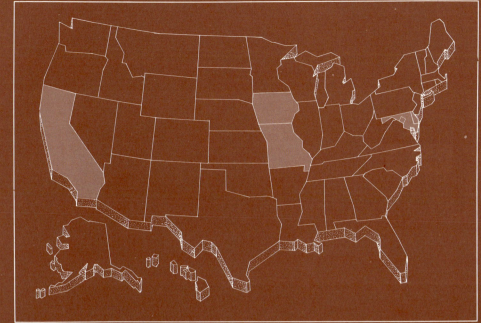

PART 4

Part 4 utilizes the now-familiar pattern of work organization that you used in Part 3:

1. Each unit includes two work-experience projects, separated by two short skill drives and followed by a skill clinic.

2. Each project contains about an hour's business typing, and each is presented in narrative form, so you must pick out the important details, just as you must in an office.

3. Each project occurs in a different location, as indicated in the map above.

Unless your teacher directs otherwise, you are to correct any errors you make in your production assignments (not drills or timed writings). Correct them expertly; make them undetectable.

4. At the start of each practice period, turn to this page and type the Warmup: From each set of sentences below, select one sentence and type it four or more times.

Part 4 is going to be very interesting: You will make arrangements for your employer to take both a short trip and a long one; then you will be introduced to "graphics" typing.

SPEED RECALL	1A It is the duty of the eight men to cut down the right oaks.	12
	1B The chairman of the panel may wish to amend the audit form.	12
	1C She got the land and the eighty oaks, but Bob got the lake.	12
ALPHABET RECALL	2A The expert quickly noted five bad jewels among the zircons.	12
	2B The next question emphasized the growing lack of navy jobs.	12
	2C I was quickly penalized five or six times by the big major.	12
NUMBER RECALL	3A Report Friday on Sections (10), (28), (39), (47), and (56).	12
	3B Use a diagonal, /, when typing 1/0, 2/8, 3/9, 4/7, and 5/6.	12
	3C No. 10 was 28 mm wide, 39 cm long. It weighed 47 kg, 56 g.	12
THINKING WHILE TYPING Edit these lines.	4A martha placed her coat hat muffler and boots in the closet.	13
	4B ann our president ordered paper erasers carbons and rulers.	13
	4C yes the boss mr. hall passed the order to bob the salesman.	13

|1 |2 |3 |4 |5 |6 |7 |8 |9 |10 |11 |12

Directions: *Spacing—1. Line—60. Tab—5.*
Warmup—page 190.

**PRETEST
5-MINUTE
WRITING**

Spacing—2.

1   Texas is so big that it leads all other states in many   12
2 ways and products. In size it is second only to Alaska; it   24
3 is longer north to south and east to west than the distance   36
4 from New York City to Chicago. It has a county the size of   48
5 Connecticut and Rhode Island combined. It is so large that   60
6 it was given the right, when it joined the Union, to divide   72
7 into five separate states if or when it decides to do that.   84
8   Among the products in which Texas is first are cattle,   96
9 sheep, oil, and cotton (which explains why the Cotton Bowl,   108
10 scene of so many great athletic contests, is in Texas), and   120
11 cities--yes, cities: Texas has 11 cities with over 100,000   132
12 people, which (of course) is more than any other state has.   144
13   Texas has known six flags: Spain, France, Mexico, its   156
14 own, Confederacy, and the United States. It is the one and   168
15 only state to have once been a nation, recognized by United   180
16 States and other nations that sent in their ambassadors.   191
17   The name of Texas as a place and a people came from an   203
18 Indian word with the meaning "friends and allies." Spanish   215
19 conquistadors pronounced it Tejas, and this anglicized into   227
20 the name Texas.   230

SI 1.43N

Speed markers are
for 5' TW.
Circled figures are
1' goals.

■ 5'/2e

PRACTICE

Type three times each the lines
indicated in this chart.

Errors in Pretest	0–2	3–5	6–+
Lines to practice	21–26	22–27	23–28

Speed.

21 big all has was oil why yes any six its own and the one for   12
22 name came from that send only have once been more than size   24
23 leads other north south large given right among which means   36

Capitals.

24 United States Rhode Island Confederacy Alaska Texas This It   12
25 New York City Connecticut Cotton Bowl Chicago Texia When In   24

Accuracy.

26 conquistadors distance products combined 100,000 Tejas (11)   12
27 ambassadors (of course) recognized separate contests Mexico   24
28 cities--yes pronounced anglicized athletic whenever Spanish   36

POSTTEST

Repeat the Pretest, score your work and note your improvement.

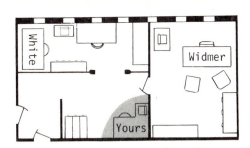

Directions: Spacing—1. Line—60.
Warmup—page 79; then begin Job 37-1.

JOB 37-1: EXPENSE ACCOUNTS

Workbook 95 or plain paper

☐ ■ 15'/0e

"Welcome to the Board of Education!" exclaims Ellen Widmer, supervisor of a bureau at the board. "First off, I want to file expense accounts for a trip I took a week or so ago and for one that my assistant, Gary White, took for us."

1. On October 3, I had these expenses: Taxi to railroad station, 2.60 / Metroliner to New York City, 24.00 / Taxi to hotel, 1.80 / Meals (per bylaws), 12.00 / Hotel (receipt attached), 32.00. Then on October 4, I had these expenses: Meals (per bylaws), 7.00 / Taxi to the New York City railroad station, 1.60. / Metroliner to Baltimore, 24.00 / Taxi from the railroad station, 2.50, totaling 107.50. My address for use in the heading is "Board of Education Building, 3 East 25 Street, Baltimore 21218."

You go to Mr. White's office. "Ms. Widmer said you had a trip expense account you would like me to type for you," you say. "Would you like me to do it now?"

"Fine," he replies. "Let me give you the information":

2. My trip was to Hagerstown, Maryland, where I went to interview someone for the Board of Education. I spent—let me see, here it is—$5.00 for the limousine to the airport. The ticket for the flight was $56—that is, $28 each direction. My meals (per bylaws) were $12.00. I had an entertainment bill of $4.50 for my guest's lunch; he is Dr. James Carlson. I returned to Baltimore the same day, so that's another $28 for the flight. And I took the limousine back from the airport, of course, and that is another $5.00. When you total that, you get $82.50. Oh, my address is right here, the same as Ms. Widmer's address.

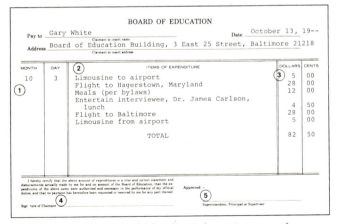

Expense-report form provides heading information, space for ① date of expenditure, ② items paid for, ③ amount of each item, ④ certifying signature of person applying for repayment, and

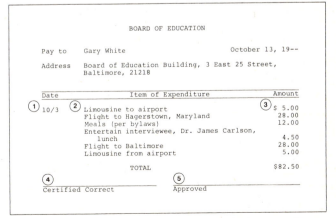

⑤ approval signature by higher authority. Similar forms can be duplicated or, as above, can be typed in an arrangement that parallels the form and looks like an invoice.

JOB 90-1: COVERAGE LETTER
(Continued)

to wait until the State Fire Marshall issues 136
his report; but as soon as we have this, Ms. 145
Rivera will be in touch with you to com- 153
plete the paperwork for your claim. 160

As you are aware you have a $200 de- 168
ductible policy, which means that you will 177
pay only the first $200 of the claim, while 186
Shawnee will cover all the balance. Thank 195
goodness we can help! / Cordially yours, / 204
Rebecca L. Allen / Supervisor of Claims / 216

urs / cc Ms. Rivera and add the following 220
postscript (without the letters "PS"): By the 223
way, you should go ahead at once to con- 231
tact two or more contractors to give you an 240
estimate of the cost of repairing the house. 249
You will need the estimates to reach a 256
settlement with Ms. Rivera. 262

JOB 90-2: COMPLETION CARDS
5" x 3" cards or slips □ ■ 5'/0e

```
JOB 90-1: CLAIMS LETTER
1. Typed by Wilma O'Daugherty
2. Proofread with June O'Brien
3. No problems in producing this job.
```

■ To type 46 or more
wam for 3'/1e.

**12-SECOND
SPRINTS**

Four 12" TWs
per sentence.

Directions: *Spacing—1. Line—60. Tab—5.*
Begin 12-second sprints at once.

```
You should know that Oklahoma
    always seems able to boast about great football teams.   17
    has taken the bison, or buffalo, for its state animal.   17
   .has the wealthiest city per capita in America:  Tulsa.   17
```
12" WAM: 45 50 55 60 65 70 75 80 85

**PRETEST FOR
PIECEMEAL
PRACTICE**

Take a 3-minute writing on this selection. Do your very best to finish it within the 3 minutes, without making more than one error.

**Speed markers are
for 3' TW.
Circled figures are
1' goals.**

```
         1               2               3             4
    Those who live in Oklahoma are proud that the state is    12
      5          6              7              8
rich in the heritage of the American Indian.  Even the name   24
       9            10            11            12
of the state is from Indian words meaning "red people," and   36
        13            14            15 (1)
there are Indian museums all through the state.               46
         16            17            18            19
    Thanks to oil and the quality of the soil, Oklahoma is    58
      20          21            22            23
now one of our wealthy states with lush grazing lands, rich   70
       24            25            26            27
cotton farms, and pulsing oil derricks, all of which mark a   82
        28            29            30      (2)
recovery from the drought years of the Depression.           92
        31            32            33            34
    When the state was opened for settlement back in 1889,   104
       35            36            37            38
about 50,000 lined up, then swarmed in at the exact signal.  116
      39            40            41            42
Some people slipped in sooner; ever since then, Sooners has  128
      43            44            45      46 (3)
been the jocular name for people from this state.            138
|1   |2   |3   |4   |5   |6   |7   |8   |9   |10  |11  |12   SI 1.40N
```

■ 3'/1e

PRACTICE

Take ten 1-minute timings, advancing as you type each paragraph within 1'/0e.

POSTTEST

Repeat the Pretest, score your work, and note your gain over the Pretest.

JOB 37-2: SCHEDULES

Workbook 97 (or type as a table)
□ ■ 20'/0e

SPECIAL EVENTS SCHEDULE FOR _Ellen Widmer_

WEEK OF _September 24-28_

DAY	TIME	EVENT
Monday	9:00 a.m.	Regular monthly meeting of department heads, Room 200.
Wednesday	1:00 p.m.	Philadelphia: NEA committee meeting, Temple.
Thursday	2:30 p.m.	Chair discussion of conflicts between new state and city consumer education outlines, Room 200.
	7:30 p.m.	Attend retirement dinner for Oscar Starer at the Lord Baltimore Hotel.
Friday	10:00 a.m.	Citywide testing conference, Room 200.

Many offices duplicate their own forms, like this schedule sheet, to standardize their procedures.

Mr. White continues, as he looks over his notes and reminders, "Please get one of those Special Events Schedule forms and fill it in for me for the week of November 1–5, as follows":

Tuesday morning at 10:00, Staff conference, Room 115A: State audit of record of supplies used last spring. Afternoon at 2:00, Visit of State Senators Joan Church and Thomas LeJeune: Should we have a citizenship award? 39 52 62 73 84 86

Wednesday at 12:00 noon, Retirement luncheon for Evangeline Foxx at Downtown Holiday Inn. 94 102 107

Thursday morning at 8:15, Arrive Roosevelt High School for special assembly. 116 124

Friday afternoon at 2:30, Attend "individualized instruction" exhibit of new publications, Room 200. Evening at 8:00, Curtain for "My Fair Lady" at Roosevelt High School. 132 143 152 160 161

"Good idea! I have one of those, too," says Ms. Widmer. "Let me dictate it to you":

Monday morning at 10:00, in Washington, D.C., for ACE conference. Afternoon at 2:00, in Washington, D.C. for CB conference. 44 54 62

Wednesday morning at 8:45, Midterm visit to Edmondson High School, / 501 Athol Avenue. Morning at 10:30, Midterm visit to Douglass High School, / 2301 Gwynns Fall Parkway. 70 79 88 98 102

Thursday morning at 8:30, Midterm visit to Forest Park High School, / 4300 Chatham Road. Morning at 10:30, Midterm visit to Dunbar High School, / 1400 Orleans Street. 111 121 130 140

Friday evening at 8:00, Curtain for "My Fair Lady" at Roosevelt High School. 149 156

JOB 38-1: ITINERARIES

Workbook 99 (or type as a table) □ ■ 15'/0e

"I have worked out the details for two trips I have agreed to take in November," says Ms. Widmer, "and I'd like to ask you to type

LESSON

38

Directions: Spacing—1. Line—60. Warmup—page 79; then begin Job 38-1.

them for me, with a carbon for the Superintendent."

"How do you want it arranged?" you ask her.

She finds a recent itinerary and gives it to you [top, next page] to review, then dictates:

JOB 89-3: COVERAGE LETTER

(Continued)

formation that you would like to have. /   146
Cordially yours, / Ray Palotti, Supervisor /   163
Motor Vehicle Division / urs / cc Ms. Rivera   174
/ Oh, please add the following postscript,
but do so without using the usual "PS"
letters—just type the paragraph without the   ..
PS. We will soon have a booklet about   152
teenage drivers, and we will send you a   190
copy when it is available.   195

JOB 89-4: COVERAGE LETTER

Workbook 213 □ Body 117 □ SI 1.61H
□ ■ 10'/0e

"The second letter," says Mr. Palotti,
"is to be arranged like the first one.
Let me dictate it":

Miss Mina M. Neitzke / 3518 Mills Acres /   16
Pawnee, Oklahoma 74058 / Dear Miss   22
Neitzke: /   24

In response to your inquiry about cover-   34
age on your 1977 Kawasaki [*comma?*] the   40
following is provided: [*Now the enumer-*   45
ation.]   ..

1. "A, B Bodily Injury/Property Damage"   54
protects you from claims for injury to other   64
persons or to their personal or real prop-   74
erty.   75

2. "C Collision" protects you from loss as   85
a result of damage to your vehicle from   94
collision.   96

3. "D Comprehensive" protects you from   105
loss to your vehicle from any cause other   115
than collision.   118

4. There are, of course, other coverages   127
that you could obtain if you wish to have   137
them.   138

For any additional details [*need comma?*]   144
please contact Mr. Alex Swantz, our agent   153
in Pawnee. He will be able to give you any   162
information that you would like to have.   170

Cordially yours and so on, just as in the   175
last letter, except there's no postscript.   198

JOB 90-1: COVERAGE LETTER

Workbook 215 □ Body 161 + 39 PS
□ SI 1.36N □ ■ 15'/0e

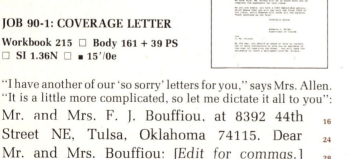

"I have another of our 'so sorry' letters for you," says Mrs. Allen.
"It is a little more complicated, so let me dictate it all to you":
Mr. and Mrs. F. J. Bouffiou, at 8392 44th   16
Street NE, Tulsa, Oklahoma 74115. Dear   24
Mr. and Mrs. Bouffiou: [*Edit for commas.*]   28

When you phoned me this afternoon I   36
was sorry to learn about the fire and smoke   45
damage to your house, but I was glad that   53

Directions: *Spacing—1. Line—60.
Warmup—page 190. Editing—comma after
introductory clause or phrase.*

I could confirm that you are protected by   62
your Shawnee policy.   66

After checking your policy I contacted   75
Ms. Adele Rivera, the claims agent who   83
serves your part of the city. If she is not   92
able to reach you please phone her at   100
272-4501 to make an appointment for her to   109
see the kitchen and photograph the damage.   117
As this is a high dollar loss we are required   127

(Continued on next page)

TRIP 1, Monday, 11/1:   13

    8:58 a.m. Depart Baltimore railroad station.   23

    9:34 a.m. Arrive Washington.   29

    10:00 a.m. Conference at American Coun-   36

cil on Education, 1785 Massachusetts Avenue   46

N.W.   47

    2:00 p.m. Conference on College Boards in   56

third floor auditorium, Union Trust Building,   66

740 15th Street N.W.   70

    5:00 p.m. Depart Washington railroad station.   79

    5:42 p.m. Arrive Baltimore.   85

TRIP 2, Tuesday, 11/9:   99

    10:15 a.m. Depart Baltimore railroad station.   108

    11:12 a.m. Arrive Wilmington, Delaware.   117

    1:30 p.m. Address Delaware Consumers'   124

League on "What Schools Should Do to   132

Create Good Buymanship," Hilton Inn, I-95.   141

    4:06 p.m. Depart Wilmington railroad station.   151

    4:54 p.m. Arrive Baltimore.   157

```
               ITINERARY FOR  Gary White*
    _____

    DAY      DATE     TIME                EVENT
    _____

    Tuesday  10/24  10:15 a.m.   Annapolis:  SACA conference.
                    Night        Annapolis:  Hilton Inn, St. Mary's Street.

    Wednesday 10/25  1:30 p.m.   Cambridge:  Dorchester County conference.
                    7:30 p.m.    Ocean City:  Worcester County conference.
                    Night        Ocean City:  Harrison Hall Hotel, Board-
                                 walk.

    Thursday 10/26  1:15 p.m.    Dover:  Kent County conference at Quality
                                 Inn South, 222 South Du Pont Highway.
                    8:00 p.m.    Wilmington:  New Castle County conference
                                 at Hotel du Pont, 11th and Market Streets.
                    Night        Hotel du Pont, 11th and Market Streets.

    Friday   10/27  1:00 p.m.    Return to Board of Education office.


    *Road map attached.
```

Itinerary tells exactly when a traveler will be where.

JOB 38-2: COMPLETION CARDS

5″ x 3″ cards or slips ☐ ■ 5′/0e

```
JOB 38-1: ITINERARIES

1. Typed by Alicia McMahon.

2. Proofread with Carrie Taule.

3. It was hard to set up the tab stops
   and type the columns so that all of
   the column heads were centered over
   their columns.
```

---

goal B

■ **To type at least 43 wam for 3′/2e.**

3-MINUTE PIECEMEAL PRACTICE

Routine:
Ten 1′ TWs.
One 3′ TW.

Circled numbers
are 1′ TW goals.

■ 3′/2e

Directions: Spacing—1. Line—60. Tab—5.

Read the copy and practice any words that look difficult. Then use these three paragraphs for Piecemeal Practice as described on page 41.

1 Delaware is a small state. It has the least number of		12
2 citizens and the second smallest extent of land, but it has		24
3 more historical sites and shrines per square mile than does		36
4 any other. It is a living museum. ①		43
5 Delaware is in between the Chesapeake Bay and Delaware	12	55
6 Bay at the top of the Delmarva Peninsula. It has farms and	24	67
7 plants and fishing fleets. It has a huge tourist trade for	36	79
8 its racetracks and sandy beaches. ②	43	86
9 The state is quite a center for finance. It has head-	12	98
10 quarters for a lot of national firms. It also has a lot of	24	110
11 banks. The major field of good jobs is the chemical field,	36	122
12 but food canning is also big time. ③	43	129

|₁ |₂ |₃ |₄ |₅ |₆ |₇ |₈ |₉ |₁₀ |₁₁ |₁₂   SI 1.38N

④ **38**   82

JOB 89-1: CLAIMS LETTER

This letter is to Mr. David P. Bennett / 3218 East Pine Street / Tulsa, OK 74110 / Dear Mr. Bennett: /

When you phoned me last night, [*comma after introductory clause*] I was sorry to learn about the smoke damage to your kitchen, but I was glad that I could confirm that you are protected by your Shawnee policy.

After checking your policy, [*comma after introductory adverbial phrase*] I contacted Ms. Adele Rivera, the claims agent who serves your part of the city. If she is not able to reach you, please phone her at 272-4501 to make an appointment for her to see the kitchen and complete the paperwork for your claim. She knows about the fire, of course.

As you are aware, [*comma after introductory clause*] you have a $100 deductible policy, which means that you will pay only the first $100 of the claim, while Shawnee will cover all the balance. Thank goodness we can help!

Cordially yours, / Rebecca L. Allen / Supervisor of Claims / urs / cc Ms. Rivera

JOB 89-2: CLAIMS LETTER

☐ Workbook 209 ☐ Body 129 + PS 30 ☐ SI 1.40N ☐ ■ 10'/0e

"I have another letter so much like that one," says Mrs. Allen, "that you can copy it and just make substitutions."

This letter is to Mrs. Nadine L. Logan, of 6915 Lapeer Road in Sapulpa, Oklahoma, ZIP 74066. She had a water pipe break this morning, so the problem is water damage instead of smoke.

The claims agent is Mr. Leslie V. Prince, whose phone number is 488-2324. He has to see the water damage, of course.

The policy is a $50 deductible, not $100, so Mrs. Logan will pay only the first $50 of the claim; Shawnee pays the balance.

Oh, let me add a postscript: As you requested, [*comma after introductory "as" clause*] I checked to see whether your policy would also cover the plumber's bill. I am sorry to tell you that it does not, only the damage.

JOB 89-3: COVERAGE LETTER

☐ Workbook 211 ☐ Body 96 + PS 20 ☐ SI 1.54FH ☐ ■ 10'/0e

"And now," says Mr. Palotti, "I have two letters about coverage to be answered."

The first is to Mr. R. A. Schauland, of 6832 Clinton Road, Tulsa, Oklahoma 74113. Dear Mr. Schauland: In response to your inquiry about coverage on your cars and motorboat,

[*comma after long introductory phrase*] the following is provided: [*Arrange these four numbered paragraphs as an enumeration.*]

1. Drivers with reckless or drunk-driving records are not insured by Shawnee.

2. Premiums can be spread through the year.

3. Rates are lower for teenagers who have successfully passed a driver-education program.

4. Shawnee takes pride in the speed with which it settles all claims.

For any additional details, [*comma after introductory phrase*] please contact Ms. Adele Rivera, our agent in your part of the city. She will be able to give you any in-

(Continued on next page)

3-MINUTE TW

Spacing—2.
Line—60.
Tab—5.

Speed markers
are for 3' TWs.

■ 3'/2e

1   Maryland is in two halves separated by Chesapeake Bay.   12
2 The outer half is on the Delmarva Peninsula, where it wraps   24
3 around Delaware and links Maryland to the ocean.   The inner   36
4 half wraps around three sides of the city of Washington and   48
5 stretches south and west, a giant wedge upon its neighbors.   60
6   Nearly half the people in Maryland are in two sections   72
7 that are forty miles apart.   One of these is Baltimore; the   84
8 other is the net of towns that surround Washington and pro-   96
9 vide homes for those who work in the Capital: College Park   108
10 and Silver Spring and Chevy Chase, for examples.   The whole   120
11 section is built up, Baltimore to Washington. ■   129
12   There are a lot of truck gardens in Maryland, but get-   141
13 ting crabs and oysters and fish out of the bay has proved a   153
14 bigger business than farming.   Half the state is covered in   165
15 forests, so lumber is good business, too.   The leading min-   177
16 eral is cement, which is a good thing: this state has more   189
17 miles of concrete highways than others twice its size.   200

|1 |2 |3 |4 |5 |6 |7 |8 |9 |10 |11 |12   SI 1.41N

5-MINUTE TW

Spacing—2.
Line—60.
Tab—5.

Speed markers
are for 5' TWs.

■ 5'/3e

18   Washington was the first capital in the world that was   12 | 212
19 planned before it was built.   Most capitals are a result of   24 | 224
20 chance, but not Washington.   It was planned in detail, then   36 | 236
21 built to its design: streets that radiate like spokes of a   48 | 248
22 wheel from certain key locations, huge buildings with green   60 | 260
23 lawns, graceful monuments to people and events, parks large   72 | 272
24 and small, big trees and broad streets, elegance all about.   84 | 284
25   The original District of Columbia was ten miles square   96 | 296
26 and stood on both sides of the Potomac River, carved partly   108 | 308
27 from Maryland and partly from Virginia.   Fifty years later,   120 | 320
28 the Virginia part, about a third of the District, was ceded   132 | 332
29 back to the state, leaving Washington with 68 square miles.   144 | 344
30   The city, which is ninth in size in the United States,   156 | 356
31 is dominated by three structures—the Capitol building, the   168 | 368
32 Washington Monument, and the White House.   The White House,   180 | 380
33 you might not know, was not always white; after the British   192 | 392
34 burned it in 1814, it was painted white to cover the scorch   204 | 404
35 marks and has been called the White House ever since.   215 | 415

|1 |2 |3 |4 |5 |6 |7 |8 |9 |10 |11 |12   SI 1.41N

Are "proximates" or "left-handers" harder for you? To find out, take two or three 1-minute timings on lines 1–3. Average the scores; then do the same on lines 4–6.

Proximates.
1 Walt knows a final printing goes to press in a few minutes. 12
2 The banks have been very fine in presiding over five cases. 24
3 Those five timber claims have been given very high reviews. 36
|1 |2 |3 |4 |5 |6 |7 |8 |9 |10 |11 |12

Left-Handers.
4 Edward was aware of the wasted gas and deferred extra fees. 12
5 Margaret agreed to trade places at that next water contest. 24
6 Everett agreed to save the cabbage to serve to their staff. 36

PRACTICE

Type drills for harder motions three to six times each; type the others two to four times each.

Proximates.
7 apple being child files climb grief drill lakes light makes 12
8 wise slip rise nail lose mild hose bent aims dues file give 24
9 word uses till wife thin sent ship rose plea pail obey nine 36
10 ail his cry bin aim dry gem fin jaw him ill leg mid peg use 48
|1 |2 |3 |4 |5 |6 |7 |8 |9 |10 |11 |12

Left-Handers.
11 treat severe dresses cabbage afterward addressee exaggerate 12
12 trade tweed wears agreed career starts assets awards better 24
13 cares carts darts deeds fares grade grass great reads staff 36
14 tree area bags read bass rare cars were data vast east fast 48

POSTTEST

Repeat the Pretest completely. Score your work as before and note your improvement.

goal A

■ **To produce two routine letters within 20'/0e.**

UNIT 23

LESSON 89

Directions: *Spacing—1. Line—60. Warmup—page 190. Editing—comma after introductory clause or phrase.*

JOB 89-1: CLAIMS LETTER

Workbook 207 ☐ Body 127 ☐ SI 1.37N ☐ ■ 10'/0e

You work in the Tulsa office of the Shawnee Insurance Company as aide to Rebecca L. Allen, supervisor of claims, and Ray Palotti, sales supervisor in Shawnee's Motor Vehicles Division.

Shawnee uses the standard letter arrangement with one slight change and two special requirements. The change: position the date so it ends at the right margin (pivot it). The requirements: always use "Cordially yours" as the complimentary closing and always make a cc for the agent, if one is named in the letter.

"My first letter for you," says Mrs. Allen, "is one of the 'we are sorry' letters we send to someone who has experienced some sort of disaster that will lead to a claim for reimbursement."

(Continued on next page)

goal A

■ To type at least 43 wam for 5'/3e.

Directions: *Spacing—1. Line—60. Warmup—page 79; then begin below.*

PRETEST

Take a 5-minute writing on lines 18–35, page 83. Goal: 43 wam/5'/3e.

PRACTICE ON TW VOCABULARY

Type, four times each, the drill lines indicated in this guide table.

Pretest errors	0–2	3–4	5–6	7–+
Type lines	4–8	3–7	2–6	1–5

For accuracy.

1 first fifty third ninth three tenth state city four 1814 68   12
2 structures dominated graceful elegance painted street marks   12
3 Washington Monuments District Columbia Capitol United River   12
4 locations, building, design: details, events, white; part,   12

For speed.

5 small trees large parks green lawns built wheel since world   12
6 ever know city size back from both huge like that then been   12
7 was the are its key and gib all ten not has for if it or to   12
8 in the|it was|of the|to its|was the|but not|was ten|and the   12

POSTTEST

Repeat the Pretest. Score your work and note your improvement.

goal B

■ To produce a business trip report.

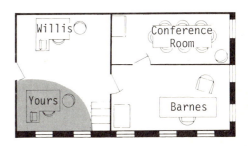

Directions: *Adjust machine for Job 39-1.*

JOB 39-1: TRIP REPORT

Spacing 1 □ ■ **15'/0e**

Your employer is J. Blake Barnes, regional manager for Qwik-Key Calculators.

"I recently took a trip to Washington," he tells you, "and I want to turn in my report to the home office. Last night I drafted it."

He gives you the report on page 85.

"Please type this for me," he says. "I will need an original to mail in and three carbon copies—one for the file and one for each of the two men I traveled with."

JOB 39-2: INFORMAL NOTE

5" x 3" card □ ■ **5'/0e**

Mr. Barnes continues, "When you finish the report, please attach an ordinary 5 by 3 card to it with this message":

Bob Jorgensen: Please do <u>something</u> about the ads and mailings on the T7. It is a shame to neglect that wonderful calculator.

goal B

▪ To produce a ruled table within 15′/0e.

JOB 88-2: RULED TABLE

Plain paper, turned sideways for pica typewriter ☐ ▪ 15′/0e

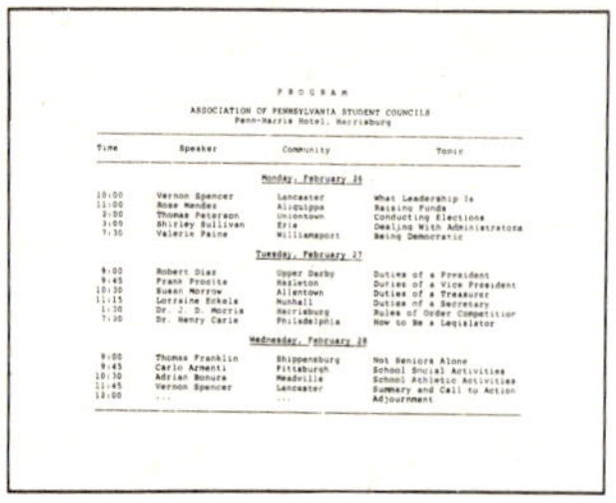

"If you'll type just one more table for me," says Dr. Morris, "we'll be caught up with the conference details."

The ruled lines enclose the important listed information and hold the table together.

JOB 88-3: COMPLETION CARDS

5″ x 3″ cards or slips of paper ☐ ▪ 5′/0e

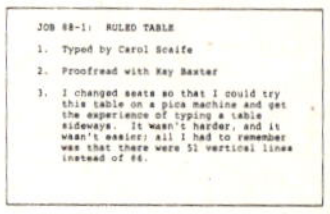

P R O G R A M 10

ASSOCIATION OF PENNSYLVANIA STUDENT COUNCILS 40

Penn-Harris Hotel, Harrisburg 59

center column headings

Time	Speaker	Community	Topic	91
		Monday, February 26		131
10:00	Vernon Spencer	Lancaster	What Leadership Is	145
11:00	*Rose Mendez*	*Aliquippa*	Raising Funds	156
2:00	Thomas Peterson	Uniontown	Conducting Elections	169
3:00	Shirley Sullivan	Erie	Dealing with Administrators	182
7:30	*Valerie Paine*	*Williamsport*	*Being Democratic*	195
		Tuesday, February 27		218
9:00	Robert Diaz	Upper Darby	Duties of a President	232
9:45	*Frank Procita*	*Hazleton*	Duties of a Vice President	245
10:30	*Susan Morrow*	*Allentown*	Duties of a Treasurer	258
11:15	Lorraine Eckels	Munhall	Duties of a Secretary	271
1:30	*Dr.* J. D. Morris	Harrisburg	Rules of Order Competition	285
7:30	Dr. Henry Carle	Philadelphia	How to Be a legislator	299
	center Wednesday, February 28			324
9:00	Thomas Franklin	Shippensburg	*Not Seniors Alone*	338
9:45	Carlo Armenti	Pittsburgh	School Social Activities	352
10:30	*Adrian Bonura*	*Meadville*	School Athletic Activities	366
11:45	Vernon Spencer	Lancaster	Summary and Call to Action	384
12:00	—	—	Adjournment	391

410

goal

▪ To find which of two motions is harder, then to practice them both proportionately to increase your skill.

ACTIVITIES	20 MIN.	40 MIN.
Warmup, page 190	3′	5′
4 Pretest 1-minute TWs	5′	—
6 Pretest 1-minute TWs	—	10′
Practice drills 3 times	7′	—
Practice drills 6 times	—	15′
Repeat Pretest	5′	10′

CLINIC 15

Directions: *Spacing—1. Line—60. Warmup—page 190.*

FIELD TRIP IN WASHINGTON AREA   30

Purposes   33

The purposes of this swing through Washington, Arlington, and Alexandria   46
were (1) to help the two new men and (2) to get a feel for   61
customer reaction to our new T7 calculator.   70

WASHINGTON   73

Joel Cass and I went to these dealers on Monday and Tuesday: 85

      Foster-Karamian, Inc., F Street N.W.   95
      George Steele Sons, K Street N.W.   103
      Winkler and Wessels, 12th Street N.W.   119

      Jayne Johnson Co.; New York Avenue

All four have done business with us before and were interested   133
in reviewing the whole line. Unfortunately none knew anything about   146
the T7—had not received our flyer or seen any of our ads. As   158
expected, they were not impressed with my one working model.   170

ARLINGTON AND ALEXANDRIA   176

Bill Swan took me to four dealers on Wednesday and Thursday: 190

      Highlands Business Machines, Arlington   200
      Kraddock Specialty, Alexandria   212
      John Monk and Son, Inc., Arlington   220
      Rosemont Business Machines, Alexandria   229

Our reception was similar to what I had found in Washington—   242
much interest in HAND CALCULATORS, little interest in the T7.   255

THE NEW MEN   258

Joel and Bill are very fine men and should do well.   270
Both are skilled in using our machines. They can demonstrate them   283
and talk about them with that calm confidence that we like.   296

The New T7 Calculator   301

If our Promotion Depart-   307
ment does not get information about T7 to our dealers within   318
two weeks, we can forget about doing any Christmas business this year.   333

                           _____   343

                          J. Blake Barnes   349

November 3, 19--   352

(Continued)

use to sign in for the conference. Here (*below*) is one from last year. It was all right, but crowded. Redesign it, please, and type a master copy with three forms to the page. We had four last time—that's why it was crowded.''

You note that a third of a page would be 22 lines.

NAME Marmo, Lynn T.

HOME ADDRESS 93 River Street

Easton, PA 18042

HOME TELEPHONE (215) 859-1957

GRADUATION MONTH, YEAR June, 1977

SCHOOL Easton High School

SCHOOL ADDRESS 25th at William Penn

Easton, PA 18042

SCHOOL TELEPHONE (215) 258-4321

POSITION Member

---

goal A

■ To produce a ruled table from a draft.

JOB 88-1: RULED TABLE

Plain paper, turned sideways for pica typewriter □ ■ 20'/0e

LESSON 88

Directions: *Spacing—1. Line—60. Warmup—page 190. Then adjust your machine for Job 88-1.*

''Next,'' says Dr. Morris, ''here is a list of the audiovisual equipment our speakers will need, along with the names of the high schools that are going to send the equipment for our use.'' Remember to turn the paper sideways.

AUDIOVISUAL SCHEDULE
ASSOCIATION OF PENNSYLVANIA STUDENT COUNCILS
Penn-Harris Hotel, Harrisburg

Day	Speaker	Equipment Needed	High School Providing	
Monday	Vernon Spencer	Tape Recorder	Steelton	160
Monday	Rose Mendez	16 mm Movie Projector	Hershey	173
Monday	Shirley Sullivan	Overhead Projector	Palmyra	187
Tuesday	Frank Procita	Cassette Player	Marysville	200
Tuesday	Lorraine Eckels	Overhead Projector	Palmyra	213
Wednesday	Adrian Bonura	Video Tape Recorder	Mechanicsburg	228
		and Slide Projector	Duncannon	236
Wednesday	Vernon Spencer	Overhead Projector	Palmyra	250

26
55
75
115
127

Directions: *Spacing—1. Line—60.
Warmup—page 79; then begin Job 40-1.*

JOB 40-1: TWO LETTERS

Workbook 101–104 □ Body 151
□ SI 1.43N □ ■ 20′/0e

"Thank you," says Mr. Barnes when you finish the report.
"Now I must write to Joel and Bill":

Mr. Joel F. Cass, Jr. / 213 Tenley House /   16
5700 Connecticut Avenue, NW / Washing-   23
ton, DC 20015 /   26

Dear Joel: / I was delighted to be with   34
you last week, and I want to thank you for   44
meeting me at the station, hauling me   51
around, and in general looking after me.   59

I hope the experience of calling on your   68
customers with me was helpful to you and   76
that you were truly impressed with the high   85
degree of respect with which they treat our   94
machines. Our product line is a fine one,   102
and your customers seem to know it.   110

When I was with you, I promised to send   119
you the names and addresses of "principal   127
customers" (ones who purchased at least   135
$7,500 from us last year) in your territory.   144
Well, the list is enclosed. These firms   153
account for about half your total business   161
and merit a visit at least once each two   170
months.   171

Our annual sales meeting will be in   180
February. I hope to spend a couple more   188
days with you before then. / Cordially   198
yours, / J. Blake Barnes / District Manager /   210
URS / Enclosure   214

"I want to send the same letter to Bill Swan," says Mr. Barnes.
"It will need two changes. Do you know what the changes are?"

"Well," you say, "one change would be the salutation—it
would be 'Dear Bill' instead of 'Dear Joel.' What is the other
change?"

"Good for you!" he says, "The other: he met me at the hotel,
not the station. His address":

Mr. William L. Swan / Apartment 317 / 288
South Kent Street / Arlington, VA 22202

PRINCIPAL CUSTOMERS	Page 13

WASHINGTON DISTRICT (J. Blake Barnes, Mgr.)

Firm	Amount
Blumenthal, Inc.; 1800 River Road; Green Acres, MD	$11,600
Davis and Young, Inc.; 1870 East Capitol Street; Washington, DC	14,300
Everett Ellis and Sons; 975 Mill-ville Road; Bethany Beach, DL	14,100
Foster-Karamian, Inc.; 1250 F Street N.W.; Washington, DC	12,500
Gordon Business Machines; 67 Frank Street; Baltimore, MD	13,800
Highlands Business Machines; 90 Highland Avenue; Arlington, VA	9,000
Jayne Johnson Co.; 750 New York Avenue; Washington, DC	12,700
Kraddock Specialty; 19 Quaker Lane; Alexandria, VA	15,200
Leslie and Lewis Co.; 1120 Chewold Avenue; Smyrna, DL	14,100
McCord and Klein Inc.; 861 Jefferson Street; Hyattsville, MD	12,800
John Monk and Son, Inc.; 377 Madison Street; Arlington, VA	11,600
North Shore Business Machines; 711 34th Street N.W.; Washington, DC	9,500
Rosemont Business Machines; 16 Hume Street; Alexandria, VA	10,800
George Steele Sons; 1575 K Street N.W.; Washington, DC	11,500
Thomas Brothers, Inc.; 1475 Monroe Street; Alexandria, VA	10,600
Victory Business Machines; 700 Pershing Drive; Arlington, VA	14,200
Winkler and Wessels; 371 12th Street N.W.; Washington, DC	16,700
Wylie Brothers, Inc.; 265 Leland Street; Bethesda, MD	14,100
ZZZ Business Machines; 707 Duke Street; Alexandria, VA	8,900

Speed markers are
for 5' TW.
Circled figures are
1' goals.

1 Pennsylvania is and has always been an important force 12

2 in our national destiny, from colonial days to the present. 24

3 The state became known as the Keystone State, since it 36

4 held the central or keystone position in the first thirteen 48

5 colonies. Its major town, Philadelphia, was the site where 60

6 our founding fathers began the dangerous fight for freedom. 72

7 That same city is, today, the fourth largest in the nation. 84

8 In fact, the whole state is a giant in almost anything 96

9 you name. It makes more steel than any other state. Farms 108

10 rank in the top third or fourth for hay, barley, corn, rye, 120

11 oats, and food for the table. Mining is equally high--this 132

12 state produces almost all the hard coal there is, plus much 144

13 of the soft coal as well. And this is the state, remember, 156

14 where oil was discovered and the first oil derricks set up. 168

15 Industrial center or not, Pennsylvania is also a giant 180

16 in the tourist trade. Millions come to visit Valley Forge, 192

17 Gettysburg, Independence Hall, and other shrines. 202

18 And one cannot speak of this state without bringing up 214

19 the fact that it is where they always have many of the very 226

20 best sports teams. 230

|1 |2 |3 |4 |5 |6 |7 |8 |9 |10 |11 |12   SI 1.42N

■ 5'/2e

goal B

■ To design and
produce a registration
form.

JOB 87-1: ORIGINAL FORM

Plain paper □ ■ 20'/0e

You work for Dr. J. D. Morris, in the state's Department of Education, Harrisburg. "We are cooperating with the Association of Pennsylvania Student Councils in conducting a leadership conference," she tells you, "and 'cooperating' means

Directions: *Adjust your typewriter for Job 87-1 and then begin it.*

that we are taking care of a lot of the technical details. For example, we need a duplicated form that each person can

(Continued on next page)

JOB 40-2: TWO OPEN TABLES

Plain paper □ ■ 15′/0e

"Now we have to prepare those names and addresses," says Mr. Barnes. He gives you the listing shown on page 86.

"This is a confidential list of the best customers in my district," he explains. "Please go down the list for customers in Joel's territory: the 'DCs.' Copy (1) their names and (2) street addresses. Then for Bill copy the (1) names, (2) street addresses, and (3) cities of the principal customers in *his* territory, the state of Virginia: the 'VAs.' Oh, show the sales figures too."

JOB 40-3: COMPLETION CARDS

5″ x 3″ cards □ ■ 5′/0e

goal

■ To use intensive drill to improve basic skill.

ACTIVITIES	20 MIN.	40 MIN.
Warmup, page 79	3′	3′
Drive 1 Pretest	4′	4′
Drive 1 Practice	9′	9′
Drive 1 Posttest	4′	4′
Drive 2 Pretest	—	5′
Drive 2 Practice	—	10′
Drive 2 Posttest	—	5′

CLINIC

Directions: Spacing—1. Line—60. Warmup—page 79; then begin Drive 1.

DRIVE 1

PRETEST 1

Take two 1-minute timings on lines 1–4. Proofread both; then average the scores.

Left-hand runs, no double letters.

1 Stewart deserves to get a big reward after saving the girl. 12
2 Seven bears rested at the water's edge after the hard swim. 24
3 Barbara wore a dark red sweater to the fair in Texas today. 36
4 Edward said the test was extra hard and feared the results. 48
|₁ |₂ |₃ |₄ |₅ |₆ |₇ |₈ |₉ |₁₀ |₁₁ |₁₂

PRACTICE 1

Make four copies. If you averaged two or fewer Pretest errors, repeat individual lines for speed gain; otherwise, repeat each block of lines for accuracy gain.

Left-hand runs, no double letters.

5 afterwards beverages greatest started drafts cards west act 12
6 decreased rewarded erasers created acreage serve gates read 12
7 after areas eager brave fever aware grave seats state tract 12

8 wears weave stage fewer great saved tests verbs waste texts 12
9 safe fact verb grew ward star text rare acre base dear eats 12
10 wet tax cat ear are bar bet war tea wax dad ads bed age sad 12

POSTTEST 1

Repeat the Pretest. Score your work and note your improvement.

1 The small state of New Jersey
2   is only 46th in size of area but is 8th in population. 17
3   stands out first in railroad trackage per square mile. 17
4   is first in miles of highways per square mile of area. 17

12" WAM:
45 50 55 60 65 70 75 80 85

**3-MINUTE SKILL
BLITZ**

To achieve the 46 wam/3'/1e goal, take a 3-minute writing, practice any portions
that were troublesome, and then repeat the 3-minute writing.

5   The small size of New Jersey makes it quite easy to go 12
6   The small size of New Jersey makes it quite easy to go 24

Circled figures are
1' goals.

7   The small size of New Jersey makes it quite easy to go 36
8 all over it. You can drive across it, east to west, in two ① 48
9 all over it. You can drive across it, east to west, in two 60
10 all over it. You can drive across it, east to west, in two 72

11 hours or less, and you can drive from top to bottom in less 84
12 hours or less, and you can drive from top ② to bottom in less 96
13 hours or less, and you can drive from top to bottom in less 108

14 than four hours, all of it a most exciting drive. 118
15 than four hours, all of it a most exciting drive. 128

■ 3'/1e

16 than four hours, all of it a most exciting drive. ③ 138
|1 |2 |3 |4 |5 |6 |7 |8 |9 |10 |11 |12   SI 1.14VE

goal A

■ To type 46 wam
for 5'/2e.

87

Directions: Spacing—1. Line—60. Tab—5.
Warmup—page 190.

PRETEST

Take a 5-minute writing on lines 1-20 at the top of page 195. Score carefully.

PRACTICE

Type three times each the lines
indicated in this chart.

Errors in Pretest	0–1	2–3	4–5	6–+
Lines to practice	17–22	18–23	19–24	20–25

Speed.

17 visit giant first third fight table makes other steel force 12
18 fact that they have many very best come this food soft coal 12
19 and has our the was you any top for hay rye all oil set not 12

Punctuation and
spacing.

20 colonies. present. valley. state. table. teams. well. 12
21 remember, destiny, barley, today, state, forge, corn, oats, 12
22 freedom. shrines. nation. trade. well. hall. up. so. 12

Capitals.

23 Philadelphia Pennsylvania Keystone Mining State Farms These 12
24 Independence Gettysburg Industrial Valley Forge Hall The In 12

Doublets.

25 thirteen freedom derricks millions valley equally steel all 12

POSTTEST

Repeat the Pretest. Score your work carefully and note your progress.

8 | 86 | 87 | 194

PRETEST 2

Up reaches, no right-hand runs.

Take three 1-minute timings on lines 11–14. Proofread them; then average the scores.

11   I was confident that all packages were delivered with care.   12
12   Eleven local farmers departed during the first of the week.   24
13   The judge gave us the rules to use for the sporting events.   36
14   The guide lowered the ropes to those standing on the ledge.   48

|1 |2 |3 |4 |5 |6 |7 |8 |9 |10 |11 |12

PRACTICE 2

Make four copies. If you averaged two or fewer Pretest errors, repeat individual lines for speed gain; otherwise, repeat each block of lines for accuracy gain.

15   president confident packages handled license grade deck who   12
16   departure operators surgical secured quarter spray farm how   12

Up reaches, no right-hand runs.

17   early farms cloth lower guide fixed parts moved seals typed   12

18   sense rules plant ready means grass judge legal local extra   12
19   show past lost ours send sole does gets idea lift hose feed   12
20   bed eat get kit par tag use hot way fat lie red sea dry are   12

POSTTEST 2

Repeat the Pretest. Score your work and note your improvement.

goal A

■ **To produce an itinerary from a revised draft.**

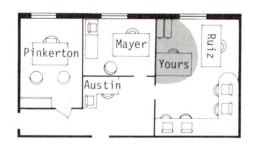

UNIT 11

LESSON

41

Directions: Spacing—1. Line—60.
Warmup—page 79; then begin Job 41-1.

JOB 41-1: ITINERARY

**Plain paper □ 5-inch line
□ Tab 5 □ ■ 20'/0e**

Michael Pinkerton is commandant (senior officer) of the Iowa district of the National Veterans Association, with offices in Davenport, Iowa. He is also your employer and has welcomed you to the NVA offices in Davenport.

"I am planning a trip to a number of our local NVA posts," Mr. Pinkerton says, "but my plans are not yet complete. I have drafted a proposed itinerary and want you to type it expertly. Then we'll make copies to send to each post to determine whether what I have planned is okay with each of them."

He gives you the draft on page 89.

You note that it should be centered vertically. The line lengths are so irregular that it would be difficult to center it horizontally, so you'll try using a 5-inch line for the body. You also note that the times line up at the colon and are followed by 2 blank spaces.

Directions: *Spacing—1. Line—60.*
Warmup—page 190. Edit to add needed commas
in series.

JOB 86-1: DICTATED LETTER

Workbook 203 □ **Body 137** □
SI 1.43N □ ■ **8'/0e**

"Here's another letter," says Ms. Caruso, "with another enumeration."

This letter is to Ms. Pauline E. Persch at ⟨12⟩
the Princeton Civic Theater at 11 Circle ⟨19⟩
Drive in Princeton, New Jersey. The ZIP is ⟨23⟩
08540. Dear Ms. Persch: ⟨29⟩

I am happy to learn that we will be able ⟨38⟩
to use your theater for our jazz concert on ⟨47⟩
Friday, June 17. The terms you have indi- ⟨56⟩
cated for the rental are fine. ⟨62⟩

In order that we may begin to make ⟨70⟩
plans for the jazz concert, please send me ⟨79⟩
the following details: *Arrange the following* ⟨83⟩
numbered paragraphs as an enumeration, ⟨..⟩
and watch for commas in series. ⟨..⟩

1. Diagram of the auditorium to show the ⟨93⟩
exits the aisles the seating arrangement and ⟨103⟩
so on. ⟨105⟩

2. Directions that can be distributed to ⟨114⟩
those who come to the theater from differ- ⟨124⟩
ent routes—train bus auto on foot from ⟨133⟩

local hotels and motels. ⟨138⟩

3. List of hotels motels inns restaurants ⟨148⟩
dining facilities and so on. ⟨156⟩

4. The name of the firm that prints your ⟨165⟩
tickets. ⟨167⟩

I look forward to working with you dur- ⟨176⟩
ing the next weeks as we make and fulfill ⟨184⟩
our plans for the show. ⟨189⟩

Sincerely yours and so on. ⟨208⟩

JOB 86-2: DICTATED LETTER

Workbook 205 □ **Body 137** □
SI 1.43N □ ■ **7'/0e**

"I want to send that same letter to another addressee," says Miss Caruso.

Send the same letter, except for inside address and salutation, to Mr. Oscar Fitzgerald, General Manager of the Lambertville Music Circus in Lambertville, New Jersey, ZIP 08530. Oh, the date is different too: Monday and Tuesday, June 20 and 21. Otherwise, the same letter.

JOB 86-3: COMPLETION CARDS

5" x 3" cards or slips of paper
□ ■ **5'/0e**

JOB 86-1: DICTATED LETTER

1. Typed by Denise Barney
2. Proofread by Jimmy Jenkins
3. I forgot to tab in on the enumerations several times, so I had to do a lot of erasing.

STROKING CHECKLIST

□ *Strokes firm but unhurried.*
□ *Strokes made without arm motion.*
□ *Strokes made by curved fingers.*
□ *Strokes are distinct, separate.*

Directions: *Spacing—1. Line—60. Tab—5.*

PROPOSED ITINERARY FOR MICHAEL PINKERTON

To the *Iowa* Posts of the National Veterans Association

Monday, December 8

    8:00 Depart Davenport on US 61 North.
  10:00 Arrive Dubuque.
  12:00 Lunch with Dubuque Post.

    2:30 Depart Dubuque on US 151 South.
    4:30 Arrive Cedar Rapids.
    6:30 Dinner with Cedar Rapids Post.

Tuesday, December 9

    9:00 Depart Cedar Rapids on Interstate 380 West.
  10:30 Arrive Waterloo.
  12:00 Lunch with Waterloo Post.

    2:00 Depart Waterloo on US 20 West.
    5:00 Arrive Fort Dodge.
    6:30 Dinner with Fort Dodge Post.

Wednesday, December 10

    8:00 Depart Fort Dodge on US 20 West.
  11:00 Arrive Sioux City.
  12:00 Lunch with Sioux City Post.

    2:30 Depart Sioux City on Interstate 29 *South*.
    5:00 Arrive Council Bluffs.
    6:30 Dinner with Council Bluffs Post.

~~THURSDAY~~, December 11

    8:00 Depart Council Bluffs on *Interstate 80 East*.
  11:00 Arrive Des Moines.
  12:00 Lunch with Des Moines Post.

    2:30 Depart Des Moines on US 65 South, then on
          US 34 *East*.
    5:30 Arrive Ottumwa.
    6:30 Dinner with Ottumwa Post.

Friday, December 12

    8:00 Depart Ottumwa on US 34 East.
  10:00 *Arrive* Burlington.
  12:00 Lunch with Burlington Post.

    2:00 Leave Burlington on US 61 *North*.
    5:00 Return to Davenport and home.

One of many possible arrangements for an itinerary.

JOB 85-2: DICTATED LETTER

(Continued)

The number of members you have the number of chapter meetings you have held and the number of concerts you have sponsored were factors in making your chapter the winner. You and your members should be proud of the record your club has

achieved.

So our plaque and our best wishes go to you to your fellow officers and to all the members of the Trenton Chapter for becoming the Chapter of the Year [*underscore that*] for the state of New Jersey.

Okay. Wind it up as you did the other.

98
106
114
122
131
139
140
150
159
167
176
186
204

goal B

■ To produce two letters from dictation within 20'/0e.

Directions: *Adjust your machine for Job 85-3. Edit where needed to add commas in series.*

JOB 85-3: DICTATED LETTER

Workbook 199 □ Body 125 □
SI 1.41N □ ■ 10'/0e

Now you take letters from Sharon Caruso, Teen Jazz scheduling agent, who says, "This one will have an enumeration in it."

This letter goes to John Graham, make that Mr. John Graham, Leader [*that's a title just as Manager would be*] of the Lively Gents Jazz Group, at 385 Linden Lane, Camden, New Jersey, ZIP 08101.

Dear Mr. Graham: Thank you for writing and asking us if your group, Lively Gents, could be part of the jazz concert we will sponsor in Camden in July. Please send us the following data about your group: *Arrange these four numbered paragraphs as an enumeration, with numbers hanging out. And watch for commas in series.*

1. Names ages and addresses of each member of your group.

2. List the performances your group has given this year. Give the date location and an estimate of the number of persons in each audience.

3. Send us the name address and phone number of your manager or agent.

12
13
14
21
24
34
43
51
60
67
··
··
··
76
82
91
102
111
114
125
131

4. Indicate any dates for which you are now committed for the month of July.

When we receive the above information from you, we will be happy to consider your group for the concert in Camden.

Sincerely yours and identify me simply as Scheduling Agent under my signature. My name goes in the reference position. Good.

140
148
157
165
172
179
187
192

JOB 85-4: DICTATED LETTER

Workbook 201 □ Body 125 □
SI 1.41N □ ■ 10'/0e

Pleased with your work, Ms. Caruso says:

I must write to another person who has a musical group that I would like to have perform at our Camden program. It is Miss Lorraine Pfeiffer, the Managing Agent of—now get this name!—"The Rockjazz Combo." Her address is 2102 Gifford Towers, in Jersey City, New Jersey, ZIP 07340.

Send her the same letter you just typed, but with these changes: (1) fix the salutation, (2) fix the group name in the first sentence, and (3) delete the paragraph about the agent—we know who she is. You will have to renumber the remaining paragraphs. Okay? Fine.

■ To produce nine transmittal cards.

```
                                         11 November 19--

             Adjutant of the Cedar Rapids Post:

             The attached itinerary is the schedule for
             the annual inspection of the personnel,
             records, facilities, and equipment of each
             Post.  If there is any reason why your Post
             cannot accommodate the inspection at the
             indicated time, let me know at once.  This
             informal notice will be followed by a for-
             mal one when all Posts have confirmed.

                         Michael Pinkerton, Commandant
             URS
```

JOB 41-2: TRANSMITTAL CARDS

5″ x 3″ cards or slips □ ■ **20′/0e**

"I need nine transmittal cards like this one," says Mr. Pinkerton as he gives you the card at the right, "one for the adjutant [administrator] of each of the nine NVA posts named in the itinerary. They are alike except that the name of the post is changed in each salutation."

You nod: nine posts, nine cards, nine salutation changes. Then you ask, "Mr. Pinkerton, the date—the day before the month?"

He smiles. "That is the military style of expressing the date.

Transmittal card (5″ x 3″) explains the paper attached to it. Note military style date.

All our military services use it, and so do we: day, month, year, no commas, no abbreviations. Please use it."

A veterans' association *would* use it, of course.

---

goal A

■ To produce an organization chart.

JOB 42-1: CHART

Paper turned sideways □ ■ **15′/0e**

"Please retype this chart," says Mr. Pinkerton as he gives you the organization chart below.

The line is 63 spaces long. Set tab stops at the start, middle, and end.

LESSON 42

Directions: *Spacing—1. Line—60. Warmup—page 79; then begin Job 42-1.*

JOB 42-2: COMPLETION CARDS

5″ x 3″ cards or slips □ ■ **5′/0e**

```
                    Col. Michael Pinkerton, USAFR
                            Commandant
```

Col. Carl Hennrikus, USAFR	Capt. Michael E. Kekker, USNR	LCol Frank R. Green, USAR
Adjutant	Director, Post Affairs	Director, Member Services
Lt.Col. T. W. Patton, BGen M. K. Glick, USMCR	Capt. C. G. Hayman, USCGR	(Col. Nita Vick, USMCR)
Deputy	Deputy	*Maj. Alice Ki, USAF* Deputy

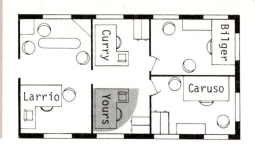

goal A

■ To produce two letters from dictation within 20'/0e.

Directions: Spacing—1. Line—60. Warmup—page 190. Edit where needed to add commas in series.

You work for Roy Bilger and Sharon Caruso at the national headquarters of Teen Jazz Clubs, Inc., and will type letters for them. They use standard letter arrangement with one exception: they want only their title under their signature; the name goes in the reference position:

Sincerely yours,

Roy Bilger

Chairman, Awards Committee

Roy Bilger/urs

JOB 85-1: DICTATED LETTER

Workbook 195 □ Body 155 □
SI 1.43N □ ■ 10'/0e

Mr. Bilger says, "Please transcribe the following dictation. Ready?"

This letter is to Ms. Linda Palumbo. She is 12
leader of The Magic Five. Her address is 25
8113 Diamond Spring Road, Newark, New 22
Jersey 07102. Okay. Dear Ms. Palumbo: 28

Your group, The Magic Five, has been de- 37
clared the winner of the East Coast contest 46
held in Atlantic City on Saturday, February 54
8. This was determined by the number of 62
mail ballots we received from the viewing 71
audience. *Watch for commas.* 73

I should like to extend sincere congrat- 82
ulations to you to Steve to Amy to Andy 90
and to Molly. Your group was truly out- 99
standing, and I know that the TV audience 107
enjoyed your show as much as did the 114
audience in that huge Atlantic City ball- 123
room. 124

Now we must make firm plans for the 132
international contest to be held in New 140
Orleans in June. Since you are regional 150
winner, you are invited to be part of this 158
contest. We will take care of the expense of 166
your travel your meals and your lodgings. 175

Please return the enclosed form to me by 184
March 10 so that the final plans will be 192
sure to include a presentation by your 201
group. 202

Sincerely yours, and just use my title, 207
Chairman, Awards Committee, with my 217
name, Roy Bilger, in the reference position. 223

JOB 85-2: DICTATED LETTER

Workbook 197 □ Body 126 □
SI 1.39N □ ■ 10'/0e

Mr. Bilger says, "Here is another 'good news letter' for you to record and transcribe today."

This letter goes to Mr. Thomas Rice, who is 11
president of the Trenton Teen Jazz Club. 18
The address is 3811 Market Street, in Tren- 23
ton, New Jersey, ZIP 08609. Dear Tom: 29

Congratulations! Your group has made it 38
to the top! When we finished tallying the 46
results of the survey we conducted in 54
December, we found that your group has 62
won [*underscore these four words*] Chapter 68
of the Year honors for New Jersey. You will 81
be entered in the East Coast Sweepstakes. 89
Watch for commas.

(Continued on next page)

Directions: Spacing—1. Line—60. Tab—5.
Begin the 12-second sprints that follow.

12-SECOND SPRINTS

Take four 12-second sprints on each of these three sentences.

1 The state of Iowa is the state
2   with the highest percent of its land in working farms. 17
3   with one-quarter of the top-grade farmland in America. 17
4   with the deepest layer of fine topsoil, known as loam. 17

12" WAM 40 45 50 55 60 65 70 75 80 85

30-SECOND DRIVES

Speed is number under which you stop after typing 30 seconds.

Take three half-minute drives on this alphabetic paragraph.

                02   04   06   08   10   12   14   16   18   20   22   24
5 The rolling plains of Iowa are so fertile that the farms of 12
                26   28   30   32   34   36   38   40   42   44   46   48
6 this famous state, which is almost exactly average in size, 24
                50   52   54   56   58   60   62   64   66   68   70   72
7 produce a tenth of all the food produced on American farms. 36
                74   76   78   80   82   84   86   88   90   92   94   96
8 That's the equivalent of breakfast for just about everyone. 48

3-MINUTE TW

Speed markers are for 3' TW.

                    1   2   3   4
9 When you think of Iowa, you think of great farms, with 12
                    5   6   7   8
10 fields of corn or wheat as far as the eye can see; but once 24
                    9   10   11   12
11 the state had the world's largest deposits of lead and zinc 36
                    13   14   15   16
12 and was more widely known for its mines than for its farms. 48
                    17   18   19   20
13 Iowa has more than four thousand manufacturing plants, 60
                    21   22   23   24
14 and the value of what they produce exceeds the value of the 72
                    25   26   27   28
15 farm output. The plants are spread all over the state, but 84
                    29   30   31   32
16 they tend to center around the half dozen principal cities. 96
                    33   34   35   36
17 The state is a great meat producer, too: just about a 108
                    37   38   39   40
18 quarter of all our pork is raised there, while Iowa markets 120
                    41   42   43
19 more beef than does any other American state. 129

|1 |2 |3 |4 |5 |6 |7 |8 |9 |10 |11 |12   SI 1.30FE

☐ *Check: feet on floor.*
☐ *Check: back erect.*
☐ *Check: shoulders level.*
☐ *Check: fingers curved.*
☐ *Check: eyes on copy.*

LESSON 43

Directions: Spacing—1. Line—60. Tab—5.
Warmup—page 79.

The six projects of
Part 8 have as their
locale:
Unit 22: New Jersey,
Pennsylvania
Unit 23: Oklahoma,
Texas
Unit 24: Oregon,
Washington

PART 8

Parts 1–6 of this book concentrate on the many different kinds of typing that clerk-typists do in offices: forms, rough drafts, tables of many kinds. Part 7 is chiefly a review. Now, in Part 8, there will be a change: the concentration will be more on the typing that secretaries do—correspondence and documents. As part of the emphasis on secretarial work, a great deal more editorial attention is required. You will gradually be required to provide the capitals, punctuation marks, paragraph indentions, and so on, that you would have to fill in if you were typing from either shorthand notes or a dictation machine.

In other regards, Part 8 is like its predecessors: Each of the six projects is located in a different state; each project has about 1½ periods of production and a ½ period of skill building.

Your skill goal in Part 8 is to type 46 words a minute for 5 minutes within 2 errors.

Turn to this page at the start of each practice period for the Warmup exercise.

SPEED RECALL	1A The auditor with their firm is proficient with audit forms.	12
	1B He is to go to work for the pane firm by the eighth of May.	12
	1C Kay is busy with the signs for their big social but may go.	12
ALPHABET RECALL	2A Liza quit her new job, packed six bags, and moved far away.	12
	2B Bill gave McKay a six-quart jug as the prize for Wednesday.	12
	2C Have you queried Jack Flagg about his experiment with zinc?	12
NUMBER RECALL	3A She sold 1,234 in June, 3,456 in July, and 7,890 in August.	12
	3B Sections 10, 28, and 39 are very much better than 47 or 56.	12
	3C I read from pages 10, 28, and 39; Joe took pages 47 and 56.	12
THINKING WHILE TYPING Insert needed commas.	4A Indeed he said we all of us shall plan I think to go.	12
	4B George Pete and Willis bowl ride and swim on Saturdays.	12
	4C Jim Dot Bob and Jane drove to Boston Troy and Buffalo.	12

|1 |2 |3 |4 |5 |6 |7 |8 |9 |10 |11 |12

Type for 5 minutes at the rate of at least 43 wam within 3 errors.

1	The state of Missouri is the crossroads of America; it	12
2	lies where air, land, and water transportation networks all	24
3	intersect. The water network is the key thing; the joining	36
4	of the Missouri and Mississippi Rivers created a good place	48
5	for a fort that became a village that became a city that is	60
6	now St. Louis, whose importance for two centuries made it a	72
7	gateway to the West. Through it came millions who traveled	84
8	by boat up the rivers, by prairie schooner across the level	96
9	plains, by car along the web of national highways. Others,	108
10	of course, opted to stay in St. Louis or built its suburbs.	120
11	The construction of enormous dams in many parts of the	132
12	state did three things: built lakes, gave a source of low—	144
13	cost power, and cut floods. As a result, recreation became	156
14	an industry, plants and mills sprang up everywhere, and the	168
15	banks of the rivers, so frequently flooded in days gone by,	180
16	became solid farmlands. Missouri can take care of its own.	192
17	Industry is the big wheel, more than all other incomes	204
18	combined, making more than six billion dollars a year.	215

|1 |2 |3 |4 |5 |6 |7 |8 |9 |10 |11 |12 | SI 1.42N |

Select five lines that you did not finish, that you made errors in, and/or that you found troublesome for any reason. Type each line three times.

Repeat the Pretest. Score your work and note your improvement.

goal B

■ To organize and produce a table from unarranged data.

JOB 43-1: TABLE

Plain paper □ ■ 20'/0e

Directions: *Begin Job 43-1 at once.*

You work for Vincent Broseley, registrar and dean at River

Bend Technical College, a private school in Jefferson City, Missouri. He says to you, "Well, it is time to gear up our recruit-

goal

■ **To experience creative thinking, accurate typing, and cooperation in a work atmosphere.**

☐ *In this Co-Op you will be working with material that is very familiar to you—the parts of a typewriter and the parts of a formal business letter.*

☐ *The final task will be to develop a table. Data for the table will be obtained from your classmate.*

☐ *Give your teacher a copy of the note, memo, and table that you prepare for this Co-Op.*

CREATIVE CO-OP 7: DEVELOPING A TABLE

TYPIST A

Your assignment is to prepare a table entitled "Familiar Parts of a Typewriter." Follow the instructions below in obtaining information for the table and in typing the final draft:

TYPIST B

In this Co-Op you will prepare a table entitled "Familiar Parts of a Business Letter." Follow the instructions below in obtaining information for the table and in typing the final draft:

1. MAKE YOUR REQUEST

Throughout this course or in other typing courses, you have learned various parts of your typewriter. Write a note to Student B in which you list five familiar parts of the machine. Ask student B to provide definitions for the five parts that you have listed.

1. MAKE YOUR REQUEST

In this course you have studied various parts of a formal business letter. Write a note to Student A in which you list five familiar parts of a formal business letter. Ask Student A to provide definitions for the five parts you have listed.

2. RESPOND TO TYPIST B

Provide definitions for the words Typist B has identified. The definitions should specify the purposes of the parts that Typist B listed.

2. RESPOND TO TYPIST A

Define the typewriter parts that Typist A has identified. The definitions should specify the purpose or use of the typewriter parts Typist A listed.

3. TYPE THE TABLE

After you receive from Typist B the definitions for the words you submitted, put them in alphabetic order and arrange them in a two-column table. Place the name of the typewriter part in Column 1 and the definition in Column 2 (use a 30-space line for typing the definitions). Single-space the lines of each definition, but double-space before starting the next definition.

3. TYPE THE TABLE

When Typist A returns your list with appropriate definitions, put them in alphabetic order and arrange them in a two-column table. Place the name of the letter part in Column 1 and the definition in Column 2 (use a 30-space line for typing the definitions). Single-space the lines of each definition, but double-space before starting the next definition.

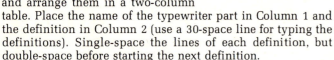

ment team for the spring semester. I am taking charge personally of our effort in Southeast Missouri. Please type this table."

He dictates while you pencil a draft.

COUNTIES ASSIGNED TO EACH TEAM   18

Team 1 / <u>Marianne Lowery, Leader</u> / Billie   54
Sanford has Washington, Crawford, and   62
Phelps (counties). Stanley Marquand has   67
Perry, Ste. Genevieve, and St. Francois.   75
Carolyn LaMotte has Dent, Texas, and   82
Howell.   83

Team 2 / <u>Dennis Hutchinson, Leader</u> /   116
Diana Krause has Butler, Wayne, and   125
Madison. Rene Courtois has Iron, Reynolds,   131
and Carter. Herbert Vaughan has Ripley,   138
Oregon, and Shannon.   141

Team 3 / <u>Maria Figueroa, Leader</u> / Suellen   175
Richland has Stoddard, Cape Girardeau, and   182
Bollinger. Robert Brownfield has New   189
Madison (North), Mississippi, and Scott.   196
Laura Caruth has Pemiscot, Dunklin, and   204
New Madrid (South).   207

goal A

■ To produce an organization chart from a draft.

Directions: Spacing—1. Line—60. Warmup—page 79; then begin Job 44-1.

JOB 44-1: CHART

Plain paper □ ■ 20'/e

"So that each member of each team will know to whom everyone reports, I need an organization chart that I can duplicate and distribute to everyone at our conference in December.

"I found a chart from last year. I have patched it, ready for retyping. Please make a good copy that we can duplicate."

When you study the draft, you estimate that the underscore line is about 55 or 60 spaces long; you decide to clear all tab stops and set new ones at the start, center, and end of such a line. Every item in the table, therefore, can be centered horizontally from one or another of those three tab stops. Rather easy!

THE SOUTHEAST MISSOURI RECRUITMENT TEAM ↓3

Vincent Brosley
Director

| Marianne Lowery | *Dennis Hutchinson* | Maria Figueroa |
| Leader 1 | Leader 2 | Leader 3 |

Billie Sanford	Herbert Vaughan	Suellen Rich*land*
Stanley Marquand	*Rene Courtois*	Robert Brownfield
Carolyn La⌒Motte	Diana Krause	Laura Caruth

4   **43**   **44**

REVIEW JOB 2: BUSINESS FORMS

Workbook 194 ☐ ■ 10'/0e

If you do not have the workbook forms, omit this assignment.

1. Expense voucher for Ben Kearns, to be delivered to him at the History, Inc., offices as reimbursement for his February 9 trip.

Round trip, Virginia City and Bozeman (166 miles @ $.20) . . . 33.20

Room at Sheridan Inn . . . 18.00

Meals . . . 10.00

Total . . . 61.20

2. Voucher check addressed to Ben Kearns for $61.20 for his 2/9/-- Bozeman trip. On the memo line note "Reimbursement for your February 9 trip to Bozeman, per your February 12 expense voucher."

Address the check to Mr. Kearns at 191 Deer Lodge Road, Virginia City, MT 59755.

REVIEW JOB 3: INCOME STATEMENT SUMMARY

Plain paper ☐ **Spacing 1** ☐ ■ 15'/0e

Center the statement on a full page.

The Sunny Surfboard Company		18
INCOME STATEMENT SUMMARY ~~(WORKSHEET)~~		36
For the Month ~~/Quarter~~ Ended January 31, 19--		61
SALE OF GOODS	$ 15,300	73
DEDUCT COST OF GOODS SOLD		79
Goods in Shop January 1, 19--	$ 6,293	89
Goods Purchased During Month	3,722	102
Total Available Goods for Sale	$ 10,015	111
Goods in Shop January 31, 19--	5,260	124
Cost of Goods Sold	4,755	138
GROSS PROFIT ON GOODS SOLD	$ 10,545	150
DEDUCT EXPENSES		154
Employee Wages	$ 850	164
Rent of Shop Space	200	173
Heating, Electricity, Phone	128	183
Maintenance and Cleaning	100	196
Total Expenses	$ 1,278	210
NET INCOME FOR MONTH OF January	$ 9,267	224
		231

7 | 7

goal B

■ To produce a letter containing a list you are to compile.

JOB 44-2: LETTER WITH LIST

Workbook 105 □ Body 103 + display
□ SI 1.64H □ ■ 15'/0e

"I phoned the motel where we will hold our recruitment conference," says Mr. Broseley, "and everything is fine. They want a letter of confirmation, so let's prepare it." He dictates:

Address this to the Reservations Manager / ₁₂
Southern Inn / U.S. Highway 60 / Poplar ₁₉
Bluff, MO 63901 / Dear Madam or Sir: / ₂₈
This letter is in confirmation of my tele- ₃₇
phone request for reservations for single ₄₅
rooms for each of the following persons for ₅₄
the night of December 3: ₅₉

Please list alphabetically all the names that appear on the organization chart.

These persons will arrive singly on the ₁₂₃
morning of December 3 and depart at 3:30 ₁₃₄
the following afternoon. Each will pay his ₁₄₁
or her own bill; payment is assured by this ₁₄₉
college. ₁₅₂

Please make note, also, that you have ₁₆₀
guaranteed us a meeting room for both ₁₆₈
dates adequate for 20 persons. / Yours very ₁₈₀
truly, ₁₈₁

Vincent Broseley / Registrar and Dean / ₁₉₄
urs ₁₉₅

JOB 44-3: COMPLETION CARDS

5" x 3" cards or slips □ ■ 5'/0e

---

goal

■ To use intensive drill to improve basic skill.

ACTIVITIES	20 MIN.	40 MIN.
Warmup, page 79	3'	3'
Drive 1 Pretest	4'	4'
Drive 1 Practice	9'	9'
Drive 1 Posttest	4'	4'
Drive 2 Pretest	—	5'
Drive 2 Practice	—	10'
Drive 2 Posttest	—	5'

CLINIC 8

Directions: *Spacing—1. Line—60. Warmup—page 70; then begin Drive 1.*

DRIVE 1

PRETEST 1

Take two 1-minute timings on lines 1–4E (electric machines) or lines 1–4M (manual machines); then average your speed scores and error scores.

Electric only:

Stress ups without ins.

1E Their friends are obliged to vote for members of the media. 12
2E The wives apologized to the police for the gifts they sold. 24
3E The rules and bylaws permit authors to request fewer pages. 36
4E The members of the museum facility are permitted no delays. 48

|1 |2 |3 |4 |5 |6 |7 |8 |9 |10 |11 |12

Manual only:

Stress downs without jumps.

1M A big rabbit, located by the black dog, was able to escape. 12
2M Can you avoid cashing a blank check from the one old local? 24
3M Max once took off his cap and jacket at a capacity banquet. 36
4M She can buy a blank checkbook in a big bank or a small one. 48

|1 |2 |3 |4 |5 |6 |7 |8 |9 |10 |11 |12

goals

- To produce usable copies of a letter, expense voucher, voucher check, and financial statement.
- To type at least 45 wam/5'/2e.

Directions: Spacing—1. Line—60. Tab—5. Warmup—page 163.

5-MINUTE WRITING

Spacing—2.
Line—60.
Tab—5.

Speed markers are for 5' TW.

■ 5'/2e

```
 1   Dear Mr. Clark: Thank you for inquiring about the new sponsor-          12
 2   ships that were announced in newspapers last Sunday. Our               24
 3   organization would be pleased to have you as a sponsor.                36
 4       There are two main kinds of sponsorships: those for a room         48
 5   and those for an item of furniture. In each case, the name of the      60
 6   sponsor is engraved on a silver plate that will be attached to the     72
 7   room door or some part of the furniture.                               84
 8       For the gift of a thousand dollars or more, a donor is made the    96
 9   sponsor of a whole room; a choice of the available rooms is           108
10   given. The gift of five hundred dollars makes one cosponsor of        120
11   a room, sharing the honor with another sponsor who has con-           132
12   tributed equally. They choose the room jointly.                       144
13       The sponsorships for pieces of furniture involve gifts of smaller 156
14   amounts, of course, and the size of the piece is proportionate to     168
15   the size of the donation. The gift of one hundred dollars makes       180
16   a donor the sponsor of a cabinet or a sofa or a bed. A fifty- or      192
17   sixty-dollar gift will make the donor the patron of a chair or        204
18   some other small furnishing.                                          216
19       What will you be sponsor to, Mr. Clark?                           225
```

SI 1.37N

REVIEW JOB 1: LONG LETTER WITH SUBJECT LINE AND CC NOTATION

Workbook 193 □ Body 230 including allowance for subject line □ SI 1.38N □ ■ 15'/0e

The timed writing above provides the salutation and body of a letter. Other details:

1. Insert <u>Subject: A History, Inc., Sponsorship</u>.

2. Use today's date, your initials.

3. Indicate that a cc goes to Dr. Keene.

4. Address is Mr. Frank G. Clark, who lives at 1633 Jeffers Road, in Butte, MT 59701.

5. The writer of the letter is Susan Fox, Treasurer.

6. Since this is a long letter, use a 6-inch line of typing.

Make four copies (each line, for speed; each group, for accuracy) of lines 5–8E if
your machine is electric, lines 5–8M if your machine is manual.

Electric only:

**Stress ups
without ins.**

5E	highway obliged friends vessel titled third voted talk wife	12
6E	folders demands members secure speaks refer sites rule left	12
7E	shelves whereas apology museum police fewer media shop sold	12
8E	utility permits covered bylaws author names dealt gift coil	12

Manual only:

**Stress downs
without jumps.**

5M	radical payable warmly scales track local vast axis bat lab	12
6M	escaped located carved hazard table favor bawl navy tab cap	12
7M	ability banquet jacket rabbit knack scale knee vain bad mix	12
8M	cashier packers abacus blanks ankle basis base able van bay	12

POSTTEST 1

Repeat the Pretest. Score your work and note your improvement.

DRIVE 2

PRETEST 2

Take three 1-minute timings on lines 9–12E (electrics) or lines 9–12M (manuals);
then average your speed scores and error scores.

Electric only:

**Stress lefts,
minimize ins.**

9E	Eva saw that fewer trees and weeds grew in the arid desert.	12
10E	All the crews dressed and were then fed and served dessert.	24
11E	The excess cases of red erasers were reserved for each day.	36
12E	The reserves deserved better results than we were assessed.	48

|1 |2 |3 |4 |5 |6 |7 |8 |9 |10 |11 |12

Manual only:

**Stress downs
without adjacents.**

9M	We think only cars and vans can act as taxicabs or coaches.	12
10M	She needs cake, film, bulbs, slacks, and fabric in the bag.	24
11M	Examine exactly what caused a yacht to sink as it embarked.	36
12M	Unlike the vacant spaces, walnut tables can be given value.	48

PRACTICE 2

Make four copies (each line, for speed; each group, for accuracy) of lines 13–16E
if your machine is electric, lines 13–16M if your machine is manual.

Electric only:

**Stress lefts,
minimize ins.**

13E	reverse desert cases based deeds beds base free wax tax red	12
14E	erasers excess fewer serve crews drew bass were bed bee eve	12
15E	dressed drawee grass taxed sever verb case weed saw was fed	12
16E	reserve served seeds trees sewed ever free fees see gas ram	12

Manual only:

**Stress downs
without adjacents.**

13M	taxicab radical cattle embark space coach vary only tax van	12
14M	contact exactly varied walnut think yacht sink lack act bat	12
15M	payable heavily inland firmly haven caves rave film can tab	12
16M	examine science fabric causes bulbs abide cake axle bag car	12

POSTTEST 2

Repeat the Pretest. Score your work and note your improvement.

JOB 84-2: NEWSLETTER

Plain paper ☐ ■ 15'/0e

"It's time to produce the March issue of the Newsletter," says Professor Keene, "so I drafted it, ready for you to retype."

The newsletter is not difficult: the line equals the width of the banner heading.

JOB 84-3: COMPLETION CARDS

5″ x 3″ cards or slips ☐ ■ 5'/0e

JOB 84-2: NEWSLETTER

1. Typed by Vera Wyatt
2. Proofread with Enid Jackson
3. No problems in producing this job.

                    ←—6″—→   12

2#
H I S T O R Y ,   I N C .   N E W S L E T T E R   45
2#
                                                            59

PUBLISHED MONTHLY   March, 19--   66

                                                              78
S.   2#
THOMAS, KEENE ELECTED PRESIDENT   87
         1#   of
Dr. Thomas S. Keene, Western Montana College of Education, in   100
Dillon, has been elected president of HISTORY, INC. (Prof.)   112
Keene succeeds Mr. Joseph Hill, who has served the organization since   125
it's beginning (25) years ago. (Prof.) Keene brings experience to the   140
position: he has been projects coordinator, for the past (10) years.   158
                                    for History, INC.,
          2#
EDWARD WILBERTS DONATES TWO RUSSELL PAINTS ING   236
         1#   Edward
The Virginia City historical Museum is the recent recipient of two   250
new paintings. Mr. Wilberts, who is a lifetime resident of Virginia   264
City, has donated two superb Frederic R. Russell paintings, "Stam-   276
pede" and "Roundup," to the Museum because "I want them to be where   289
the whole town can enjoy them, he told the Newsletter.   296

          2#
Wayne Sorensen TO SPEAK AT STATE CONFERENCE VENTION   169
         1#
Dr. Wayne Sorensen HISTORY, INC., vice president will be the featured main   185
speaker at the Montana State Historical Society convention at the   198
museum on March 20. He will speak on "How to Restore More for   210
Less." He will also conduct a discussion session at the convention   225

          2#
BEN KEARNS TO DESIGN NEW PROJECT   305
         1#
A brand new plan to restore the West Wing of the old Virginia City   318
Hotel is being designed by Ben Kearns. He is the projects coordi-   331
nator for HISTORY, INC. He is also a great, great, great grandson   344
of the Sam Smothers who built the hotel.   353
BE SURE   2#
          TO SEE CHANNEL 12 on MAY 1   362
              1#
Miss Robin Leigh, of the public relations committee, reports that   375
the story of the splendid efforts of HISTORY, INC., to restore the   386
town
city of VIRGINIA City will be featured in an hour-long show on   399
(CH) 12 at 8:30 p.m. on Wednesday, May 1.   408

7 | 84   186

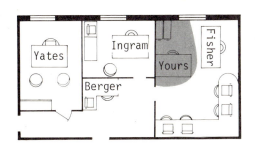

JOB 45-1: ART TYPING PROCEDURES

Plain paper □ ■ 20'/0e

In the Graphic Arts Department you meet James Yates, Ed Berger, and Jan Ingram. Then you begin work with Susan Fisher, head of the typing lab.

She gives you the display below. "To review art typing (artistic typing) procedures we often use here, copy these exercises. You don't have to turn in a slick copy; just stay with each exercise until you get the knack of doing it."

You study the assignment carefully and note:

1. The date is pivoted (backed up from) one space after the end of the line of underscores.

2. Using the underscore and diagonal to make large letters is not hard—just tricky.

3 and 4. To type the small m's close together as shown here, you need a typewriter with half spacing. Skip them if your machine does not half-space.

5 and 6. These are self-descriptive. Copy them both, letter for letter and space for space.

7. Decorations like this are fun to make.

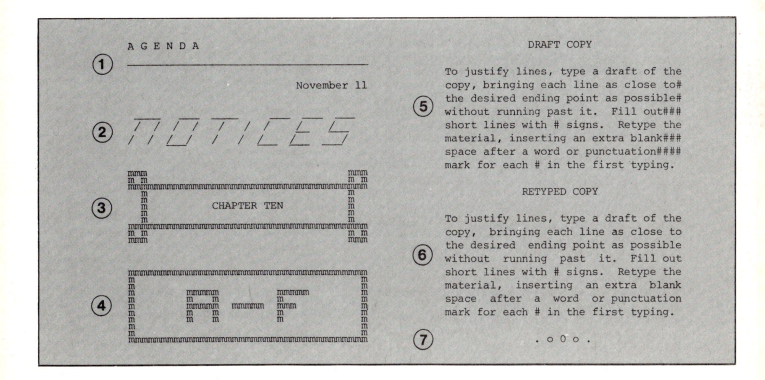

Display typing: ① *Aligning words at the start and end of underscored line.* ② *Using underscores and diagonals for lettering.* ③ *Using small m's, half-spaced, for a decorative border and* ④ *lettering.*

⑤ *Justifying lines (spreading them to equal length) requires a draft, then* ⑥ *retyping and inserting the extra spaces.* ⑦ *Decorating with periods and large and small o's.*

JOB 83-2: DISPLAY TYPING

Plain paper □ ■ 10′/0e

"I'm impressed!" says Professor Keene when he looks at your display page. "Let me tell you another idea for one of these displays. Start with a heading in one or two lines to say something like":

Do Your Share for History

"Then have a message, nicely justified, like":

HISTORY, INC., cordially invites you to join us in making the historical events of past years live once more in our beautiful Virginia City. We have restored eleven landmarks in the city during the past twenty-five years and are now busy at work on a twelfth one.

Membership in HISTORY, INC., is open to everyone in Virginia City who has an interest in our history and wants to share ideas about it.

Call us today. Become a member. Do your share for HISTORY, INC.

"Sign the message," Professor Keene continues, "with our name and address":

HISTORY, INC. / 191 Deer Lodge Road / Virginia City, MT 59755.

---

goal A

■ To produce a graphic chart.

JOB 84-1: GRAPHIC CHART

Plain paper □ ■ 20′/0e

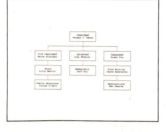

Directions: *Spacing—1. Line—60. Warmup—page 163. Review—pages 151, 152. Then produce Job 84-1.*

LESSON **84**

"Mr. McComas got started on this chart of the organization of History, Inc.," says Professor Keene, "then was pulled away to do something else. Will you type it for me? Thanks."

Each box is 19 strokes wide by 4 lines deep.

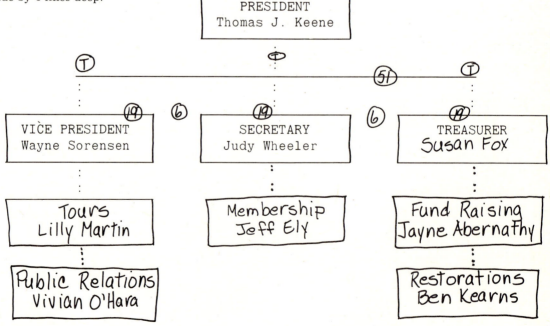

■ To produce two bulletin board notices using display typing.

Directions: *Adjust your machine for Job 45-2 and begin it at once.*

JOB 45-2: BULLETIN BOARD NOTICE

Half page □ Spacing 2 □ ■ 10'/0e

"I began this notice, complete with number signs for justifying," says Miss Fisher. "Please center it on a half page so we can display it on the employees' bulletin board. You know how to use the # signs as a justifying guide?"

You do know: Each # indicates a space that you must insert when you retype the lines.

```
          N O T I C E                                           2

          _____            15


          The Women Employees Association and the Men Employees  27
          Association are jointly sponsoring the formation of a  38
          glee club.  If you enjoy singing and would like to###  49
          join the club, come to the first meeting.  It will be  59
          held in the large conference room off the lobby at###  70
          six o'clock on Thursday, November 14.  Please come.##  80


          _____            91

              Y O U   A R E   I N V I T E D !                  111
```

JOB 45-3: BULLETIN BOARD NOTICE

Half page □ Spacing 1 □ ■ 10'/0e

"Here is another of the same sort of bulletin board notice," says Miss Fisher. "Center it, too, on a half page. When notices are short, we would just as soon have them on half pages as on full-size ones, for they take less room on the bulletin board. Please single-space the body of this one. It would fit on a half page in double spacing, but it would look crowded; in single spacing, I think it will look proportionate to the page and therefore very good."

```
          H E N R Y   G .   F L E M I N G                       6

          _____            19

          Dr. Fleming is a psychologist who is also one of the  30
          most fascinating speakers and humorists that you####  40
          will ever have a chance to hear.  He is a specialist  51
          in helping office employees get along with their####  61
          employers and each other.  Dr. Fleming will be with#  72
          us in the lobby conference room from 4:30 until 5:30  83
          on Friday, November 15.  You are invited to hear him  93
          speak on "How to Win Every Argument."                101

          _____            112

              D O N ' T   M I S S   H I M !                    131
```

goal A

■ To type 45 or more wam for 5'/2e.

Directions: Spacing—1. Line—60. Tab—5.
Warmup—page 163.

PRETEST

Take a 5-minute TW on lines 13–31, page 183, to establish your typing base.

PRACTICE

Type three times each the lines indicated in this chart.

Errors in Pretest	0–1	2–3	4–+
Lines to practice	1–7	2–8	3–9

Speed.

1 earth house scoop first money found known tales miles tribe 12
2 lift huge bite size uses hill real made city gold camp fled 12
3 was the two our big met his led out for too but one top you 12

Doubles.

4 Grasshopper trapped Bannack little copper Butte inner added 12
5 Cheyenne occurred slipped digging biggest upper bluff creek 12

Capitals.

6 Regiment Custer's Cavalry Montana General Sioux Stand Chief 12
7 Anaconda Virginia Seventh Indians Oregon Joseph Custer Horn 12

Accuracy.

8 prospectors world——one equipment discover traveled richest, 12
9 interesting best-known campaigns resisted other their lands 12

POSTTEST

Repeat the Pretest, score your work, and note your improvement.

goal B

■ To produce two displays with lines justified.

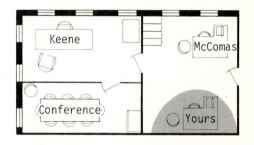

Directions: *Adjust machine for Job 83-1.*

JOB 83-1: DISPLAY TYPING

Plain paper □ ■ **10'/0e**

"Welcome to History, Inc.," says the president and main organizer of this Montana historical society, Professor Thomas J. Keene.

"I'd like a page that we can enclose with every letter we mail," Professor Keene says, "to invite people to contribute to our society."

He shows you the adjacent typing. "Could you make this a fancy display," he asks, "maybe with an elaborate 'H E L P' in dollar signs over the paragraph and our address below it?"

Address: 191 Deer Lodge Road, Virginia City, MT 59755. *Need to review pages 96–98?*

HISTORY, INC., is more than half///
finished with the work needed to///
restore the Daly home. All of us//
in Virginia City are looking for-//
ward to the day when this home will
be another historical landmark in//
our community.

We need your support to raise the//
remainder of the money to complete/
this project. Won't you please////
help us with your generous contri-/
bution?

goal A

■ To produce two notices with display lettering.

Directions: *Spacing—1. Line—60.*
Warmup—page 79; then begin Job 46-1.

JOB 46-1: BULLETIN BOARD NOTICE

Plain paper □ **Spacing (body) 2** □ ■ **8'/0e**

"Please center this display on a full sheet," says Miss Fisher. "Leave a half inch of space between each of the four sections. Note that the lettering does *not* involve half spacing."

```
$$$$$  $$$$$  $      $  $$$$$  $
$      $   $  $      $      $  $
$$$$$  $$$$$  $      $    $$$  $
    $  $   $  $  $  $    $     $
$$$$$  $   $    $     $$$$$  $
```

```
Save your money by investing what
you can spare in the Employees'##
Credit Union.  Every penny helps!

Save your money by borrowing, if#
borrow you must, from that same##
Employees' Credit Union--it costs
you less and makes money for your
investment.

Call Jan Ingram on Extension 339.
```

JOB 46-2: BULLETIN BOARD NOTICE

Plain paper □ **Spacing (body) 2** □ ■ **7'/0e**

"Here's another of the same sort," says Miss Fisher, "if you can manage half spacing."

```
mmmmm  mmmmm  mmmmm  mmmmm   m
m   m      m  m   m  m   m   m
mmmmm      m  m   m  mmmmm   m
    m      m  m   m      m   m
mmmmm      m  mmmmm      m   m
```

```
Look!  Listen!  If you want a
happy, warm glow all through#
this holiday season, here is#
your chance to get it.  We###
need a lot of helping hands##
to pack boxes and wrap gifts.
Will you help us?  If you####
will, meet us in the lobby###
conference room on Monday,###
November 18, at 5:00, and let
that wonderful, lovely glow##
```

```
mmmmm mmmmm mmmmm mmmmm mmmmm
m   m     m m   m m   m     m
mmmmm     m mmmmm mmmmm     m
    m     m m   m     m     m
mmmmm     m m   m m   m     m
```

JOB 46-3: COMPLETION CARDS

5" x 3" cards or slips □ ■ **5'/0e**

```
JOB 46-1:  ART TYPING PROCEDURES

1. Typed by Mary Reeves

2. Reviewed with Martha Wells (you can't
   "proofread" work of this kind).

3. Since it's a different kind of typing,
   I found it hard to do.  I had to con-
   centrate on getting the spacing right.
```

goal B

■ To type 43 wam for 3'/2e.

Directions: *Spacing—1. Line—60. Tab—5.*
Begin the 12-second sprints.

12-SECOND SPRINTS

```
1  Speaking of California, it is
2      the state that raises the most food for dinner tables.   17
3      the state with the greatest number of new automobiles.   17
4      the state whose citizens catch and sell the most fish.   17
```

12" SPEED: 45 50 55 60 65 70 75 80 85

3-MINUTE WRITING
Lesson 82.

Speed markers are for 3′ TW. Circled figures are 1′ goals.

```
 1   If you live in Idaho, or if you have a chance to spend      12
 2   time there, you can do almost anything you want when fun is  24
 3   your goal. Grab those skis and head for the slopes. Idaho    36
 4   has one of the most famous ski resorts in the entire world.  48
 5   Pack up your gear and go by foot, by horseback, by boat, or  60
 6   by light plane to some of the most awesome and scenic camp-  72
 7   sites in our land. If hunting is your game, Idaho has some   84
 8   of the largest hunting grounds in the states. Antelope and   96
 9   deer are quite common, and some moose and elk join them. A   108
10   few lynx, grizzlies, and cougar are also there. If fishing   120
11   brings a twinkle to your eyes, trout are just waiting for a  132
12   big frying pan.                                              135
```

■ 3′/1e

SI 1.20E

5-MINUTE WRITING
Lesson 83.

Speed markers are for 5′ TW. Circled figures are 1′ goals.

```
13   If you like digging into the past of a state, you will      12 | 147
14   discover that Montana was the site of two of the best-known  24 | 159
15   Indian campaigns in our history. Sioux and Cheyenne tribes   36 | 171
16   met General Custer near the Little Big Horn and wiped out a  48 | 183
17   part of the Seventh Cavalry Regiment in the famed "Custer's  60 | 195
18   Last Stand." The other campaign occurred when Chief Joseph   72 | 207
19   resisted orders to transplant his tribe from their lands in  84 | 219
20   Oregon. The entire tribe slipped away and fled through the   96 | 231
21   state of Montana. The chief led about eight hundred of his  108 | 243
22   tribe in a retreat in which they traveled day and night for 120 | 255
23   miles only to end up trapped near the border.               129 | 264
24   The tales of mining are an interesting part of Montana      141 | 276
25   history also. Virginia City and Bannack are the best-known  153 | 288
26   gold camps, but prospectors first found gold in Grasshopper 165 | 300
27   Creek. First gold and then silver were found, but the real  177 | 312
28   money was made in copper. The city of Butte perches on top  189 | 324
29   of "the richest hill on earth." The Anaconda Mine uses the  201 | 336
30   biggest digging equipment in the world—one scoop can seize  213 | 348
31   and lift a huge bite of earth the size of an average house. 225 | 360
```

■ 5′/2e

SI 1.40N

Capitals.

Type three copies of each line. Start slowly each time and gradually pick up speed.

```
5   California Riverside Gonzales Burbank Ventura Oxnard Culver    12
6   Capistrano La Quinta El Cajon Wheeler Springs Pomona Quartz    12
7   Santa Cruz San Diego Alhambra La Brea Beverly Laguna Corona    12
8   Buena Park Pendleton Pasadena Redondo Anaheim Orange Centro    12
    |1    |2    |3    |4    |5    |6    |7    |8    |9    |10   |11   |12
```

SKILL BLITZ

Take a 3-minute TW, follow with corrective practice, and then repeat the timed writing.

```
9       Few states have the natural gifts of California:  rich    12
10      Few states have the natural gifts of California:  rich    24
11      Few states have the natural gifts of California:  rich    36
```

Circled numbers are 1' goals.

```
12  soil, fine climate, all the water it needs for great crops,   48
13  soil, fine climate, all the water it needs for great crops,   60
14  soil, fine climate, all the water it needs for great crops,   72

15  and endless bounties of gas, oil, and precious metals.  The   84
16  and endless bounties of gas, oil, and precious metals.  The   96
17  and endless bounties of gas, oil, and precious metals.  The   108

18  Golden State is what it is called.                            115
19  Golden State is what it is called.                            122
20  Golden State is what it is called.                            129
    |1    |2    |3    |4    |5    |6    |7    |8    |9    |10   |11   |12   SI 1.35N
```

■ **3'/2e**

goal A

■ **To type 43 or more wam for 5'/3e.**

LESSON 47

ASK SOMEONE TO CHECK YOU

☐ *Feet are apart, firmly on floor.*
☐ *Body is erect, leaning forward.*
☐ *Shoulders are level.*
☐ *Elbows are in.*
☐ *Wrists are low.*

Directions: *Spacing—1. Line—60. Tab—5. Warmup—page 79.*

DRIVE 1

Type each of lines 1–3 three times; then take a 5-minute writing on Selection 1, next page. Your goal: 43 or more wam/5'/3e. Be careful on lines 7, 8, and 9.

Preview practice.

```
1   San Francisco American Chicago Founded Father Serra Our Bay    12
2   Porciuncula El Pueblo New York Nuestra Senora Queen City It    12
3   Los Angeles San Diego Junipero Oakland Angels While Flag Of    12
```

DRIVE 2

Type each of lines 4–6 three times; then take a 5-minute writing on Selection 2, next page. Your goal: 43 or more wam/5'/3e.

Preview practice.

```
4   professional Sutter's (itself) Spanish tourism racing horse    12
5   fourteenth obscurity baseball neighbor Mexican nation zoos;    12
6   California explorers commerce tourists hundred sports motel    12
```

The Snowcap Ski Shoppe
SUMMARY BALANCE SHEET
For the Month Ended January 31, 19--

A S S E T S

```
Cash in Register ......................... $  102.17
Cash in Bank .............................   8,219.16
Accounts Receivable, Customers ...........     460.92
Supplies for Displays ....................      27.17
Goods for Sale in Shop ...................   2,476.18

TOTAL ASSETS .............................              $11,285.60
```

L I A B I L I T I E S

```
Accounts Payable, Ski Equipment ......... $1,246.18
Accounts Payable, Ski Clothing ..........    943.12

TOTAL LIABILITIES ........................             $ 2,189.30
```

O W N E R S '   E Q U I T Y

```
Capital (Ted Darrell's Money in Shop) .... $1,771.28
Capital (Robin Leigh's Money in Shop) ....  1,771.28
Net Income From Sale of Goods ............  5,553.74

TOTAL OWNERS' EQUITY .....................               9,096.30
TOTAL LIABILITIES AND OWNERS' EQUITY .....             $11,285.60
```

12-SECOND SPRINTS

Four or more 12″ TWs on each sentence.

Directions: *Spacing—1. Line—60. Tab—5.*

Type each sentence until you achieve at least 45 wam without error for 12 seconds.

```
1  You should know that Idaho is
2      in first place in America in producing white potatoes.   17
3      also in first place when it comes to producing silver.   17
4      the site of many of the best ski slopes in the nation.   17
```

12″ WAM: 45 50 55 60 65 70 75 80 85

1-MINUTE WRITING

Take 1-minute TWs until you complete the paragraph without error in 1 minute.

```
5      We know that Idaho grows a potato uniquely special for   12
6  baking, but you may not realize that it is just one of many  24
7  products that come from the rich mineral deposits, the fine  36
8  soil, and the dense forests of the Gem State.                45
```

|1 |2 |3 |4 |5 |6 |7 |8 |9 |10 |11 |12   SI 1.40N

■ 1'/0e

5-MINUTE TW
(SELECTION 1)

Spacing—2.
Line—60.
Tab—10 for
paragraph
indentions.

Speed markers are
for 5′ TW.

■ 5′/3e

1 The Golden State is the only state with more than a lone city in 14

2 the top fifteen in the nation. It has three of the fifteen: Los Angeles, 29

3 San Francisco, and San Diego. 35

4 Third in the nation, behind New York and Chicago, Los Angeles 48

5 is a huge and beautiful and busy city. Founded some two hundred 61

6 years ago, as one in the group of missions set up by Father Junipero 75

7 Serra, the settlement was given a long name: El Pueblo do Nuestra 89

8 Senora la Reina de Los Angeles do Porciuncula (The City of Our 102

9 Lady the Queen of the Angels of Porciuncula). Some sixty years later 116

10 the mission was a large town with a shorter name, Los Angeles, 128

11 when the United States acquired it, and it became an American prize. 142

12 While many a major city is losing citizens to the suburbs, Los 156

13 Angeles is still growing. It has nearly three million now and is likely 170

14 to reach that figure fairly soon. 177

15 The city of San Francisco, with its three-fourths of a million 191

16 people, ranks thirteenth. It lies at the very tip of a land point that 205

17 is the southern one of the pair of arms that almost circle San Fran- 218

18 cisco Bay, and it is linked over the bay to the north by the famous 232

19 Golden Gate Bridge. 236

|1 |2 |3 |4 |5 |6 |7 |8 |9 |10 |11 |12 |13 |14   SI 1.44N

5-MINUTE TW
(SELECTION 2)

Spacing—2.
Line—60.
Tab—10 for
paragraph
indention.

Speed markers are
for 5′ TW.

■ 5′/3e

20 San Francisco was founded by Spanish explorers at about the 14 250

21 same time that Los Angeles was started. It was a small fort until gold 27 263

22 was found at the nearby Sutter's Mill and the Gold Rush began; then 41 277

23 people flocked in by land and sea from all over. The Rush lasted only 55 291

24 five or six years, but long enough for San Francisco to come out of 69 305

25 obscurity. 71 307

26 San Diego, the third giant city in the state, has grown to rank 85 321

27 fourteenth in the nation, just one step below San Francisco. The city 99 335

28 is more than two hundred years old and got its roots as one of those 113 349

29 missions by Father Serra. It has lived under four flags: the Spanish, 127 363

30 Mexican, Californian (when the state was a nation itself), and 140 376

31 American. 142 378

32 For good reasons, San Diego has become not only a center of in- 155 391

33 dustry and commerce but also of tourism: there are more hotel and 169 405

34 motel rooms in San Diego city than there are in all of Hawaii. The 182 418

35 big appeals to tourists are many and include all kinds of sports, 195 431

36 from professional baseball to horse racing and deep-sea fishing; many 209 445

37 famous zoos; and visits to Mexico. 216 452

|1 |2 |3 |4 |5 |6 |7 |8 |9 |10 |11 |12 |13 |14   SI 1.44N

The Snowcap Ski Shoppe

INCOME STATEMENT SUMMARY ~~(WORKSHEET)~~

For the Month ~~Quarter~~ Ended January 31, 19--

SALE OF GOODS . . . . $ 10,250.71

DEDUCT COST OF GOODS SOLD

    Goods in Shop January 1, 19-- . . . . $ 4,231.18

    Goods Purchased During Month 2,507.00

    Total Available Goods for Sale . . . . $ 6,738.18

    Goods in Shop January 31, 19-- 2,476.18

      Cost of Goods Sold 4,262.00

GROSS PROFIT ON GOODS SOLD . . . . $ 5,988.71

DEDUCT EXPENSES

    Employee Wages . . . . $ 200.00

    Rent of Shop Space 150.00

    Heating, Electricity, Phone 72.80

    Maintenance and Cleaning 12.17

      Total Expenses . . . . $ 434.97

NET INCOME FOR MONTH OF January . . . . $ 5,553.74

goal A

■ To produce a
summary balance
sheet.

JOB 82-1: BALANCE SHEET

Plain paper □ ■ 15'/0e

"Janet Tao typed this summary balance sheet in single spacing," says Miss Monez, giving you the work shown at the top
of page 182, "but we still need a copy in which the items in the
body are all double-spaced. At least you can work from her
single-spaced copy instead of having to figure everything out
from handwriting or a worksheet!"

Directions: _Spacing—1. Line—60._
Warmup—page 163; then begin Job 82-1.

"How much space is left above and below the spread-centered
headings?" you ask.

"Oh, 2 blank lines above, 1 below."

JOB 82-2: COMPLETION CARDS

5″ x 3″ cards or slips □ 5'/0e

goal B

■ To produce a letter with a coupon on it.

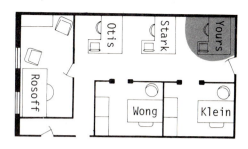

JOB 47-1: COUPON LETTER

Workbook 109 □ ■ 20'/0e

Directions: *Prepare your machine for Job 47-1.*

You work in the Los Angeles headquarters office of the National Association of Creative Jewelers, Inc. Your employer is Charles M. Rosoff, director of the Association.

"We have to prepare a couple of letters to show members of our Convention Committee," he says. "The first letter is a coupon letter to send to jewelers who will attend our conven-

tion in San Francisco next month. We want to get them to pay their dues before going to the convention so we will have more money to use for the convention."

He gives you the draft on the next page.

"Please type this on our stationery," he says, "with three carbons for reworking the draft."

goal A

■ To produce a letter with a coupon on it.

JOB 48-1: COUPON LETTER

Workbook 111 □ ■ 20'/0e

LESSON 48

Directions: *Spacing—1. Line—60.*
Warmup—page 79; then begin Job 48-1.

"Now let's do a letter that we might send to those coming to the convention to arouse their interest in the tours and help them save money," says Mr. Rosoff. "You see, they can get a discount if they buy their tickets in advance."

He continues, "Type this material with a coupon at the bottom, somewhat like the first letter. Incidently, I prefer the tear line at the top of the coupon to be made of underscores and spaces rather than hyphens."

"Three carbons, Mr. Rosoff?" you ask.

"Yes, please," he replies. "This one has the same heading as the other, then continues with":

There will be three hospitality tours for the   32
families of the jewelers attending the NA/CJ   41
convention in San Francisco: 47

1. The Harbor Boat is a three-hour   66

circle tour of the harbor, 9:00 and 1:00   74
daily. See the skyline, bridges, buildings,   84
Alcatraz, Treasure Island, the Golden Gate.   94

2. The Golden Gate Tour is a two-hour   113
sightseeing bus tour, daily at 9:30 and 2:00,   122
for a round trip over Golden Gate Bridge   131
and visits to Golden Gate Park and the   141
Presidio.   142

3. The Chinatown Visit is a four-hour bus   161
tour that includes a Chinese luncheon or   171
supper at Cathay House and visits to Nob   178
Hill and Telegraph Hill, daily at 10:30 and   187
5:30.   188

(Continued on page 103)

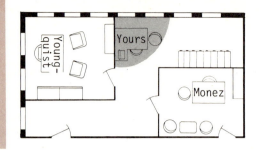

goal A

■ To produce an accounts receivable list in two arrangements.

You begin working for an accountant, Charles Youngquist, who is away on vacation. You report to Anita Monez, who is temporarily acting as office supervisor.

JOB 81-1: ACCOUNTS RECEIVABLE STATEMENT

Plain paper □ ■ 20'/0e

"We're all working on the Snowcap Ski account," says Miss Monez. "Please type this for us." She hands you the penned list in the adjacent column.

You ask, "Spacing? Leaders? Alphabetic?"

She replies, "Alphabetic, yes; leaders, yes; but spacing I'm not sure of—so type it both ways: once single-spaced, once double-spaced. Each time leave an extra blank line after each group of four names."

The Snowcap Ski ~~Lodge~~ Shoppe

ACCOUNTS RECEIVABLE

As of January 31, 19—

Customer	Amount Due
Lyndon Spangenberg	$ 25.17
Lois V. Shannon	31.98
Sandra Marcelle Henkel	54.20
Susan T. Ahern	21.93
Margaret Ann Fulwiler	16.87
Marilyn K. Kramer	27.89
Ruth Etta Anglemyer	61.37
Frederick Caton	34.17
Lucy Maxton Crum	29.94
D. David McDaniel	51.15
Jan Hustad	42.53
Thomas William Cale	63.72
Total Outstanding Accounts	$460.92

goal B

■ To produce an income summary in two arrangements.

JOB 81-2: INCOME STATEMENT SUMMARY

Plain paper □ ■ 20'/0e

Giving you the draft at the top of page 181, Miss Monez says, "Here's an income statement summary that needs typing. Again, use leaders, but you needn't alphabetize. I don't like to have you type things twice, but I can't always help it. So please type it once single-spaced and once double-spaced."

NATIONAL ASSOCIATION OF CREATIVE JEWELERS, INC.

17 Olvera Street
Los Angeles, California 90012

November 17, 19-- ↓4   4

                                                        7

To All NA/CJ Members   12
Who Plan to Attend the   17
San Francisco convention: 22

This letter is to remind you that only paid-up members of the   36
association will be admitted to the sessions of the convention   48
we will hold next month at the Mark Hopkins Hotel. Dues can, of   61
course, be paid at the door, but the charge there will be $10   72
more per person than dues paid in advance. We urge you,   85
therefore, to pay your dues in advance--in fact, right now.   97

You may use the coupon below. Just Fill it in, attach your check   111
for $50 (company group membership) or $25 (individual member-   123
ship), and mail them in the enclosed envelope to us in Los   135
Angeles. Your membership card will be forwarded at once.   147

                 Thanks for your cooperation! ↓3   155

                                                        157

                 Charles M. Rosoff, director   165

-   180

                 Date _____ ↓2   189

                                                        190

National Association of   195
    Creative Jewelers, Inc.   200
17 Olvera Street   204
Los Angeles, CA 90012   208

Enclosed is a check for $_____ in payment of membership dues   221

for _____   235
    Company or personal name   241

                                                        254
    _____
    address   zip   265

Please send convention credentials and membership card(s).   278

                                                        279

    _____   287
                 Authorized Signature   292

Business letter with an order coupon.

4   48   102

goal

■ To use intensive
drill to build skill.

CLINIC

14

ACTIVITIES	20 MIN.	40 MIN.
Warmup, page 163	3'	3'
Drive 1 Pretest	5'	5'
Drive 1 Practice	7'	7'
Drive 1 Posttest	5'	5'
Drive 2 Pretest	—	5'
Drive 2 Practice	—	10'
Drive 2 Posttest	—	5'

Directions: Spacing—1. Line—60.
Warmup—page 163.

DRIVE 1

PRETEST 1

Take two 1-minute timings on lines 1–3 and average your scores; similarly, take two 1-minute timings on lines 4–6 and average your scores. Compare the two averages.

Stress on out motions.

1 Each dairy farm gave a two-month notice when raising rates. 12
2 Our family now takes that trip each month to the local bay. 24
3 Ships at sea can now call ports and talk to their shippers. 36
   |1 |2 |3 |4 |5 |6 |7 |8 |9 |10 |11 |12

Stress on alternates.

4 They may make their eighth visit to their big lake to fish. 12
5 The city paid for the title to six of the eight land signs. 24
6 Henry did make a profit with the signs he got for the city. 36

PRACTICE 1

Type each line three times; then repeat three more times either lines 7–9 (if you scored lower on lines 1–3 than you did on 4–6) or lines 10–12.

Stress on out motions.

7 bases whose doors bulbs easel fails shoot quota metal horse 12
8 easy hogs draw bulk cash bass weak bank tips rank plea jobs 24
9 day fan gas who not rip two mob nod raw bay can cup hoe job 36

Stress on alternates.

10 dials sight forms goals ivory panel right shape their works 12
11 paid rich sign them when also both city down firm chap hand 24
12 air big cut did end for ham icy got jam key lay nap oak may 36

POSTTEST 1

Repeat the Pretest. Score your work and note your improvement.

DRIVE 2

PRETEST 2

Take two 2-minute timings on lines 13–16; proofread both and average the scores.

Stressing the hyphen.

13 We may make eighty-six signs for the social for a neighbor. 12
14 Their auditor may pay the right-hand man to do their audit. 24
15 Their torn-down bus is so worn it may pay to own a bicycle. 36
16 We gave them up-to-date information they needed by Tuesday. 48
    |1 |2 |3 |4 |5 |6 |7 |8 |9 |10 |11 |12

PRACTICE 2

Make four copies of each line.

Stressing the hyphen.

17 banana— burlap— chairs— bushel— height— eighth— pays— rush— 12
18 naught— enamel— pajama— formal— panels— memory— hand— snap— 24
19 mirage— parade— ramrod— remain— narrow— mature— fame— malt— 36
20 recall— danger— female— onward— matrix— dampen— mane— rant— 48

POSTTEST 2

Repeat the Pretest. Score your work and note your improvement.

JOB 48-1: COUPON LETTER

(Continued)

Use the coupon below. If you mail it before 198
December 10, you may take 10 percent off 206
your check. 209

              Thanks for reserving early! ↓3 218
              Charles M. Rosoff, Director 231

-- 246

Dear Mr. Rosoff: Please send me tickets for 267
the following tours: 271
_____ Harbor Boat Ride @ $5.00 . $_____ 284
_____ Golden Gate Tour @ $3.00. _____ 296

_____ Chinatown Visit and Meal 303
    @ $7.50 .... _____ 308
Total price of requested 315
    tickets .... _____ 320
10% discount if mailed by 327
    December 10 .... _____ 332
    Amount on check enclosed . _____ 344
Send the tickets to: 349
    Name _____ 361
Address _____ 373
       _____ 385

JOB 48-2: COUPON LETTER

Workbook 113 □ ■ 15'/0e

"I like coupon letters," says Mr. Rosoff, "so we're going to do one more. Make the following letter in coupon arrangement; then we'll make enough photocopies to mail to everyone who is on the Convention Committee. This is the letter":

Ladies and Gentlemen / Of the San Fran- 16
cisco / Convention Committee: / With this 26
letter I am sending you copies of two letters 35
that I have drafted as a result of our last 44
meeting. Because time is getting short, I ask 53
you to review the two letters and then indi- 61
cate on the coupon at the bottom whether 71
you approve them. 72
    1. The dues letter is the result of the sug- 89
gestion by Hilary Salk and, I think, puts 99
just the right amount of pressure for imme- 107
diate action by the person who receives it. 117
    2. The tours letter is the result of the 135

suggestion by Frank Liebert. You will recall 145
that we get a 20 percent rebate on tickets 155
we sell; giving a 10 percent discount to 161
those who buy tickets early not only will 171
let us make a margin but will also guaran- 182
tee that we have the required minimum. 189
    When you have filled in the coupon 198
below, please detach it and send it back to 206
me in the envelope that is enclosed. / I 217
appreciate your help. ↓3 Charles M. Rosoff, 230
Director 231

-- 247

Dear Mr. Rosoff: / Here are my evaluations 258
of the two letters. 262
    1. The dues letter is acceptable ( ) is 279
not acceptable ( ). Suggestion for improv- 288
ing it: _____ 296
_____ 309
    2. The tours letter is acceptable ( ) is 326
not acceptable ( ). Suggestion for improv- 335
ing it: _____ 343
_____ 356
Date   Signed 376

JOB 48-3: COMPLETION CARDS

5″ x 3″ cards or slips □ ■ 5'/0e

JOB 80-1: VOUCHER CHECKS

Workbook 185–187 □ ■ 20'/0e

Mr. Brundage sends you next to the treasurer's office where Miss Flacon, the supervisor, tells you "We have some bills to pay. Please prepare voucher checks for":

No. 2-63. Mr. Charles W. Wigent / Wigent and Dupreaux, Inc. / 32 Metonga Street / Rhinelander, WI 54501 / $250.00 for expenses and gratuity for trip to Fond du Lac, January 6–13, for conference on new freezers.

No. 2-64. Mr. Richard T. Fremont / 2717 Fisk Road / Oshkosh, WI 54902 / $2,780.75 full payment of back salary as ordered by Judge George Hunker, Common Pleas Court of Wisconsin, January 21, 19--.

No. 2-65. Ms. Mary M. Horbatuk / 628 Overlook Drive / McFarland, WI 53558 / $57.50 reimbursement in full for expenses (50 miles @ $.15, + $50 replacement of day's wages) for trip to Fond du Lac on January 22 for employment interview.

JOB 80-2: EXPENSE ACCOUNTS

Workbook 189 □ ■ 15'/0e

Reporting back to Mr. Brundage after the brief stay in the treasurer's office, you are sent next to Mr. William Shreiber, an employment recruiter in the Personnel Department. He visits schools and colleges to interview likely candidates for jobs. He is paid for his expenses.

"I'm glad to see you," says Mr. Shreiber. "I am far behind in turning in my expense accounts for two trips I took recently. Could I dictate the information to you and have you prepare the two expense vouchers for me?"

You've typed expense accounts before (page 80) and so you can say "Yes." Mr. Schreiber dictates:

No. 1. I, William Shreiber, am the claimant, and I want the payment sent to my office here in the Personnel Department, 7th Floor North. Now for one set of expenses:

Jan. 11 Drive to Green Bay (70 miles @ $.15), $10.50 / Meals, $12.00 / Room at Holiday Inn, $22.50.

Jan. 12 Drive to two vocational training cen-

Directions: Adjust machine for Job 80-2.

ters, $1.50 / Meals, $12.00 / Room at Holiday Inn, $22.50.

Jan. 13 Drive from Green Bay (70 miles @ $.15), $10.50. Meals, no, make that just simply Breakfast, $2.00.

TOTAL $93.50.

No. 2. This is a different trip and goes on a separate voucher. Same heading.

Jan. 17 Drive to Milwaukee (64 miles @ $.15), $9.60 / Drive to Madison (61 miles @ $.15), $9.15 / Meals, $12.00 / Room at University of Wisconsin Student Union, $10.00.

Jan. 18 Meals, $12.00 / Room at University of Wisconsin Student Union, $10.00.

Jan. 19 Meals, $6.00 / Drive from Madison (60 miles @ $.15), $9.00.

TOTAL $77.75.

JOB 80-3: COMPLETION CARDS

5" x 3" cards or slips □ ■ 5'/0e

Directions: *Spacing—1. Line—60. Warmup—page 79; then readjust machine for the timed writing.*

goals

- To type at least 43 wam for 5'/3e.
- To produce an itinerary.
- To produce a letter with a listing.
- To produce a justified display.

5-MINUTE TW

Spacing—2. Line—50. Tab—5.

Speed markers are for 5' TW.

SPECIAL KEYS

! ° [ ] ±

SPECIAL STYLES

ORATOR
Courier
Artisan
Italic
Prestige
Gothic

- 5'/3e

SPECIAL SPACING

1 1½ 2 2½ 3
1
1 1½ 2
1 1½ 2½ 3
1 1½ 2
1 1½ 2 2½
1 1½ 2 3

Take a 5-minute writing, copying line for line as shown.

1 When buying a new typewriter, a customer has 10
2 many options and choices regarding a machine. An 20
3 office typist is likely, therefore, to run into a 30
4 machine with unique features that are unexpected. 40
5 Special keys may be substituted for standard 50
6 keys, such as the degree sign for an asterisk, a 60
7 one-eighth key for the capital period, etc., with 70
8 lots of choices. One can get a business's trade- 80
9 mark on a key, accent marks, mathematics symbols, 90
10 scientific symbols--each in many types and sizes. 100
11 Special print styles can be found, too. The 110
12 shape and size of the characters can be in any of 120
13 a wide range of designs: forward slant, backward 130
14 slant, script, two sizes of capital letters, bold 140
15 or heavy, tall and thin, or broad and squat, etc. 150
16 The standard type is best for general office use. 160
17 Special sizes of print can be obtained, too. 170
18 The normal sizes are pica (ten spaces to an inch) 180
19 and elite (twelve spaces to an inch), but one can 190
20 get tiny print with fifteen spaces to an inch and 200
21 giant print with eight or nine spaces to an inch. 210
22 Special vertical spacing may be built into a 220
23 machine. Normal spacing is six lines to an inch, 230
24 but some makes of machine have five lines or five 240
25 and a fraction lines to an inch. As to automatic 250
26 spacing, you can get machines that space one, one 260
27 and a half, two, two and a half, and three lines. 270

SI 1.41N

goal B

■ To produce an invoice, a credit memo, and a monthly statement within 20'/0e.

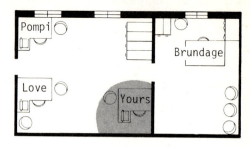

JOB 79-1: BILLING FORMS

Workbook 183–185 □ ■ 20'/0e

You are one of the "emergency squad" typists working for Wesley Brundage at Wisco, Inc., in Fond du Lac, Wisconsin. He beckons to you "Please go down to the Billing Department," he says. "They need your help."

The billing supervisor welcomes you and says, "Can you rush this for us, please. We sent an invoice, then a credit memo, then a statement to an addressee, but the name was misspelled and the address was incorrect. So make new copies, please."

The customer is L'Epicerie, Inc., with both a shipping and a mailing address of 2200 Trempeauleau Drive / La Crosse, WI 54601. This is Invoice 1-3922, to be labeled "(Duplicate)" in the box where you type the invoice number and dated January 8, 19--. Delivery is via our truck. There are four items on this invoice:

```
1 DF1 Display freezer, style 1,
    @ $1,465.00, amount ........... 1,465.00
2 DF8 Display freezer, style 8,
    @ $1,868.50, amount ........... 3,737.00
4 DF2 Display freezer, style 11,
    @ $927.50 ..................... 3,710.00
```

```
1 HBK Maintenance Manual, no charge
    Total ................ 8,912.00
    Delivery ............   210.00
    Total amount due .... 9,122.00
```

Next, the customer is to be given a credit memo, No. CM 1-38, labeled "(Duplicate)" and dated January 14. There is just one item:

```
1 DF8 Display freezer, style 8,
    inoperative on delivery, @
    $1,868.50, amount .............. 1,868.50
    Amount credited ................ 1,868.50
    Delivery charge refund ........    30.00
    Total amount credited .......... 1,898.50
```

Finally, the customer is to be given a new statement, dated January 31 and labeled "(Duplicate)." Data are as follows:

```
Jan.  1  Brought Forward ..........     0.00
Jan.  8  Invoice 1-3922,
         charges $9,112.00 ......... 9,112.00
Jan. 14  CM 1-38
         credits $1,898.50 ......... 7,213.50
Jan. 21  Payment on Account
         credits $5,000.00 ......... 2,213.50
Jan. 31  AMOUNT NOW DUE ...... 2,213.50
```

REVIEW JOB 1: ITINERARY

Workbook 115 or use plain paper and arrange it as shown on page 89

☐ ■ 15'/0e

Also see illustration on page 104.

Itinerary for Ms. M. J. Donaldson   21

Sunday, December 10 *(Use short form, 12/10, if you use the workbook form.)*   35

9:35 a.m., CST Depart Memphis on United 433.   42 / 44

1:02 p.m., PST Arrive San Francisco.   51

Hotel Reservations at Mark Hopkins Hotel.   60

5:30 p.m. Depart hotel for Chinatown visit.   69

9:30 p.m. Return hotel from Chinatown visit.   78

Monday, December 11 (or 12/11)   91

..... Convention at Mark Hopkins Hotel.   101

Tuesday, December 12 (or 12/12)   114

..... Convention at Mark Hopkins Hotel.   124

Wednesday, December 13 (or 12/13)   139

2:00 p.m. Depart hotel on Golden Gate tour.   149

4:00 p.m. Return hotel from Golden Gate tour.   157 / 158

Thursday, December 14 (or 12/14)   172

10:30 a.m. Depart hotel for airport.   180

12:00 noon, PST Depart San Francisco on United 700.   187 / 190

7:15 p.m., CST Arrive Memphis.   195

REVIEW JOB 2: LETTER

Workbook 116 ☐ Body 132 ☐ SI 1.36N ☐ ■ 15'/0e

Ms. M. J. Donaldson / 61 North Fernway Road / Memphis, TN 38117 / Dear Ms. Donaldson: / I am delighted to tell you that we have been able to plan your trip to the NA/CJ convention in San Francisco so that you can do all the things that you told us you wished to do.   15 / 23 / 32 / 41 / 49 / 58 / 62

1. You are free to go to the convention meetings on Monday, Tuesday, and Wednesday mornings.   71 / 78 / 83

2. You can leave on Sunday morning and return on Thursday evening.   92 / 99

3. You can enjoy the Chinatown visit and the Golden Gate tour without missing any of the meetings.   108 / 116 / 121

A copy of your schedule is enclosed. If you want us to make your hotel and flight reservations, please let us know within the next day or two. Throughout the month of December, there are so many travelers that rooms and flights are not always easy to get.   130 / 138 / 147 / 155 / 164 / 173 / 174

May I hear from you soon? / Frank E. Farrell, Agent / urs / Enclosure   186 / 195

REVIEW JOB 3: DISPLAY
TYPING WITH JUSTIFIED LINES

Plain paper ☐ Retype the display, providing the indicated number of spaces to make lines end even ☐ Spacing 2 ☐ ■ 15'/0e

WHERE ARE YOU GOING? ↓₁   4

   14

Wherever it is, you should know that   22

your travel agent can make reserva–#   29

tions for you without charge. The##   37

hotels, motels, airlines, buses, and   44

just about everyone else pays us to#   52

handle the arrangements for them.###   60

We have copies of all the schedules#   67

and all the rates. We save those###   75

companies so much money by acting as   82

their agent that they save money by#   90

paying us to help. So don't think##   97

it costs a bundle to ask us to help#   105

you--it does not cost you one cent!# ↓₁   113

   122

FARRELL & MULLINS AGENCY   139

Memphis 555 - 3343   152

goal A

■ To type at least 45 wam for 5'/2e.

CHECK YOUR POSTURE

☐ *Both feet are on the floor.*
☐ *Body is erect, leaning forward.*
☐ *Head is turned toward copy.*
☐ *Wrists are motionless.*
☐ *Fingers are curved like hooks.*

Directions: Spacing—1. Line—60. Tab—5.
Warmup—page 163. Then start 30" timings.

30-SECOND SPEED CHECK

Speed is number under which you stop typing.

Set the pace of your typing by taking three 30-second timed writings.

```
          01      03      05      07      09      11      13      15      17      19      21      23
1  The main image of Wisconsin as a dairyland is so vivid that          12
          25      27      29      31      33      35      37      39      41      43      45      47
2  it is hard to realize that it has, at Superior, the largest          24
          49      51      53      55      57      59      61      63      65      67      69      71
3  dock in the world for loading ore directly onto lake ships.          36
   |1   |2   |3   |4   |5   |6   |7   |8   |9   |10  |11  |12
```

5-MINUTE WRITING

Spacing—2.

Maintain your 45-wam pace for 5 minutes, with as few errors as possible.

```
                    1
4      Wisconsin produces more milk and cheese than any other          12
                                                  2
                3
5  state and so is recognized as the dairyland of America; the          24
                                              4
        5                        6
6  dairy farms of the state take care of more than two million          36
                                                  7
              8
7  milch cows.  The state also leads in the production of food     48
                                                  9①
          10                        11
8  for livestock:  hay such as alfalfa.  Four out of each five    60
                                                        12
                              13
9  Wisconsin farms are dairy farms.  Not quite half of all the   72
                                              14
                    15                16
10  workers in the state work with dairying or food processing.   84
        17                    18②                          19
11      But, dairy state or not, Wisconsin has a great deal of    96
                    20                    21
12  industry, too, with lumber, tools and machinery, automobile  108
                22                        23                    24
13  parts, and paper among its many products.  Shipbuilding and  120
                          25                    26
14  shipping are two more of its exceptional sources of income.  132
                  27③
15      One of the things about Wisconsin for which persons in   144
                                              28
        29                    30                    31
16  this course should cheer is the fact that the first working  156
                    32                        33
17  typewriter was invented in Milwaukee.  It was in 1868.  The  168
          34                        35                        36④
18  inventor was a Christopher L. Sholes, a printer who enjoyed  180
                              37                    38
19  working with tools.  He invented a machine that would print  192
                  39                        40
20  consecutive numbers on tickets and sales slips.  After that  204
        41                        42                        43
21  he was urged to see what he could do with the alphabet, and  216
                        44                    45⑤
22  what he could do turned out as a typewriter.                 225
   |1   |2   |3   |4   |5   |6   |7   |8   |9   |10  |11  |12    SI 1.40N
```

Routine:
1. 5' timing.
2. Corrective practice.
3. 5' timing.

Speed markers are for 5' TW. Circled numbers are 1' goals.

■ 5'/2e

goal

□ You (Typist A) and a classmate (Typist B) work in the corporate headquarters of DATRON, Inc., in San Francisco, California.

□ Divisional offices for DATRON are in Albuquerque, Boise, Cheyenne, Denver, Los Angeles, Phoenix, Portland, and Salt Lake City.

□ Typist A works for the general sales manager; Typist B works in the accounting office.

CREATIVE CO-OP 3: DEVELOPING TABULAR INFORMATION

TYPIST A: SALES MANAGER'S OFFICE

Your employer is planning to visit some of the divisional offices next month. To plan the trip, you need the following information: (a) the amount of travel funds available; (b) the air fare to fly to each of the divisional offices.

TYPIST B: ACCOUNTING OFFICE

This year a limit of $700 will be allowed for travel to divisional offices. Air fare to each of the offices is as follows:

Albuquerque: $165   Los Angeles: $51
Boise: $130   Phoenix: $146
Cheyenne: $102   Portland: $120
Denver: $170   Salt Lake City: $133

WHY MUST YOU WRITE TO TYPIST B?

The Airline Guide you had been using is out of date, so you disposed of it. Write to Typist B and ask for the new fares. Also ask how much travel is permitted this year.

WHY MUST YOU WRITE TO TYPIST A?

You are asked to compare last year's fares (Typist A has them) with the above fares. Write to Typist A for the old fares, and enclose the above fares with your note.

WHAT DO YOU DO WHEN YOU HEAR FROM TYPIST B?

You no longer have the Airline Guide. However, you do remember that there was a 10 percent increase in fares. To give Typist B an *estimate* of the old fares, take 10 percent of the new fares and subtract those amounts from the new rates. Send these estimates to Typist B.

WHAT DO YOU DO WHEN YOU HEAR FROM TYPIST A?

Only $700 is available for tickets! Recommend only five trips for which Typist A should plan, but do not exceed the maximum funding allowed. Choose those trips that would most closely approach full use of the $700 travel funds.

WHAT DO YOU DO WHEN YOU RECEIVE THE INFORMATION YOU PREVIOUSLY REQUESTED FROM TYPIST B?

Develop a flight schedule (in table form), based on Typist B's information. Give the table an appropriate title and use a subtitle to identify the travel dates from January 15 to January 23 (one city every other day). Use column headings; include air fares.

WHAT DO YOU DO WHEN YOU RECEIVE THE INFORMATION YOU PREVIOUSLY REQUESTED FROM TYPIST A?

Devise a table listing last year's and this year's fares. Name the cities and both years' rates. Use an appropriate table title and a subtitle (to indicate current prices as of December 15, 19--). Use column headings and double-space the items within columns. Round off fares to even dollars.

JOB 78-1: BOOK MANUSCRIPT PAGE

(Continued)

ductory clause that begins with if or when 156
or a similar term: When Stanton made the 165
field goal for the Vikings, the fans went 173
wild. If he had missed the goal, they would 182
have been even wilder. 187

8. Use the comma to set off an introduc- 196
tory phrase that is followed by a breath 204
pause: To count all 15,000 lakes in Min- 212
nesota, the bureau had to use a helicopter. 221

9. Use the comma after the complimen- 230
tary closing of a letter: Yours very truly, 239
Sincerely yours, etc. 243

10. Use the comma to separate a title 252
from the name in the inside address or 266
writer's identification of a letter: Ralph 275
Jones, St. Paul Manager. 279

JOB 78-2: COMPLETION CARDS

5″ x 3″ cards or slips □ ■ 5′/0e

---

goal B

■ To type 45 wam
for 3′/1e.

Directions: *Spacing—1. Line—60. Tab—5.*
Begin the 12-second sprints.

**12-SECOND
SPRINTS**

**Four 12″ timings
on each sentence.**

1 Many people call Minnesota the
2 North Star State for its motto is "Star of the North." 17
3 Gopher State in honor of its prairie ground squirrels. 17
4 Bread and Butter State to honor its farms and dairies. 17

12″ WAM: 45 50 55 60 65 70 75 80 85

**3-MINUTE
PIECEMEAL
PRACTICE**

Take ten 1-minute TWs, staying on each paragraph until it is typed 1′/0e; then
take a 3-minute writing on the entire selection to type 45 wam/3′/1e.

5 Minnesota is rich in its mines, forests, prairies, and 12
6 water, but it is probably best known for its fabulous mines 24
7 of iron ore: nearly two-thirds of the iron ore produced in 36
8 the United States comes from this one region. ① 45

9 In the northern timber country, loggers fell mountains 57
10 of trees each year. It was here Paul Bunyan and his prized 69
11 helper, Babe the Blue Ox, could pull crooked roads straight 81
12 with a quick jerk, according to the legends. ② 90

**Speed markers are
for 3′ TW. Circled
figures are 1′ goals.**

13 Water is a big resource. The state has something over 102
14 fifteen thousand lakes the size of at least ten acres. The 114
15 headwaters of three large river systems rise in Minnesota—— 126
16 the Mississippi, the Red, and the St. Louis. ③ 135

1 2 3 4 5 6 7 8 9 10 11 12

SI 1.39N

■ 3′/1e

---

7 | 78

175

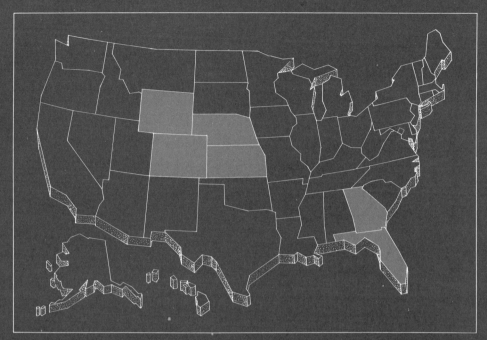

The six projects of Part 5 use the following states as their locale:
Unit 13: Florida, Georgia
Unit 14: Kansas, Nebraska
Unit 15: Colorado, Wyoming

PART 5

Part 5 continues the working plan that you used in Part 4:

1. There are two work-experience projects in each unit, separated by two short skill drives and followed by a skill clinic.

2. There is about an hour's typing in each project. Each project is presented in narrative form to give you experience in listening to and following directions.

3. Each project occurs in a different location, as indicated in the map above.

4. You are to correct all errors in your production work (unless your teacher directs otherwise). Make corrections so expertly that they are undetectable.

5. Turn to this page at the start of each practice period and type a Warmup of your own design: Select one sentence from each of the four groups below and copy it four or more times.

You will find the production exercises interesting, for your work is now becoming closer and closer to the financial and management side of business operations.

SPEED RECALL	1A I am to go to work for the audit firm by the eighth of May.	12
	1B Their men wish to blame us for most of their big work jams.	12
	1C She is busy with the work but is to go to town for the pen.	12
ALPHABET RECALL	2A Wolf gave Jake an extra dozen quarts, but he can't pay him.	12
	2B Seizing the wax buffers, Jensen quickly removed a big spot.	12
	2C Judy gave my boy quite an exciting gold prize for his work.	12
NUMBER RECALL	3A Arnie read pages 10 through 28, 39 through 47, and page 56.	12
	3B They got rooms 10 and 28. We got rooms 39, 47, and 56 too.	12
	3C The room went from 10° to 28° to 39° to 47° to 56° Celsius.	12
THINKING WHILE TYPING **Spell the numbers.**	4A We need 3 more men, 8 altogether, on duty at 7.	12
	4B We want 4 or 6 chairs for the next 3 or 4 days.	12
	4C Please send us 9 clerks, 4 typists, and 1 secretary.	12

|1 |2 |3 |4 |5 |6 |7 |8 |9 |10 |11 |12

5

JOB 77-3: BOOK MANUSCRIPT PAGE

Workbook 176 visual guide ☐ **Plain paper** ☐ ■ **20'/0e**

After you have done the rearranged version of page 38, Mrs. Smith says, "Okay, here is page 42 of our handbook. You're on your own!"

CHAPTER XII   20

Punctuation in a Nutshell   37

Some punctuation marks are used more 47
often in business work than others. The 55
purpose of this chapter is to review with 63
you the punctuation uses that office workers 73
should know. 75

Section 182: The Period   92

1. Use the period to end a simple de- 101
clarative sentence: I am glad I live in 109
Minnesota. 111

2. Use a period to end a polite request: 121
Will you send the Twin Cities Report at 129
once, please. 131

3. Use the period after an initial or 140
abbreviation: Do you know Mr. T. B. Clark 149
of St. Cloud? 152

4. Do not use a period in a cluster of 161
initial letters: He joined the YMCA in 169
Duluth. 171

Section 183: The Comma   187

1. Use the comma before the conjunction 196
that connects two complete clauses in one 204
sentence: The Obijah Indians were in the 212
east part of Minnesota, and the Sioux were 222
in the west. 224

2. Use the comma to separate words, 233
phrases, or other elements in a series: 241
Minnesota excels in raising corn, wheat, 249
barley, and a number of other grain crops. 257

JOB 78-1: BOOK MANUSCRIPT PAGE

Workbook 176 visual guide ☐ **Plain paper** ☐ ■ **15'/0e**

"And here is page 43," says Mrs. Smith, when you have completed page 42. On you go. Did you remember to make a carbon of page 42?

3. Use the comma to set off contrasts: 18
In Minnesota, fishermen hope to catch trout, 27
not bass. 29

4. Use the comma to separate two or 37
more adjectives that precede the same noun 46
when the word "and" is implied but is not 54
given: A cool, brisk breeze came in from 63
Lake Superior. 66

LESSON 78

Directions: *Spacing—1. Line—60. Warmup—page 163; then begin Job 78-1.*

5. Use the comma to set off appositives 75
(words explaining or identifying other 83
words or terms): St. Paul, the capital of 92
Minnesota, is located at the Falls of St. 100
Anthony. 102

6. Use the comma to set off an adjective 111
clause that is not essential to the complete- 120
ness of the sentence: Bemidji, which is in 128
the iron ore part of Minnesota, is a northern 138
city. 139

7. Use the comma to set off an intro- 148

(Continued on next page)

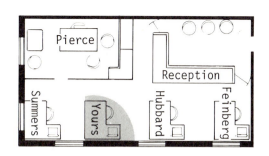

Pierce

Reception

Summers

Yours

Hubbard

Feinberg

Directions: *Spacing—1. Line—60.*
Warmup—page 107; then begin Job 49-1.

JOB 49-1: INCOME STATEMENT

Plain paper □ Center □ ■ 15'/0e

You meet Paul Pierce, an accountant, who shows you around the office and then gives you the page of work shown below.

"This is one of two income statements I need right away," he says, "so please type it while I draft the next one."

You notice that it is typed on a 60-space line. You are to copy it line for line.

```
          Jacksonville Tile and Shingle Company              24
                     Income Statement                        36
           For the Month Ended August 31, 19--   ↓₁      ①   57
                                                             70
                                                     ②  ↓₂   71
Revenue From Sales:               T----------T--------       74
                                                             75
     Sales .................... $9,160.00                    85
     Less:  Returns and Allowances ....    200.00            91
     Net Sales .................           $8,960.00         113
                                                             114
Cost of Goods Sold ...................  ③   5,832.00         130
                                                             131
Gross Profit on Sales ...........  ④        $3,128.00        142
                                                             143
Operating Expenses:                                          148
                                                             149
     Cash Short ......... $    18.50                         159
     Delivery Expense ........    64.75                      169
     Insurance Expense .........  29.75                      179
     Payroll Taxes Expense ...   175.50                      189
     Salaries Expense ........ 2,000.00                      199
     Supplies Expense .........  114.36                      209
     Utilities Expense .......   195.64                      219
     Miscellaneous Expense ....   25.00                      234
     Total Operating Expense .......   $2,623.50             250
                                                             251
Net Income ........................    $   504.50           271
```

Financial statements are often typed on a limited line to match what is used in accompanying papers; here a 60-space line is used. In such cases: ① set margins for desired line (some firms want a line typed, as here); ② backspace from the right margin to set tab stops for the money columns, with ③ 2 spaces between money columns; and ④ fill in between columns 1 and 2 with leaders (periods). Leader line must start and end with 1 blank space.

Start on line 13 → CHAPTER IX

Put on line 7 → Page 38

Quick
A Review of Capitals

2# here →

Do not indent first paragraph

One of the language *mechanics* ~~niceties~~ that ~~everyone who works in an~~ office, *workers must* ~~ought to~~ know well and use correctly is Capitalization. Some of the ~~essential~~ rules that must be known and *used* ~~applied~~ at all times are the *se:* ~~following.~~

2# here →

Section 174 : The Capital

1. Use a capital in the first word of *a* sentences, and of ~~each~~ direct quotation. Also capitalize the first word in each line of *an outline or a* poem. [1]

¶ 2. Use a capital in the name of a particular person and a word ~~that may be~~ substituted for such a name: Joe Wilson, Buddy Wilson, Big Brother, Mr. Simpson, J. P. and so on.

3. # Use a cap*ital* in the title of a particular person; ~~too.~~ Ms. Welsh, Dr. Jones, President Kennedy, *and so on* ~~etc.~~ Don't cap a title that follows a name in a sentence *(other than* ~~unless the name is that of~~ a very, very high-ranked public official*)*: Robert Evans, our Mayor; Mr. Hall, ~~the well known~~ state senator from Mille Lacs County. [2]

1½" margin on this side; 1" on other →

4. # Use a cap*ital* in the name of a particular place: In Minnesota, in Rochester, at the Mayo Clinic, ~~over~~ on Poe Street, ~~etc.~~

5. Use a capital for *the name of* a particular thing: a bowl of Wheaties, a Ford, a Chevelle, a Concorde.

[1] William A. Sabin, <u>The Gregg Reference Manual</u>, 5th ed., McGraw-Hill Book Company, New York, 1977, p. 71.

[2] Ibid., p. 76.

JOB 77-2: ONE-PAGE MANUSCRIPT

Workbook 175 visual guide □ Plain paper □ ■ 10'/0e

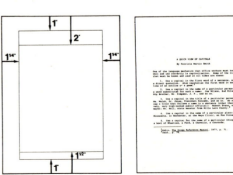

Mrs. Smith looks at your work and says, "It will be a long time before we have printed copies of our handbook. This material on capitalization is so good that I am going to ask you to type another copy I can have duplicated."

Mrs. Smith continues, "Type it as an ordinary report—centered 6-inch line, single spacing. Insert my name as a by-line: Patricia Martin Smith. Omit the side heading line. Center the work on a full page, and condense the footnotes."

Condense footnotes? See page 279.

Standard report: Margins are the same as for book manuscript pages (see page 172) except that sides are even, 1¼" each. Spacing—1. Only 1 space above and below side headings, if any.

7 77

goal B

■ To produce an
income statement
from a draft.

JOB 49-2: INCOME STATEMENT FROM DRAFT

Plain paper ☐ **Line—60** ☐ ■ **20′/0e**

"Here is the second income statement," says Mr. Pierce. "This
one is 'For the Month Ended September 30' instead of 'August
31,' but in all other regards it should be arranged just like the
first statement."

Revenue from sales:

Sales	$9,875.00	
Less: returns and allowances	215.50	
Net sales		$9,659.50
Cost of goods sold		6,009.90
Gross profit on sales		$3,649.60

Operating expenses:

Cash short	$ 26.80	
Delivery expense	104.80	
Insurance expense	29.75	
Payroll taxes expense	175.50	
Salaries expense	2,000.00	
Supplies expense	69.40	
Utilities expense	205.35	
Miscellaneous expense	25.00	
Total operating expense		$2,636.60
Net income		$1,013.00

70
71
74
75
85
91
113
114
130
131
142
143
148
149
159
169
179
189
199
209
219
234
250
251
271

goal A

■ To produce a
two-page letter
within 15′/0e.

LESSON **50**

Directions: *Spacing—1. Line—60.*
Warmup—page 107.

"I have analyzed the two income statements," says Mr. Pierce,
"and now I want to dictate a long letter about them. The letter
must be addressed to the president of the company, but carbons
are to be sent to each of the three families that own the company's stock."

PRETEST 2

Take three 1-minute timings on lines 11–14. Proofread all and average the scores.

11 Frank knows about the campus campaign to back a labor vote. 12
12 Carol gave six tubs of shrubs to enable the band to travel. 24
13 Scott and Elmer called the track coaches about those races. 36
14 Benjamin will carry about nine heavy carts to the big barn. 48

|1 |2 |3 |4 |5 |6 |7 |8 |9 |10 |11 |12

PRACTICE 2

Use the same practice pattern you used in Practice 1.

15 bay mad tax map tab mar van nab car ink can jam bat jab man 12
16 baby mast vary mall sack pack care jack bank hymn tack jobs 24
17 enemy vault blame clams mulch bands madam track bulbs nails 36

18 cab mob bag mix vat men bin lob act inn bar nob may bad vim 12
19 back maze bake navy calm mast many came zany cage bend mint 24
20 meant coach manly basic naval cable lemon canal money candy 36

POSTTEST 2

Repeat Pretest 2. Score your work and note your improvement.

goal A

■ To produce a one-page manuscript in two arrangements.

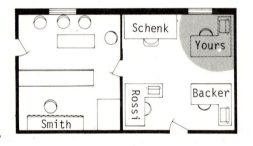

JOB 77-1: BOOK MANUSCRIPT PAGE

Workbook 176 visual guide □ Plain paper □ ■ 10'/0e

Directions: Spacing—1. Line—60. Warmup—page 163. WB 177–178.

The Training Department of a large insurance company in Minneapolis is preparing a handbook for its office workers. The person coordinating the project is Mrs. Patricia M. Smith. You and Lola Schenk are brought in to assist Bob Rossi and Phyllis Backer in typing the manuscript so it may be sent to the printer for composition.

Giving you the manuscript page shown on page 173, Mrs. Smith says, "This is the start of Chapter Nine. Please retype it, and make one carbon copy too."

Seeing the perforations on your copy, you ask, "When it is done, it will go in a binder?"

"Yes," replies Mrs. Smith.

"And double-spaced, I see," you add, "with the side heads in underscored cap and small letters."

"Right," confirms Mrs. Smith.

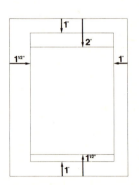

Book manuscript page: Top margin is 1" on all pages except chapter opener, which is 2". Side margins are 1½" on binder side and 1" on right. Bottom margin is at least 1", preferably 1½". Spacing—2. Page number is on line 7 at the right margin, with or without the word "page."

(Continued on next page)

JOB 50-1 AND JOB 50-2: TWO-PAGE LETTER

Workbook 117 □ 316 Words □ SI 1.41N □ ■ 15′/0e

Today's date / Mr. Richard Cohen, Presi- 13
dent / Jacksonville Tile and Shingle Co. / 22
8091 21st Street NW / Jacksonville, FL 28
33024 / 29

Dear Mr. Cohen: / I have gone over the 39
books for the month of September and can 47
report to you and the owners that you have 55
had a most successful month: a net income 64
of $1,013.00 on sales of $9,659.50, which 73
is 10.5 percent. I tip my hat to you and 82
your staff. 84

A comparison of the August and Septem- 92
ber figures shows that, with just about the 101
same sales, you doubled the net income in 109
September. Here are the summary figures 116
for the two months: *Indent 5 on each side.* 121

	August	September	
Net Sales	$8,960.00	$9,659.50	146
Cost of Goods Sold .	5,832.00	6,009.90	164
Gross Profit	$3,128.00	$3,649.60	175
Operating Expenses	2,623.50	2,636.60	194
Net Income	$ 504.50	$1,013.00	207

This comparison shows that with only 227
$700 more sales than in August, you 234
were able to hold the line on expenses 243
and therefore transfer $500 of the $700 250
to the bottom line as more net income. 258
An income statement for each month is 267
enclosed. 268

I looked into your expense items but 277
could find no weak spot. Your delivery 285
expenses went up about $50 more than 293
expected, but supply cost was down 299
about $50, which made a standoff. It 307
seems to me that you really are working 315
close to the line. 319

Be on guard for the bottom margin. ..
Use plain paper and standard heading on ..
page 2. ..

As you know from our many confer- 326
ences, you must get your sales to the 334
$10,000 mark each month to stay in the 342
black and up to the $12,000 mark if you 375
are to give the owners the return that 383
they need to sustain their confidence in 391
your management. The benefit that came 399
from the $700 increase proves the point. 407

So it seems to me that you will have 415
to take some big steps to boost your 423
sales. I know of no way you can cut 431
expenses more than you have; indeed, I 438
think that you may have to set up a 445
sales promotion account as a new ex- 452
pense, for more sales will require expense 461
in attracting them. They won't just hap- 469
pen. / *Closing phrase:* 470

Congratulations on a good month! / 479
Paul Pierce, Management Consultant / 490
Florida Accounting Services, Inc. / urs / 500
cc Mr. James Green / cc Mr. Arthur 506
Green / cc Mrs. Clara Green Downs 512

JOB 50-3: COMPLETION CARDS

5″ x 3″ cards or slips □ ■ 5′/0e

---

goal B

■ **To type at least
44 wam for 3′/2e.**

Directions: *Spacing—1. Line—60. Tab—5.*
Begin the 12″ sprints on the next page.

TOP SALES ITEMS
Tennessee Handicraft Association

75
83
93
135
145
155
165
175
185
194
236

Item Number	Description	Amount Sold	Percentage of Total
#78	Corn Husk Dolls	$12,869	9.8
#12	Heritage Quilts	10,118	7.7
#89	Hand-Painted Jewelry	8,907	6.8
#45	Quilted Pillows	8,389	6.4
#29	Crocheted Shawls	7,206	5.5
#19	Hanging Pottery	7,198	5.5

Boxed tables: Vertical lines are drawn after table is typed. Horizontal rules are extended 3 spaces on each end. Leave 1 blank line above and below each ruled line.

goal

■ To use intensive drill to improve basic skill.

ACTIVITIES	20 MIN.	40 MIN.
Warmup (page 163)	3'	3'
Drive 1 Pretest	4'	4'
Drive 1 Practice	9'	9'
Drive 1 Posttest	4'	4'
Drive 2 Pretest	—	5'
Drive 2 Practice	—	10'
Drive 2 Posttest	—	5'

Directions: Spacing—1. Line—60. Warmup—page 163.

DRIVE 1

PRETEST 1

Take two 1-minute timings on lines 1–4. Proofread both and average your scores.

Stress on in-motions.

1 Mark ought to clear enough money from our pipes to go home.   12
2 Carl bought a sixty-pound crate of cotton from that farmer.   24
3 Leonard wrote to you last month about coming to our picnic.   36
4 I doubt Ruth won a hat as one of the prizes at the meeting.   48
  |1 |2 |3 |4 |5 |6 |7 |8 |9 |10 |11 |12

PRACTICE 1

Make four copies. Repeat individual lines for speed gain if you averaged two or fewer Pretest errors; otherwise, repeat each block of lines for accuracy gain.

Stress on in-motions.

5 you won pin out add sad are fly one hat mar ate coy mat lye   12
6 toys adds tone clad spur flag come glad song size pure road   24
7 wrong adapt woman flags doubt touch roads ought prize spurs   36

8 the jab rat you rot yes red ore vat her nor hat big lit aft   12
9 long hats pure mets gone navy club part bond jack flue puff   24
10 ghost earth ready virus think teach spunk vague yearn yacht   36

POSTTEST 1

Repeat the Pretest. Score your work and note your improvement.

Take four 12-second timings on each of the three complete sentences.

1 You should know that Florida
2   raises more than six million tons of oranges each year.   17
3   raises almost two million tons of grapefruit each year.   17
4   raises more citrus fruits than do all the other states.   17

12" WAM: 40 45 50 55 60 65 70 75 80 85

3-MINUTE PIECE-MEAL PRACTICE

Take ten 1-minute timings, staying on each paragraph until you type it within 1'/0e; then take a 3-minute writing that targets on the goal: 44 wam/3'/2e.

Spacing—1 for 1' TWs.
Spacing—2 for 3' TW.

Speed markers are for 3' TW. Circled numbers are 1' goals.

5   Thanks to the subtropical climate that Florida enjoys,   12
6 the state leads the nation in its fine crops of grapefruit,   24
7 oranges, tangerines, and limes. It is also one of the best   36
8 for tobacco and all kinds of vegetables. ①   44
9   That great climate, when mixed with some of the finest   12 | 56
10 beaches in the world, is the big lure which draws in nearly   24 | 68
11 thirty million visitors a year, a great number of whom like   36 | 80
12 it so well that they move to Florida. ②   44 | 88
13   The state is almost equally famed for its Cape Kennedy   12 | 100
14 launchings of missiles, capsules, and satellites. When you   24 | 112
15 think of men on the moon, you always remember that the Cape   36 | 124

■ 3'/2e

16 is where the astronauts take off from. ③   44 | 132

1 2 3 4 5 6 7 8 9 10 11 12   SI 1.39N

goal A

■ To type 44 wam within 5'/3e.

FOR THE SAKE OF ACCURACY

☐ Sit clear back in the chair.
☐ Sit erect, leaning forward.
☐ Brace feet, apart, on the floor.
☐ Hold wrists low, together.

LESSON 51

Directions: Spacing—1. Line—60.
Warmup—page 107.

PRETEST PRACTICE

Take a 5-minute writing from page 112. Count your errors carefully.

Type the designated drills three times each.

Pretest errors	0–2	3–5	6–+
Drills to type	1–6	2–7	3–8

Speed.

1 worth value grown trade north roads along those pines resin   12
2 with from city only sign fact that what made more than land   24
3 only of also of sign of fact of what is made in sits in the   36

Technique.

4 Southeast Savannah Atlanta, Athens United States South They   12
5 Peachtree Valdosta Columbus Albany Empire Plains State It A   24

(Continued on next page)

RULED TABLES

☐ *Heading line(s) centered.*
☐ *Column headings centered.*
☐ *Column headings not underscored.*
☐ *Column headings even at bottom.*
☐ *One blank line above and below each ruled line.*
☐ *Rules even with sides of table.*
☐ *Entries in natural groupings.*
☐ *Lines organized in some system (here by pages in yearbook).*

Supplier	Location	Space in Yearbook
Dunaway, Inc.	Pittman Center	¼ page
M & R Crafts	Elkmont	¼ page
Woods & Stuff	McCookville	¼ page
Pottery Unlimited	Pigeon Forge	½ page
Appalachian, The	Prospect	1 page
Doll House, The	Middle Creek	1 page
Hollaway House	Pine Grove	1 page
Mountain Crafts	Sevierville	1 page

JOB 76-2: RULED TABLE

Plain paper ☐ ■ 10'/0e

Giving you the adjacent table, Miss Hall says, "I found this table in a newspaper. I will need copies for a talk I'm to give at the convention. Please type it for me."

"Do you want it in ruled form like the table I just finished," you ask, "or do you want it in open style?"

"Ruled," she says, "and alphabetic, please."

TENNESSEE HANDICRAFT ASSOCIATION
Average Yearly Sales Since 1975

Sales Areas By Cities	Outlets	Amount
Nashville	4	$ 21,174
Kingsport	2	18,292
Clarksville	2	18,173
Murfreesboro	1	15,421
Bristol	3	14,331
Jackson	2	12,794
Knoxville	2	11,439
Oak Ridge	1	9,770
Memphis	4	9,478
TOTAL	21	$130,872

goal B

■ **To produce a boxed table within 15'/0e.**

JOB 76-3: BOXED TABLE

Plain paper ☐ ■ 15'/0e

"I have another table that I will need for my talk in Nashville," says Miss Hall.

She gives you the table (top of page 171) and adds, "You know, I like this arrangement with the vertical lines as well as the horizontal ones. Could you type it that way?"

Remembering page 154 in this book, you know that of course you could type it that way.

"That arrangement is called 'boxed,'" you reply. "It's just a little more complicated than the ruled tables I have been typing."

You continue, "Do you wish this one alphabetized, too, as you did the others?"

She ponders. "No," she says, "the important thing is the amount sold. Type it as it is."

JOB 76-4: COMPLETION CARDS

5" x 3" cards or slips ☐ ■ 5'/0e

```
 6   production buildings conquest industry amazing magical name    12
 7   turpentine factories striving thriving finance exceeds also    24
 8   throughout principal highways quarters network world's sits    36
```

POSTTEST   Repeat the Pretest. Score your work and note your improvement.

5-MINUTE TW

```
 9        Georgia!  It is a magical name.  It is a magical dream    12
10   about the Old South, complete with the sounds of banjos and    24
11   singing in the night.  It is the magic of Peachtree Street,    36
12   the amazing conquest from the village of Plains.              44
13        It is also the thriving new Empire State of the South,    56
14   with the city of Atlanta as capital not only of Georgia but    68
15   also of the whole Southeast.  A sign of the change through-    80
16   out the state is the fact that the value of what is made in    92
17   her factories is more, now, than the value of what is grown   104
18   on the land; and the worth of her buildings now exceeds the   116
19   worth of the land itself--it is a striving, thriving state.   128
20        Atlanta, the center of commerce and industry and trade   140
21   and finance, sits in the middle north of the state, circled   152
22   by a network of roads to the principal cities--to Columbus,   164
23   to Albany, to Valdosta, to Savannah, to Augusta, to Athens.   176
24        Along those highways are pines, pines, and more pines,   188
25   for Georgia production of resin and turpentine is more than   200
26   half of all the world's supply and is three-quarters of the   212
27   supply produced in the United States.                        220
     |1   |2   |3   |4   |5   |6   |7   |8   |9   |10   |11   |12   SI 1.33FE
```

Speed markers are for 5′ TW. Circled numbers are 1′ goals.

■ 5′/2e

goal B

■ To produce the first page of a three-page report.

JOB 51-1: REPORT (PAGE 1)

□ ■ 15′/0e

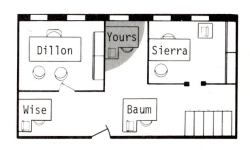

Directions: *Adjust the typewriter for Job 51-1. Spacing—2. Line—6 inches. Tabs—5 and center.*

"Welcome to Georgia Power," says Kent Dillon, president of the company. "You're just in time to type my stockholders' report for the third quarter." He gives you the first page. (See page 113.)

JOB 75-2: OPEN TABLE

Plain paper □ ■ 10′/0e

"Next," says Miss Hall, "please type this table in the style you used for the last one."

Headquarters of the Tennessee Handicrafts Association in Gatlinburg, Tennessee.

List of Exhibitors
Tenth Annual Handicrafts Festival
Hermitage Hotel
Nashville, Tennessee
May 9 Through May 11, 19—

Exhibit	Representative	Booth
Amy's Mountain Crafts	Amy C. Wallingford	7
Bluegrass Handicrafts	Edward Carson	2
Bristol Pottery Store	Jo Ann Bristol	1
Gatlinburg Specialties	Sara McCoy Weir	6
Heritage Furniture, Inc.	Truman Hammer	4
Polly's Quilt Shop	Polly Scott Gee	3
Smith's Wood Crafts	John C. Smith, IV	5
Stitch N Chatter	Eloise Dreyfuss	8

13
35
46
60
78
99
115
124
133
143
153
162
172
180

---

goal A

■ To produce two ruled tables.

JOB 76-1: RULED TABLE

Plain paper □ ■ 10′/0e

Miss Hall gives you the ruled table shown at the top of page 170 and says, "Please retype this for me. It is now arranged by space in the yearbook, and I want it arranged alphabetically instead."

She continues, "Please add these entries":

LESSON 76

Directions: *Spacing—1. Line—60. Warmup—page 163; then begin Job 76-1.*

Leather Thong	Cove Creek	1 page
Fruit of the Forest	Cedar Bluff	1 page

"Ruled form, please, double-spaced," Miss Hall adds.

THE ~~ACTING~~ PRESIDENT'S REPORT   Line 13   15

On Operations in the ~~Second~~ *third* Quarter ↓3   Line 15   38

     Georgia Fuel and Power provides electric service to most   52

parts of Georgia, ~~We also provide~~ oil service to the top half   61

of the state, and steam heat service in the ~~area~~ *five counties* around Atlanta.   77

     High lights for the ~~second~~ *third* quarter are ~~displayed~~ *shown* in ~~the~~   87

~~first two columns~~ *columns 1 and 2* of the following table. ~~The third~~ column 3   97

shows the comparable figures for *the third quarter of* ~~last~~ year.   110

   126

FINANCIAL HIGH LIGHTS

	This Year	Last Year	
			139
	$3,234,800	$3,043,800	151
Net sales	228,000	272,600	164
Net Earnings	5.00	5.90	176
Per Share of Common Stock	86,100	76,700	188
Cash Dividends Paid	2.00	1.75	200
Per Share of Common Stock	1,492	1,398	212
Common Share Owners' Equity	32.93	30.35	225
Per Share of Common Stock	442,100	536,200	237
Working Capital	1,274,200	717,300	249
Long-Term Debt	677,100	627,300	261
Payroll and Employee Benefits	49,491	51,030	273
Full-Time Employees, *September* ~~June~~ 30	76,761	78,964	286
Share Owners, *September* ~~June~~ 30			

Indent 5 (for Per Share of Common Stock)

     The third quarter was an ~~exceptional~~ *difficult* one for Georgia (F&P), as it was   322

for ~~a lot of~~ *some* other firms too. The slump in business in July and August   336

led *at once* to a decline in power use, making even weaker a year that had ~~been~~ *known*   352

~~predicted to be a year of lower~~ *only low* demand.   355

     Our firm responded *to the market sag* by tailoring power output to ~~equal~~ *fit* customer's   372

needs. We *also* reduced *our* inventory and doubled our effort to keep *our* costs under   396

close control. The net result *of our response* was earnings of $5 a share.   405

STEPS TOWARD GROWTH   411

     The key development in the third quarter was our acquiring Macon Oil,   426

Inc., a most successful firm. With *n*o ~~serious~~ loss of staff, our group   439

Watch for the bottom margin!

JOB 52-1:
REPORT
(PAGE 2)
(See page 114)

goal A

- **To type 45 wam for 5'/2e.**

Directions: Spacing—1. Line—60. Tab—5.
Warmup—page 163.
WB 173–174.

PRETEST

Take a 5-minute TW on lines 13–31, page 167. Score your work carefully.

PRACTICE

Type three times each the lines indicated in this chart.

Errors in Pretest	0–1	2–4	5–+
Lines to practice	1–6	2–7	3–8

Speed.

1 which gives great river ports farms ideal homes grand blend 12
2 also lead most rich from make folk gait take over made give 24
3 and has new way old you the are oak was far big its one use 36

Commas.

4 why, made, wood, miles, horse, dolls, world, first, banjos, 12

Periods.

5 new. life. over. said. ports. years. power. country. 24

Accuracy.

6 Tennessee potteries flooding settin' brooms narrow will all 12
7 Knoxville hardwoods feelings bottoms middle across wood off 24
8 Nashville bluegrass flooring fiddles offers smooth doll see 36

POSTTEST

Repeat the Pretest and note how much your scores have improved.

goal B

- **To produce two open tables.**

JOB 75-1: OPEN TABLE

Plain paper ☐ ■ 10'/0e

You work for Miss Kate Hall, executive secretary for the Tennessee Handicraft Association with headquarters in Gatlinburg.

"Hello," she says. "We have a state convention coming up and a number of things to get ready for it."

"How can I help?" you ask.

She gives you the table shown at the right. "You'll note," she says, "that this is arranged alphabetically. Please retype it, arranging it by time—the nine o'clock program first, then the ten o'clock, then the one, and so on."

```
                Schedule of Demonstrations             18
             TENTH ANNUAL HANDICRAFTS FESTIVAL         40
                     Hermitage Hotel                   51
                  Nashville, Tennessee                 65
                     May 10, 19--                      75
                                                       77

        Event            Location          Time        89
     Furniture         Room 137           1:00         95
→
     Painting          Room 234           2:00        102
     Pottery           Room 254          10:30        108
     Stitchery         Room 173           4:00        114
     Weaving           Room 126           9:00        121
     Wood Carving      Room 256           3:00        128
```

Open table: Title lines are centered; column headings are centered over their columns and underscored. Columns are 6 spaces apart; the whole table is centered.

goal A

- To produce page 2 of a report.

goal B

- To produce page 3 of a report.

LESSON

52

Directions: *Spacing—1. Line—60.*
Warmup—page 107; then continue the
three-page report.

and the Macon group are now operating successfully as ① unit. Macon Oil   454

was important ⌃to us because of the fine storage tanks and the modern equipment   469

with which the firm worked in serving their customers.   475

491
505
518
530
536

*We have two other projects under study by the Board. One is a $150 million
expansion of the Jekyll Island plant, which would serve the eastern part
of the state. The other project would be a $175 million expansion of the
La Grange plant to serve the rest of the state. Expansion proposals
costs less than new plants.*

**Watch for the
bottom margin!**

REORGANIZATION   541

        The plan prepared last winter was introduced on July 1: each   555
profit center in our firm now operates under one general manager with   567
full command of the marketing, the engineering, and so on, We were   581
delighted to find that the plan went into effect with no difficulty.   591

With three months' experience with the new organization plan,   624
we now see far more assets in the plan than we did before: 635

    1. There is an increased focus on making a profit.   647

    2. We are using our land and buildings better.   668

**JOB 52-2:
REPORT
(PAGE 3)**

    3. We can respond quicker to customer needs.   657

    4. We have uncovered a great deal of new business.   679

    5. There is improved control of all the budgets.   691

    6. We have reduced the layers of management from five rows   704
to two, which means better team work, of course.   713

    7. There is more efficient use of all of our equipment.   726

(Continued on next page)

3-MINUTE
WRITING

Lesson 74.

Speed markers are
for 3′ TW. Circled
numbers are 1′ goals
at 45 wam.

Take a 3-minute TW on this unpracticed copy to reconfirm your skill.

1 The Ohio River was a roadway for the settlers who came 12
2 by flatboats and scows and rafts. One of the best known of 24
3 the settlers was Dan Boone, the man who blazed the trail to 36
4 the middle of Kentucky and became a legend. 45
5 Kentucky has had many famous sons, but none were famed 57
6 more than the two who led opposite sides in the Civil War-- 69
7 Abraham Lincoln and Jefferson Davis. Another great one was 81
8 Henry Clay, a star in all the history books. 90
9 Of many lakes and parks and other attractions, the one 102
10 for which Kentucky is best known is Mammoth Caves, and they 114
11 really are mammoth, with 150 miles of passageways, ceilings 126
12 up to 200 feet in rooms like football fields. 135

■ 3′/1e

|1 |2 |3 |4 |5 |6 |7 |8 |9 |10 |11 |12   SI 1.35N

5-MINUTE
WRITING

Lesson 75.

Speed markers are
for 5′ TW. Circled
numbers are 1′ goals
at 45 wam.

13 Because it's long and narrow and stretches across more 12 | 147
14 than four hundred miles, Tennessee has a mixture of scenery 24 | 159
15 and ways of life. It is a grand blend of both old and new. 36 | 171
16 Gatlinburg, deep in the Smokies, is the center of many 48 | 183
17 of the handicrafts of the country. You will gaze for hours 60 | 195
18 as craftsmen make brooms, pottery, dolls, carvings of wood, 72 | 207
19 and an old mountain "settin' chair" which is said to last a 84 | 219
20 hundred years. Near Knoxville are TVA projects that secure 96 | 231
21 the state from flooding and give power. Also nearby is Oak 108 | 243
22 Ridge, where atomic power was made, refined, and unleashed. 120 | 255
23 It is not far to the middle of the state where horses, 132 | 267
24 bluegrass, and music take over. Big farms make ideal homes 144 | 279
25 for the Tennessee walking horse, unique for its smooth gait 156 | 291
26 which gives riders a gliding feeling. Guitars, banjos, and 168 | 303
27 fiddles make country and western folk music from Nashville. 180 | 315
28 Western Tennessee offers rich river bottoms and one of 192 | 327
29 the great river ports. Memphis is most famous for its lead 204 | 339
30 in the cotton markets of the world, but it is also a center 216 | 351
31 for hardwoods used in flooring and furniture. 225 | 360

■ 5′/2e

|1 |2 |3 |4 |5 |6 |7 |8 |9 |10 |11 |12   SI 1.38N

JOB 52-2: REPORT (PAGE 3)

(Continued)

We make no claim that the new plan 734
is perfect, but we are working on the few 742
points of concern and taking great satis- 750
faction in the instant success that our 758
plan has enjoyed. 762

LOOKING AHEAD 767

The next two quarters are ones in 775
which the weather and an expected pick- 783
up in production in the cotton mills will 791
mean a sharp improvement in our sales 799
and, therefore, our profits. 805

Your company executives at headquar- 813
ters have rededicated themselves to the 821
precepts and principles on which our 828
company was founded and by which it 831
has grown to serve the whole state. We 839
are grateful for the support of our stock- 847
holders. 849

Respectfully submitted, ↓4 858
Kent Dillon, President 865

JOB 52-3: COMPLETION CARDS

5″ x 3″ cards ☐ ■ 5′/0e

■ To use intensive drill to improve skill.

ACTIVITIES	20 MIN.	40 MIN.
Warmup, page 107	3′	3′
Pretest (two 2′ TWs)	5′	—
(or four 2′ TWs)	—	10′
Practice (lines—3)	7′	—
(or lines—6)	—	17′
Posttest (repeat Pretest)	5′	10′

Directions: *Spacing—1. Line—50. Tab—5. Warmup—page 107; then begin the Pretest.*

PRETEST

Weighted with right-hand and alternate-hand combinations.

Speed markers are for 2′ TWs.

Take 2-minute timings and average your scores to set the base for practice.

```
1        Did you ever think of the phenomenon that normally the    12
2    fish is a truly active animal?  Some fish do the minimum of    24
3    swimming, but the group is small; the busy fish abides in a    36
4    hungry bowl, and the fish that slows down is soon devoured.    48
5        The body of the fish is designed to handle the dangers    60
6    of such a world.  The supple spine whips about from side to    72
7    side.  The mighty muscles empower quick motions.  The slick    84
8    skin aids the body in slipping through the water.  Finally,    96
9    the chest fins allow quick turns and slow or halting moves.   108
```

PRACTICE

Weighted with right-hand consecutives.

```
10   ion nation motion station portion rations position donation   12
11   oin points joints coining appoint joining pointing adjoined    24
12   min mining minute minting minimum mineral trimming minerals    36
13   imp import impose imposes imports impress imposing imported    48
14   ill chills drills fulfill willing billing goodwill waybills    60
```

(Continued on next page)

JOB 74-1: LETTER

(Continued)

answer the question you asked about copy-41
right laws. The wording used in the state-49
ment in each book is one that has been57
worked out by the courts to guard the65
rights of authors and publishers. We do not73
invent the words; they are prescribed. These83
are the words used in all of our books:91

An extended quotation like this one is ..
indented 5 spaces on each margin. ..

All Rights Reserved. No part of this101
publication may be reproduced, stored109
in a retrieval system, or transmitted,118
in any form or by any means, elec-125
tronic, mechanical, photocopying, re-133
cording, or otherwise, without the prior142
written permission of the publisher.151

After the quotation, be sure to move the ..
margin stops back to where they were. ..

You will find these words on either the159
front or the back of the title page in each169
Maps of America book. / Sincerely yours, /180
Nancy T. Rothberg / Editor in Chief / urs194

A postscript is introduced with "PS:" ..
and is typed as an "added on" paragraph. ..

PS: If you will look at the title pages204
of books by other firms, you will find a212
similar statement in their books.218

JOB 74-2: COMPLETION CARDS

5" x 3" cards or slips □   ■ 5'/0e

JOB 74-1: LETTER WITH QUOTATION AND PS
1. Typed by Roberta Siebmann
2. Proofread with Denise Childs
3. While typing the quotation, I kept
   forgetting to tab in 5 spaces, so I
   had to do a lot of erasing.

3-MINUTE PIECEMEAL PRACTICE

Skill goals in Part 7 remain at 45 wam for speed but reduce the number of errors in timings, allowing only one in a 3-minute TW, two in a 5-minute TW.

Directions: *Spacing—1. Line—60. Tab—5.*

Spacing—1 for
1' TWs. Spacing—2
for 3' TW.

Take ten 1-minute TWs, typing each paragraph until you can type it within 1'/0e; then take a 3-minute writing on the entire selection to type 45 wam/1e.

```
 1        If you gave a quiz on Kentucky to a lot of people, you      12
 2   would probably find that more of them know about the Derby,      24
 3   Churchill Downs, and bluegrass than know that Kentucky also      36
 4   is first in the nation in gold, third in coal.                   45

 5        The gold, of course, is the billions in Fort Knox, the      57
 6   snug sanctuary a dozen miles south of Louisville.  The coal      69
 7   is mined by stripping, which means peeling off the soil and      81
 8   scooping out the thick veins of coal beneath.                    90

 9        The Ohio River squirms around in a sweeping arc across     102
10   the top half of the state.  Cities and factories are spread     114
11   all along its banks.  Industry brings in two billion a year     126
12   to give manufacturing first place for income.                   135
```

Speed markers are for 3' TW. Circled numbers are 1' goals.

■ 3'/1e

|1 |2 |3 |4 |5 |6 |7 |8 |9 |10 |11 |12

SI 1.35N

15	for	got	with	then	moths	world	handle	bushel	neither	visitor	12
16	aid	but	body	rich	turns	amend	mighty	signal	visible	trouble	24
17	ham	icy	town	fish	abide	signs	social	repair	supreme	profits	36
18	the	aid	such	busy	eight	fancy	owners	normal	signals	perhaps	48
19	and	did	work	down	giant	ought	entire	bought	further	channel	60

|1 |2 |3 |4 |5 |6 |7 |8 |9 |10 |11 |12

POSTTEST

Repeat the Pretest, score your work, and note your improvement.

goal A

■ **To produce a stockholders' notice and an agenda.**

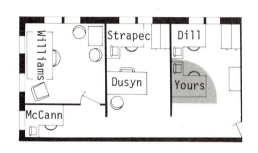

JOB 53-1: ANNOUNCEMENT

Plain paper ☐ Line 5″ ☐ Spacing 2
☐ Top margin 1½″ ☐ SI 1.36N
☐ ■ 10′/0e

"I am grateful to Personnel for sending you to help us," said George Williams Jr., president of Farm Technology, Inc. "We have decided, suddenly, to have a special meeting of our stockholders. We do not have time to get things printed in the usual way and will have to duplicate, by offsetting what you type for us, the copies we need to get in the mail. So this is rush!"

He continues, "First, we must prepare the stockholders' announcement. I have drafted it." He gives you the work below.

You discuss the assignment with Terri Dill, who sits just behind you. "What I'd do," she says, "is use a 1½-inch top margin, a 5-inch line of writing, and single spacing. I had an assignment like this once before, and that's what worked for me."

Today's date ↓5   4

SS (Dear Stockholder of   12

Farm Technology, INc.:   17

We
^ ~I~ have three things to report to you in this, our third message   31

of the Year.   34

⌐ ← 1.# It has been only a mediocre year so far. A year ago we   64

told you that we were quite concerned about the business scene   76

for the next year. Our concern was well placed: *We are* ~~trapped~~ *caught* *in a*   90

squeeze between rising costs and *firm* *resistance to rising prices.*   104

(Continued on next page)

JOB 73-3: LETTER WITH ATTENTION LINE AND TABLE

Workbook 167 □ **SI 1.42N** □
Body 124* □ ■ **10'/0e**

Miss Nancy T. Rothberg, editor in chief at Maps of America, also needs your help.

"I have two letters to send to printers, asking them to bid on some new map books that we will produce," she says. "Here is the first one":

The Danville Press / 2121 College Street / **16**
Danville, KY 40422 / Attention Paul M. **24**
Davis / *An attention line should be typed in* **26**
all caps at the left margin, a double space ..
under the inside address. / Gentlemen: / **29**

This is written to confirm my phone call **38**
today. We wish to know what delivery **45**
schedule you could offer for each of four **54**
books of maps, each book to consist of 64 **63**
pages, 11 by 15 inches, with art cover, in **71**
four colors, if the manuscripts for the books **81**

*An average letter (line–5") becomes a long one (line–6") when the body includes a table, quotation, or other major space-taking display.

are brought to you on this schedule: **88**

County Maps of Kentucky	March 15	**97**
City Maps of Kentucky	May 10	**105**
County Maps of Tennessee	April 15	**115**
City Maps of Tennessee	June 12	**123**

Please try to let me have your firm esti- **132**
mates not later than February 15. They **140**
should be addressed to this company and to **149**
my attention. We are making this same **156**
request of several other printers and expect **166**
to award the contract by March 1. / Yours **177**
very truly, / Nancy T. Rothberg / Editor in **192**
Chief / urs **194**

JOB 73-4: LETTER WITH ATTENTION LINE AND TABLE

Workbook 169 □ **SI 1.43N** □
Body 124 □ ■ **10'/0e**

"I want to send the same letter to another printer," says Miss Rothberg.

"Here is the opening":

Select Printing & Binding / 1800 Render **16**
Road / Beaver Dam, KY 42320 / Attention **24**
June O. Blake / Ladies and Gentlemen: / **32**

JOB 74-1: LETTER WITH QUOTATION AND PS

Workbook 171 □ **SI 1.40N** □
Body and PS 142 □ **15'/0e**

"Can you do one more?" asks Miss Rothberg.

Sure, you nod.

"I want to answer a question raised by a social studies teacher," she says. She begins:

LESSON 74

Directions: *Spacing—1. Line—60.*
Warmup—page 163; then adjust machine for Job 74-1.

Mr. Ronald D. Brown / Wilson High School **16**
/ 700 South Ridge Road / Louisville, KY **23**
40205 / Dear Mr. Brown: / I am pleased to **33**
(Continued on next page)

As the enclosed statement shows, the results of that squeeze has   117

been a lower sales volume and, therefore, less profit and lower   130

net earnings *per* share; however, we have turned the corner and expect   145

the rest of the year to be normal, *or even better than normal.*   157

Single space 2. We have completed the expansion *and office space* of our plant, have moved   188

into the new building wing, and are enjoying a production boost   201

as a result. We are all set, now *for at least ten more years.*   214

3. Two *new* things are on the Planning Board. One is a study of   245

the panels that could be ~~installed~~ *used* on barn roofs to harness solar   257

energy; *and* the other is a study of the need for us to add larger   270

storage units to our line, *now that farmers are storing so much grain.*   285

These and other matters will be on the agenda of a Special   297

Meeting of Stockholders on (Dec.) 9 in the *Sunflower Central Hotel.* ~~headquarters office.~~ We   312

urge ~~ask~~ you to attend or, *if you cannot,* to be sure to mail the enclosed proxy.   326

Respectfully submitted,   333

George Williams, Jr.   341
President   344

---

5 | 53

JOB 53-2: MEETING AGENDA

Plain paper □ **Spacing 1** □ **Line 5″**
□ **Tabs 5 and center** □ **Top 3″**
□ **SI 1.47FH** □ ■ **10′/0e**

Mr. Williams also gives you the following agenda. "Arrange it in enumeration style," he says, "so that the numbers hang out."

AGENDA / Special Meeting of the Stockholders / 10:00 a.m., December 9, 19-- /   27 / 53

1. Report by George Williams Jr. on operations of the Company in the last quarter and forecast for the next two quarters.   63 70 79 82

2. Presentation by Mr. John F. Cooke, of Cooke & Wheeler, Inc., on current research in the use of solar panels for powering grain dryers.   92 99 107 113

3. Report by Anne W. Jepsen on the estimated cost that would be incurred if and when Farm Tech were to expand its line to include solar collectors and other solar units.   122 130 139 146 152

4. Further discussion of the solar project; then a vote on the question.   161 169

5. Luncheon in the Blue Room, Second Floor of the Sunflower Central Hotel.   178 186

6. Tour of the new plant and office facilities. A bus will shuttle from the hotel to the plant.   195 202 207

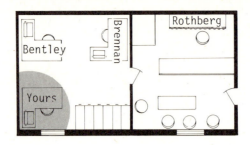

goal A

■ To type two letters with subject lines and other technical features.

JOB 73-1: LETTER WITH A SUBJECT LINE

Workbook 163 □ SI 1.45N □ Body 130 + Subject 20 + cc's 20 □ ■ 10'/0e

You are working at Maps of America, Inc., in Lexington, Kentucky. Mr. Bentley, the sales manager, has two letters for you.

"Please take the following letter," Mr. Bentley says; then he dictates:

Mr. Harry McGee, President / Kentucky Edu-   16
cation Association / 225 State Street / Frank-   24
fort, KY 40601 / Dear Mr. McGee: /   31

Subject: KEA Convention in May *Please*   51
start the subject line at the left margin
and underscore it. As we have done for   56
each of the past 18 years, Maps of America   65
will be pleased to exhibit at your conven-   73
tion in Bowling Green on May 3, 4, and 5.   82
Please ask the exhibit chairperson to send   91
me the contract for a two-unit space.   98

Please also ask him or her to send all the   108
details about the facilities (chairs, tables,   117
electric outlets, and so on) to the person   126
who will be in charge of our exhibit: 134
Ms. Bethel Lawton, 313 Third Street, Glas-   142
gow, KY 42141.   145

KEA always has a good convention, and I   154
know that this year's will be as good as or   163
better than previous ones. We are grateful   172
that you have asked us to participate. We   181
extend our sincere best wishes. / Sincerely   191

yours, ↓4 / Roger Bentley / Sales Manager /   203
urs / cc Ms. Lawton / cc Miss Toll / bcc   225
Mr. French.   227

Some suggestions: Start the date and closing
lines at the center. Type the bcc notation on
line 7 at the left margin after you remove the
original copy and first sheet of carbon.

JOB 73-2: LETTER WITH A SUBJECT LINE

Workbook 165 □ SI 1.44N □ Body 132 + Subject 20 + cc's 20 □ ■ 10'/0e

"I've another letter just like that one," says Mr. Bentley. "You can copy from the one you just typed if you remember to make these changes in it":

This letter is to Mr. John W. Creche, President / Kentucky Private Schools Association / Ashland School of Business / Ashland, KY 41101 / Dear Mr. Creche: /

Subject line is the same except that the initials are KPSA instead of KEA.

First paragraph is the same except that the convention will be at Mammoth Cave National Park, not Bowling Green; and the dates are May 10, 11, and 12.

Second paragraph is the same.

Third paragraph is the same except that the initials are KPSA instead of KEA.

The closing lines are identical to the first letter, including the two cc notations and the bcc notation at the top of the page (but not on the letterhead!).

JOB 53-3: STATEMENT OF OPERATIONS

Plain paper □ Line 60 □ ■ 20'/0e

"Next," says Mr. Williams, "please type this statement [below] of operations."

It should be double-spaced and centered, with leaders to spread it out to 60 spaces.

FARM TECHNOLOGY, INC.

Consolidated Statement of Operations

For the Quarter Ended September 30, 19--

Summary Items	This Year	Last Year	
Net Profit After Taxes	$ 48,247	$ 123,642	114
Federal and State Income Tax	10,700	128,521	126
Sales	2,241,507	2,285,474	139
Resale Material Sales Cost	136,825	153,596	151
Delivery Sales Cost	137,314	89,542	163
Installation Sales Cost	392,910	395,923	175
Net Plant Sales	1,514,458	1,646,413	187
Orders	2,193,966	2,392,743	200
Backlog	932,605	1,042,329	212
Employees	70	67	224
Stockholders	127	128	236
Stock Investment	182,915	183,915	248
Shares	16,855	16,772	261
Book Value per Share	22.18	19.42	273
Net Earnings per Share	2.86	7.52	285

(margin numbers: 14, 38, 64, 78, 88, 102, ... 299)

CHECK YOUR POSTURE

□ Sit tall, erect.
□ Lean forward slightly.
□ Keep shoulders down, elbows in.
□ Hold wrists steady, motionless.
□ Set feet apart, braced on floor.

LESSON 54

Directions: Spacing—1. Line—60.
Warmup—page 107.

The six projects of Part 7 have as their locale:
Unit 19: Kentucky, Tennessee
Unit 20: Minnesota, Wisconsin
Unit 21: Idaho, Montana

PART 7

Part 7 marks the midpoint in *Typing 2* and the start of a new semester. To help newcomers who may enter the class and to give reassurance to others, Part 7 reviews what a typist should know at this point about typing letters, tables, forms, reports, financial statements, and several kinds of graphic display.

In other regards, Part 7 is like its predecessors. Each unit of four lessons includes two work-experience projects of an hour's typing, two skill drives of 20–25 minutes, and a skill-builder clinic. As before, the work of each project focuses on one state.

You are to correct all errors in your production work unless your teacher directs otherwise. Your corrections must be professional.

At the start of each period, turn to this page and type a Warmup: Select any one sentence from each of the four groups below and type it four or more times.

SPEED RECALL	1A	I envy them the big sign they got the man to make for them.	12
	1B	The profit she got for the corn and hay may make them rich.	24
	1C	It is the duty of the eight to cut the oaks down right now.	36
ALPHABET RECALL	2A	Squad Sixteen was puzzled by the vigor of the major attack.	12
	2B	The jewelers quickly made up five boxes in the right sizes.	24
	2C	Old Ben may give quite a few extra prizes for their jacket.	36
NUMBER RECALL	3A	Are 123 sales out of 456 contracts as good as 789 of 1,100?	12
	3B	The winning bulletins were numbered 10, 28, 39, 47, and 56.	24
	3C	The five lengths are 10 mm, 28 mm, 39 mm, 47 mm, and 56 mm.	36
THINKING WHILE TYPING	4A	jack smith came from akron; bill dowe came from fort worth.	12
	4B	mr. owens met ken vance at the sheridan hotel in texarkana.	24
Each line needs seven capitals.	4C	tom caron won the indianapolis five hundred over bob towne.	36

|1 |2 |3 |4 |5 |6 |7 |8 |9 |10 |11 |12

7

JOB 54-1: PROXY

Plain paper ☐ Spacing 2 ☐
Top 1½" ☐ Line 6" ☐ ■ 15'/0e

"One more task. Then we will have this wrapped up," says Mr. Williams. "I want you to type this proxy for me.

I have updated a computer card that we used the last time, but now just type it as an ordinary display document. That will be just as 'legal' as a computer card would be. Thanks a lot."

JOB 54-2: COMPLETION CARDS

5" x 3" cards ☐ ■ 5'/0e

Spreadcaps

~~Elmer T. Fawcett~~

PROXY) KNOW ALL MEN BY THESE PRESENTS that the undersigned does hereby constitute and appoint George Williams Jr., John S. Haines, Anne W. Jepsen, and ~~Glynn M. Kelly~~ and each of them, the true and lawful attorneys, agents, and proxies of the undersigned, with full power of substitution and revocation, for and in the name, place, and stead of the undersigned, to vote upon and act with respect to all the shares of Common Stock without par value of FARM TECHNOLOGY, INC. standing in the name of the undersigned on the books of the Company as at the time of the meeting, at the Special Meeting of the Stockholders of the Company to be held at the Sunflower Central Hotel in Clay Center, Kansas, on Friday, December ⑦, 19 —, at ⑪:00 a.m. and at any and all adjournments thereof, with all the powers the undersigned would possess if personally present, hereby ratifying and confirming all that said attorneys, agents, and proxies or any of them, shall do or cause to be done by virtue hereof.

9   10

WITNESS the hand and seal of the undersigned this_____day of_____, 19_____.

Signature: _____

■ To type 44 wam for 3'/2e.

Directions: *Spacing—1. Line—60. Tab—5. Drills—4.*

PRETEST   Take a 3-minute writing on the first paragraph, page 120, and score your work.

PRACTICE ON TW VOCABULARY   Type the designated drills four times each.

Pretest errors	0–2	3–5	6–+
Drills to type	1–4	2–5	3–6

Speed.

1   farm huge next rank near coal lead zinc food fine soap feed   12
2   known money value towns least large plays major flour mills   24
3   for its are top ten oil gas has lot dot big too see why all   36

Accuracy.

4   stockyards processing windmills soybeans farming silos corn   12
5   meat-packing livestock buildings sorghum state's giant tons   24
6   manufacturing canneries jostling western section miles zinc   36

POSTTEST   Take a 3-minute writing on the second paragraph, page 120, and compare your scores.

goal

■ **To experience creative thinking, accurate typing, and cooperation in a work atmosphere.**

☐ *You and another classmate will work together in Creative Co-Op 6 to develop an organizational chart. One of you is Typist A; the other, Typist B.*

☐ *The chart each of you develops will be similar in format to the one developed in Job 68-1, p. 151.*

☐ *Give your teacher a copy of the memo and chart that you prepare and attach a brief note verifying the accuracy of your work. Proofread carefully!*

CREATIVE CO-OP 6: DEVELOPING A BLOCK DIAGRAM

TYPIST A

1. DRAFT A MEMO

Send a memo to Typist B asking for a list of 12 U.S. cities (four each from the western, central, and eastern thirds of the country).

2. RESPOND TO TYPIST B

Respond to Typist A's request when you receive it. Arrange your answer in tabular form on a card, as it will be easier for Typist A to use this information in planning an organizational chart of the cities.

3. DEVELOP THE CHART

Type an organizational chart from the information received from Typist B, following the guidelines below. Identify a city (other than one of those given to you by your classmate) as your headquarters.

TYPIST B

1. DRAFT A MEMO

Type a memo to Typist A. Ask for a list of 12 cities in the United States (four each from the western, central, and eastern thirds of the country).

2. ANSWER TYPIST A'S REQUEST

Answer Typist B's request as soon as you receive it. Provide your answer in a tabular format on a card, as it will be easier for Typist B to create an organizational chart from the tabulated information.

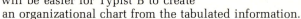

3. DEVELOP THE CHART

Type a chart from Typist A's data, following the guidelines given below. Identify a city (other than one of those given to you by your classmate) as your headquarters and include it in the first block of your chart.

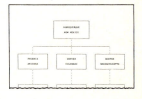

GUIDELINES FOR DEVELOPING ORGANIZATIONAL CHART

1. Start the chart on line 9. Center the city and state within each block, double-spacing the names so they are easier to read.

2. Leave 6 vertical lines between each row of blocks and 6 horizontal spaces between each column of blocks.

3. Center the headquarters in all caps within the block at the top of the chart. Block dimensions are 24 underscores, 5 vertical lines.

4. Follow Job 68-1 as a sample for typing the 4 cities within 3 regions (one city will be a regional office; the others are area offices).

5. *Regional Offices:* Type in all caps in a block that is 20 underscores in length and 6 vertical lines in depth.

6. *Area Offices:* Type with initial caps below regional offices in blocks with dimensions of 20 underscores, 5 vertical lines.

1 Take a quick glance at Kansas, and you will be able to 12

2 see why it ranks at the top of the states in output of farm 24

3 goods. About five million cattle graze on the farms in the 36

4 western section of the state. Wheat grows in all counties. 48

5 The golden fields, marked with windmills, tall grain silos, 60

6 and clumps of trees hiding signs that buildings exist, take 72

7 off across the flat plains for miles and miles, telling why 84

8 Kansas is the Wheat State. Huge combines sweep through the 96

9 wide fields jostling crisp heads of wheat from their stems. 108

10 Later on, giant groups of farm equipment invade the fields, 120

11 and hay, sorghum, soybeans, and corn are reaped for market. 132

SI 1.23E

12 Although Kansas is known for its farm products, mining 12 144

13 and manufacturing are just as worthy as sources of money in 24 156

14 the state. The state's mineral sources are next to farming 36 168

15 in value, and Kansas ranks at least near the top ten states 48 180

16 in the value of mineral output. Its sources of mineral are 60 192

17 oil, cement, natural gas, coal, lead, and zinc. Because of 72 204

18 the large farm output, the state plays a major role in food 84 216

19 processing. Kansas has a lot of fine flour mills and a lot 96 228

20 of plants which make tons of feed for livestock. Many huge 108 240

21 meat-packing plants, stockyards, and canneries dot the main 120 252

22 towns of Kansas. The state is quite a large soapmaker too. 132 264

SI 1.32FE

LESSON 55

Directions: Spacing—1. Line—60. Tab—5. Warmup—page 107.

1 The big state of Nebraska has

2 the only state legislature with one house, its senate. 17

3 the highest percent in the nation of land under crops. 17

4 great pastures and farms where once was a huge desert. 17

12" WAM: 35 40 45 50 55 60 65 70 75 80 85

REVIEW JOB 1: MEMO

Workbook 137 □ **SI 1.39N** □ ■ **15'/0e**
Type the page 160 TW selection (including lines 6, 19, and 28) as a memorandum to:

THE SALES STAFF *in all caps,* today's date, *from* Preston E. Johnstone / National Sales Manager / *on the subject of* Staff Promotions and Possible Plan for Reorganizing /↓₃

REVIEW JOB 2: BOXED TABLE

Plain paper □ **15'/0e**

MOCCASIN FOOTWEAR COMPANY, INC.
Central Southwest District
Charlton Vincent, Regional Director

Region	Product Line Supervisors		Supervisor
	Girls and Women	Boys and Men	
Arizona	L. Bahr	J. Stewart	D. Crane
Colorado	S. Schrumpf	R. Vorndran	T. Swanson
New Mexico	A. Preston	S. Rodgers	D. Ladwig
Utah	E. Scott	J. Graf	R. Bentley

REVIEW JOB 3: CHART

Plain paper □ **15'/0e**

MARKETING ORGANIZATION FOR
EXPERIMENTAL CENTRAL SOUTHWEST DISTRICT

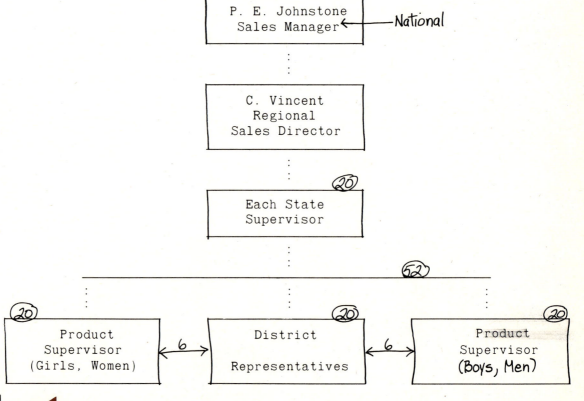

1 Nebraska is one of our great states in the plains. It is one of the   15
2 best agricultural and livestock states. On a fertile, stone-free earth   29
3 grow more native grasses than are found elsewhere; most of them   42
4 are valuable for food. Crops of major importance start with corn;   55
5 this is raised on about thirty percent of the tillable farmland.   68
6 Wheat is second, and oats, barley, rye, alfalfa, potatoes, sorghum,   82
7 and soybeans are next in market value. The North Platte Valley is   96
8 known for its extremely high yield per acre of sugar beets.   108
9 Although Nebraska holds claim to being largely a state which is   122
10 agricultural in nature, a major part of its income is gained from   135
11 sources other than the farm. The processing of food is the main   148
12 source of money, with flour, dairy, and meat products being a   160
13 large slice of it. Nebraska produces much of the livestock food for   173
14 the nation; and an expanding list of other goods and services   187
15 such as insurance, leather and plastics, bricks, farm equipment,   200
16 machine tools, drugs, and textiles all show that Nebraska is grow-   213
17 ing as a leader in industry as well.   220

|1 |2 |3 |4 |5 |6 |7 |8 |9 |10 |11 |12 |13 |14

SI 1.42N

Speed markers are
for 5' TW. Circled
numbers are
1' goals.

Routine:
1. 5' timing.
2. Corrective
practice.
3. 5' timing.

■ 5'/3e

goal B

■ To produce four
interoffice memos,
each within 5'/0e.

JOB 55-1: INFORMAL MEMOS

Plain paper (half sheets)
☐ ■ 20'/0e

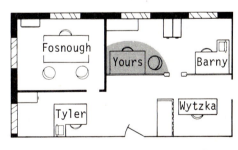

Directions: *Adjust the machine for Job 55-1.
Spacing—1. Line—5". Tabs—10 and center.*

"I really need help!" exclaims Daniel Fosnough, of the Personnel Department. "I am secretary of the Employee Relations Committee of this company, and I am very late in preparing the minutes from our last committee meeting."

He continues, "While I finish the minutes, please type four memos, addressing them to the four persons who attended the meeting":

Sally Edison, Training Department   7
Richard Hester, Union Relations   13
Elliot Sanderson, Maintenance-Security   21
James Zeller, Corporate Affairs   27

"Now," Mr. Fosnough continues, "each of these persons is very important and therefore should have an individually

goals

- To type 45 or more wam for 5′ within 3e. ■ To produce a long memo, a boxed table, and an organization chart.

5-MINUTE WRITING

Spacing—2.
Line—50.
Tab—5.

Omit lines 6, 19, 28.

Speed counters are for 5′ TW.

■ 5′/3e

Directions: Spacing—1. Line—60.
Warmup—page 136; then adjust machine for TW.

1 We are pleased to announce a number of staff promotions that   13

2 will take place on May 1, as part of an experiment by which we   26

3 hope to find whether our plan for reorganizing our marketing   38

4 effort is or is not a good one that will work in the field. First,   51

5 let me tell you about the experiment plan.   60

6 A NEW DESIGN   ..

7 At the present time most of our regions have half a state. For   74

8 example, in Utah there are two regions—the north half and the   86

9 south half. What we wish to do is to determine whether it might   99

10 be better to split each state into two product lines instead of two   113

11 regions. It is an interesting and debatable idea that is worth an   126

12 experimental run.   130

13 In each state, therefore, we are promoting a woman who will   143

14 help the field staff in efforts to sell our shoes for girls and   156

15 women, plus a man to do the same for our line for boys and   168

16 men. These persons will give up their present territories so that   181

17 our service to their customers will not lag; we will be hiring their   195

18 replacements for March 1.   200

19 THE PROMOTIONS   ..

20 Promoted from his post as supervisor in Utah is Charlton Vin-   213

21 cent, who will be our new district sales director for Arizona,   226

22 Colorado, New Mexico, and Utah. Mr. Vincent will work towards   238

23 figuring out for us whether our plan is a good one or not.   250

24 The others who have won their chance to play a role in this   263

25 field test are listed on the table that follows. I congratulate each   277

26 of them, and I am sure that all members of our staff do so also.   290

27 Let's all aid our colleagues in every way we can.   300

28 PEJ / urs / Enclosure   304

|1 |2 |3 |4 |5 |6 |7 |8 |9 |10 |11 |12 |13 |14

SI 1.35N

typed message, but all the messages are to be alike. You know who the memos are *TO*. They are *FROM* me, Dan Fosnough—"

You interrupt, "'Dan,' not 'Daniel'?"

"Yes," he says, "'Dan.'" *DATE* the memos today. The *SUBJECT* is 'Minutes of Employee Relations Committee Meeting of September 18.' *BODY*":

I am terribly sorry to be so late in prepar- 68 ing the minutes of our last meeting. I 76 apologize. I hope you will help me by 84 glancing over these minutes and letting me 92 know whether they seem correct. If I do not 101 hear from you by Friday, I will assume that 108 they are correct. Thanks for your help. / 117 DF ↓₁ / urs / Enclosures 126

goal A

■ **To produce a set of minutes within 15'/0e.**

JOB 56-1: MINUTES

Plain paper □ SI 1.54FH
□ ■ 15'/0e

Directions: *Spacing*—1. *Line*—60. *Warmup*—page 107; then begin Job 56-1.

"Well, I have the minutes ready," says Mr. Fosnough, giving you the work below and a three-ring binder of past minutes. Looking in it you see that a 6-inch line is used, with the first 15 spaces reserved for side headings. You also note that each page has a 1½-inch top margin.

	Minutes of the Meeting	15
	EMPLOYEE RELATIONS COMMITTEE	35
	September 18, 19--	49
THE CALL TO ORDER	The monthly meeting of this Committee was held on *Thursday,* *September 18, 19--* in the Board Room. It was called to order by the chairman, *James Zeller,* at *9:30 a.m.*	66 82 92
ATTENDANCE	Those present were *S. R. Edison, R. F. Hester, E. J. Sanderson, J. L. Zeller,* and the secretary. Missing from the meeting were *E. C. Rolling and R. J. Wells*	109 117 131
APPROVAL OF MINUTES	The minutes of the meeting of *August 16, 19--,* were read and were approved *as read*	146 155
Telephone Course	*Sally Edison told about the nature and purpose of the review course in good telephoning that will be sponsored by Training and will be conducted by the Central Telephone Company. All employees will be invited to attend the one-hour session on December 12, but no one will be required to attend.*	171 185 200 213 226
Employee Turnover	*Elliott Sanderson gave a report on the results of the survey of employee turnover. A copy of the figures from the survey is*	242 257

(Continued on next page)

JOB 72-2: MEMO

Workbook 135 ☐ **Line 6"** ☐ ■ 10'/0e

"And here is another memo to type," he says.

Memo to Utah Representatives / from me, Charlton Vincent, about [subject] Annual Winter Sales Conference. /　21

We will hold our annual winter sales conference on February 21, 22, and 23. We will hold it at the Bruin Peak Lodge, which　47

is just a stone's throw north of Dragerton. Please plan your trip to arrive for dinner on February 20. We will finish with a luncheon on February 23.　78

This year's conference is about three weeks earlier than we have held it in other years. We have moved it up so that we can have Ken Flood with us, as he is moving to Florida the following Sunday.　120

A tentative agenda is enclosed. Please note your part in it.　133

CV / urs / Enclosure　139

JOB 72-3: AGENDA

Plain paper ☐ **Use original layout, not necessarily the one shown** ☐ ■ 15'/0e.

"Here is the agenda for our sales conference," says Mr. Vincent. 'Since you're new here, why not try to set up the program in some new way!"

PROGRAM　10
Sixteenth Annual Winter Sales Conference　37
' Utah Sales Representatives　55
Moccasin Footwear Company, Inc.　76

Monday, February 21　82
8:30–10:00 <u>Session 1</u>: Stella Gottlieb, from the home office, will review the new expense forms that we will now use because of the new IRS voucher requirements.　122

10:30–12:00 <u>Session 2</u>: Visda Arat, from the factory in Seattle, will review the new summer and fall lines.　151

<u>Afternoon</u>: Mrs. Gottlieb will audit with northern reps while southern reps ski, swim in the lodge pool, etc.　176

7:00–10:00 <u>Dinner</u>: Speaker, Charlton Vincent, "What Moccasin Has Meant to Utah."　198

Tuesday, February 22　204

8:30–10:00 <u>Session 3</u>: Panel of Joe Graf, Ken Flood, and Chairman Bill Walmach, "Problems and Answers in Selling Winterwear."　238

10:30–12:00 <u>Session 4</u>: Panel of Ray Bentley, Em Scott, and Chairwoman Bev Miller, "P&A in Sportswear."　266

<u>Afternoon</u>: Mrs. Gottlieb will audit with southern reps while northern reps ski, swim in the lodge pool, etc.　292

7:00–10:00 <u>Dinner</u>: Speaker, Preston T. Johnstone, "What Utah Has Meant to Moccasin."　314

Wednesday, February 23　320
8:30–10:00 <u>Session 5</u>: Panel of Joe Graf, Ken Flood, and Chairwoman J. T. Crane, "P&A in Juvenile Footwear."　351

10:30–12:00 <u>Session 6</u>: Panel of Em Scott, Bev Miller, and Chairman Ray Bentley, "P&A in Selling Accessories."　379

12:00 <u>Lunch</u>: Lunch and adjournment.　387

JOB 72-4: COMPLETION CARDS

5" x 3" cards or slips ☐ ■ 5'/0e

enclosed and is to be considered a part of these minutes.   271

ADJOURNMENT   The meeting came to a close at _____11:00_____ . The next   284
                meeting will be held on _____October 22_____ .↓₃   295

                                                                    305

                                Daniel Fosnough, Secretary   313

goal B

■ To produce a four-column ruled table within 15'/0e.

Sanderson's handwriting, but I think you can make it out well enough to type it."

You note that it's just a standard ruled table—double-spaced, with 6 spaces between columns.

When you proofread, check to make sure that the left margin on the minutes is (as it should be) wide enough for the binder.

JOB 56-2: RULED TABLE

Plain Paper □ ■ 15'/0e

"The last part of this project is to prepare the survey data that go along with the minutes," Mr. Fosnough says. "It's in Mr.

JOB 56-3: COMPLETION CARDS

5" x 3" cards □ ■ 5'/0e

Survey of Employee Turnover June Through August, 19--			
Department	June	July	August
Administration:			
Dividends	1	2	0
Premium Notices	0	1	0
Compensation	3	2	4
Policy Holder Services:			
Cash/Loan Settlement	1	5	0
Claims	1	0	2
Beneficiary Assignment	2	0	0
Central Information	12	17	10
Cash Control	0	0	2
Underwriting	0	0	0
Actuarial	1	0	1
Totals	21	27	19

18
36
50
59
73
77
85
94
101
106
117
124
135
144
151
159
166
180
186
200

REGION: Northern Utah

SUPERVISOR: Charlton Vincent
HEADQUARTERS CITY: Salt Lake City
DATE OF THIS REPORT: *(today's date)*

Give each representative's name, home city, and territory.

DISTRICT 1	DISTRICT 2	DISTRICT 3	DISTRICT 4
Joseph Graf Logan	*Michael Davis* ~~Ken Flood~~ Ogden	J. T. Crane Salt Lake City	Beverly Miller Tooele

Counties of:
  Box Elder
  Cache
  Rich
	Counties of:
	  Davis
	  Morgan
	  (Summit) ──→
	  Weber
		Counties of:
		  Daggett
		  Salt Lake
		  [ ]
			Counties of:
			  Tooele
			  Juab

Always try to leave at least 1 blank space between vertical lines and the typing.

JOB 71-2: FILL-IN FORM

(Continued)

District 2: Emma V. Scott, Richfield. Counties of Beaver, Emery, Grand, Millard, Piute, Sevier, and Wayne.

District 3: William Walmach, Cedar City. Counties of Garfield, Iron, Kane, San Juan, and Washington.

District 4: None. *Type "None" in the middle.*

goal A

■ To produce two memos on forms, each 10'/0e.

JOB 72-1: MEMO

Workbook 135 □ **Line 6"** □ ■ **10'/0e.**

"Now we must send the two reports to national headquarters," says Mr. Vincent.

Memo to Preston T. Johnstone / National Sales Manager / from Charlton Vincent / on the subject Report on Sales Territories. /

With this memo I am pleased to send you two reports on sales territories—one for the northern Utah region and one for the southern Utah region. There are no changes in

LESSON 72

Directions: *Spacing—1. Line—50.*
Warmup—page 136; then adjust machine for Job 72-1.

the southern, but there are two changes to report for the northern region:

1. Ken Flood has retired after 27 years with Moccasin; he has been replaced by a fine young man, Michael Davis.
2. Summit County, which was part of Ken's district, is now part of Jacqueline Crane's district. Making this change more nearly equates the two districts.

CV / urs / 2 Enclosures

goal

- To use intensive drill to build more skill.

ACTIVITIES	20 MIN.	40 MIN.
Warmup	3'	—
Warmup, Plus	—	6'
Drive 1 Pretest	4'	4'
Drive 1 Practice	9'	9'
Drive 1 Posttest	4'	4'
Drive 2 Pretest	—	4'
Drive 2 Practice	—	9'
Drive 2 Posttest	—	4'

Directions: *Spacing—1. Line—60. Follow the adjacent schedule of activities.*

WARMUP, PLUS

Edit line 2.

1 When they come back here next week, see that he meets them.   12
2 Does al like wheaties frosted flakes or rice crispies more?   12
3 The woodsmen quietly kept just five dozen big axes in cars.   12
4 Their auto races are for 10, 28, 39, 49, and 56 kilometers.   12

12" SPEED: 30 35 40 45 50 55 60

DRIVE 1

Take two 1-minute timings on lines 5–8. Proofread both and average the scores.

PRETEST 1

Accent up reaches with no runs on left hand.

5 We spoiled the values of thrift analysis by charity drives.   12
6 My golf clubs are a very poor sample of American ingenuity.   24
7 Dora likes to dig up soil and plant things that will bloom.   36
8 Yes, Andrews took the ropes and hooks for use on the hoist.   48

1 2 3 4 5 6 7 8 9 10 11 12

PRACTICE 1

Accent up reaches with no runs on left hand.

Make four copies, repeating either individual lines for speed gain (if you averaged two or fewer Pretest errors) or whole sets for accuracy gain.

9   adjoins telling smiled thrift likes hotel hope golf dry hit   12
10 spoiled analyze always baking ropes shift dyed club log mat   12
11 airline apology totals depend taken hooks list role use yes   12

12 justify banking wisely theirs waits daily plow only ran joy   12
13 grouped charity golden surely token cliff told wife kit lot   12
14 amounts costing values liquid hoist major wail talk kid low   12

POSTTEST 1

Repeat the Pretest. Score your work and note your improvement.

DRIVE 2

PRETEST 2

Average two 1' timings.

15 Someone must review the mistake to perfect the main device.   12
16 It was wrong to think that the closing balances were fixed.   24
17 Why not join the best debate teams and have fun as you win?   36
18 Our members were trying their best, but they could not win.   48

1 2 3 4 5 6 7 8 9 10 11 12

PRACTICE 2

Accent jump reaches without doubles.

19 mistake reviews verify trying wrong think acre very act pin   12
20 someone perfect reveal paints pound river over main gun bed   12
21 furnace extreme member extent movie kinds text from ton mix   12

22 drawing created levels ignore fixed doubt best join not won   12
23 closing balance device atomic above copes have much any ice   12
24 animals country coding debate brown among twin save fun son   12

POSTTEST 2

Repeat Pretest 2. Score your work and note your improvement.

5 10

goal A

■ To type 45 wam
for 5'/3e.

Directions: *Spacing—1. Line—60.*
Warmup—page 136.

PRETEST

Take a 5-minute writing on lines 24–41 on page 156. Score carefully.

PRACTICE

Type three times each the lines
indicated in this table:

Errors in Pretest	0–2	3–5	6–+
Lines to practice	1–8	2–9	3–10

Speed.

1 notch shape lakes miles water owned parks visit enjoy mined   12
2 Utah song ever have task find deep city also part just land   24
3 and put all you the for own has but one are way job can who   36

Numerals.

4 1 11 21 31 41 51 61 5 55 15 25 35 45 55 9 99 49 59 69 79 89   12
5 2 22 32 42 52 62 72 6 66 16 26 36 46 56 0 00 50 60 70 80 90   24
6 3 33 43 53 63 73 83 7 77 27 37 47 57 67 $\frac{1}{2}$ 1$\frac{1}{2}$ 2$\frac{1}{2}$ 3$\frac{1}{2}$ 4$\frac{1}{2}$ 5$\frac{1}{2}$ 6$\frac{1}{2}$ 36
7 4 44 54 64 74 84 94 8 88 38 48 58 68 78 $\frac{1}{4}$ 1$\frac{1}{4}$ 2$\frac{1}{4}$ 3$\frac{1}{4}$ 4$\frac{1}{4}$ 5$\frac{1}{4}$ 6$\frac{1}{4}$ 48

Accuracy.

8 population northeast national minerals largest related Salt   12
9 rectangular northwest religion biggest natural produce Lake   24
10 government different minerals admitted federal workers City   36

POSTTEST

Repeat the Pretest. Score your work and note your progress.

goal B

■ To produce two
fill-in forms, each
within 10'/0e.

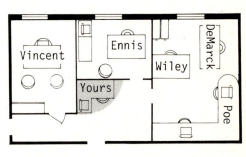

Directions: *Adjust machine for Job 71-1.*

JOB 71-1: FILL-IN FORM
Workbook 133 or plain paper □ ■ 10'/0e

You work for Charlton Vincent, in Salt Lake City. He is supervisor of both the northern Utah and southern Utah regions of Moccasin Footwear Company. "Each year about now," he says, "we report to our national office the names and territories of our field representatives."

He gives you the revised list at the top of page 158. "Please type this for me," he says.

If you do not have the preprinted workbook form, arrange the material as a boxed table as shown in the small illustration above.

JOB 71-2: FILL-IN FORM
Workbook 133 □ ■ 10'/0e

"Next," he says, "the similar report for our *southern* Utah region. I have another office in Richfield that is our headquarters for the southern. Other information:

District 1: Ray Bentley, Provo. Counties of Carbon, Duchesne, Sanpete, Uintah, Utah.

(Continued on next page)

goal A

■ To produce two
tax itemizations.

JOB 57-1: INCOME TAX ITEMIZATION

Plain paper □ ■ 10′/0e

"Welcome to the world of accounting and income taxes!" says Fred B. Obernberger, a tax specialist for whom you will work. "Right now we're working on the tax reports for Dr. Mariucci. Please type this itemization of expenses for laboratory fees."

You think, "I'll put the two columns 6 spaces apart, then fill in with leaders."

Joseph N. Mariucci, D.D.S.

EXPENSE ITEMIZATION

Laboratory Fees

For the Year Ended December 31, 19--

Denver General Hospital	$ 269.00
Denver University	67.50
Gonska Laboratories	145.32
Hagerty Dental Services, Inc.	4,189.87
Medical Research Associates	376.23
TOTAL	$5,047.92

JOB 57-2: INCOME TAX ITEMIZATION

Plain paper □ ■ 10′/0e

"And here is another expense itemization," says Mr. Obernberger. "Double up each item, as shown."

Joseph N. Mariucci, D.D.S.

EXPENSE ITEMIZATION

Wages and Salaries

For the Year Ended December 31, 19--

Mary L. Hayes, Bookkeeper	$ 8,748.27
Runetta E. Jackson, Dental Assistant	9,430.27
Janet A. Sundblad, Receptionist/Secretary	9,156.90
Arthur D. Tessmer, Dental Assistant	8,623.45
TOTAL	$35,958.89

goal B

■ To produce two
tax itemizations.

JOB 57-3: INCOME TAX ITEMIZATION

Plain paper □ ■ 10′/0e

"There is one more expense itemization to be typed for Dr. Mariucci," says Mr. Obernberger, "but I'll have to dictate it, since I don't have it written down for you. This one is for dues and meetings, and it should be arranged like the last itemization you typed. Ready?"

5-MINUTE WRITING

Lesson 70.

Spacing—2.

Line—60.
Lines end even.
Speed counters are
for 5′ TW. Circled
figures are 1′ goals.

Procedure:
1. 5′ writing.
2. Corrective
   practice.
3. 5′ writing.

■ 5′/3e

5   If you would like to live in a place where there would not be   13
6   too many people, you might want to look into Nevada. The 1970   26
7   census indicates that Nevada is 47th in the number of people who   39
8   live there, with close to 570,000 people. It has a density of 5.2   52
9   people per square mile, which ranks it high in amount of room   65
10   per person living there. However, a large number of people have   78
11   begun to realize that Nevada is a great place to live—it leads all   91
12   50 states in percent of people who are moving in to become   103
13   residents.   105

14   The name of this state is derived from a Spanish word; it   118
15   means "snowcapped." When you travel through this state, you   130
16   will quickly see how it got its name. It is located in the heart of   144
17   the dry Great Basin, and most of the land is a part of high pla-   156
18   teau country; the average elevation through the state is 5,500 feet.   170
19   On all sides you view a good many mountain peaks that rise   182
20   nearly 8,000 feet more. Ranges of such size give scenic sights of   195
21   snow-clad peaks. Nevada is more than just beauty, though: it has   209
22   such exciting things to enjoy that millions of tourists come visit-   222
23   ing each year.   225

|1 |2 |3 |4 |5 |6 |7 |8 |9 |10 |11 |12 |13 |14

SI 1.33FE

5-MINUTE WRITING

Lesson 71.

Spacing—2.

Line—60.
Lines end even.
Speed counters are
for 5′ TW. Circled
figures are 1′ goals.

Procedure:
1. 5′ writing.
2. Drills on
   page 157.
3. 5′ writing.

■ 5′/3e

24   Utah, We Love Thee is the state song of the 45th state to be ad-   15 | 240
25   mitted to the union. Utah is 11th in area size and 38th in popula-   27 | 252
26   tion. If you ever have pieces of a puzzle of all 50 states to put   40 | 265
27   together, it will be a simple task for you to find Utah: it is rec-   54 | 279
28   tangular in shape, except for a deep square notch in the northeast   67 | 292
29   corner.   69 | 294
30   Salt Lake City is the biggest city in the state and is also known   83 | 308
31   as the world center of the Mormon religion. The Great Salt Lake   96 | 321
32   is in the northwest part of Utah, and it is one of the largest natu-   110 | 335
33   ral lakes in the United States. The lake covers more than 1,000   123 | 348
34   square miles and provides water sports and fun for many people.   135 | 360
35   Just about 2/3 of the land in Utah is owned by the federal govern-   149 | 374
36   ment. Thus you would find that Utah has more national parks for   162 | 387
37   you to visit and enjoy than all other states but one.   172 | 397

38   The workers in this state are kept active in different ways. A   186 | 411
39   large number of workers are needed to help produce all the min-   198 | 423
40   erals that are mined in Utah. All types of jobs related to mining   212 | 437
41   can be found. Raising cattle and growing crops also provide jobs.   225 | 450

|1 |2 |3 |4 |5 |6 |7 |8 |9 |10 |11 |12 |13 |14

SI 1.36N

JOB 57-3: INCOME TAX ITEMIZATION

(Continued)

Denver Central Association Dues $80.00

American Dental Association Dues $300.00

Colorado Association of
  Dental Surgeons Dues $100.00

Colorado Association of
  Dental Surgeons Convention $465.76
  TOTAL $945.76

JOB 57-4: INCOME TAX ITEMIZATION

Plain paper ☐ **Spacing 2**
☐ ■ **10'/0e**

Mr. Obernberger says, "Next, here is a depreciation schedule."

To have 6 spaces between columns, you may need to turn the paper sideways.

Joseph N. Mariucci, D.D.S.
Depreciation Schedule
For the Year Ended December 31, 19—

Property	Cost	Total Life	Prior Depreciation	Depreciation This Year
Office Desk	$ 140	10 years	$ 42	$ 14
Dental Unit	2,500	8 years	938	313
Typewriter	470	5 years	188	94
Dental X-Ray Unit	2,000	10 years	800	200
Calculator	300	5 years	240	60
Cabinets	800	15 years	320	53
Total				$734

goal A

■ To produce an income statement.

JOB 58-1: INCOME TAX STATEMENT

Plain paper ☐ **Spacing 2**
☐ ■ **15'/0e**

After Mr. Obernberger has reviewed the four financial statements you typed for him, he says, "This is one more sheet to type for Dr. Mariucci—the summary income statement."

Your mind flicks back to the income statements you typed previously [pages 108, 109]. "Oh, with totals in a third column," you reply.

"Right!" says Mr. Obernberger, "with the totals in a third column. Okay then, here is the information for the statement":

LESSON 58

Directions: *Spacing—1. Line—60. Warmup—page 107; then adjust machine for Job 58-1.*

goal A

■ To produce a boxed table with a braced heading.

JOB 70-1: BOXED TABLE

Plain paper (sideways for pica) □ ■ 15'/0e

Directions: *Spacing—1. Line—60.*
Warmup—page 136; then begin Job 70-1.

"I thought this table (below) was done," says Mr. Schellinger, "but the Carson City manager phoned in the sales of one more agent. . . ."

JOB 70-2: COMPLETION CARDS

5″ x 3″ cards or slips □ ■ 5'/0e

SALES BY AGENTS DURING FOURTH QUARTER

Carson City Branch

Agent	Type of Life Insurance			Total
	Whole Life	Term	Endowment	
James Mancini	$ 61,250	$ 40,850	$13,700	$115,800
Roger Allgor	57,675	35,675	14,960	108,310
Pamela Stevens	53,850	31,110	12,800	97,760
William Lopez	48,960	29,865	12,665	91,490
Herbert Gaston	42,555	24,860	13,950	81,365
Patricia Smith	39,242	19,840	11,360	70,442
Leonard Cyrus	36,150	15,500	10,250	61,900
TOTAL	$339,682	$197,700	$89,685	$627,067
	~~$303,532~~	~~$282,200~~	~~$79,435~~	~~$565,167~~

goal B

■ To type 45 wam for 5'/3e.

30-SECOND SPRINTS

Take three timings. Try for 60 wam! Or type three copies.

Directions: *Spacing—1. Line—60. Tab—5.*

```
     01    03    05    07    09    11    13    15    17    19    21    23
1  Nevada contains some 110,540 square miles of land, so it is    12
     25    27    29    31    33    35    37    39    41    43    45    47
2  seventh in size among the states.  It has nearly 26,000,000    24
     49    51    53    55    57    59    61    63    65    67    69    71
3  visitors a year who spend nearly $783,900,000 in Nevada for    36
     73    75    77    79    81    83    85    87    89
4  their food, lodging, and vacation enjoyment.                   45
```

Joseph N. Mariucci, D.D.S.
INCOME STATEMENT
For the Year Ended December 31, 19--

RECEIPTS

Professional	$118,261.00	
Other	432.52	
Gross Income		$118,693.52

EXPENSES

Rent for Office	$ 6,120.00	
Utilities	734.67	
Wages and Salaries	35,958.89	
Telephone	326.90	
Office Supplies, Stamps ...	856.11	
Professional Supplies	3,456.78	
Laboratory Fees	5,047.92	
Professional Insurance	4,890.00	
Dues and Meetings	945.76	
Books, Journals	147.65	
Laundry, Cleaning	387.09	
Goodwill	140.00	
Depreciation	734.00	
Total Expenses		$ 59,745.77
NET INCOME		$ 58,947.75

JOB 58-2: COMPLETION CARDS

5″ x 3″ cards ☐ ■ 5′/0e

JOB 58-1: INCOME TAX STATEMENT
1. Typed by Joan Anderson
2. Proofread with Amy Boelke
3. No problems in producing this job.

■ **To type 44 wam for 3′/2e.**

12-SECOND SPRINTS

Four 12″ timings on each sentence.

Directions: Spacing—1. Line—60. Tab—5.
Begin the 12-second sprints at once.

```
1  You should know that Colorado
2      built more than twenty thousand miles of water canals.   17
3      is the highest state; it's called "top of the nation."    17
4      has half the one hundred highest peaks in the country.    17
```

12″ SPEED: 45 50 55 60 65 70 75 80 85

3-MINUTE PIECE-MEAL PRACTICE

Routine:
Ten 1′ timings.
One 3′ timing.

```
5      The mountains of Colorado add a good bit to the wealth    12
6  of this state.  It has been said that there are over ninety   24
7  types of fish in its streams, lakes, and reservoirs.  There   36
8  are wide valleys, and deep fresh lakes, and awesome canyons   48
9  which draw people from near and far.  Those who try to whiz   60
10 down the ski slopes find this a great way to tax the lungs!   72
11     The state has real quality that can be shared by those    84
12 who enjoy the open air.  But there are now large industrial   96
13 plants in the east which make it a state with more than raw  108
14 resources.  There are new jobs that have been brought about  120
15 by this growth.  Colorado is one state that is on the move.  132
```

Speed markers are for 3′ TW. Circled figures are 1′ goals.

■ **3′/2e**

1 2 3 4 5 6 7 8 9 10 11 12   SI 1.20E

JOB 69-1: BOXED TABLE
(Continued)

FOURTH QUARTER LIFE INSURANCE SALES
Nevada Branches

Branch	This Year	Last Year	Difference	Change
Carson City	$ 627,067	$ 594,376	$ 32,691	+ 5.5%
→ Elko	263,440	243,926	19,514	+ 8.0%
Las Vegas	2,401,450	2,193,105	208,345	+ 9.5%
Reno	1,688,225	1,713,934	(25,709)	− 1.5%
Sparks	1,174,595	1,135,972	38,623	+ 3.4%
TOTAL	$6,154,777	$5,881,313	$273,464	+ 4.6%

Boxed table is ruled table with two changes: (1) vertical lines are penned in after table is completed and (2) each horizontal line is extended an extra 3 spaces at each end, to balance with the 3 spaces on each side of the vertical lines.

goal B

■ **To produce a boxed table with braced heading.**

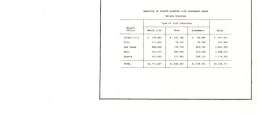

JOB 69-2: BOXED TABLE

Plain paper (sideways if pica) ☐ ■ 20′/0e

Giving you the table below, Mr. Schellinger says cheerfully, "Here's another one. Watch out for that braced heading." Be careful when you draw the vertical lines, especially the two short ones in the center section.

ANALYSIS OF FOURTH QUARTER LIFE INSURANCE SALES
Nevada Branches

Branch Office	Type of Life Insurance			Total
	Whole Life	Term	Endowment	
Carson City	$ 339,682	$ 197,700	$ 89,685	$ 627,067
→ Elko	137,850	76,230	49,360	263,440
Las Vegas	980,000	735,750	685,700	2,401,450
Reno	765,675	496,900	425,650	1,688,225
Sparks	547,800	337,685	289,110	1,174,595
TOTAL	$2,771,007	$1,844,265	$1,539,505	$6,154,777

When boxed table has a braced heading like Type of Life Insurance, leave space for it, then come back to insert it after typing the underscore line (including 3 extra spaces at each end) under it. The braced heading is centered over the underscore line that is also the top line for the column heads. Like the column headings, the braced heading should be preceded and followed by 1 blank line.

goal A

- To type 44 wam for 5' within 3e.

Directions: *Spacing—1. Line—60. Tab—5.*
Drills—3. Warmup—page 107.

PRETEST

Spacing—2.

Take a 5-minute writing and score it as a base for intensive practice.

1   Wyoming is north of Colorado and has a like landscape: the   13
2 Rockies in the west and wide plains in the rest, and an outdoor   26
3 life all over. There are just about one-third of a million persons   39
4 living in the state; more than that come in as tourists to see   52
5 Yellowstone Park and that famous geyser, Old Faithful, or to   64
6 camp a while among the Teton Mountains.   72
7   This is a state of few people, little industry, and no large   85
8 cities, but its citizenry are numbered among the most progressive   98
9 in the nation: they were the first to give the vote to their women   112
10 and the first to have a woman governor, Nellie Ross. Wealthy   124
11 with wool, cattle, and oil, the state has always held firmly to its   138
12 sense of frontier equalities.   144
13   The history of Wyoming provides many of the themes you rec-   157
14 ognize in a typical Western book, movie, short story, or TV pro-   169
15 gram. Quarrels between sheepmen and cattlemen, raids by rustlers,   183
16 wars between Indians and settlers, fights over mines—all these and   196
17 many more can be traced back to actual events that happened   208
18 along the routes on which the railroad would one day arrive.   220

|1 |2 |3 |4 |5 |6 |7 |8 |9 |10 |11 |12 |13 |14   SI 1.40N

Speed markers are for 5' TW. Circled figures are 1' goals.

- 5'/2e

PRACTICE

Take two 1-minute TWs on each of the lines indicated in this chart.

Errors in Pretest	0–2	3–5	6–+
Lines for 1' TWs	19–22	20–23	21–24

Speed.

19 The chairman of both firms paid for the eight ancient maps.   12
20 When did she go to the eight men and pay for the oak panel?   24
21 I am to go to the firm and work for them if they pay right.   36

|1 |2 |3 |4 |5 |6 |7 |8 |9 |10 |11 |12

Accuracy.

22 Bob quickly mixed strawberries over the frozen grape juice.   12
23 Your folks who got the money prizes were vexing to Jacques.   24
24 She trained a brown fox to jump quickly over a dozen gates.   36

POSTTEST

Repeat the Pretest, figure your scores, and note your improvement.

Make four copies of each drill. Remember: Space twice after each period.

```
 5   world.  usual.  visit.  proxy.  theme.  rush.  pale.  goal.   12
 6   audit.  black.  chair.  dozen.  eight.  form.  name.  gown.   24
 7   claim.  bored.  table.  nurse.  seven.  gull.  jobs.  give.   36
 8   rakes.  giant.  shame.  third.  drill.  into.  self.  tape.   48
 9   basic.  grant.  world.  finds.  table.  play.  step.  ride.   60
```

Repeat the Pretest. Score your work and note your improvement.

DRIVE 2

Take three 1-minute timings on lines 10–13. Average your scores.

Stressing question mark.

```
10   Did they blame the dog?  Did they blame him for the attack?   12
11   When did the auditor come here?  Did he fix the audit form?   24
12   What is the theme?  Is it apt to irk the men on the panels?   36
13   Why did he give away that money?  Did he owe it to someone?   48
    |1   |2   |3   |4   |5   |6   |7   |8   |9   |10  |11  |12
```

Make four copies of each drill. Remember: Space twice after each question mark.

```
14   angle?  claim?  blend?  shape?  dials?  push?  them?  rich?   12
15   forms?  handy?  giant?  ivory?  fight?  burn?  worn?  torn?   24
16   towns?  score?  hopes?  coins?  hilly?  noun?  hymn?  honk?   36
17   pupil?  nylon?  milky?  garbs?  shake?  blue?  door?  high?   48
18   onion?  rifle?  shell?  panel?  doors?  rugs?  clue?  take?   60
```

Repeat the Pretest. Score your work and note your improvement.

goal A

- To produce a boxed table.

UNIT 18

LESSON **69**

Directions: Spacing—1. Line—60. Warmup—page 136; then begin Job 69-1.

JOB 69-1: BOXED TABLE

Plain paper (sideways for pica) □ ■ 20'/0e

You report to Edward Schellinger, statistician of the Freedom Insurance Company. He introduces you to Mrs. Greene and Mr. Sprague. Then he says, "We are knee-deep in statistics on insurance sales for the past quarter year."

He gives you a table (top of page 154).

"Please type this for me," he says.

You study it; it is almost the same as many of the *ruled* tables you typed in other assignments.

(Continued on next page)

goal B

■ To produce a
long one-page letter
within 15'/0e.

JOB 59-1: LONG LETTER

Workbook 121 □ Body 233
□ SI 1.33FE □ ■ 15'/0e

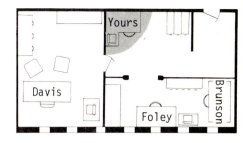

Directions: *Adjust the machine for Job 59-1:
Spacing—1. Line—6". Tab—center.*

You work for Darrell E. Davis, owner of an auto parts supply store in Casper, Wyoming. He is chairman of the Metric Study Team, a committee of the Wyoming Auto Parts Association which is studying the advisability of the industry's conversion to the metric system.

"I want you to type the team's report," says Mr. Davis, "but first let's prepare the letter that accompanies the report":

Mr. Joe R. Revazza, President / Wyoming   16
Auto Parts Association / Heath Rubber Co.,   24
Inc. / 2177 Ute Street West / Cheyenne, WY   32
82001 /   33

Dear Joe: The Metric Study Team of the   43
WAPA is pleased to turn in the enclosed   51
report. The team has met two times a   58
month for the past six months. All mem-   66
bers of the team feel that what we are rec-   74
ommending is what we should, that the   83
whole auto parts industry in our state   90
should adopt what we recommend, and that   98
WAPA should take our plan to the next   106
national meeting.   110

We believe that our report is clear, Joe,   119
but we hope that you and the other officers   128

of WAPA will turn to us with questions   136
that you may have before you take official   145
action. We hope you will note that the   152
United States has made a great deal of   160
progress toward the metric system. We will   169
be sadly out of step if our industry does not   178
move along with the others.   184

The Metric Study Team hopes that you,   193
as president of WAPA, will present our re-   201
port to the Board of Directors and will add   210
your voice to ours in urging that it be   217
adopted.   219

Joe, there is real need for leadership in   229
this matter, both on the state and the na-   237
tional level; and your Metric Study Team   245
believes that you are the person who can   253
demonstrate it. If there is any help that we   263
can give you, we shall be proud to do so.   271
Please let us know that WAPA will lead to   281
metrics. / Sincerely yours, ↓3 / Darrell E.   295
Davis / Chairman of the Team / urs /   302
Enclosure   304

goal A

■ To produce page 1
of a two-page report
within 20'/0e.

LESSON 60

Directions: *Spacing—1. Line—60. Warmup—page
107; then adjust machine for Job 60-1: Spacing—2.
Line—6". Tabs—5 and center.*

goal B

■ To produce an organization chart.

JOB 68-2: CHART

Plain paper ☐ ■ 15'/0e

"This is the other chart," says Mr. McCullough. "Type it to look just like the first one."

Turn paper sideways if machine is pica but not if it is elite.

When you compare the second chart with the first, you note that they are the same size—the boxes are the same width, they have the same number of lines, and so on. All the placement aids and calculations you used in the first chart apply also to the second. Just be careful to observe the changed wording in some boxes.

JOB 68-3: COMPLETION CARDS

5" x 3" cards or slips ☐ ■ 5'/0e

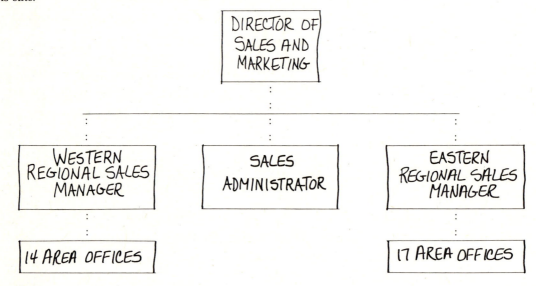

PROPOSED MARKETING ORGANIZATION

goal

■ To use intensive drill to build more skill.

ACTIVITIES	20 MIN.	40 MIN.
Warmup, page 136	3'	3'
Drive 1 Pretest	4'	4'
Drive 1 Practice	9'	9'
Drive 1 Posttest	4'	4'
Drive 2 Pretest	—	5'
Drive 2 Practice	—	10'
Drive 2 Posttest	—	5'

Directions: *Spacing—1. Line—60.*
Warmup—page 136.

DRIVE 1

PRETEST 1

Stressing periods.

Take two 1-minute timings on lines 1–4. Proofread both and average the scores.

```
1  Pamela Rush is very busy.  She works for some antique firm.   12
2  Rodney paid for the audit and for a map.  He paid the city.   24
3  Jane got six authentic antiques.  She got them at a social.   36
4  Len is at the store.  He is paying for groceries they sent.   48
   |1   |2   |3   |4   |5   |6   |7   |8   |9   |10  |11  |12
```

"Well," says Mr. Davis, "I have written the report for you to copy. Please type this in standard business-report form for me."

You know that standard business-report form means single spacing, a 6-inch line, side headings in all caps, a bottom margin of 1 to 1½ inches, and a top margin of 12 lines on the first page and 6 lines on the other pages.

JOB 60-1: REPORT

If time permits, take a 5-minute TW to compare with your scores on normal copy.

On guard for the bottom margin!

Wyoming Auto Parts Association — 20
Report of the Metric Study Team — 42
Darrell E. Davis, Chairman — 61
This committee finds that the time has come — 71
for WAPA to "go metric." This report will tell why we — 83
believe it is so. — 85

EARLY HISTORY — 91

The metric system that is up for adoption in the — 102
United States had its start in France. A decimal plan — 114
for measures and weights was proposed as early as 1670. — 125
France passed a law in 1837 to require that the metric — 136
system be used. — 140

Thomas Jefferson proposed a decimal system — 149
for coins and paper money for the new, young nation, — 161
and Congress adopted it in the late 1700s. His proposal — 172
for a decimal system for weights and measures did — 182
not fare as well; it was rejected. — 190

CONCERNS — 192

More than 90 percent of the world uses the — 202
metric system. More than 80 percent of the world trade — 214
is conducted under the metric system. Metrics deal — 224
with the physical qualities of length, of weight, of — 235
volume, and of temperature. — 241
Con Arguments. People who are opposed to — 257
metrics seem to be concerned with the high cost of — 267
conversion and anxiety about how hard it would be — 277
for all of us to learn the metrics. They like to hint — 288
that there is something un-American about the system, — 298
as though we were kowtowing to outside influence. — 309
Pro Arguments. Those who favor metrics — 324
dismiss those three reasons, pointing out that the cost — 335
of metrication will be absorbed like any other change — 346

5 | 60

130

JOB 67-1: BUSINESS REPORT

(Continued)

1. The twelve district offices that are now 169 supervised by the midcontinent office will 177 report to the other regions—six to the 185 western and six to the eastern. 192

2. The Des Moines office will be closed, 202 and the staff will be reassigned or released. 212

3. The sales manager of the midcontinent 222 region and six members of her staff will be 231 invited to come to East Cleveland and set 239 up the new sales service department. 247

4. All of the support services that can be 259 nationalized will be drawn from the two 266 regional offices and put under the direction 275 of the new sales administrator. 282

Finances / It is estimated that about 295 $400,000 a year will be saved by the 304 closing of the Des Moines office. This 312 saving will not occur the first year since it 321 will be used for severance pay, leases, and 330 so on, but will be actual after one year. 338

Align the three identification lines at the .. *center. Richard Sinclair / Director of Sales /* 350 *and Marketing / Today's date* 360

---

goal A

■ **To produce an organization chart.**

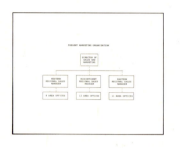

JOB 68-1: CHART

Plain paper □ ■ 20'/0e

Directions: Spacing—1. Line—60. Warmup—page 136; then adjust machine for Job 68-1.

"Here's the first of two charts," says Mr. McCullough. "After typing this, use a pen to draw in the sides of the boxes." (Examine the chart on page 152 to see how the boxes will look.)

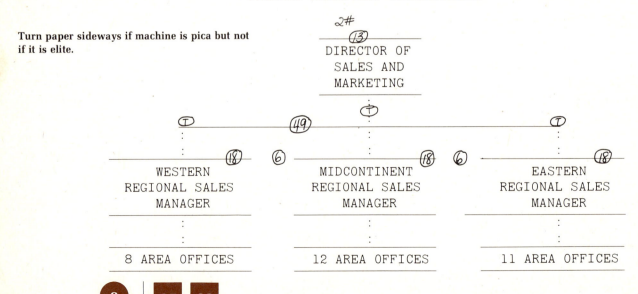

PRESENT MARKETING ORGANIZATION

Turn paper sideways if machine is pica but not if it is elite.

```
                              2#
                             (13)
                       DIRECTOR OF
                       SALES AND
                        MARKETING

       (T)         (49)         (T)                        (T)
            (18)   (6)               (18)   (6)              (18)
     WESTERN              MIDCONTINENT              EASTERN
  REGIONAL SALES         REGIONAL SALES         REGIONAL SALES
     MANAGER                MANAGER                MANAGER


  8 AREA OFFICES         12 AREA OFFICES        11 AREA OFFICES
```

goal B

■To produce page 2
of a report within
15'/0e.

You will need to watch closely for the bottom of the first page. When you start the second page, type "Page 2" at the right margin on line 7—that is the only heading on the second page. Leave 2 blank lines below it and then continue the narrative of the report.

JOB 60-2: REPORT (PAGE 2)

Plain paper □ SI 1.50FH □ ■15'/0e

JOB 60-3: COMPLETION CARDS

5" x 3" cards □ ■5'/0e

JOB 60-1: REPORT (PAGE 1)
1. Typed by Donald B. Marble
2. Proofread with Sandra Collins
3. I don't like typing from handwriting.

Can you make a better 5' TW score on this page than you did on page 130?

of model into the cost of the product. They point | 10
out that metrics are not at all hard to learn. | 20
They laugh off the whole idea of foreign influence. | 30

This Committee believes that the ages have | 41
it. The business that is lost in trade with the rest | 52
of the world, because the rest of the world is Metric | 63
in all things from payments to tools, must run into | 73
billions of dollars that would help payrolls and | 83
employment in thousands of towns in our America. | 93

The metric system is simple and logical. | 103
It's a decimal system that is based on units of ten, | 114
just like our money is, with ten cents making a dime | 125
and ten dimes making a dollar. Educators, some | 134
bureaus of the government, and some firms are in the | 145
fore of the firm move to shift to the metric system. | 156

RECENT U.S. DEVELOPMENTS | 162

The Metric Conversion Act of 1975 has been | 173
referred to by many as the point where the United | 183
States made its decision to go metric. Under this act | 194
the conversion will be voluntary for the next ten years. | 205
By 1980 it is expected that we will be mostly, if not | 216
exclusively, a metric nation. | 222

After all, the medical field made the | 231
change over fifteen years ago, and with little fuss. | 243
Metrics are standard in science too. More than half | 253
our canned goods are labeled both in traditional | 263

5 | 60

131

Directions: *Spacing—1. Line—60.*
Warmup—page 136.

goal A

■ To type 45
wam/5'/3e on
normal copy.

PRETEST

Take a 5-minute writing on lines 25–43, page 149. Score your work carefully.

PRACTICE

Spacing—1.

Type three times each the lines
indicated in this table:

Errors in Pretest	0–2	3–5	6–+
Lines to practice	1–6	2–7	3–8

Speed.

1 state glass ships other their blimp built claim glean shape   12
2 know city huge plus well both fame also know many more coal   24
3 you one two was the now and can who own for its any get his   36

Capitals.

4 Steubenville Canton Toledo Dayton Wright Again Ohio Pro For   12
5 Kitty Hawk Garfield Goodyear Football Hayes Akron Grant One   24

Accuracy.

6 presidents organized brothers library flights league famous   12
7 interesting residents balloons founder answer flying museum   24
8 distinctions registers located doesn't served rubber nation   36

|1 |2 |3 |4 |5 |6 |7 |8 |9 |10 |11 |12

POSTTEST

Repeat the Pretest. Score your work and note your improvement.

goal B

■ To produce a
business report
within 20'/0e.

JOB 67-1: BUSINESS REPORT

Plain paper □ **SI 1.44N**
□ ■ **20'/0e**

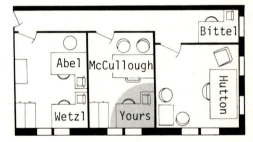

Directions: *Adjust machine for Job 67-1:*
Spacing—1. Line—6". Tabs—5 and center.

"I am pleased to have your help," says J. Mark McCullough, assistant to the director of sales and marketing, Richard Sinclair. "We have been developing a plan for reorganizing our sales administration and are finally ready to put it down on paper. So first of all, let me dictate to you the plan itself":

A PROPOSED PLAN FOR REORGANIZ-   19
ING / OUR MARKETING EFFORT ↓3 /   36
Purpose / The proposed plan has two aims: /   51

1. To effect savings in the cost of sales   61
administration by closing the midcontinent   70
office in Des Moines.   74

2. To improve our service to our custom-   84
ers and our field staff by centralizing all   93
the support services that we can.   100

Procedure / While the changes to be made   115
day by day are still to be worked out, the   123
steps will be to switch from the organiza-   131
tion shown on the attached chart of the   139
present arrangement to that shown on the   148
chart for the proposed plan. Steps would   156
include: 158

(Continued on next page)

and metric units. The Ford Motor Company has intro- 274
duced metric engines in its Pinto and its Mustang II. 285
All about us are signs that America is going metric. 295

OUR RECOMMENDATION 300

    The Metric Study Team believes that the time 311
has come for WAPA to support a firm move to the 321
metrics. We recommend that WAPA form a metric task 331
force to make plans for conversions to metric that 341
will affect our whole industry in this state. The 352
full acceptance of metrics by 1980 should be the 361
goal of WAPA. 364

      Respectfully submitted, 370
      Darrell E. Davis, Chairman 378
Lauren O. Linds Foster J. Jehle 383
      Thomas T. Thomas 389
           394

goals

■ To type 44 or more wam for 5'/3e. ■ To produce a technical memo, an agenda, and a financial statement.

Directions: *Spacing—1. Line—50. Warmup—use lines below, selectively.*

WARMUP

Type three times each either lines 1–3, to give an accuracy momentum to your work in the review, or lines 4–6, to give a speed momentum to it.

For accuracy.

1 Mr. Wilbert cannot pay for the dozen extra quarts Jack gave him. 12
2 Joel quickly amazed the audience by giving six fine new reports. 24
3 The next question emphasized the growing lack of very good jobs. 36
   1 2 3 4 5 6 7 8 9 10 11 12

For speed.

4 Rickey did not wish to pay them the usual duty for the fur pelt. 12
5 Jane may pay the profit of eighty bushels of corn for the chair. 24
6 He may end the land fight if they sign for the oaks by the lake. 36

3-MINUTE
WRITING

Spacing—2.
Line—60.
Tab—5.

Speed markers are
for 3' TW. Circled
figures are 1' goals.

13 The upper peninsula in Michigan is about half the size   12
14 of the lower half and is rich in forests and mines; whereas   24
15 the lower peninsula, twice as big but with twenty times the   36
16 number of people, is farms, factories, cities.   45

17 The product for which the state is best known is cars,   57
18 for the plants in Detroit, Pontiac, and Flint turn out end—   69
19 less rows of shining new cars, trucks, and buses you see in   81
20 the showrooms and on the highways of America.   90

21 The state makes half the autos made in America, but it   102
22 is also famous for other things. For example, it is number   114
23 one in cherries, number one in lake fishing, and almost top   126

■ 3'/2e
24 in lumber, copper, gypsum, salt, and dairying.   135

|1 |2 |3 |4 |5 |6 |7 |8 |9 |10 |11 |12   SI 1.40N

5-MINUTE
WRITING

Spacing—2.
Line—60.
Tab—5.

Speed markers are
for 5' TW. Circled
figures are 1' goals.

25 Do you know which state has given us seven presidents?   12   147
26 The answer is Ohio. One unique thing is that three of them   24   169
27 served in a one, two, three order: Grant, Hayes, Garfield.   36   181

28 What state was father to professional football? Again   48   193
29 the answer is Ohio; the first football league was organized   60   205
30 at a meeting in the city of Canton, which is where the Hall   72   217
31 of Fame of Pro Football is now located. This is a huge and   84   229
32 interesting museum plus library in the shape of a football.   96   241

33 What state was the founder of flying? Well, since the   108   253
34 Wright brothers were Dayton residents both before and after   120   265
35 their famed flights in Kitty Hawk, again the answer: Ohio.   132   277
36 The state can claim fame also because of the giant balloons   144   289
37 built in Akron, and who doesn't know of the Goodyear blimp?   156   301

38 Ohio can claim many distinctions, thanks to its cities   168   313
39 and their unique natures. For example, Akron is the rubber   180   325
40 capital of the nation. Toledo is famous for its glass, its   192   337
41 scales, its coal——it ships more coal than any other city in   204   349
42 the nation. Steubenville is famous for glass. ·Dayton gets   216   361

■ 5'/3e
43 honors for registers. What a state Ohio is!   225   370

|1 |2 |3 |4 |5 |6 |7 |8 |9 |10 |11 |12   SI 1.44N

5-MINUTE
WRITING

Spacing—2.
Line—60.
Tab—5.

Speed markers are
for 5' TW.

■ 5'/3e

Take and score a 5-minute writing. Lines should end even on a 60-space line.

1 When people speak of safety, most of them think of big factories, which   15
2 they believe are full of dozens of hazards like boxes in the aisles, whir- 30
3 ring belts, loose bolts, etc. Actually, of course, none of these things   44
4 is permitted; you frequently discover more risk in the office than in a   59
5 mill.   60

6 For example, no lathe or crane in a factory is riskier than a file   74
7 cabinet. Let a telephone buzz when somebody is filing and up the person   89
8 jumps to answer it, leaving a wide drawer extended so any passing person   104
9 will collide with it. If the person filing was sitting on a stool, then   118
10 the stool is out in the aisle, too, for the next person to trip over; and   133
11 someone, roused by the telephone, is sure to come then.   144

12 Some desks in today's office have a maze of wires that spread in all   159
13 directions. Your telephone and your electric typewriter both have wires. So   173
14 does your pencil sharpener, so does your calculator if you have one.   188
15 Wind up the wires around the desk legs, loop them to sockets across   202
16 aisles or doorways, and note how the squiggles of wire make an expert   216
17 jungle trap that will snare at least one person every week.   228

18 Even the chair that secretaries sit on is another vast hazard. How   243
19 many office workers have had a bad jolt when a foot caught on the pedestal,   258
20 or when the chair unexpectedly rolled back or tilted? It happens to all   272
21 of them sometime.   276

22 No one can say that an office is exactly a safe haven; it is probably   291
23 better than a factory—but not by very much!   300

|1 |2 |3 |4 |5 |6 |7 |8 |9 |10 |11 |12 |13 |14 |15   SI 1.37N

REVIEW JOB 1: STOCKHOLDERS' REPORT

**Plain paper □ Spacing 2 □ Line 6″ □ Tabs 5 and center
□ Start line 11 □ SI 1.43N □ ■ 15'/0e**

January 1, 19-- ↓5   4

To Our Stockholders: 12

I am pleased to report that the Wyoming   20
Automobile Fixit Company has just com-   29
pleted the best year since it was founded   37
in 1960. The new gas stations contributed   46
to that success.   49

Finances. Our net income for the past   62
year was $27,289, which is a gain of $5,341,   70
or 24 percent, over the figure for the preced-   79
ing year, $21,948. Gross revenues for the   88
year are $419,032, which is $34,473 more   96
than for the year before.   101

Earnings per share for the year came to   111
$1.10, compared to $.89 in the year before.   120
The recent increase in the price of our stock   129
reflects the improved earnings of the firm.   138

(Continued on next page)

JOB 66-2: MEMO

Workbook 129 □ Line 4″ □ SI 1.44N □ ■ 7′/0e

"The second memo," says Mr. Greco, "is to":

Saul E. Vogel / Bureau of Engineering /   10
Saul, we have put together the figures of   34
our campsite survey, and I am happy to let   42
you know that your support has made a   50
real difference in the number of campsites   58
that have electric power.   67

    The survey shows that 12,382 of the   75
14,419 campsites, or 86.1 percent, now have   84
electric power. This is a gain of 503   92
modernized camps since 1975, the last year   100
for which we have detailed data. This gain   109
is divided among the three regions: 116

Region I	137	126
Region II	304	130
Region III	62	136
Increase	503	141

interoffice memorandum

Date   July 14, 19--

To   Ms. Hildreth J. Joyce
      Library, Parks Division

From   Joseph Greco
       Coordinator of Camping

Subject   Putting Survey on Tape

When we do our next survey of campsites in

Mr. Greco's memo style: vertical half page, 4-inch line, tab stops at heading alignment and at the center.

On behalf of the tens of thousands who   150
now use the electric power in those 503   158
additional sites, thanks! / JG / urs   169

JOB 66-3: COMPLETION CARDS

5″ x 3″ cards or slips □ ■ 5′/0e

JOB 66-2: MEMO
1. Typed by Andrea Reiter
2. Proofread with Betty Meehan
3. No problems in preparing this job.

goal B

■ **To type at least 45 wam for 3′/2e.**

3-MINUTE SKILL BLITZ

Circled figures are 1′ goals.

Directions: *Spacing—1. Line—60. Tab—5.*

To achieve the goal, take a 3-minute writing, practice any words or phrases that were troublesome, and then repeat the 3-minute writing.

1	Michigan is made up of two peninsulas that come within	12
2	Michigan is made up of two peninsulas that come within	24
3	Michigan is made up of two peninsulas that come within	36
4	five miles of one another at the Straits of Mackinac, where ①	48
5	five miles of one another at the Straits of Mackinac, where	60
6	five miles of one another at the Straits of Mackinac, where	72
7	they are joined by one of the longest suspension bridges in	84
8	they are joined by one of the longest suspension bridges in ②	96
9	they are joined by one of the longest suspension bridges in	108
10	the United States and perhaps in the world.	117
11	the United States and perhaps in the world.	126
12	the United States and perhaps in the world. ③	135

|1 |2 |3 |4 |5 |6 |7 |8 |9 |10 |11 |12   SI 1.41N

■ **3′/2e**

3-MINUTE WRITING

Confirm your blitz score with the timing on lines 13–24 at the top of page 149.

REVIEW JOB 1: STOCKHOLDERS' REPORT

(Continued)

    Gas Stations. We now have three stations `151`
in the chain we are building in Casper. `160`
Each is leased to the person who operates `169`
it. The company gets income from the rent, `177`
from the sale of our brand products, and `185`
from a small percent of the net profit that `194`
is earned by the operation of that station. `203`

    A Look Ahead. With sales and service up `217`
at each of our profit centers, we expect `225`
the next year to be just as good as the `234`
past year or perhaps even better. `240`

            Darrell E. Davis, President `247`

REVIEW JOB 2: LETTER TO STOCKHOLDERS

Workbook 123 ☐ **Body 194**
☐ **SI 1.43N** ☐ ■ **15'/0e**

Retype the stockholders' report as a letter. Some changes to make:

1. Add a complimentary closing, "Respectfully submitted."

2. Add a 2-line enclosure notation:

Enclosure:
    Summary Statement

REVIEW JOB 3: RULED FINANCIAL STATEMENT

Plain paper ☐ **Spacing 2** ☐ **Line 60**
Style as a ruled table ☐ ■ **15'/0e**

        Wyoming Automobile Fixit Company

         Summary of Financial Results

       For the Year Ended December 31, 19--

Summary Items	This Year	Last Year
Operating Revenue	$419,032	$384,159
Income Before Taxes on Income and Minority Interests	57,894	44,525
Provision for Taxes on Income	29,957	22,194
Minority Interest in Earnings of Subsidiaries	648	383
Net Income	$27,289	$21,948
Average Number of Common Shares	24,960	24,582
Earnings per Common Share	$1.10	$0.89

PARKS CAMPSITES
DATA

1975	Change From 1970	1970	Change From 1965	1965
2,701	+ 7	2,694	+ 17	2,677
16	0	16	0	16
15	0	15	0	15
2,438	+ 18	2,420	+ 48	2,372
6,505	+ 37	6,468	+ 11	6,457
30	0	30	0	30
30	0	30	0	30
5,975	− 14	5,989	− 15	6,004
5,546	−119	5,665	− 15	5,680
25	+ 10	15	− 10	25
22	0	22	0	22
4,198	− 93	4,291	− 37	4,328

LESSON 66

Directions: Spacing—1. Line—60.
Warmup—page 136.

goal A

■ **To produce two memos within 15'/0e.**

JOB 66-1: MEMO

**Workbook 129 □ Line 4" □ Tab 10 □
SI 1.37N □ ■ 8'/0e**

"Now, two memos about the survey," says Mr. Greco. "Arrange them this way." He gives you the illustration at the top of page 148.

"Each memo is from me," he continues. "Each is on the subject of 'Survey of Campsites.' Each is dated today. The first is to":

Dr. L. A. Bierlein / Chief, Parks Division /   10
I am pleased to forward to you a copy of   42
the results of the survey we made last   50
fall of the campsites in our state.   57

    You will be gratified by the gains that   66
this bureau of the division has made in   74
the past year. Compared to the count in   83

1975 (the last year we had a survey as   91
full as this one), we have a 4 percent gain   100
in the number of campsites. These gains are   109
divided among the regions: 115

Region I	120		120
Region II	337		125
Region III	116		131
Increase	573		137

If there is anything else I could provide   146
in support of the budget request, I would be   155
happy to provide it at once. / JG / urs /   167
Enclosure   169

goal

■ **To experience creative thinking, accurate typing, and cooperation in typing correspondence.**

☐ You and another student are members of a business club in your respective high schools. One of you is a member of Alpha Chapter; the other is a member of Beta Chapter.

☐ Your respective chapters have asked each of you to obtain certain recommendations from the other's chapter concerning a trip that the business club is planning to take.

☐ After obtaining data and recommendations from each other, both of you will prepare a table to be presented to your respective chapters at the next chapter meeting.

CREATIVE CO-OP 5: DEVELOPING MEETING REPORTS

STUDENT A: ALPHA CHAPTER

1. TYPE A NOTE TO TYPIST B

Type a note to Student B asking for five suggestions on ways the business club could earn some money for its annual trip. Suggest that Typist B recommend activities in which all the club members could participate. Also indicate that each activity should take no longer than one day.

2. RESPOND TO STUDENT B

After hearing from Student B, draft a note recommending <u>five</u> attractions the business club could visit. Determine the transportation costs for visiting each attraction. Assume an average per student cost of 10 cents a mile (there are 30 members in the club, so assume $3 a mile when estimating). Estimate as closely as you can the total miles to each of the five attractions you suggest. Do *not* list any attraction in the county where you live. In your note, give the names of the attractions, the distances, and your estimate of the round-trip costs.

3. DEVELOP A TABLE FOR ALPHA'S MEETING

After receiving your information from Student B, prepare a table on a half sheet of paper. Your table should include (1) the identification of the project, (2) the profit expected, and (3) the estimated expenses for each project. If you can add a sixth, seventh, or even more projects to the list, go ahead and do so.

STUDENT B: BETA CHAPTER

1. TYPE A NOTE TO TYPIST A

Write to Student A asking for five suggestions his or her chapter might have on places to visit for the annual trip. Tell Typist A that Beta Chapter wishes to visit scenic attractions in the state and that you would appreciate it if Alpha Chapter would make their recommendations with this preference in mind.

2. RESPOND TO STUDENT A

After hearing from Student A, recommend <u>five</u> projects that could be completed to earn funds for this year's trip. Provide Student A with a breakdown of gross profits and expenses for each project. For example, for a project of washing cars on a Saturday afternoon, list the gross profit (price charged for each wash times the estimated number of cars washed) and the expenses (for such things as soap, cleaners, cloths). Allow yourself only 5 minutes for your reply. If you can't think of five projects, send fewer (and apologize!); don't delay Alpha!

3. DEVELOP A TABLE FOR BETA'S MEETING

Prepare a table from the information you receive from Student A. Place the table on a half sheet of paper and include (1) the names of the attractions, (2) the distance (in miles) to each, and (3) the round-trip cost to visit each attraction. If there are additional attractions that you'd like to include, do so.

spread it as neatly as possible across the two adjacent pages. Have you typed two-page tables before?"

You assure him that you have.

He gives you the material below. "Here is the first page," he says. "You can start it while I check over the data on the second page."

MICHIGAN STATE

SUMMARY ←2#→

REGION I	←#6→	Last Year	←#7→	Change From 1975	←#6→
Total campsites		2,821		+120	
Parks with campgrounds		16		0	
Parks with lotted campsites		15		0	
Sites with electricity		2,575		+137	
REGION II					
Total campsites		6,168		−337	
Parks with campgrounds		29		− 1	
Parks with lotted campsites		29		− 1	
Sites with electricity		5,671		−304	
REGION III					
Total campsites		5,430		−116	
Parks with campgrounds		25		0	
Parks with lotted campsites		24		+ 2	
Sites with electricity		4,136		− 62	

goal B

■ To produce the second page of a two-page table.

Directions: Clear the machine and reset it for Job 65-2.

JOB 65-2: TABLE (PAGE 2)

Match page 1 □ **Plain paper** □ ■ **20'/0e**

"And here is the second page," says Mr. Greco, giving you the material on the next page. "Be sure it lines up evenly with the first page and has equal space between the columns."

On page 1 you backed up from the right edge of the paper; on page 2 you will space forward from the left edge of the paper.

(Continued on next page)

PART 6

Part 6 continues the same plan of organization that was used in previous parts:

1. Each unit of four lessons includes two work-experience projects, two skill drives of 20–25 minutes each, and one skill-builder clinic.

2. Each project includes about one hour's typing. The project is presented to you in a narrative form to give you experience in listening to and following directions.

3. Each project occurs in a different location, as indicated in the map above.

4. You are to correct all errors in your production work unless your teacher directs otherwise. Make your corrections professionally.

5. Turn to this page at the start of each practice period and type a Warmup of your own design: Select one sentence from each of the four groups below and type it four or more times.

You will type many kinds of tables in Part 6, including some that spread out over two pages and some that require both horizontal and vertical ruled lines.

SPEED RECALL	1A Jane's neighbor kept the dog and also paid for the big pen.	12
	1B He and Jay may aid the man and cut the hay for the big cow.	24
	1C The men may fix their antique auto and go downtown with it.	36
ALPHABET RECALL	2A Jack quietly moved up front and seized the big ball of wax.	12
	2B As Elizabeth requested, Jack will pay for fixing my silver.	24
	2C Roxie picked off the yellow jonquils by the amazing cavern.	36
NUMBER RECALL	3A He has 10 or 28. She has 39 or 47. I have 10 or maybe 56.	12
	3B Add 234, plus 456, plus 678, minus 890, for a total of 478.	24
	3C Five camps are 10, 28, 39, 47, and 56 kilometers from here.	36
THINKING WHILE TYPING	4A The popular ADDING–LISTING machine is a TEN–KEY calculator.	12
	4B The "home position" on the TEN–KEY is on the 4–5–6–key row.	24
	4C Is ACME–APEX the brand of that company, or is it APEX–ACME?	36

|1 |2 |3 |4 |5 |6 |7 |8 |9 |10 |11 |12

PRACTICE 1	Make four copies. If you averaged two or fewer errors in Pretest 1, repeat individual lines; otherwise, repeat each block (lines 5–7 and 8–10) for accuracy gains.	
Accent jump reaches and no alternate-hand runs.	5 joining matched utmost saying zones place unit text act run	12
	6 protect routine season invest women river pins mill inn nor	24
	7 utilize younger paying refund serve thing army live won bid	36
	8 fortune exposed making prompt using prize done none ton gun	48
	9 correct defects gained detect minor night save much now son	60
	10 appoint citizen finish import aimed catch once soon fun ice	72

|1 |2 |3 |4 |5 |6 |7 |8 |9 |10 |11 |12

POSTTEST 1 Repeat Pretest 1. Score your work and note your improvement.

DRIVE 2

PRETEST 2 Take three 1-minute timings on lines 11–14 and average the scores.

Accent jump reaches and no adjacent-key strokes.

11 She informs me that the mob was running to the office room.	12
12 Just for the fun of it, I gave my aunts one cent for lunch.	24
13 We have to admit that the stones somehow broke the windows.	36
14 Tod doubts the main brakes have a chance of working anyhow.	48

|1 |2 |3 |4 |5 |6 |7 |8 |9 |10 |11 |12

PRACTICE 2 Use the same procedure you followed for Practice 1 above.

Accent jump reaches and no adjacent-key strokes.

15 windows somehow timely office print night tiny pain act nor	12
16 unknown tactful prompt stones round smoke skin main sun any	24
17 orchard shelves lesson motive hints exact room noon mob run	36
18 primary running expand having lunch knife inch aunt ice cry	48
19 leading mounted chance driven bench count gave from win beg	60
20 informs helping anyhow brakes doubt admit have cent fun one	72

|1 |2 |3 |4 |5 |6 |7 |8 |9 |10 |11 |12

POSTTEST 2 Repeat Pretest 2. Score your work and note your improvement.

goal A

■ To produce the first page of a two-page table.

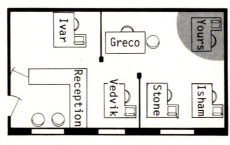

LESSON 65

Directions: *Spacing—1. Line—60.*
Warmup—page 136.

JOB 65-1: TABLE (PAGE 1)

Plain paper ☐ ■ 20'/2e

"I hope you will like your work here in the Parks Department," says Joseph Greco, camping coordinator for the state of Michigan. He introduces you to your colleagues and shows you your desk.

Getting down to business, he says, "In order to get state appropriations for the camping program, we make an annual survey of our total camp facilities. We have just compiled our data for the past year and are ready to put it into a two-page table that our department chief can include in his annual budget request. We want to make the table as impressive as we can, so we

(Continued on next page)

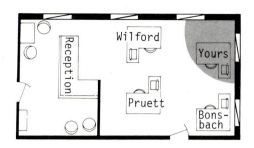

You work for Jenny Bonsbach, manager of the Maine branch of the New England Tourist Association, in Augusta. You meet Bill Wilford and Joe Pruett, then settle down to your work.

JOB 61-1: TWO-PAGE RULED TABLE

Plain paper ☐ **Spacing 2** ☐ ■ **20'/0e**

"For a survey I am making," says Mrs. Bonsbach, "I need a tally sheet like this one."

She gives you the samples shown in the illustration below. You study them very carefully.

"Note that they list the name of each town, give its population, and provide three write-in columns of underscores."

You comment, "Then what I need for this are the names of the communities and the population of each one. If I have those, I

can manage the lines for 'Yes,' 'No,' and 'Growth' with no difficulty. Where can I get the names and populations?"

"I will dictate them to you," she says, and begins:

Auburn	24,200	Old Town	9,100
Augusta	21,900	Orono Center	9,100
Bangor	33,200	Portland	65,100
Bath	9,700	Presque Isle	8,500
Belfast	6,000	Rockland	8,500
Biddeford	20,000	Rumford	
Brewer	9,300	Compact	6,200
Brunswick Center	10,900	Saco	11,700
Caribou	10,200	Sanford Center	10,500
Gardiner	6,700	Scarborough	7,700
Houlton Center	6,800	Skowhegan	
Kittery Center	7,400	Center	6,600
Lewiston	31,800	South Portland	23,300
Lisbon	6,400	Waterville	18,200
Millinocket		Westbrook	14,400
Center	7,600	Windham	6,600
Old Orchard		Winslow	7,500
Beach	5,300	York	5,700

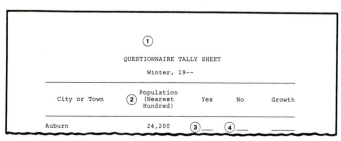

On first page: ① 1″ top margin; ② column headings are detailed; ③ underscores: 3, 3, 6; ④ 6 spaces between columns.

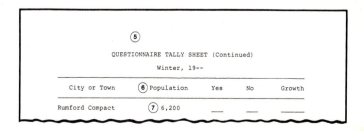

On second page: ⑤ 1″ top margin; ⑥ column headings are shortened; ⑦ stops are same.

■ **To produce a letter with an approval line.**

JOB 64-2: LETTER

Workbook 127 □ **Body 122 +**
Coupon □ **SI 1.36N** □ ■ **15'/0e**

"I'm ready now to dictate the letter that will get us permission to mail the questionnaire," says Mr. Filbin. He begins:

Mr. Thomas T. Scott / Managing Director /   16
County Council of Vermont and New Hamp-   23
shire / 250 Wadley Falls Road / Portsmouth,   30
NH 03801 / Dear Tom: /   36

Enclosed is the new form for us to use   44
this year in getting data from the county   53
agents. It is similar to the one we used last   62
year and should get us all the data we need   70
for the page in the yearbook.   77

Please review the form and return it to   86

me. If you have ideas for improving it or   95
see things that need to be corrected or   102
changed, please indicate right on the form   111
the improvements to be made to it.   118

If the form meets with your approval and   127
if I have your permission to proceed with   131
mailing it to all of our county agents,   144
please sign on the line at the bottom of   152
this letter and return it to me. *Arrange the*   158
following sentence as a two-line compli-   ..
mentary closing: When are you coming for   165
the / skiing lesson I promised? / Kenneth   179
Filbin / Office Manager / urs / Enclosure↓2   187

Type a line of hyphens across the page,   199
margin to margin. Then type at the margin: ..
The questionnaire and its / mailing are ap-   209
proved. ↓2 *Type a line of 34 underscores;*   211
under it type: Thomas T. Scott, Managing   225
Director   227

JOB 64-3: COMPLETION CARDS

5″ x 3″ cards or slips □ ■ **5'/0e**

---

goal

■ **To use intensive drill to build more basic skill.**

ACTIVITIES	20 MIN.	40 MIN.
Warmup, page 136	3'	3'
Drive 1 Pretest	4'	4'
Drive 1 Practice	9'	9'
Drive 1 Posttest	4'	4'
Drive 2 Pretest	—	5'
Drive 2 Practice	—	10'
Drive 2 Posttest	—	5'

CLINIC
11

Directions: *Spacing—1. Line—60. Warmup—page 136; then begin Pretest 1.*

DRIVE 1

PRETEST 1

Accent jump reaches and no alternate-hand runs.

Take two 1-minute timings on lines 1–4. Proofread both and average the scores.

1 The river runs in every season but not once has ice formed.   12
2 The women were given a refund and made a fortune in prizes.   24
3 It is much too soon to detect minor defects in the new car.   36
4 Now is the moment to save and protect our younger citizens.   48

|1 |2 |3 |4 |5 |6 |7 |8 |9 |10 |11 |12

■ To produce a
two-page table
within 20'/0e.

JOB 61-2: TWO-PAGE RULED TABLE

Plain paper □ **Spacing 3** □ ■ **20'/0e**

"Here's another two-page table for you to type," says Mrs. Bonsbach. "In this one, the two pages go side by side. Be sure they line up so they can be read straight across, as if they were on one page."

She gives you the two illustrations below.

"It's easier than it seems to be," she says. "I did a little to show you how I'd like it to look."

You study the problem carefully. You will be very careful with the drop to the first line of typing on both sheets.

LEFT-HAND PAGE

1. Lines end 1 or 1½ spaces from edge.
2. Separate the columns by 6 spaces.
3. Leave 1 blank line above and below the city names.
4. In triple spacing, leave 2 blank lines between sections.

HIGHWAY GUIDE TO PRINCIPAL

HIGHWAY	Augusta	Bangor	Biddeford	Houlton
US 1	..	..	X	X
US 2	..	X	..	X
US 202	X	X	..	..
I 95	X	X	X	X
Maine Turnpike	X	..	X	..

TRAFFIC CENTERS IN MAINE

Lewiston	Portland	Portsmouth	Rochester	Waterville
..	X	X	..	..
..	..	..	..	..
X	X	..	X	X
..	X	X	..	X
X	X	X	X	..

RIGHT-HAND PAGE

5. Lines begin 1 or 1½ spaces from edge.
6. Lines must match exactly the lines on opposite page.
7. The X lines up with the first period.

LESSON **64**

JOB 64-1: ENVELOPE LABELS

Workbook 125 ☐ ■ 20'/0e

Directions: *Spacing—1. Line—60. Warmup—page 136; then do Job 64-1.*

"After we get an okay on the questionnaire," says Mr. Filbin, "we will duplicate it and mail copies to the county agents. Right now, please address an envelope mailing label to each of these recreational agents."

He gives you the mailing directory below.

You do not type the county name, of course. If you do not have the workbook page, make a similar sheet: type a line of hyphens every six lines, edge to edge; then turn the paper sideways and type two long lines of hyphens on lines 17 and 34. Result: 24 small labels.

County	Recreational Agent	Address	ZIP	
STATE OF NEW HAMPSHIRE				..
Belknap	Celia Golden (Miss)	341 Granite Road, Laconia, NH	03246	15
Carroll	Marcia Rubin (Mrs.)	96 Church Street, Ossippee, NH	03864	30
Cheshire	Bensley Jonson	321 Marble Avenue, Keene, NH	03431	45
Coos	Esther Jung (Mrs.)	11 Atlantic Park, Lancaster, NH	03584	60
Grafton	Frederick J. Paul	660 Third Street, Woodsville, NH	03785	75
Hillsborough	Olive Strang (Miss)	183 Pine Avenue, Nashua, NH	03060	92
Merrimack	~~Quincy Stork~~ Thomas Bank	10 Bennington Street, Concord, NH	03301	107
Rockingham	Freda Wring (Mrs.)	935 Glebe Road, Exeter, NH	03833	122
Stratford	Frank Liebert	81 Mansfield Avenue, Dover, NH	03820	136
Sullivan	Stella Rodgers (Mrs.)	898 Court Street, Newport, NH	03773	152
STATE OF VERMONT				..
Addison	Francis E. Fiske	222 Village Square, Middlebury, VT	05753	169
Bennington	Eloise Sumner (Miss)	141 Third Street, Bennington, VT	05201	186
Caledonia	Hiram Victor	793 Peace Park, St. Johnsbury, VT	05819	201
Chittenden	Wesley H. Forscht	2 Park Place, Burlington, VT	05401	216
Essex	Thursa V. Adams (Mrs.)	750 East Northside, Guildhall, VT	05905	232
Franklin	Kermit Ducey	110 South Street, St. Albans, VT	05478	248
Grand Isle	Glenn Rose, Jr.	74 Harbor Outlook, North Hero, VT	05474	263
Lamoille	T. T. Draughon (Miss)	700 Mountain Lane, Hyde Park, VT	05655	280
Orange	Ed Christopher	16 Leavit Hill, Chelsea, VT	05638	293
Orleans	John P. Jones	1800 Beebe Plain Road, Newport, VT	05855	308
Rutland	J. G. Fields (Mrs.)	238 South Main, Rutland, VT	05701	324
Washington	Richard Robinson	Route 100, Montpelier, VT	05602	339
Windham	Richard Rainey	465 West Street, Newfane, VT	05345	353
Windsor	Mark T. Scott	45 Market Lane, Woodstock, VT	05091	366

goal A

To produce a
two-page table
within 20'/0e.

LESSON **62**

JOB 62-1: TWO-PAGE RULED TABLE

Plain paper ☐ ■ 20'/0e

"One more two-page table," says Mrs. Bonsbach, giving you the dual illustration below. "This is a carbon of what I used last year, and I'd like you to type a new copy for me. It is another survey tally sheet, of course."

You say, "Look at that—six columns of underscores! Well, they'll be easy to type."

"Maybe the names of counties and county seats are not clear," she says. "Let me review them":

Androscoggin and Auburn . . . Aroostook and Houlton . . . Cumberland and Portland . . . Franklin and Farmington . . . Hancock and Ellsworth . . . Kennebec and Augusta . . . Knox and Rockland . . . Lincoln and Wiscasset . . . Oxford and South Paris . . . Penobscot and Bangor . . . Piscataquis and Dover-Foxcroft . . . Sagadahoc and Bath . . . Somerset and Skowhegan . . . Waldo and Belfast . . . Washington and Machias . . . York and Alfred.

ANNUAL SURVEY OF HOTEL

This 8-column tally sheet takes two pages of 4 columns each. Six of the columns, however, consist only of headings and 16 lines of 5 underscores. Between columns: usual 6 spaces.

County	County Seat	January-March	April-June
Androscoggin	Auburn	_____	_____
Aroostook	Houlton	_____	_____
Cumberland	Portland	_____	_____
Franklin	Farmington	_____	_____
Hancock	Ellsworth	_____	
Kennebec	Augusta	_____	
Knox	Rockland	_____	
Lincoln	Wiscasset	_____	
Oxford	South Paris	_____	
Penobscot	Bangor	_____	
Piscataquis	Dover-Foxcroft	_____	
Sagadahoc	Bath	_____	
Somerset	Skowhegan	_____	
Waldo	Belfast	_____	
Washington	Machias	_____	
York	Alfred	_____	

AND MOTEL REGISTRATIONS

July-September	October-December	Total	Year's Change
_____	_____	_____	_____
_____	_____	_____	_____
_____	_____	_____	_____
_____	_____	_____	_____
_____	_____	_____	_____
_____	_____	_____	_____

JOB 63-1: QUESTIONNAIRE

Plain paper □ ■ 20′/0e

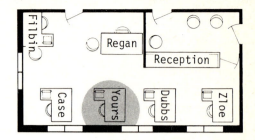

Directions: *Adjust the machine for Job 63-1.*

Your employer is Kenneth Filbin, office manager for the County Council of Vermont and New Hampshire. He shows you your desk and says, "It is time for us to request the annual report on recreation facilities in our states. I have a copy of the questionnaire we used last year."

He gives you the questionnaire shown below.

"I have made some changes on it, as you see, but I think that you can follow its form, arrangement, spacing, and so on. At least, it gives you a model with which to work."

Studying it carefully, you note: (1) The form is double-spaced except for the column headings, which are single-spaced and ruled with no spaces. (2) Six spaces are left between columns. (3) Each underscore line is 9 strokes long.

Because of its shape and size, this job would look better if typed with the paper sideways.

ANNUAL REPORT OF RECREATION FACILITIES

County _____ County Clerk _____

Address _____

Indicate the number of facilities of each category in your county:

Facility	Residents Only	Residents Primarily	Visitors Primarily	Total
Camping grounds	_____	_____	_____	_____
Fishing	_____	_____	_____	_____
~~Golfing~~ Hiking trails	_____	_____	_____	_____
Hunting *lodges*	_____	_____	_____	_____
Picnic grounds	_____	_____	_____	_____
~~Riding stables~~	_____	_____	_____	_____
Riding trails	_____	_____	_____	_____
~~Skiing~~ *lifts*	_____	_____	_____	_____
Ski trails Swimming	_____	_____	_____	_____
Trailer park	_____	_____	_____	_____

Mail this report before ~~January 15~~ *February 1* to County Council of Vermont and New Hampshire
1165 South Atlantic Street
Concord, New Hampshire 03301

Directions: *Spacing—1. Line—60. Tab—5.*
Begin the 12-second sprints.

12-SECOND SPRINTS

Four 12" timings
on each sentence.

1	Did you know that Maine is the	
2	state where the first ship in America was constructed?	17
3	source of one out of every twelve potatoes in America?	17
4	one state that has a border with just one other state?	17

12" SPEED: 40 45 50 55 60 65 70 75 80 85

3-MINUTE SKILL BLITZ

Routine:
1. 3' writing.
2. Corrective practice.
3. 3' writing.

Circled figures
are 1' goals.

5	You might think that most workers in Maine tend to the	12
6	You might think that most workers in Maine tend to the	24
7	You might think that most workers in Maine tend to the	36
8	lobster pots, but really most of them work in ① the factories	48
9	lobster pots, but really most of them work in the factories	60
10	lobster pots, but really most of them work in the factories	72
11	that line the banks of the rivers that flow down to the sea	84
12	that line the banks of the rivers ② that flow down to the sea	96
13	that line the banks of the rivers that flow down to the sea	108
14	from the White Mountains of northern Maine.	117
15	from the White Mountains of northern Maine.	126
16	from the White Mountains of northern Maine. ③	135

1 2 3 4 5 6 7 8 9 10 11 12   SI 1.19E

■ 3'/2e

3-MINUTE WRITING

Speed counters are
for 3' TW. Circled
figures are 1' goals.

17	Once the settlers of early Maine had established their	12
18	homes and food supplies, they turned to shipbuilding as the	24
19	first industry they set up, for the forests about them were	36
20	full of tall pines; Maine is called the Pine State, you may	48
21	know. Ships of all sizes soon set forth from Maine, and in	60
22	a few quick years Maine ships were seen all over the world.	72
23	Forests are still important; they mean lumber, pulp, paper.	84
24	There is extensive farming in the southeast section of	96
25	the state. Maine is recognized as the blueberry capital of	108
26	the nation. Other crops are beans, oats, peas, apples, and	120
27	potatoes. One by-product: lots of jobs in food processing	132
28	and storage.	135

1 2 3 4 5 6 7 8 9 10 11 12   SI 1.34FE

■ 3'/2e

goal A

■ To type 45 or more wam for 5'/3e.

Directions: *Spacing—1. Line—60.*
Warmup—page 136.

PRETEST

Spacing—2.
Line—60.
Tab—5.

Take a 5-minute writing to set the base for intensive practice.

1   New Hampshire and Vermont are so much alike in terrain and   13

2 size and history that you could almost call them twins.   24

3   Both are rugged, with mountains and gorges, rivers and lakes,   37

4 fields for small gardens and slopes for fast skiing. All summer   50

5 long the cool of the forests and lakes makes the states into sum-   63

6 mer resorts, and all winter long the skating and skiing make them   76

7 into winter resorts. And all the year long they turn out electric   90

8 equipment and products from the hundred and one small factories   102

9 along the many river banks.   108

10   The two states are almost the same size: each is just a trifle   122

11 more than nine thousand square miles. Vermont has a slight edge   135

12 of almost a hundred or so extra square miles.   144

13   New Hampshire was ninth among the original colonies to join   157

14 the united effort against England. Vermont became the first new   170

15 state in the nation after the War of Independence and therefore   183

16 ranks as the fourteenth of the United States.   192

17   The two states also have nicknames that seem akin, the Green   205

18 Mountain State for Vermont, and the Granite State for New Hamp-   219

19 shire; yes, just like twin neighbors.   225

|1 |2 |3 |4 |5 |6 |7 |8 |9 |10 |11 |12 |13 |14   SI 1.36N

Speed markers are for 5' TW. Circled figures are 1' goals.

PRACTICE

Spacing—1.

Type three times each the lines indicated in this table:

Errors in Pretest	0–2	3–5	6–+
Lines to practice	20–25	21–26	22–27

Speed.

20 square slight almost became skiing summer winter trifle ago   12

21 alike could twins lakes small makes along river banks miles   24

22 much size that call them edge fast long cool year turn nine   36

Capitals.

23 Independence Vermont Granite States Still They Both All War   12

24 Hampshire Mountain England United Green State Thank The New   24

Accuracy.

25 fourteenth nickname thousand terrain history rugged, gorges   12

26 mountains neighbors electric resorts gardens forests nation   24

27 equipment therefore original colonies hundred united effort   36

|1 |2 |3 |4 |5 |6 |7 |8 |9 |10 |11 |12

6   63   141